Death and Mortality in Contemporary Philosophy

This book contributes to current bioethical debates by providing a critical analysis of the philosophy of human death. Bernard N. Schumacher discusses contemporary philosophical perspectives on death, creating a dialogue between phenomenology, existentialism, and analytic philosophy. He also examines the ancient philosophies that have shaped our current ideas about death. His analysis focuses on three fundamental problems: (1) the definition of human death, (2) the knowledge of mortality and of human death as such, and (3) the question of whether death is "nothing" to us or, on the contrary, whether it can be regarded as an absolute or relative evil. Drawing on scholarship published in different languages and from distinct currents of thought, this volume represents a comprehensive and systematic study of the philosophy of death, one that provides a provocative basis for discussions of the bioethics of human mortality.

Bernard N. Schumacher received his Ph.D. in philosophy and his Habilitation from the University of Fribourg in Switzerland, where he currently teaches. He has served as a visiting professor at the University of Chicago; Providence College, Rhode Island; and the University of Lugano. He is the author of *A Philosophy of Hope* (2003) and has edited and co-edited numerous scholarly works, including *L'humain et la personne* (2008, translated into German as *Der Mensch und die Person*) and *A Cosmopolitan Hermit: Modernity and Tradition in the Philosophy of Josef Pieper* (2009).

Death and Mortality in Contemporary Philosophy

BERNARD N. SCHUMACHER
University of Fribourg

Translated by Michael J. Miller

CAMBRIDGE
UNIVERSITY PRESS

CAMBRIDGE UNIVERSITY PRESS
Cambridge, New York, Melbourne, Madrid, Cape Town, Singapore,
São Paulo, Delhi, Dubai, Tokyo, Mexico City

Cambridge University Press
32 Avenue of the Americas, New York, NY 10013-2473, USA

www.cambridge.org
Information on this title: www.cambridge.org/9780521171199

First published in French as *Confrontations avec la mort. La philosophie contemporaine et la question de la mort* by Cerf, Paris 2005
Published in German as *Der Tod in der Philosophie der Gegenwart* by
Wissenschaftliche Buchgesellschaft, Darmstadt 2004
Revised English edition published by Cambridge University Press 2011

Printed in the United States of America

A catalog record for this publication is available from the British Library.

Library of Congress Cataloging in Publication data
Schumacher, Bernard N.
Death and mortality in contemporary philosophy / Bernard N. Schumacher.
p. cm.
Includes bibliographical references and index.
ISBN 978-0-521-76932-7 – ISBN 978-0-521-17119-9 (pbk.)
1. Death. I. Title.
BD444.S3936 2010
128′.5–dc22 2010030606

ISBN 978-0-521-76932-7 Hardback
ISBN 978-0-521-17119-9 Paperback

to Michele Marie

This award-winning book received the
Prince Franz-Joseph II of Liechtenstein Prize.

Contents

Preface

In order to safeguard his happiness, contemporary Western man has contrived to stop thinking at all about death and, more particularly, about his own death, to deny it in a way by maintaining a stony silence with regard to it. Some philosophers end up taking part in this masquerade by considering the subject taboo or by declaring that it is not philosophical. Whereas the act of philosophizing was understood in the philosophical tradition as a preparation for death, as a rumination on life and death, many contemporary philosophers set aside the very question of man's relation to "his own death". Does this habit of averting their eyes originate in a fear of death? Is it due to a shift of attention away from radical questions concerning the meaning and ultimate foundation of human life, in both its personal and its social dimension, so as to focus on particular and local problems? Whatever the reason, it seems that philosophy would have everything to gain if it once again centered its theoretical and practical reflections on such fundamental themes, for they are at the heart of human existence.

When they heard that I was writing a book on death, most of my colleagues smiled ironically; they just couldn't understand how a young philosopher could "waste" several years of his life meditating on death, given that the subject eludes all philosophical investigation and there is no hope whatsoever of arriving at definitive answers. But isn't philosophy, in some sense, a waste of time? Like true leisure and love, philosophy cannot be evaluated in terms of profitability, and I am glad that I devoted time to contemplating a philosophical subject that of course continues to elude me but that nonetheless is evident under the aspects of the incomprehensible and the frontier.

The years that I spent meditating on death have certainly enabled me to tame it somewhat, to understand it a little better by clarifying certain points and by dispelling several false notions with regard to it. While eluding thorough comprehension, it nevertheless remains one of the most troubling mysteries for philosophical reflection. Writing the present volume did not lay to rest my philosophical and existential musings; I am still seeking a better understanding of death and, more particularly, my death and the death of those whom I love.

I am extremely grateful to my wife, Michele Marie, without whom this book could not have been written. During her patient and painstaking reading of the various drafts of the manuscript, she managed with great perspicacity to identify a number of problems in my arguments, suggesting excellent comments and corrections and offering many pertinent arguments and criticisms. I am very grateful to her for those long and stimulating discussions that shaped the present volume, as well as for her constant support over the course of those many years. I dedicate this book to her as a token of my profound gratitude. I likewise thank my older daughter, Myriam, for her patience, during the final months of composition, with a Dad who was absorbed in his reflections, and also for her regular visits with her mother to the library to look up references. I am likewise very thankful for my three other children, Sophia, Teresa, and Nicolas, who helped me, along with Myriam, to understand better what it means to live.

My thanks also to Evandro Agazzi for his generous support and his availability, as well as for his valuable comments and suggestions; to Martine Nida-Rümelin, Daniel Schulthess, and Jean-Claude Wolf for their helpful remarks; to the late Jorge Arregui for the long and stimulating discussions that we had on several themes treated in this work; to Jacinto Choza, Günther Figal, John Martin Fischer, Thomas Flynn, Paul Griffiths, Otfried Höffe, Thomas De Koninck, Thomas Nagel, Gregory Reichberg, and Ronald Santoni for their discussions and their excellent critiques; to the anonymous reviewers of the manuscript for their very helpful comments and enlightening points; to Michael J. Miller not only for his excellent translation but also for his marvelous synthesis of professional and human qualities including his dedication and true kindness; and finally to the staff of Cambridge University Press – especially Beatrice Rehl, editor; Emily Spangler, assistant editor; and Regina Paleski, production editor – for their helpful comments, fine work, and patience. This monograph was also made possible thanks to the financial assistance of the Humboldt Foundation and of the National Swiss

Foundation for Scientific Research. Finally, I am very grateful to the students of the University of Fribourg (Switzerland) and the University of Chicago who attended my seminars and my lectures on death and on the notion of person for their questions and comments, which stimulated my personal reflection.

The present work constitutes a revised edition of the original French and German editions. The first part of this English edition has been entirely rewritten and the first chapter of the second part (treating the knowledge of death and mortality of the animal, the "primitive" human being, and the child) of the original editions does not appear here.

Introduction

Although it is widely discussed within the framework of bio- and medical ethics, sociology, history, and literature, at the dawn of the third millennium death is the subject of a taboo that has been epitomized by the expression "the pornography of death".[1] Public practices and discourse pertaining to death are no longer connected to the "private" experiences and feelings of those who die or are in mourning.[2] After holding a prominent place for thousands of years at the very heart of human culture, death has vanished from everyday communications, and contemporary Western society even tends to suppress anything that calls it to mind. It has become rare to see someone die. People no longer die at home, but rather at the hospital; the dead are, in a way, excluded from the community of the living. As for burial, it has been disguised so as not to recall too explicitly the victory of death that awaits everyone, as though the important thing were to camouflage or mask that victory. Meditation on death is avoided like the plague, because we prefer to occupy ourselves with things that are less lugubrious and, one might add, less obscene. Death causes those who speak about it to shiver and to experience an uneasiness mingled with a fear of their own death or of the death of a loved one; it is mentioned only in cloaked terms; Montaigne noted that people "take fright at the mere mention of death, and [...]

[1] See Geoffrey Gorer, "The Pornography of Death"; Herman Feifel, "Death". In recent years, however, we have witnessed a slow, surreptitious renaissance of death. See Tony Walter, *The Revival of Death*.

[2] Changes in family ties and the separation of the public from the private sphere have likewise brought about a privatization of mourning in the Westernized world.

cross themselves [...] as at the name of the devil".[3] Pascal emphasizes that "as men are not able to fight against death, misery, ignorance, they have taken it into their heads in order to be happy not to think of them at all".[4] Freud notes that "we [contemporary men and women] [have] showed an unmistakable tendency to put death to one side, to eliminate it from life. We have tried to hush it up".[5]

Thus the human being is deprived of his death. We constantly lie to ourselves, saying that it is always someone else who dies, but never myself.[6] The individual is content to live day by day in what Heidegger calls inauthenticity [*Uneigentlichkeit*], in a recognition that "one dies" that is never taken personally but is invariably perceived as someone else's business. This notion that "one dies" dominates everyday life and expresses "an indefinite something which, above all, must duly arrive from somewhere or other, but which is proximally *not yet present-at-hand* for oneself, and is therefore no threat".[7] Such an attitude does not acknowledge death but tries to neutralize it by denying it. The death of a loved one, in particular, is seen – through a reaction of fear – as a mere happenstance, an accident, and is no longer viewed from the positive perspective as an existential shock that enables the survivor to transcend his everyday attitude of activity for activity's sake and to open himself to reflecting upon the meaning of his existence, personally and communally. Contemporary philosophy on the subject of death, or "thanatology", aims to awaken the human being from the drowsiness resulting from this negation or this rejection of death; it tries to bring the human being to face his own mortality. It also seeks to tame death somewhat by confronting it directly, by seeking to understand the typically human attitude toward it, and by questioning the rationality of the fears that it arouses.

3 Michel de Montaigne, *The Complete Essays of Montaigne*, p. 58 [*Essais*, vol. I, chap. xx, p. 130: *"on s'en signe, comme du nom du diable"*].

4 Blaise Pascal, *Pensées*, no. 168, p. 60 [p. 119: *"N'ayant pu guérir la mort", les êtres humains "se sont avisés, pour se rendre heureux, de* n'y point penser"]. See Georg Simmel, "Zur Metaphysik des Todes", p. 32. It should be noted, however, that the flight from death expresses a human attitude that is quite natural and healthy; Max Scheler described it as a "metaphysical recklessness" [*"metaphysischen Leichtsinn"*] (*Tod und Fortleben*, p. 28). Such repression of death makes human action in the world possible, which otherwise would be paralyzed by the constant thought of death.

5 See Sigmund Freud, "Thoughts for the Times on War and Death", p. 289 [p. 49].

6 An attitude exemplified by the Leo Tolstoy character Ivan Llitch.

7 Martin Heidegger, *Being and Time*, p. 297 [p. 253: *"Ein unbestimmtes Etwas, das allererst irgendwoher eintreffen muss, zunächst aber für einen selbst noch nicht vorhanden und daher unbedrohlich ist"*].

Despite the opinion of Schulz and Scherer,[8] who insist that death does not constitute a relevant theme in contemporary philosophy, or, in contrast, that of Gray and Wyschogrod that during the twentieth century it was "rediscovered as a philosophical idea and problem",[9] for my own part I maintain that contemporary philosophers, on the contrary, have taken to heart the importance of the theme of death, which nevertheless is the subject of many very pertinent reflections by philosophers from the past. Contemporary philosophy has treated death on the theoretical level (on which the present analysis is chiefly situated) as well as on the ethical level. We can distinguish two main periods: on the one hand, the thanatological debate in the first half of the twentieth century, chiefly among adherents to the philosophy of life ("vitalism"), phenomenology, or existentialism; on the other hand, the recent controversy in analytical philosophy, which is marked by a disregard for the arguments set forth during the first period. Indeed, it is not uncommon that the analytical philosophers propose, without any citation whatsoever, theses and arguments that strangely resemble those developed by the phenomenologists and existentialists; in other cases, the citation refers the reader to works of secondary literature, which do not always interpret the primary sources exactly.

Contrary to Schulz's suggestion that they are definitively a thing of the past,[10] metaphysical questions about an eventual afterlife have certainly not been rejected so readily by contemporary philosophy; nor do I think that the classical metaphysics of death are of nothing more than *antiquarian interest* today, as Hügli claims,[11] or at best of existential interest to the contemporary philosopher. Furthermore it is incorrect to describe contemporary philosophical reflection in terms of what Ebeling calls an irreversible "thanatological inversion",[12] that is to say, a

[8] See Georg Scherer, "Philosophie des Todes und moderne Rationalität", p. 507.

[9] J. Glenn Gray, "The Idea of Death in Existentialism", p. 114: "The question of death has occupied a surprisingly small place in modern thought. [...] In the twentieth century, death was rediscovered as a philosophical idea and problem". See Edith Wyschogrod, "Death and Some Philosophies of Language", p. 255; Otto Friedrich Bollnow, "Der Tod des andern Menschen", p. 1257.

[10] See Walter Schulz, "Wandlungen der Einstellung zum Tode", pp. 99, 104; "Zum Problem des Todes", pp. 313, 324; *Subjektivität im nachmetaphysischen Zeitalter*, p. 143.

[11] See Anton Hügli, "Zur Geschichte der Todesdeutung", pp. 2–3.

[12] Hans Ebeling, ed., *Der Tod in der Moderne*, p. 12. "Before Heidegger, philosophical thanatology had still maintained the hope for a sort of immortality. With Heidegger, that hope was abandoned. And since Heidegger it has no longer been possible to restore it by means of philosophy" ["*Vor Heidegger hatte auch die philosophische Thanatologie die Hoffnung auf eine Unsterblichkeit noch bewahrt. Mit Heidegger ist sie preisgegeben. Und*

systematic bracketing off of questions concerning immortality and metaphysics, questions that are deprived of meaning for a post-Heideggerian philosophy and that should be relegated from now on, according to Fuchs, to the realm of magic, the archaic, the primitive, and religion: in a word, to the domain of the irrational.[13] I distance myself from such an assessment of the situation of contemporary philosophical thanatology, which is only partially and not entirely postmetaphysical. Furthermore, inquiry into the possibility of an afterlife did not cease with Scheler;[14] far from being outmoded, it is currently the subject of very interesting speculative philosophical reflections.[15]

Even so, in the present study I will not address the metaphysical questions concerning an eventual afterlife. I will focus my attention instead on three problems: the problem of the nature of human personal death in the context of the biomedical debate, the problem of the knowledge of (my) mortality and of human death as such, and finally the problem of determining whether death is nothing to us or, on the contrary, whether it can be regarded as an evil. In order to do this, I limit myself to a careful reading of the classical texts of contemporary philosophy from the two periods just mentioned, while referring to the ancient philosophers as well, and especially to Epicurus and his provocative thesis of the "nothingness of death". I have opted for a dialogue and a critical integration of the various positions rather than for a historical and chronological presentation of the thanatologians of contemporary philosophy.

It seemed to me necessary to begin by discussing in Part One of this study the definition of human personal death, which has important

seit Heidegger ist sie mit Mitteln der Philosophie nicht mehr zu restaurieren", p. 11]. See also *Rüstung und Selbsterhaltung*, pp. 84–5. See Walter Schulz, "Zum Problem des Todes", pp. 313 f.; *Subjektivität im nachmetaphysischen Zeitalter*, pp. 125 f.

[13] See Werner Fuchs, *Todesbilder in der modernen Gesellschaft*, pp. 50 f.

[14] As Walter Schulz interprets him in "Zum Problem des Todes", p. 324; *Subjektivität im nachmetaphysischen Zeitalter*, pp. 125 f.

[15] Within the framework of the phenomenological, existential, and neo-Thomistic debate, as well as in the discussion of the Anglo-Saxon analytical tradition concerning personal identity and the various sorts of afterlife (personal immortality, reincarnation, etc.). See John Donnelly, ed., *Language, Metaphysics, and Death*; Fred Feldman, *Confrontations with the Reaper*; John Martin Fischer, ed., *The Metaphysics of Death*; Anthony Flew, *The Logic of Mortality*; Peter Geach, *God and the Soul*; Hywel D. Lewis, *The Self and Immortality*; Ronald W. K. Paterson, *Philosophy and the Belief in a Life after Death*; Terence Penelhum, *Survival and Disembodied Existence*; Roy W. Perrett, *Death and Immortality*; Ted Peters, John Russell, and Michael Welker, eds., *Resurrection*; Josef Pieper, *Death and Immortality*; Jay F. Rosenberg, *Thinking Clearly about Death*.

ethical repercussions. Unlike the establishment of functional criteria and tests for determining the death of a human being, such a definition is situated at the level of a philosophical anthropology that serves as the starting point for an ethical discussion about the end of life. The definition of human personal death ultimately refers to the definition of the person. In order to do this, I analyze, first, against the background of the distinction between "human being" and "person", those theories that situate death exclusively on the biological level or, on the contrary, solely on the personal level, that is, without any reference to the human body. I will then address the proposal to shift the question of defining human personal death to the ethical level and investigate whether a living human being who is irreversibly deprived of the exercise of the so-called personal properties, such as self-consciousness, could be considered as dead. I propose to examine critically these different definitions of death in connection with the definitions of person and to show the weakness of the dualist position that distinguishes "human death" and "personal death".

Part Two of this study is devoted to a reflection on the knowledge of (my) mortality and of human personal death. In attempting to grasp the specific difference between the human being and other living beings – more specifically, animals – with regard to their relations to (their) death, thinkers have cited the human abilities to abstract and to form concepts; to laugh; to construct a language; to invent, fabricate, and use a tool, as well as the human capacity for self-consciousness, which makes possible a knowledge of death and mortality, both universal and personal. Only the human being who has attained a certain level of mental development would be aware of his mortality and of death, which would imply that a child below a certain stage of maturity lacks this ability.[16] Thus, for Heidegger,[17] the spokesman for an entire tradition, an animal that is, in his opinion, devoid of consciousness and language can merely perish; only a human being is conscious that he *must* and *can* die; humans are likewise characterized by their relation to the dead, which

[16] See Susan Carey, *Conceptual Change in Childhood.*

[17] See Martin Heidegger, *Being and Time*, p. 291 [p. 247]. In *On the Way to Language*, p. 107, Heidegger appears to connect the ability to relate to death with language, thus distinguishing between man and the animals: "Mortals are they who can experience death as death. Animals cannot do so. The essential relation between death and language flashes up before us, but still remains unthought" [p. 215: *"Die Sterblichen sind jene, die den Tod als Tod erfahren können. Das Tier vermag dies nicht. Das Wesensverhältnis zwischen Tod und Sprache blitzt auf, ist aber noch ungedacht"*].

is evident in their various beliefs in an afterlife, in funeral rituals, as well as in their rebellion against death. It would appear, then, that the awareness and knowledge of death and of mortality express, to use Gadamer's phrase, "the ontological honor"[18] proper to the human being.

This "honor" that is expressed in the *cogitatio mortis* is the source of a paradox that Pascal summarizes as follows: "All I know is that I must soon die; but what I know least is this very death which I cannot escape".[19] The first statement raises the question about the origin of our knowledge and awareness of our mortal condition, as well as the question of its degree of certitude. How does one have an awareness of it? Whence does such knowledge spring? Is it acquired, or already present in the unconscious mind and thus the object of a Platonic reminiscence? Is it a matter of foreknowledge, an intuitive knowledge, or is it, on the contrary, the result of experiencing the death of someone else? How does one arrive at the declaration that death is "the only certainty"[20] or that "my death", as Heidegger puts it, is the basis for my very certitude that I exist?

Pascal's second statement accentuates the enigmatic character of death as such, as opposed to dying. What do we know about death, which cannot be experienced? Can we think about it and measure it? Is it not, rather, inconceivable? Wouldn't rational thanatological discourse be devoid of meaning and doomed to failure? Despite the fact that death cannot be grasped intentionally (by means of rational cognition) and that it is not a phenomenon, can we nevertheless delve somewhat into this enigma by approaching death from the perspective of the passivity of its occurrence and with the help of the concept of frontier? Would the thesis of death *in* life, as a part of life, make it possible to experience death and to grasp it better? Or is it not in fact completely beyond the realm of life? Are we not faced with a no man's land? Is a phenomenology of death possible, starting from the premise that the states of life and death are mutually exclusive, as Epicurus and Wittgenstein have noted? Does the predication "my death" have any meaning? Is it possible to speak of death "in" life?

Part Three of our study deals with the axiological question of thanatology: is death nothing to us – as Epicurus admirably maintained – or,

18 Hans-Georg Gadamer, "La mort comme question", p. 21: *"l'honneur ontologique"*.

19 Blaise Pascal, *Pensées*, fragment 194, p. 68 [pp. 125–6: *"tout ce que je connais est que je dois bientôt mourir; mais ce que j'ignore le plus est cette mort même que je ne saurais éviter"*].

20 Søren Kierkegaard, "At a Graveside", p. 91.

on the contrary, can it be regarded as an evil? It is not a matter of knowing whether death is an evil for the survivors, especially for those who loved the departed person, but of determining whether it is an evil for the subject himself, not while he is still living (that is, dying), but as of that moment when he is deceased, when he "finds himself" in the state of death. The question becomes all the more interesting for philosophy if one introduces – from the methodological perspective, so as to take the same point of departure as Epicurus – an *a priori* that consists of identifying death, and hence the state of being dead, with the absence of an afterlife. Assuming, then, that there is no life after death, how can it be maintained that evil or a wrong has been done to a deceased party who no longer exists? Death appears instead to be nothing to me, since as long as I am alive, my death is not, and when I am dead, I no longer am. My death, therefore, is nothing to fear. This is the challenging argument crafted by Epicurus.

For the sake of clarification, I would like to point out the fact that death is evaluated in several ways in philosophy: as something indifferent, as a good (in itself or depending on the circumstances), or finally as an evil (in itself or depending on the circumstances).

1. First, death can be understood, following Epicurus, as *indifferent*: for the dead person it would be neither a good nor an evil. This position is based on the premise that there is no such thing as a personal afterlife, and that in order for a state of affairs to be considered as a good or an evil, it is necessary for the subject to experience it.
2. The second possibility is to regard death as a *good in itself*. Here we find two trains of thought, all of which are located on a different level from the ideas associated with evolution or the death instinct. (a) The first way of thinking about death as a good in itself is illustrated by those who maintain that it is better not to be than to be and who understand existence as a curse and consider it as something that ought not to be. When King Midas asked what is the best thing in the world, the wise man Silenus replied that it "is utterly beyond your reach: not to be born, not to *be*, to be *nothing*. But the second best for you is – to die soon".[21] In a

[21] Quoted in Friedrich Nietzsche, *The Birth of Tragedy*, §3, p. 42 [p. 35: *"Das Allerbeste ist für Dich gänzlich unerreichbar: nicht geboren zu sein, nicht zu sein, nichts zu sein. Das Zweitbeste aber ist für dich bald zu sterben"*]. See Marcus Tullius Cicero, *Tusculan Disputations*, book I, xlviii (p. 139); Epicurus, *Letter to Menoeceus*, § 126–127 (p. 31); Lucius Mestrius

less pessimistic way, yet likewise emphasizing the agreeable side of a dreamless sleep, Socrates, in the *Apology*,[22] conceives of death as a "gain". Other thinkers acknowledge it as a good or as "the highest good",[23] and several anecdotes are also enlightening in this regard: the one, for example, about Cleobis and Biton, sons of an Argive priestess who asked the goddess to grant them the greatest good that a god can give to a human being and were discovered dead the next day. Plutarch adopts this idea: death is a good, because it delivers the human being from the evils and servitude of life and rewards piety.[24] The idea that life is a punishment and death is a gain is of Orphic-Pythagorean origin. These writers, however, do not offer counterarguments to the provocative thesis of Epicurus, who identifies death with nonbeing and declares that the dead man is not capable of feeling or experiencing anything. How could the dead man experience his state as something good, when he no longer exists? (b) A second line of argument proclaiming death to be a good can be found among the proponents of a metaphysics of being who affirm the personal afterlife of the subject, to whom it is given to contemplate the perfect and absolute good, that is, God, if he is judged worthy on the basis of good actions performed during his life. Ambrose of Milan,[25] for example, maintains that death is a good for the Christian, because it delivers him from life's calamities, from evils (a favorite theme of the Stoics), and leads him to the true life. Nevertheless Ambrose does not address the Epicurean challenge per se. The neo-Platonists and the pseudo-Platonists[26] likewise belong to this category.

Plutarch, *A Letter of Condolence to Apollonius*, 27, 115D ff. (pp. 179 f.); Theognis, *Elegies*, I, 425–428 (p. 111).

[22] Plato, *Socrates' Defense (Apology)*, 40c-e (pp. 24 f.).

[23] See Marcus Tullius Cicero, *Tusculan Disputations*, book I, xlvi, 110 (p. 133); xl, 95 f. (pp. 115 f.). These stories are recounted also by Lucius Mestrius Plutarch, *A Letter of Condolence to Apollonius*, 14 f., 108E f. (pp. 143 f.).

[24] See Lucius Mestrius Plutarch, *A Letter of Condolence to Apollonius*, 10 f., 106C f. (pp. 131 f.).

[25] See Ambrose of Milan, "On the Death of His Brother Satyrus".

[26] See, for example, the remarks of Axiochus about death, after he has compared immortality to being set free from the prison in which the living body finds itself. "For no longer do I have a fear of death, but now I even have a longing for it" (Plato-pseudo, *Axiochos*, 370d-e [p. 45]); "I now feel love toward it [death]. [...] Now I despise life, since I am ready to move to a better home" (372b [pp. 49–51]).

3. Third, death can be understood as *a good or an evil depending on the circumstances*,[27] which include the ability of the subject to complete his task, to accomplish projects or the plan for his life that he deems important. Often, from a utilitarian perspective that is sometimes accompanied by hedonism, there is an attempt to determine whether death is a good or an evil by means of a quantitative and qualitative calculus of the benefits and disadvantages that the subject would have experienced if he had continued to live. Given that mindset, death could easily be considered as a good in a case where it came to deliver the subject in some way from a catastrophic "quality of life". "Life is the condition of all goods, but alas it is also the condition of all evils. When continued life promises only great evils unmixed with any compensating goods, our best bet may be death".[28]
4. Without necessarily being seen by the subject as the greatest evil,[29] death can be understood as *an evil in itself*.

I will present and analyze the famous Epicurean thesis of "the nothingness of death" against the background of his three presuppositions, which are materialism, hedonism, and experientialism. The last-mentioned, together with the requirement of a subject, will be the object of a painstaking inquiry: I will discuss two sets of examples, the purpose of which is to counter both experientialism and the question of posthumous states. Distancing myself from the Epicurean understanding of evil, I will propose a concept of the evil of death as a privation. But of what does it deprive a human being? Is death always an evil? Or, on the contrary, is it an evil only depending on the circumstances? If it is an evil of privation, is that not also the case with the nonexistence preceding conception?

Ironically, it seems appropriate to conclude this introduction by adding that this study is meant to be a beginning and at the same time

[27] Among other discussions, see Anthony L. Brueckner and John Martin Fischer, "Why Is Death Bad?", p. 221; Peter C. Dalton, "Death and Evil", p. 203; Fred Feldman, *Confrontations with the Reaper*, pp. 140, 144, 149–50, 226; Jeff McMahan, "Death and the Value of Life" and *The Ethics of Killing*; Mary Mothersill, "Death", p. 92; Robert Nozick, "Dying", pp. 20 ff., and *Philosophical Explanations*, pp. 580 f.; Leonard W. Sumner, "A Matter of Life and Death"; Bernard Williams, "The Makropolus Case".

[28] Leonard W. Sumner, "A Matter of Life and Death", pp. 161–2.

[29] See Aristotle, *Nicomachean Ethics*, III, 6 (1115a 9 ff.) and I, 6 (1097b 33 ff.); Marcus Tullius Cicero, *Tusculan Disputations*, book I, v, 9 (pp. 11 f.); Augustine, *City of God*, XIII, 6 (pp. 306 f.); Ernst Bloch, *The Principle of Hope*, pp. 1103 ff. [pp. 1297 ff.]; Jean-Paul Sartre, *Being and Nothingness*, pp. 680 ff. [pp. 615 ff.]; Thomas Nagel, "Death".

a reference point for a much broader philosophical reflection. It is intended as a modest contribution to what I judge to be one of the most important philosophical inquiries, namely, the human being's relation to "his own death". To philosophize is nothing other than to get ready for death: "the whole life of the philosopher", as Plato again says, "is a preparation for death".[30]

[30] Marcus Tullius Cicero, *Tusculan Disputations*, book I, xxx, 74 (p. 87).

PART ONE

HUMAN PERSONAL DEATH

1

Definitions of Death and What We Mean by Person

1. INTRODUCTION

The recent technological discoveries that make it possible to transplant human organs and to keep a human being alive artificially with the help of machines, as well as the controversy surrounding euthanasia, have given rise to a heated debate revolving around the question of knowing when a human subject is really dead. This inquiry is nothing new. What is new are the motives driving people to look for particular *criteria* and *signs* of death that are truly reliable. Whereas people in times past were moved by the fear of being buried alive,[1] our contemporaries are afraid that their organs might be taken from them while they are still alive – that they might undergo a "vivisection",[2] to use Jonas's expression – or that they might be killed unawares by euthanasia. In order to be sure that one is not killing a human being while removing his organs, it is crucial to define the nature of human death and then to develop tests for certifying the demise. If a patient is in a so-called permanent vegetative state and is being kept alive artificially by means of mechanical support, is that human being dead? Can the same be said of Terri Schiavo, who continued to live only because of artificial feeding and hydration? Should we assume that she had passed away the moment when she was "irreversibly" plunged into that state? An anencephalic newborn has no cortex, and a human being suffering from "locked-in

[1] See A. Keith Mant, "The Medical Definition of Death"; Claudio Milanesi, *Mort apparente, mort imparfaite.*

[2] Hans Jonas, "Gehirntod und menschliche Organbank: Zur pragmatischen Umdefinierung des Todes", p. 221: "Vivisektion".

syndrome", for example, Bauby as described in his book *The Diving Bell and the Butterfly*, is conscious but imprisoned, so to speak, in what is said to be a so-called permanent vegetative state: can they or should they be considered dead?

The answer to these questions is not situated primarily at the level of establishing useful functional criteria, together with tests (procedures to be followed, medical techniques) with a view to determining when a particular human individual has died and the fact that he is dead. Certainly the choice of functional criteria has important ethical repercussions in specifying the moment after which, for example, (a) the death of "N." should be deemed a murder, (b) the transplantation of "N.'s" organs is permissible without the risk of performing a vivisection, and (c) one can bury "N." and settle his estate. Although the criteria are subject to change and certain ones can be abandoned in favor of others as scientific and technological discoveries advance, I disagree with Feldman's claim[3] that the choice of criteria is random and relative, that it is a "contingent truth" to be gauged according to the wishes of the majority and according to the success obtained in applying them to practical cases. Although the criteria depend on scientific findings that are subject to refinement and corroboration, or may be called into question again by a theory better suited to deal with problematic aspects, they are based first of all on a certain objective knowledge. It is not a question of determining, according to standards of profitability or practical utility, which criteria would be more convenient in such and such a society, group of individuals, or situation, but rather a matter of discovering objective, universal criteria for noting when death "breaks into" the life of a human being.

The question posed by Veatch – "What is it in an individual that is so significant that when it has been lost the person is no longer considered alive?"[4] – presupposes, first of all, a conceptual definition of human death gained from a philosophical analysis, more specifically from philosophical anthropology, which constitutes the point of departure for the ethical discussion.[5] This "most fundamental philosophical question

[3] See Fred Feldman, *Confrontations with the Reaper*, pp. 14 ff.

[4] Robert M. Veatch, *Death, Dying and the Biological Revolution*, p. 33. See David Lamb, *Death, Brain Death and Ethics*, pp. 1–2; Edward T. Bartlett and Stuart J. Youngner, "Human Death and the Destruction of the Neocortex", p. 200.

[5] This is maintained likewise by the physician Charles M. Culver and the philosopher Bernard Gert in *Philosophy in Medicine*, p. 179: "We believe that a proper understanding of the ordinary meaning of this word or concept [death] must be developed before a medical criterion is chosen. We must decide what is ordinarily meant by death before physicians can decide how to measure it". See also Peter D. G. Skegg, *Law, Ethics and*

about death"[6] tries to answer the query "What is human death?" Such discourse precedes debates about public policy and ethical considerations, while having important repercussions on them. The conceptual level is logically prior to the functional level. The second requires the first. Although the choice of functional criteria is the result of medical research, it implies a particular understanding of death and life, of a dead human being and of a living human being.[7] Some writers confuse these two epistemological levels[8] and use the expression "definition of death" when they are arguing on the functional level. They pretend in this way to "define" death – to answer the question about the *nature* of death, about what death is – by means of functional criteria that answer the question about *when* death occurs. However excellent and precise one's analysis of the criteria of death may be, it does not enable us to define and know the nature of death, which eludes technology and verification by empirical methods.

Certainly, any attempt to answer the ethical questions mentioned previously will be based on a conceptual definition of human death, yet it calls also for an investigation of fundamental questions, among them: what criterion defines the human person (*who is a person?*) and is that criterion all-inclusive (*are all human beings persons?*). Since what is at stake in bioethics varies according to the concept that one has of the human person, philosophy must perform its task today prior to the ethical problems that are being debated. One of the purposes of philosophy is to contribute to such a debate in modern societies.

This anthropological reflection underlying current bioethical debates rests in turn on an *a priori* that is accepted by most practicing physicians, even though some describe it as "stupid" and "useless"[9]: a human being

Medicine, p. 187. Roland Puccetti explains similarly that "you cannot offer argument as to when a person may be safely considered dead without doing philosophy. The question, of course, is whether you are doing philosophy well or badly": "Does Anyone Survive Neocortical Death?", p. 76. See also Bernard Gert, Charles M. Culver, and Danner K. Clouse, *Bioethics*, p. 290.

6 Fred Feldman, "Death", p. 818.

7 We could make a comparison here with Heidegger's ontological analysis of death, which presupposes an ontic reflection. I refer the reader to the second part of this book (chapter 2) for the distinction between "ontological" and "ontical" and the Heideggerian thesis of *Sein-zum-Tode* ["Being-towards-death"].

8 See for example Guy Durant, "Mort (bioéthique de la –)", p. 1691.

9 See Steven Pinker, "The Stupidity of Dignity", and Ruth Macklin, "Dignity is a Useless Concept", pp. 1419–20: "Dignity is a useless concept in medical ethics and can be eliminated without any loss of content". For Peter Singer "human dignity" and "mankind" are nothing but "fine phrases [...] the last resource of those who have run out of arguments" (*Applied Ethics*, p. 228).

is endowed with rights, and in particular with the fundamental right to live, because he or she has a dignity[10] that requires that this person be treated, according to the second categorical imperative of Kant, as an end in itself and never merely as a means to an end. A human person has no price; in other words, he or she eludes all instrumentalization, as emphasized by the recent report by the U.S. president's Council on Bioethics entitled *Human Dignity and Bioethics.*[11] Hence, to the extent that a newborn or a human being afflicted with severe mental retardation or profound dementia is considered a person, he or she has an inalienable right to life. If, on the other hand, he or she should not be considered a person – a position held in recent decades by a growing number of philosophers headed by Engelhardt, Harris, Lizza, McMahan, Singer, and Tooley,[12] to mention only a few – his or her death at the hands of others could not be viewed as a homicide.

The conceptual definition of human death refers to a definition of the human person, because dignity and rights, more specifically the right to life, are attributed to a being that has the status of person. For several years now a growing number of philosophers follow Engelhardt in maintaining that "crucial to these disputes is the issue of whether the death that is to be determined is the death of a person or an organism".[13] Such a statement presupposes the veracity of the underlying anthropological thesis that one must distinguish between a human being and a human person. Death would thus be reduced either to its biological dimension alone, without any reference to the disappearance of the person, or else exclusively to the so-called personal dimension, without any reference to the human body. Other philosophers propose to resolve the thanatological question by shifting it to the ethical level: the real question would then be to determine whether the life of a human being

[10] See Thomas de Koninck, *De la dignité humaine.*

[11] See Edmund D. Pellegrino, Adam Schulman, and Thomas W. Merrill, eds., *Human Dignity and Bioethics.*

[12] See, among other works, Tristram H. Engelhardt, *The Foundations of Bioethics*, pp. 135 ff., 239 ff.; John Harris, *The Value of Life*; John P. Lizza, *Persons, Humanity, and the Definition of Death*; Jeff McMahan, *The Ethics of Killing*; Peter Singer, *Practical Ethics*, pp. 85 ff., 117 ff.; Michael Tooley, "Abortion and Infanticide", *Abortion and Infanticide*, and "Personhood". See also Dieter Birnbacher, "Das Dilemma des Personbegriffs"; Peter Carruthers, *Introducing Persons*, pp. 227 ff.; Stéphane Chauvier, *Qu'est-ce qu'une personne?*; Jonathan Glover, *Causing Death and Saving Lives*; Norbert Hoerster, *Abtreibung im säkularen Staat*; Roland Puccetti, "The Life of a Person", pp. 172 ff.; Leonard W. Sumner, *Abortion and Moral Theory*; Mary Anne Warren, "On the Moral and Legal Status of Abortion", pp. 43 ff.; Robert N. Wennberg, *Life in the Balance*, pp. 31 ff.

[13] Tristram H. Engelhardt, "Redefining Death: The Mirage of Consensus", p. 320.

in a so-called permanent vegetative state is worth the trouble of living. Other philosophers, finally, advocate a diversity of definitions of death within the framework of a secular ethics. In addition to presenting and critiquing these attempts at defining death, I would like to demonstrate here the weakness of the thesis that supposes that "personal death" is different from "human death."

2. BIOLOGICAL DEATH

The so-called classical or traditional functional criterion that defines human death as the irreversible cessation of spontaneous heartbeat and respiration put physicians in a delicate situation with regard to euthanasia and the acquisition of organs for transplantation that were very much in demand. This led to an increasingly urgent need for a change of criteria defining "when" death occurs. In 1959 two French physicians, Mollaret and Goulon,[14] published an article describing *"le coma dépassé"* as the irrevocable destruction of the brain resulting from a lack of oxygen supply, while the patient is being kept alive by means of artificial respiration; about ten years later an *ad hoc* committee of Harvard Medical School – made up of theologians, lawyers, and physicians – published a report proposing a "new" functional criterion for death: irreversible coma, the cessation of cerebral activity (brain death).[15] The development of this "new" criterion was based on reasons that are recognized today as being primarily pragmatic and utilitarian, in particular for the purpose of harvesting and transplanting organs. As Engelhardt explains, "Technological advances, rising costs, and an interest in transplantation pressed the question of whether one could not hold brain-dead but otherwise living human bodies to no longer be the bodies of living persons".[16] The committee in question wished not only to facilitate organ transplants but also to protect those who unplugged equipment providing artificial life support from accusations of murder and active euthanasia.[17] It also wanted to relieve society of

[14] See Pierre Mollaret and Maurice Goulon, "Le Coma dépassé".

[15] See "A Definition of Irreversible Coma", pp. 85–8.

[16] Tristram H. Engelhardt, *The Foundations of Bioethics*, pp. 245–6. See Jeff McMahan, *The Ethics of Killing*, pp. 426–7.

[17] "A Definition of Irreversible Coma", p. 87: "It should be emphasized that we recommend the patient be declared dead before any effort is made to take him off a respirator [...] otherwise, the physicians would be turning off the respiration on a person who is, in the present strict, technical application of law, still alive".

the financial burden of providing medical treatment for "brain-dead" patients on artificial life support.[18] The proposed diagnosis of death is based on the following indications: flat-line electro-encephalograph (EEG) readings over a period of forty-eight hours, complete dilation of the pupils together with a failure of the reflex response to light, a lack of reflexes in the muscles and tendons, circulation at a standstill despite the massive injection of drugs that dilate blood vessels, carotid and vertebral angiography or arteriography, and so forth. Hence death occurs when there is a permanent cessation of all brain activities.

The encephalon (vertebrate brain) is composed of, first, the brain or neocortex, which encases the cerebral hemispheres and the basal nuclei and which makes possible the exercise of the so-called personal mental faculties; second, the brain stem, made up of the centers that regulate respiratory and cardio-vascular functions, among others; and finally, the cerebellum, which coordinates movement. To summarize quickly the current debate: on the one hand are the proponents of whole-brain death, who declare that the death of a human being takes place when all activities of the brain – the neocortex and the brain stem – are no longer functioning. They maintain that the human body is an integral part of the person, who is defined by rationality and whose brain function is essential for the existence of the personal organism. On the other hand we find the proponents of brain stem death, who follow Feldman, Perrett, and Rosenberg[19] in defining death at a strictly biological level, in other words, as the permanent cessation of the interactive functioning of the organism understood as a unity. The brain stem is of crucial significance, because unlike the neocortical structures it is responsible for the integrative capacity of the human organism understood as a unity and for the coordination of the different organs and subsystems that make up that organic unity. Bernat, Culver, and Gert declare in chorus that death is "the permanent cessation of functioning of the organism as a

[18] "Our primary purpose is to define irreversible coma as a new criterion for death. There are two reasons why there is need for a definition: (1) Improvements in resuscitative and supportive measures have led to increased efforts to save those who are desperately injured. Sometimes these efforts have only partial success so that the result is an individual whose heart continues to beat but whose brain is irreversibly damaged. The burden is great on patients who suffer permanent loss of intellect, on their families, on the hospitals, and on those in need of hospital beds already occupied by these comatose patients. (2) Obsolete criteria for the definition of death can lead to controversy in obtaining organs for transplantation". *Ibid.*, p. 85.

[19] See Fred Feldman, *Confrontations with the Reaper*, pp. 19 ff.; Roy W. Perrett, *Death and Immortality*, pp. 14 ff.; Jay F. Rosenberg, *Thinking Clearly about Death*, p. 105.

whole".[20] The U.S. president's commission emphasized in 1981 that "the brain is the regulator of the body's integration".[21] Death occurs when the brain stem irreversibly ceases to function by itself. Hence, according to Feldman, it is wrong to advocate, as a growing number of philosophers do, a concept of death that would be applicable solely to persons. Human death, he explains, is situated exclusively on the biological level.[22] Lamb specifies that "the concept of 'death' can only be applied to organisms, not persons",[23] which is to say that "death is a biological concept".[24] Since the functions proper to the brain stem can be performed independently of the neocortical functions, it follows that a human being in a so-called irreversible vegetative state without mechanical support and definitively incapable of exercising the so-called personal properties – for example, self-consciousness and moral conscience – would not be considered a cadaver but rather a living organism, even though proponents of neocortical death, as we will see in a moment, insist that there would be no presence of a human person.

This definition of brain stem death is partly called into question in certain cases of locked-in syndrome, in which a conscious human being with a normal electroencephalogram is trapped within an organism that he or she is incapable of controlling (except, in certain cases, the eyes). The activity of the neocortex that makes self-consciousness and mental activities possible is disconnected on the functional level from the activity of the brain stem.[25] Although the definitive cessation of the

[20] James L. Bernat, Charles M. Culver, and Bernard Gert, "On the Definition and Criterion of Death", p. 390. See James L. Bernat, "How Much of the Brain Must Die in Brain Death?"; Charles M. Culver and Bernard Gert, *Philosophy in Medicine*, pp. 179 ff.; David Lamb, *Death, Brain Death and Ethics*, pp. 93, 96; Michael Lavin, "How Not to Define Death: Some Objections to Cognitive Approaches"; Chris Pallis, *The ABC of Brain Death*; Tom Russell, *Brain Death*; Peter D. G. Skegg, *Law, Ethics and Medicine*; Bernard Gert and Charles M. Culver (*Bioethic*) consider 25 years later that this definition is insufficient, that it is a "mistake" (p. 293) and "inadequate" (p. 293). They propose redefining death by adding the criterion of the permanent absence of consciousness: "Death is the permanent cessation of all observable natural functioning of the organism as a whole, and the permanent absence of consciousness in the organism as a whole, and in any part of that organism" (pp. 290, 293).

[21] *Defining Death*, p. 32.

[22] See Fred Feldman, *Confrontations with the Reaper*, p. 20.

[23] David Lamb, *Death, Brain Death and Ethics*, p. 93.

[24] James L. Bernat, Charles M. Culver, and Bernard Gert, "On the Definition and Criterion of Death", p. 390. See Charles M. Culver and Bernard Gert, *Philosophy in Medicine*, p. 182.

[25] "The locked-in patient [...] suffers significant, but incomplete, destruction of the brain. Unlike the Quinlan-like patient [in a persistent vegetative state], the brain

latter – which can be replaced by mechanisms external to the organism – implies the beginning of the irreversible decline of the neocortical functions, this does not mean that such a human being is dead. A human being with locked-in syndrome is commonly considered alive.

3. SO-CALLED PERSONAL DEATH

3.1. The Distinction Between "Human Being" and "Person"

The case of locked-in syndrome, among others, leads a growing number of philosophers to define death as the irreversible loss of what is essential, not to a human organism, but to a person, in other words, the loss of the personal "self". Lizza, following the proponents of neocortical death and subtly introducing the distinction between "human being" and "person", explains that "the criteria for the death of a person or human being will therefore be determined by the loss of whatever properties are deemed essential to the nature of persons or human beings".[26] Engelhardt notes that the concept of neocortical death "implies a distinction between human biological life and human personal life, between the life of a human organism and the life of a human person".[27] Proponents of neocortical death refuse to employ the terms "human being" and "person" interchangeably and propose to define a human being according to strictly biological criteria. In effect "human being" would be the equivalent of "member of the species *Homo sapiens*". A person, on the other hand, would be defined by the actual exercise of a number of properties, in particular rationality, consciousness of oneself over time, as well as moral conscience and responsibility for one's actions. Thus, according to those philosophers, a human being is not necessarily a person solely by membership in the human species, but only to the extent that he or she is a subject who in an empirically

portions responsible for consciousness and cognition are intact. All portions of the brain stem and deep cerebral areas responsible for integration of vegetative functions have been destroyed. However, the blood supply and neural connections to the other cerebral areas, as well as the reticular activating system located in the brain stem, have been spared. Although the patient cannot spontaneously regulate respiration, blood pressure, temperature, hormonal balance and other functions, he is awake and alert. [His] life can only be maintained through the full efforts of the Intensive Care Unit staff". Edward T. Bartlett and Stuart J. Youngner, "Human Death and Destruction of Neocortex", pp. 205–6.

26 John P. Lizza, *Persons, Humanity, and the Definition of Death*, p. 32.

27 Tristram H. Engelhardt, "Medicine and the Concept of Person", p. 170.

verifiable way actually exercises rationality and self-consciousness, on the one hand, and performs moral actions, on the other hand. Harris defines a person as a human being or any other being "[actually] capable of valuing its own existence"[28] or having "the capacity to want to exist and the sort of self-consciousness that makes the possession of such a want possible".[29] The exercise of this capacity makes it possible to identify human individuals or other forms of life that have "the sort of value and importance that makes appropriate and justifies our according [i.e., granting] to them the same concern, respect and protections as we [i.e., being persons] grant to one another".[30] One of the most-read authors on the subject of bioethics in the Anglo-Saxon world, Engelhardt, explains unambiguously that "what distinguishes persons is their [present] capacity to be self-conscious, rational, and concerned with worthiness of blame and praise. [...] On the other hand, not all humans are persons. Not all humans are self-conscious, rational, and able to conceive of the possibility of blaming and praising. Fetuses, infants, the profoundly mentally retarded, and the hopelessly comatose [and, as he explains further on, senile individuals and those who have suffered severe brain damage[31]] provide examples of human nonpersons. They are members of the human species but do not in and of themselves have standing in the secular moral community".[32] The same author explicitly maintains that "not all humans are equal",[33] as Singer does elsewhere. The latter agrees with Engelhardt that "the embryo, the later fetus, the profoundly intellectually disabled child, even the newborn infant [and, one could add, the adult human being suffering from profound dementia or in a so-called vegetative state] – all are indisputably members of the species Homo sapiens, but none are self-aware, have a sense of the future, or the capacity to relate to others"[34] (and therefore they are not persons). In an article published with his colleague Kuhse entitled "Should All Seriously Disabled Infants Live?" he explicitly declares that "normal adults and children, but not fetuses and infants are persons; that is, they are self-aware and purposeful beings with a sense of the past and the future. They can see their lives in a continuing process, they can identify with

[28] John Harris, *The Value of Life*, p. 18.

[29] *Ibid.*, p. 242.

[30] *Ibid.*, p. 18.

[31] See Tristram H. Engelhardt, *The Foundations of Bioethics*, p. 239.

[32] *Ibid.*, pp. 138–9.

[33] *Ibid.*, p. 135.

[34] Peter Singer, *Practical Ethics*, p. 86.

what has happened to them in the past, and they have hopes and plans for the future. For this reason we can say that in normal circumstances they value, or want, their own continued existence, and that life is in their interest. The same does not apply to fetuses or new-born infants. Neither a fetus nor an infant has the conceptual wherewithal to contemplate a future and to want, or value, that future".[35]

This supposedly real distinction between "human being" and "person" within the human species implies that certain humans cannot expect to be treated as persons, as ends in themselves, and that means ultimately that equality among human beings is an illusion. Singer notes unswervingly that "since no fetus is a person, no fetus has the same claim to life as a person. Now it must be admitted that these arguments apply to the newborn baby as much as to the fetus".[36] A few pages later he emphasizes that everything that he says with regard to newborns within the framework of the ethical debate about infanticide can likewise "apply to older children or adults whose mental age is and has always been that of an infant",[37] namely, to the severely mentally handicapped, to human beings suffering from profound dementia, or, in the case that concerns us, a human being who is in a so-called vegetative state. Presupposing his theory of interests (discussed further on), which requires that in order to have a right, and more specifically the right to life, one must exercise interests that are empirically verifiable, the Australian philosopher states that "the life of a self-aware being, capable of abstract thought, of planning for the future, of complex acts of communication, and so on [i.e., a person], is more valuable than the life of a being without these capacities [i.e., a human being]".[38] Following Singer in lockstep, Engelhardt argues that whereas "mere human biological life is of little moral value in and of itself",[39] a human person possesses rights and dignity.[40] All human beings are not equal. "Self-consciousness", Singer

35 Helga Kuhse and Peter Singer, "Should All Seriously Disabled Infants Live?", p. 239.

36 Peter Singer, *Practical Ethics*, p. 169. "In all this the newborn baby is on the same footing as the fetus, and hence fewer reasons exist against killing both babies and fetuses than exist against killing those who are capable of seeing themselves as distinct entities, existing over time", p. 171.

37 *Ibid.*, p. 181.

38 *Ibid.*, p. 61. See p. 73.

39 Tristram H. Engelhardt, *The Foundations of Bioethics*, p. 243.

40 "Insofar as we identify persons with moral agents, we exclude from the range of the concept of person those entities which are not self-conscious. Which is to say, only those beings are unqualified bearers of rights and duties who can both claim to be acknowledged as having a dignity beyond a value (i.e., as being ends in themselves), and can be responsible for their actions. [...] It is only respect for persons in this strict

explains, "is crucial in debates about whether a being has a right to life".[41] We find the same thesis in the writings of Hoerster, who for the most part adopts the theses of Singer and opines that "only a being with such self-consciousness [i.e., one which "possesses an awareness of its identity over time and has a concept of its ego or self which remains the same over time"] can have wishes about the future and, in this respect, an interest in survival".[42] Thus only a being that is a person possesses "a serious right to life",[43] to use an expression of Tooley. The latter author emphasizes that "having a right to life presupposes that one is capable of desiring to continue existing as a subject of experiences and other mental states. This in turn presupposes both that one has the concept of such a continuing entity and that one believes that one is oneself such an entity. So an entity that lacks such a consciousness of itself as a continuing subject of mental states does not have a right to life".[44]

3.2. John Locke's Philosophical Anthropology of the Person

The proponents of neocortical death, like a number of other philosophers who promote the distinction between "human being" and "person" within the framework of bioethical debate, generally rely in an *a priori* manner and without critical analysis on the Lockean definition of the person as "de-substantialized". They assume that his philosophical anthropology of the person is accurate, whereas it is vulnerable and poses serious problems, as Finnis rightly emphasizes.[45] Locke proposes

sense that cannot be violated without contradicting the idea of a moral order in the sense of living with others on the basis of mutual respect": Tristram H. Engelhardt, "Medicine and the Concept of Person", pp. 172–3.

41 Peter Singer, *Practical Ethics*, p. 73. Helga Kuhse and Peter Singer argue that "the assertion that human beings have a right to life depends on the fact that beings generally possess mental qualities that other living beings do not possess", namely the exercise of self-consciousness: "Individuals, Humans, and Persons: The Issue of Moral Status", p. 193.

42 Norbert Hoerster, *Abtreibung im säkularen Staat*, p. 75: *"Nur ein Wesen mit einem so verstandenen Ichbewusstsein ['dass es das Bewusstsein seiner Identität im Zeitablauf besitzt, dass es einen Begriff von einem Ich oder Selbst hat, das im Zeitablauf identisch ist'] kann zukunftsbezogene Wünsche und unter diesem Aspekt ein Überlebensinteresse haben".*

43 Michael Tooley, "Abortion and Infanticide", p. 37.

44 *Ibid.*, p. 49.

45 John Finnis notes in reference to the position of John Harris: "In his case, they are little more than a definition of 'person' resting uncritically on the authority of an under-interpreted and rationally most vulnerable proposal by Locke": John Finnis, "Misunderstanding the Case against Euthanasia", p. 69. For a critical discussion of

a philosophical anthropology that can be described as revolutionary inasmuch as it begins by envisaging the person independently of any material or rational substance. His definition of person is no longer based on the self as a substance (*le moi substance*) but rather on cognition, in other words, on the actual exercise of self-consciousness and moral conscience. The term "person" is in the first place "a forensic term",[46] which is to say that it has meaning only for a moral subject who imputes to himself his own actions and renders an accounting of them to his own conscience, thereby recognizing himself as the author of his own actions and thus as responsible for them. The revolutionary Lockean idea is thus the understanding of "person" within the specific framework of a legal tribunal, and consequently the reduction of the person to one's ability to see that one's moral acts are imputed to him or her. The English philosopher reduces the person to his or her social and moral role, thereby implicitly denying this status for all who do not perform empirically verifiable moral acts. Hence the person is defined by actual self-consciousness as the unifying principle in a Self who appropriates and imputes to itself present and past thoughts and moral acts by means of the memory – and does so independently of any substance, whether material or rational. The person is, to use John Locke's expression, "a thinking intelligent being, that has reason and reflection, and can consider itself as itself, the same thinking thing in different times and places".[47] Although our philosopher is not at all concerned about questions of life and death and, more particularly, about the definition of human death, he is nevertheless unambiguous in his concept of person and declares that one and the same person can exist in several bodies or several persons in a single body. He defends first of all the thesis of the person as self-consciousness – "without consciousness [of the self], there is no person"[48] – and then the thesis that the status of person "belongs only to intelligent agents capable of law, and happiness and misery",[49] thereby formulating the thesis of the person as moral conscience. In order to be

John Locke's position, see Bernard N. Schumacher, "La personne comme conscience de soi performante au cœur du débat bioéthique: Analyse critique de la position de John Locke". Some proponents of neocortical death, however, cite also the Kantian concept of the moral person as the autonomous subject that initiates those actions that can be imputed to him, an idea that we find elsewhere in similar form in the writings of the English philosopher.

46 John Locke, "Identity and Diversity", p. 346.

47 *Ibid.*, p. 335.

48 *Ibid.*, p. 344. Locke adds immediately thereafter: "and a carcass may be a person".

49 *Ibid.*, p. 346.

a person, one must be capable of actually experiencing happiness and misery, of caring about one's own happiness, and of projecting oneself into the future as the same self. In short, only a moral, self-conscious subject is able to be a person. In the Lockean perspective, however, the certainty of being the same self over time is anchored in solipsistic subjectivity, which poses serious problems: every consciousness is trapped in "its own private mental asylum".[50] Lockean anthropology does not manage, however, to place such a certainty upon an objective foundation. Nor does it succeed in distinguishing between the authentic memories that a person really has, on the one hand, and the pseudo-memories that a person believes that he has but which belong to another person or are the product of imagination or design. Here is the difficulty: can one demonstrate with certainty, morally and forensically, that a particular thought or action which has been appropriated and imputed by a person is authentic, in other words, that it really belongs to that person? Can we rule out the possibility that this particular thought or action is in reality a pseudo-memory and that it did not really exist? Much is at stake: one can judge (and consequently reward or punish) a person for his past actions only if the person present is the same as the one who performed those acts. Indeed, it sometimes happens that we subjectively consider some pseudo-memories about ourselves to be authentic, although the content of those memories never existed in reality. Accurately describing Lockean anthropology as a "radically subjectivist view of the person",[51] Taylor explains that this "disengaged [...] Punctual Self" is made up of a "pure independent consciousness",[52] detached from the singular corporeal substance. Hence the particular human body is perceived as a random, mechanical, and functional object: Koninck calls this the "disenchantment"[53] of the body, because it no longer has dignity.

3.3. Personal Death as the Irreversible Loss of Self-Consciousness

Proponents of neocortical death who rely on such a Lockean anthropology, which can fairly be described as dualistic,[54] define the human

[50] Fergus Kerr, *Theology after Wittgenstein*, p. 82. He describes it likewise as a "picture of the solitary self-communing self, radically independent of relationships with anyone else in this world", p. 72.

[51] Charles Taylor, *Sources of the Self*, p. 172.

[52] *Ibid.*, pp. 159, 172.

[53] Thomas de Koninck, *De la dignité humaine*, p. 87: "désenchantement". See p. 95.

[54] This is true even though John Harris disputes it: John Harris, "A Reply to John Finnis", p. 41.

person by the exercise of self-consciousness, while for some of them the definition includes having moral conscience and interests. Personal death occurs, for these authors, when the person is irreversibly incapacitated and no longer exercises self-consciousness and moral conscience, in other words, upon the destruction of the neocortex. In practice this means that human beings who are irreversibly deprived of these mental functions are no longer persons. The American woman Karen Ann Quinlan in the so-called vegetative state and the anencephalic newborn, as well as a human being who suffers from severe brain damage or severe mental retardation – even though the proponents of neocortical death do not mention the last case – would then be considered as dead on the personal level but living from the point of view of their organisms, which are functioning autonomously.[55] What matters is not the death of the biological human organism, but exclusively the death of the person, which is defined, in Tooley's opinion, "either as the complete ceasing to be of a continuing subject of mental states or as the severing of all relationship between such a continuing subject and the biological organism with which it has been associated".[56] Seeking to define death in some way other than the biological approach, Veatch declares that "when this embodied capacity for consciousness or social interaction is gone irreversibly, then and only then, do I want society to treat me as dead",[57] and Truog, Fackler, and Agich follow this line precisely in maintaining that death is "the irreversible loss of the capacity for consciousness".[58] As for Green and Wikler, they determine, on the basis of the concept of personal identity, that "N." is dead when he is no longer in continuous possession of certain psychological properties over time.[59] Similarly, McMahan, relying on this anthropological dualism, maintains that "we are not organisms. We die or cease

55 See Michael Tooley, "Personhood", pp. 123–4.

56 Michael Tooley, "Decisions to Terminate Life and the Concept of Person", pp. 75–6. See p. 65. He explains in *Abortion and Infanticide* (p. 163) "that there are ways in which human persons can be destroyed without *any* destruction of the *general* capacities of any human organism".

57 Robert M. Veatch, "Whole-Brain, Neocortical, and Higher Brain Related Concepts", p. 182.

58 Robert D. Truog and James C. Fackler, "Rethinking Brain Death", p. 1711. See also George J. Agich, "The Concepts of Death and Embodiment".

59 Michael B. Green and Daniel Wikler, "Brain Death and Personal Identity", p. 127: "The death of persons, unlike that of bodies, regularly consists in their ceasing to exist. [...] We have argued, following other personal identity theorists, that a given person ceases to exist with the destruction of whatever processes there are which normally underlie that person's psychological continuity and connectedness".

to exist when our brains lose the capacity for consciousness in a way that is in principle irreversible".[60] The human person is not identical with his or her biological organism, which does not have "any intrinsic moral significance";[61] rather the person is defined as "an entity with a mental life that is strongly psychologically connected from day to day, which is possible only when self-consciousness is achieved".[62] McMahan goes so far as to say that "it is entirely natural to say that a person dies when he ceases to exist [i.e., ceases to exercise self-consciousness], even if his organism remains alive".[63] "If one ceases to be a person in this sense [i.e., loses the exercise of self-consciousness], he or she ceases to exist".[64] At issue here is not the loss of a property belonging to the person, but the loss of the person himself, in other words, his death. Zaner likewise emphasizes that "the permanent loss of personhood *is* death in the most significant sense, and it is this that should form the core of public policy or legislative statute".[65] He could not put it any more clearly than when he states that "death is the death of the person, not the body".[66] Bartlett and Youngner also, presupposing a dualistic, functionalistic (*performante*) anthropology, maintain that "the irreversible destruction of the neocortex – that is, the center of consciousness and cognition – constitutes death".[67] Shann, a specialist in anencephaly, plainly advocates the thesis "that the organ that really matters is the cerebral cortex. If the cortex is dead, there is permanent loss of consciousness and there can be no person, no personality, even though the organism may still be alive (with a beating heart, and even breathing movements). If the cortex of the brain is dead, the person is dead. I suggest that it should be legal to use the organs from the body of the dead person for transplantation".[68]

60 Jeff McMahan, *The Ethics of Killing*, p. 424. He likewise notes on page 425: "I propose to say that when a person ceases to exist by losing the capacity for consciousness, he dies". Jeff McMahan, "Brain Death, Cortical Death and Persistent Vegetative State", p. 257: "It seems that what ceases to exist with cortical death is the *mind*, and that is what we essentially are. One cannot cease to have a mind without ceasing to exist".

61 Jeff McMahan, *The Ethics of Killing*, p. 214. See p. 212.

62 *Ibid.*, p. 45. See p. 55.

63 *Ibid.*, p. 425.

64 *Ibid.*, p. 45. See p. 55.

65 Richard M. Zaner, "Introduction", p. 7.

66 *Ibid.*, p. 10.

67 Edward T. Bartlett and Stuart J. Youngner, "Human Death and Destruction of Neocortex", p. 211.

68 Frank Shann, "The Cortically Dead Infant Who Breathes", p. 30.

Lizza emphasizes, as Harris does elsewhere,[69] that from the moment when the neuro-physiological basis for cognitive functions (which enables the exercise of the so-called personal properties to be manifested empirically) has been destroyed, the person no longer exists: that is, he or she is deceased. He explicitly refers to the so-called vegetative state and notes (incorrectly) that "there is an implied consensus among philosophers in the Western tradition that these entities are not persons" and that this claim is supported by "the philosophical tradition".[70] McMahan explains that "when a person lapses into a PVS [persistent vegetative state], he ceases to exist. What remains is a living but unoccupied human organism".[71] Against the backdrop of the Lockean anthropological thesis, which renders the person insubstantial by considering the individual human body as an accident and by situating the self at the level of the exercise of self-consciousness, the American philosopher explains several pages later that "since you and I are essentially minds and are not identical with our organisms, an anencephalic infant [and one could also mention a human being who is severely mentally handicapped and irreversibly deprived of the exercise of self-consciousness or a human being with advanced Alzheimer's disease[72]] is a fundamentally different sort of thing from us [who are persons; McMahan calls a human being who throughout the past exercised self-consciousness but is now suffering from advanced Alzheimer's disease a "post-person"[73]]. It is simply an organism – a permanently unoccupied human organism. Whereas in a normal infant crib there are two distinct things – a human organism and the infant mind or self that will eventually become a person – there is only one individual in the crib of an anencephalic infant. This organism may well be alive, but it will never support the existence of a mind, self, or person".[74]

Hence proponents of neocortical death maintain that the person does not begin to exist until some time after the birth of the human organism, and that it can cease to exist before the death of the organism. The

69 John Harris, "A Reply to John Finnis", p. 42: "For example, in persistent vegetative state it is not that the person is absent from the body, it is that, as in death, the body has ceased to be the body of a person. It is a living human body [...] but it is not the living human body of a person".

70 John P. Lizza, *Persons, Humanity, and the Definition of Death*, p. 33. See also "Persons and Death", pp. 355–6, and "Conceptual Basis for Brain Death Revisited", p. 58.

71 Jeff McMahan, *The Ethics of Killing*, p. 446. See pp. 424, 428.

72 See *Ibid.*, 43–4, where he refers explicitly to Alzheimer's patients.

73 *Ibid.*, p. 55.

74 *Ibid.*, p. 451.

persistence of physical identity from the fetal stage to old age is in no way disputed. Indeed, the human being begins to exist as an individual as soon as the cells making it up start to function together in an integral, organized way – in biological terms from the moment of conception, as the embryologist Rager recently emphasized.[75] Although there is physical continuity from fetus to old man at the level of the organism, understood as a unity, this does not mean, for proponents of neocortical death, that there is any mental continuity. Indeed, the person who is conscious of him- or herself is not, according to Kuhse and Singer, the newborn that he or she "was" some years ago, just as the human being in a state of profound dementia or a so-called permanent vegetative state is in no way the person that he or she "was" before lapsing into that state. We began to live as persons, in their opinion, only from the moment when we "became continuing selves",[76] that is to say, when we started to be conscious of ourselves. Not only Puccetti[77] and Harris,[78] but also McMahan follow this line of argument, stating that "we begin to exist when our brains develop the capacity to generate consciousness [of self] and mental activity [i.e., some time after birth, specifically somewhere between the age of one and two years][79] [...] and we cease to exist when our brains lose that capacity in a way that is in principle irreversible".[80] In short, from the perspective of the personal subject, "we never existed as newborn infants or fetuses".[81] And Engelhardt raises the stakes by declaring that "mere human biological life precedes the emergence of the life of persons in the strict sense, and it usually continues for a

75 See Günter Rager, "Données biologiques et réflexions sur la personne".

76 See Helga Kuhse and Peter Singer, "Should All Seriously Disabled Infants Live?", p. 241: "But there is no mental continuity, and in this crucial sense *we* are not, and never were, infants, foetuses, or embryos. Our lives as *persons* – as self-aware and purposeful beings with a sense of the past and the future – did not begin until some time after birth, when we ceased to be beings with momentary interest and became 'continuing selves'".

77 See Roland Puccetti, "The Life of a Person", p. 170: "But if so [the person is understood as psychological continuity, as self-consciousness], how vain it seems to extend personhood beyond the loss of a capacity for conscious experience, and equally so to thrust it back in time to a stage of organic life before that capacity existed".

78 See John Harris, "A Reply to John Finnis", p. 41: "When these [the exercise of the capacity of intelligence and autonomy, in short the capacity to value existence] are lacking the person has ceased to exist (or has not yet come into being)".

79 See Jeff McMahan, *The Ethics of Killing*, pp. 44 and 46.

80 *Ibid.*, p. 439.

81 *Ibid.*, p. 44. McMahan also maintains (p. 45): "that none of us now is psychologically continuous with a newborn infant, and thus that none of us is now numerically the same individual as a newborn infant".

while after their death".[82] Luper mentions that being a person is only one episode in the life of a human being, in other words, that the term "person" applies only to those stages of human life in which the human being is conscious of himself.[83] Hence the person is deceased when self-consciousness is irreversibly gone.[84]

Those who advocate the definition of neocortical death maintain, as we have said, that the human being in a so-called permanent vegetative state is therefore no longer a person, since the person was deceased at the moment when it lost the exercise of its so-called personal properties: according to this view and this diagnosis, Karen Ann Quinlan departed from this world on April 15, 1975, whereas her whole-brain death was declared on June 11, 1985. Her quality of life over the course of that ten-year interval was in no way different from that of a corpse that had been laid to rest.[85] Indeed, according to Puccetti, there are two types of human corpses: the great majority of them are no longer capable of breathing by themselves, that is, without artificial help, and a small minority of them are capable of breathing but have irreversibly lost consciousness of themselves.[86] A human being whose neocortex no longer functions, irreversibly so, but whose body continues to live as an organic unity without the aid of machines, is considered by some authors to be a "biologically living corpse" (Engelhardt),[87] a "breathing corpse" (Gervais and Puccetti),[88] or even "a thing" (Bartlett and Youngner).[89] If the burial of such an organism that is breathing by itself but is considered dead by proponents of neocortical death were to pose a psychological problem (for many would find such an act repulsive), Puccetti[90] proposes making sure that it stops breathing. Gervais suggests injecting it with potassium chlorite, for aesthetic reasons.[91] In any case, the introduction of such a definition, neocortical death, relying

[82] Tristram H. Engelhardt, *The Foundations of Bioethics*, p. 240. See p. 243.
[83] See Steven Luper, *The Philosophy of Death*, pp. 31 ff., 35.
[84] Tristram H. Engelhardt, *The Foundations of Bioethics*, p. 250: "By making permanent loss of consciousness the point at which humans are declared dead".
[85] See Roland Puccetti, "Does Anyone Survive Neocortical Death?", p. 83.
[86] See *ibid.*, p. 85.
[87] Tristram H. Engelhardt, *The Foundations of Bioethics*, p. 248.
[88] Karen G. Gervais, *Redefining Death*, p. 176. Roland Puccetti, "Does Anyone Survive Neocortical Death?", p. 85 and "The Conquest of Death", p. 252.
[89] Edward T. Bartlett and Stuart J. Youngner, "Human Death and Destruction of Neocortex", p. 211: "the death of a thing".
[90] See Roland Puccetti, "The Conquest of Death", p. 252.
[91] See Karen G. Gervais, *Redefining Death*, p. 176.

on an anthropology of the functioning person, at the heart of a health care policy is motivated mainly by reasons of a pragmatic and utilitarian sort: it is a question of "the simplest way", as Singer emphasizes, "of achieving the desirable end of allowing organs to be taken from these infants [anencephalics and cortically dead infants]".[92]

4. THE ANTHROPOLOGICAL CHALLENGE OF NEOCORTICAL DEATH

4.1. A Dualistic Anthropology

Despite their differences concerning the definition of the nature of death, defenders of neocortical death and proponents of brain stem death agree on an anthropological dualism that views the human body as extrinsically related to the person. They deny that a particular human organism is an integral and constitutive part of the person that reveals it in time and space. For the proponents of neocortical death, the human body is reduced to "a soul-possessing receptacle of the spirit",[93] as Habermas puts it. They maintain that an organism – generally speaking and therefore not in the individualized sense – is necessary to support the exercise in time of the so-called personal properties that constitute the Self. Functional self-consciousness (*la conscience de soi performante*) is incarnated during its temporal existence in a corporeal substance, which, however, is in no way constitutive of the person. Personal individuality is fundamentally independent of any specific organism.

Therefore, according to this hypothesis, there are two modes of existence: biological and personal; this dualism originates in the reduction of the person to the active functioning of the so-called personal states, described by Elshtain as the "sovereign self".[94] This reductive view defines a person solely in terms of the empirical functioning of its so-called personal properties, the presence of which is confirmed by behavioral analysis. The person is reduced to the personal acts that it performs, in other words, to certifiable properties. In reality this functioning is only the verifiable expression of the ontological constitution that makes such a display of performance possible; in other words, to

[92] Peter Singer, *Rethinking Life and Death*, p. 47. See pp. 36 ff.

[93] Jürgen Habermas, *The Future of the Human Nature*, p. 34 [p. 63: "zu einem beseelten Gefäss des Geistes"].

[94] Jean Bethke Elshtain, *Sovereignty*, p. 172. See also Charles Taylor, *Sources of the Self.*

quote MacIntyre, we act as persons "in order to develop our powers as independent reasoners, and so to flourish *qua* members of our species".[95] A human being does not *become* a person through the actual exercise of the faculty of reason. Such exercise is simply the fulfilment of what he or she already *is*.

Proponents of brain stem death and neocortical death invert the relation between the so-called personal properties and the very being that supports them. They maintain, in effect, that the so-called personal properties, insofar as they are exercised, are the entity (*le référent*), in other words, that those properties strictly speaking determine the very being of the person. Thus they are opposed to the thesis that the person is the entity and that self-consciousness or moral conscience is one particular essential (and not accidental) property of an entity, that is, of the person. The being of the person is the very source of the property that is activated. In order that the property of self-consciousness may be exercised, there must be an entity that makes such a display possible. The person is not a property of a being that attaches itself to one or another individual organic human body, but rather it is fundamentally the substrate that makes possible the concrete, empirically verifiable exercise of the so-called personal property and that thereby manifests what the person is.

This so-called personal property is nevertheless already fully "in act", that is, realized, in the individual person who subsists in a rational human nature. We can distinguish two ways of understanding "being in act". Presupposing the differentiation between act and exercise, one can maintain that an individual who, for various reasons, does not exercise a so-called personal property nevertheless exists "in act" as a person, in other words, accomplishes the act of personal existence. Think for example of a human being who is sleeping or inebriated, to quote two examples given by Locke, or one who is in a so-called vegetative state. The question of knowing whether or not this state is irreversible in no way detracts from the distinction mentioned. The statement that Karen Ann Quinlan is in an irreversible state only allows us to maintain that the concrete exercise of her self-consciousness has become impossible, whereas her self-consciousness is still present in act at the level of her ontological constitution, even if she will never again be capable of exercising it. Karen Ann Quinlan is fully a person, but she is fundamentally deficient, not at the level of her being, but more particularly at the level

95 Alasdair MacIntyre, *Dependent Rational Animals*, p. 71. See pp. 76, 81, 83, 105.

of the concrete exercise of the so-called personal properties, which makes us "independent practical reasoners".[96] Being a human person does not admit of degrees, in the sense of more or less, any more than being a cat or a horse does. As Finnis notes with reference to the human being who no longer exercises the so-called personal properties, "He has lost the capacity (ability) to think and feel – but not the humanity, the *human* life, which until his death goes on shaping, informing, and organising his existence *towards* the feeling and thinking which are natural to human life (i.e., which human life is radically capable of and oriented towards)".[97] Proponents of neocortical death confuse (1) that which belongs to the order of the act of a *res* (a thing), namely, its constitutive ontological or radical capacity, which consists in part of the personal properties, which are in act independently of the empirically verifiable concrete exercise thereof, and (2) that which belongs to the order of the functioning (*performance*) of that *res*, which is expressed by the actual ability to exercise these personal properties; in other words, the human unfolds (*se déploie*) in his action *as* a person. They wrongly equate the person with the Self that is empirically observable through the functioning of its personal properties.

4.2. The Dead Person Recognized as a "Social" Person

Such a functional or operational anthropology centered on the exercise of self-consciousness would legitimize *per se* the possibility of treating, in certain utilitarian or consequentialist ways, a human being who does not function on the personal level as a "thing" – to use the famous Kantian distinction – the value of "which" would be relative to the interests of third persons (who are moral subjects). Hence it would be ethically permissible to make use of the vital organs of "non-personal" living human bodies, in other words, ultimately to use them merely as means for the benefit of moral persons. Harris explains that "where, however, the person no longer exists [i.e., upon the irreversible cessation of the exercise of self-consciousness, namely, neocortical death], the critical interests of the former person, while still worthy of our respect, must of necessity

96 *Ibid.*, p. 81. See pp. 76 and 83.

97 John Finnis, "Misunderstanding the Case against Euthanasia", p. 69. He likewise explains in "The Fragile Case for Euthanasia: A Reply to John Harris", p. 50: "The same organising principle which integrated a human individual and directs his or her development continues to do so until death. So this individual remains the same organic individual even if gravely impaired by immaturity, senility or illness".

give way to the significant interests or preferences of actual people [= persons]".[98] This statement is even more valid [in Harris's opinion] when there never was a person in the first place, for example, in the case of the newborn or someone who is severely mentally handicapped, because there would be no need to take into consideration the interests that the person would have had before he or she ceased to be a person.

Some philosophers who propose a real anthropological distinction between "human being" and "person", as well as the definition of neo-cortical death, are apparently uneasy with the ethical consequences of such instrumentalization; they propose granting certain rights to such human organisms that are deemed non-personal, reasoning that they once were persons or else that we should at least consider them as though they were persons. This is the notion of "social person" in the writings of Engelhardt, or of the "person since birth" in the works of Habermas.[99] These proposals in turn give rise to further problems. Let us look more closely at the thesis of "social person", which seems the most capable of giving some consideration to all human beings who would not be persons. This notion is essentially a "utilitarian construct"[100] that primarily envisages not the good of the non-personal human being, but rather the interests of the moral third person, or those of a particular community of moral persons. "The social sense of person is a way of treating certain instances of human life in order to secure the life of persons strictly. [...] A person in this sense is not a person strictly, and hence not an unqualified object of respect. Rather, one treats certain instances of human life as persons for the good of those individuals who are persons strictly".[101]

The recognition of a human being as a "social person" would be justified, according to Engelhardt, because it helps moral persons to cultivate important personal virtues, such as sympathy, solicitude, "care".[102]

98 John Harris, "Euthanasia and the Value of Life", p. 19.

99 See Jürgen Habermas, *The Future of Human Nature*, pp. 34–5 [pp. 63–5]. Habermas accepts the argument of the potential person and its (referring to the person) fundamental right to life. He calls the human embryo a "pre-personal" human life (p. 39) [p. 72: *"vorpersonalem menschlichem Leben"*] or a "second person" (p. 70) [p. 120: *"eine zweite Person"*] by virtue of an act of "anticipatory socialization" (p. 35) [p. 66], in other words, an act anticipating what it will be: a person. Such a human life, however, according to Jürgen Habermas, possesses a certain dignity that he equates, not with the dignity of a person, but with that of human corpses (pp. 35–6) [p. 67].

100 Tristram H. Engelhardt, "Medicine and the Concept of Person", p. 177. See *The Foundations of Bioethics*, pp. 147, 150, 271.

101 Tristram H. Engelhardt, "Medicine and the Concept of Person", p. 177.

102 See Tristram H. Engelhardt, *The Foundations of Bioethics*, p. 147.

It could happen nevertheless that some persons might personally think that the death of their infant or of their non-personal parent could lead to the maximization of their happiness and thus would not be contrary to their interests. It follows that one grants to the life of a human being that is a non-person a dignity by proxy, subject to the interests and preferences of third persons.[103] Such a dignity is "relative" to the interests and preferences of moral persons. An organism devoid of positive interests with respect to a closely related third party could be instrumentalized and considered as a mere means.[104]

One of the fundamental problems of the term "social person" lies in its legitimacy on the ethical level. Engelhardt elaborates this concept along utilitarian and consequentialist lines.[105] He recognizes, however, that this is a "troubling" or "disturbing"[106] element, while maintaining that these ethical models cannot be substantiated universally by reason and therefore are answerable only to a particular community of what he

[103] Within the context of his discussion of the status of the human embryo, René Frydman concedes that it deserves respect only to the extent that there is a "parental plan" (René Frydman, *Dieu, la Médecine et l'Embryon*, p. 84: *"project parental"*), with relation to "the future that it carries within it" (p. 83: *"l'avenir dont il est porteur"*). Absent a "parental desire" (p. 169: *"désir parental"*; see p. 84), it would be considered "as a thing" (p. 169: *"comme une chose"*; see p. 84). Although Frydman speaks about the embryo, his argument can be applied to any human being in a similar state, according to the criteria of the Lockean functional person. Tristram H. Engelhardt presents a similar line of reasoning in referring to newborns who can be used merely as means to the extent to which the parents gave their consent. The newborn is their property (*The Foundations of Bioethics*, p. 255), an "extension of and the fruit of one's own body", because the parents "produced it, they made it, it is theirs". His argument is equally valid for any human being who was not a person or a social person.

[104] See for example Tristram H. Engelhardt, *The Foundations of Bioethics*, p. 256, and "Medicine and the Concept of Person", p. 179. Mary Anne Warren maintains in *Moral Status*, pp. 199 and 166, that the moral status of beings who have always lacked self-consciousness – for example an anencephalic infant or someone who is severely mentally handicapped (which she does not mention) – is largely determined by the preferences of the immediate family or of those otherwise related to them. Such preferences, however, are subjectively relative: i.e., there is no question of a universal preference. As for the human being in a so-called vegetative state, his moral status depends on the preferences that he had as a person, either to continue living or not, if he ever found himself in such a situation (p. 198).

[105] Tristram H. Engelhardt, *The Foundations of Bioethics*, p. 147: "a social sense of persons justified in terms of various utilitarian and other consequentialist considerations". See p. 148.

[106] *Ibid.*, p. 150: "Still, it is disquieting that the strongest rights claims that can be advanced in favor of humans who are not persons in the strict sense can in general secular terms be at best appreciated in consequentialist, if not indeed on utilitarian, considerations established by particular formal or informal agreements".

calls "moral friends", that is, moral persons who share a common ethics based on identical values and axioms.[107]

Strangely enough, the instrumentalization of a human being who was not a social person because he was devoid of interests for a closely related third party or for the various communities is nevertheless rejected by the great majority of proponents of neocortical death. Engelhardt is one of the rare philosophers who argue consistently on the basis of the premises that they have developed: "By making permanent loss of consciousness the point at which humans are declared dead, one would be able to establish a practice that would provide uniformity in general secular moral contexts for the declaration of death for infants, the retarded, adults, and the senile [and, one might add, human beings who are in a so-called irreversible vegetative state]. Particular communities with their own understandings of death might exempt themselves".[108]

If proponents of neocortical death were consistent, they would necessarily not only defend the ethical permissibility of cloning in order to create an anencephalic infant intended mainly as an "organ bank" for a moral person (a position taken by McMahan[109]), but also consider a person in a so-called permanent vegetative state as dead and treat him as such, that is, as material to be exploited with regard exclusively to the interests of third persons. Human beings who were not deemed social persons would be considered dead on the personal level and thus ready for burial, cremation, or the harvesting of their bodily organs, as is the case for all human beings who are not persons. Such assertions, however, are profoundly counterintuitive, since in the name of a functional anthropology they justify the exploitation of a human being by his peers, that is, the instrumentalization of all human beings who are not persons.

4.3. Personal Death as the Permanent Cessation of Circulatory-Respiratory Function

Given the argumentative weaknesses of the definition of neocortical death and brain stem death, we turn to the thesis of whole-brain death. This,

[107] See *Ibid.*, pp. 45 ff.

[108] *Ibid.*, p. 250. See p. 239.

[109] See Jeff McMahan, *The Ethics of Killing*, p. 454: "it should also be permissible for a person needing a transplant to grow an anencephalic infant from his or her own genetic material via cloning technology". Further on he explains (p. 455): "It seems, rather, that the intrinsic moral status of an anencephalic clone [...] is no different from that of a collection of separately grown organs".

however, seems to be called into question, according to some authors, by recent empirical medical facts.[110] There are allegedly numerous cases, discussed by Shewmon, among others, in which a human being who was considered to be brain dead continues to manifest what some authors call integrative functions of organic unity. The two most important and crucial functions are respiration, understood as the exchange of oxygen and carbon dioxide, and nutrition, understood as the breaking down of nourishment into elementary forms that are burned for energy or else assimilated into the structure of the body. These two integrative functions are certainly more efficient when directed by the brain, but they do not disappear completely once the brain no longer functions. Such human life in a patient whose brain no longer functioned but whose body performed the functions in question would certainly be considered as very infirm, but one could not consider the patient as dead.[111] These authors maintain that a human being is defined as a holistic, integrated unity, expressed in those nerve, hormone, and immune systems that are not centered on the brain. Thus, in this view, not all organs are dependent on the brain for their functioning; the brain merely enables the different integrative organ systems to work better.[112] Hence one cannot declare a person dead, according to Potts, Byrne, and Nilges, until "the circulatory, respiratory, and nervous systems (the three most important vital systems of the body) have been destroyed".[113] DeGrazia concurs, while professing a kind of relativism with regard to the application of the definition of death in public policy (*dans la Cité*): "human death is *the permanent cessation of circulatory-respiratory function*".[114] It is likewise interesting to note that certain proponents of neocortical death, for example McMahan, maintain that a human being is considered to be alive even

[110] These medical facts are discussed also by several philosophers: Jeff McMahan, *The Ethics of Killing*, pp. 429 ff.; John P. Lizza, *Persons, Humanity, and the Definition of Death*; David DeGrazia, *Human Identity and Bioethics*, pp. 142 ff., who subscribes to the definition of human death that refers to circulation and respiration (p. 149): "that human death is *the permanent cessation of circulatory-respiratory function*".

[111] See Alan Shewmon, "The Brain and Somatic Integration: Insights into the Standard Biological Rationale for Equating 'Brain Death' with Death", pp. 464 ff.

[112] See *ibid.*, p. 471.

[113] Michael Potts, Paul A. Byrne, and Richard G. Nilges, "Introduction", pp. 2–3. See also several articles published in Calixto Machado and Alan Shewmon, eds., *Brain Death and Disorders of Consciousness.* See also Manuel M. Lavados and Alejandro M. Serani, *Etica Clinica*; Alan Shewmon, " 'Brainstem Death', 'Brain Death' and Death: A Critical Re-Evaluation of the Purported Equivalence"; Josef Seifert, "Is 'Brain Death' Actually Death?".

[114] David DeGrazia, *Human Identity and Bioethics*, p. 149.

if the brain is no longer functioning. Indeed, the human embryo before the formation of the brain is quite logically (*bel et bien*) considered a living human being, which is to say that it exhibits an integrative function that is not regulated by the brain. Thus we can conclude that "a human organism's functions need not be regulated by the brain in order for it to be alive".[115]

The reference made, for example by McMahan, to the definition of death proposed by Shewmon and other authors in no way endorses their position, but rather sides with it in denouncing the position of proponents of brain stem death. They distance themselves from the definition of death in terms of integrative functions, maintaining, on the basis of a dualistic anthropology, that the latter definition is valid only for the death of the human body and not for the death of the person. On this point they oppose Potts, Byrne, Nilges, and others who maintain that their definition of death not only applies to the death of the human being at the bodily level, but is altogether applicable to the death of the human person, which implies that the person is fundamentally constituted not only by self-consciousness, but also by a personal, individualizing body, in other words, one that is directed toward and facilitates the exercise of the so-called personal properties.

The central question, which is debated today and by no means resolved, is determining whether the mere empirical presence of respiration, nutrition, and growth really signifies the presence of an organism understood as a whole – which should be distinguished from the "whole-body" model of death requiring that all the cells and the organic system of an individual be completely dead – or merely the presence of different parts of an organism. In any case, and independently of how one resolves this question, the anencephalic newborn, or someone in a so-called permanent vegetative state, and thus by extension any human being who does not exercise or has ceased to exercise the so-called personal properties, can be considered alive, because that individual is himself capable of organizing and informing the different aspects of his biological life.

5. ETHICS AS THE CRITERION FOR DEFINING DEATH

Some proponents of neocortical death attempt to resolve their paradox by shifting the debate over the definition of death from the anthropological level to the ethical level, by asking when is it morally justifiable

[115] Jeff McMahan, "Brain Death, Cortical Death and Persistent Vegetative State", p. 255.

to treat a person as dead. Glover explains: "The only way of choosing [between competing definitions of death] is to decide whether or not we attach any value to the preservation of someone irreversibly comatose. Do we value 'life' even if unconscious, or do we value life only as a vehicle for consciousness?"[116] Singer maintains that the definition of the death of a person is above all an "ethical judgment", neglecting to mention that such a judgment is logically dependent on a Lockean anthropology that he assumes *a priori* to be true. As the Australian philosopher sees it, the key question is whether a human life that continued after the irreversible loss of the exercise of self-consciousness can be a "benefit"[117] for a particular human being, namely, for someone in a so-called permanent vegetative state or afflicted with profound dementia or even for the anencephalic newborn and, one might add, newborns in general or the very severely mentally handicapped. Rachels raises the stakes by maintaining that since it is impossible to define the moment when a person has died, then necessarily "the final decision [as to when death occurs] is determined by moral considerations, which argue for fixing the time of death at the point at which consciousness is no longer possible".[118] The central question is not to ask, "What is death?" and to determine at what moment a person has died on the basis of an anthropological definition of the person, but rather to ask, "at what point is it morally all right to declare him dead?" or even, "at what point is it morally all right to remove his organs?"[119] We ought to declare his death so that it will be morally permissible to remove his organs, even if the person should still be present. These moral considerations amount to asking, as Hoffman notes, "What minimal quality of life in a human body possesses sufficient intrinsic value to obligate us to regard it as a living person?"[120] The usual answer is that a human life permanently

116 Jonathan Glover, *Causing Death and Saving Lives*, p. 45. See Robert Veatch, "The Impending Collapse of the Whole-Brain Definition of Death", p. 21.

117 Peter Singer, *Rethinking Life and Death*, pp. 206–7. See pp. 17, 32.

118 James Rachels, *The End of Life*, p. 43.

119 *Ibid.*, p. 42.

120 John C. Hoffman, "Clarifying the Debate on Death", p. 445. Although Bernard Gert, Charles M. Culver, and Danner K. Clouser (*Bioethics*, p. 296) maintain, along with the proponents of neocortical death, that a human organism that has irreversibly lost self-consciousness, as in the case of the so-called vegetative state, would no longer be a person, they nevertheless refuse to consider such an organism to be dead. The reason that would allow society to stop caring for it and thus to use the organism as an organ bank is of an ethical and, more specifically, a utilitarian sort. Keeping alive such organisms that are no longer persons would amount to "an extravagant waste of both economic and human resources".

deprived of self-consciousness would be meaningless. Hence we would no longer have the moral obligation to consider that individual as alive and could regard him as dead. Such an assertion applies not only to Karen Ann Quinlan or to the anencephalic newborn, but also – despite the fact that proponents of neocortical death systematically omit any mention thereof within the framework of thanatological discussion – to the very severely mentally handicapped or to any human being in a similar situation. His or her value would depend, in the opinion of a large number of philosophers, on the subjective interests of moral persons, as mentioned earlier.

5.1. The Ethic of Interests

Those who advocate introducing ethical discourse into the thanatological debate confuse the level of the conceptual definition of death, which relies on philosophical anthropological reflection, with the subjective desirability of continuing a life or not, a desirability that after all is founded, for those advocates, on an assumption that is quite debatable, namely, an ethic of interests. This ethic requires not only that an individual actively exercise interests, in order to be the subject of rights, but also that one take into consideration the interests of other beings who are present. One must assign "equal weight in our moral deliberations to the like interests of all those affected by our actions".[121] An action is considered morally bad to the extent that it is "contrary to the preference of any being"[122] and, more particularly, to a preference that is consciously expressed in the case of a person. "The wrong is done", Singer explains, "when the preference [that has been expressed] is thwarted",[123] implying thereby that one can do wrong to a person only if the action runs counter to a willed, experienced, conscious preference. McMahan explains that "what is fundamentally wrong about killing, when it is wrong, is that it frustrates the victim's time-relative interest in continuing to live",[124] specifying that the stronger the interest in continuing to live, the more the killing of the individual is morally reprehensible. Tooley declares, *a priori*, the intrinsic connection between the

[121] Peter Singer, *Practical Ethics*, p. 21. See pp. 94 ff.

[122] *Ibid.*, p. 94. An action is morally reprehensible when it "violates" a preference (see p. 95).

[123] *Ibid.*, p. 99.

[124] Jeff McMahan, *The Ethics of Killing*, p. 194. See Peter Singer, *Practical Ethics*, p. 94: "Killing a person who prefers to continue living is therefore wrong".

exercise of a desire, and thus of a preference or an interest, and a right, more particularly of the right to exist. An individual has a right to something insofar as he desires something, in other words, to the extent to which he concretely exercises such a desire.[125] In order to have a right to live, a person is required to exercise a desire "to continue to exist as a subject of experiences and other mental states".[126] Although Singer, among other authors, states that there are more basic preferences, such as preferring not to suffer, there are also more fundamental interests, for example, having plans for a distant future, which requires consciousness of oneself over time. A human being who was deprived of such self-consciousness would thereafter be altogether deprived of rights. "In order for a being to have interests or rights, it must have the capacity for consciousness",[127] McMahan explains. He has a fundamental right to life insofar as he explicitly desires to continue living as a subject of experience. If he exercises such a desire to continue living, other individuals possessing the same desire have a *prima facie* obligation not to deprive him of his ability to keep living.[128] In the contrary case, exemplified by states of neocortical death, for instance of Karen Ann Quinlan or an anencephalic infant, the human being would be without rights, because he exercised no desire or preference concerning his future existence, with the possible exception of the desire not to suffer, which is situated at the bodily level.[129] If there is no conscious, willed, and expressed interest in continuing to live, no wrong would be done to him if one were to kill him, for no interest would be violated. McMahan notes that such a human being would no longer be an appropriate object of respect, either.[130] If, on the other hand, a person were to express an interest in no

[125] See Michael Tooley, *Abortion and Infanticide*, pp. 87 ff. and "Why a Liberal View Is Correct", p. 10.

[126] Michael Tooley, "Abortion and Infanticide", p. 46.

[127] Jeff McMahan, *The Ethics of Killing*, p. 447.

[128] See Michael Tooley, "Abortion and Infanticide", pp. 44 ff. "The reason it is wrong to kill persons is that they are *things that can envisage a future for themselves, and that have desires about those futures states of themselves*, and thus killing such entities makes it impossible for these desires to be satisfied"; Michael Tooley, "Decisions to Terminate Life and the Concept of Person", p. 90.

[129] "Beings who cannot see themselves as entities with a future [i.e., who are not persons] cannot have any preferences about their own future existence," notes Peter Singer, *Practical Ethics*, p. 95.

[130] Jeff McMahan, *The Ethics of Killing*, p. 451: "Because an anencephalic infant has neither the capacity nor the potential for consciousness, it is not a bearer of interests. Nothing can matter, or be good or bad, for its sake. Nor can it have rights or be an appropriate object of respect. If, therefore, the view for which I have argued is correct,

longer living, killing him would be considered a morally good act – this position is defended not only by Singer but also by Harris.[131]

This theory of interests is based on an *a priori* assumption that is accepted by a good number of philosophers who write on bioethics, namely, the thesis of experientialism, which is likewise one of the presuppositions that form the basis for the famous thesis of Epicurus concerning the nothingness of death.[132] Experientialism asserts that a state of affairs is good or bad for a subject solely to the extent that the subject experiences it. Otherwise one would not be able to say that an action brought against him would be somehow beneficial to him or would do him harm. Singer explains that "something that happens to self-conscious beings can be contrary to their interests while similar events would not be contrary to the interests of beings who were not self-conscious",[133] given that they have no awareness of having interests and they do not experience them. The only interest that one can take into consideration for a human being without self-consciousness is that of not suffering – insofar as he exercises the faculty of suffering. Following Singer,[134] Rachels emphasizes that "in the absence of a conscious life, it is of no consequence to the subject himself whether he lives or dies".[135] Once the person is irreversibly incapable of exercising self-consciousness, while his body continues to live, "we cannot possibly be harming him by removing his heart or kidney or whatever".[136] Harris presses the argument further, declaring that "creatures that cannot value their own existence cannot be wronged [...] for their death deprives them of nothing that they can value".[137]

it is difficult to see what objection there could be to taking the organs from a living anencephalic infant for transplantation – apart, of course, from objections based on the interests and rights of the parents". See also Jeff McMahan, "An Alternative to Brain Death", p. 48: "The organism [a living human being that is deprived of self-consciousness and hence not a person] itself cannot be harmed in the relevant sense; it has no rights, and it is not an appropriate object of respect in the Kantian sense".

[131] See John Harris, *The Value of Life*, p. 17.

[132] I will develop this thesis in greater depth in Part Three of this book.

[133] Peter Singer, *Practical Ethics*, p. 73.

[134] Peter Singer, *Rethinking Life and Death*, p. 207: "Without consciousness [Peter Singer explicitly mentions the human being in the so-called permanent vegetative state, the anencephalic infant, and the infant whose cortex no longer functions; he neglects, however, to mention those who are severely mentally handicapped and human beings with profound dementia and without self-consciousness], continued life cannot benefit them".

[135] James Rachels, *The End of Life*, p. 26.

[136] *Ibid.*, p. 42.

[137] John Harris, *The Value of Life*, p. 19. See also John Harris, *Clones, Genes, and Immortality*, p. 87.

Proponents of the ethic of interests and of neocortical death also maintain that there would no longer be a subject who could suffer a wrong, given, as we have seen, that no person is present, for example in the case of Karen Ann Quinlan. This assertion adopts the second Epicurean presupposition: the requirement of a subject in order to maintain that a state of affairs is an evil or a wrong. The argument proposed by McMahan is based on such a presupposition, when he maintains that "the killing of a human organism in a PVS [persistent vegetative state] is not euthanasia: there is no one there to be benefited by being killed. Nor, *a fortiori*, is there anyone there to be harmed".[138] For proponents of neocortical death, the death of the human organism that survives the decease of the person and is thus deprived of self-consciousness in no way concerns us.[139] Such an organism, exemplified by Karen Ann Quinlan, would not constitute a subject that was suffering: according to Engelhardt, "There is no one to suffer from dehydration and starvation or to derive pleasure from hydration and nutrition".[140] As we have already mentioned, certain proponents of neocortical death deduce from their premise that we can treat such an organism that is without self-consciousness as a corpse, in other words that we should have no fear of doing wrong to "it", given that there is no subject whom one could wrong. Lachs underscores that "once the human person is gone, in the faltering body there is no one there".[141] Indeed, McMahan adds, "there is no one there to be benefited by being killed. Nor, *a fortiori*, is there anyone there to be harmed".[142]

5.2. Ethics and the Definition of Death

To require that a human being manifest empirically verifiable interests in order to determine that he has been wronged is a problematic thesis, the serious consequences of which will be elaborated in Part Three of this book, which deals with the Epicurean challenge – namely, that death is not an evil, since one never experiences it – and also with the thesis of the evil of death according to the circumstances, which is defended

138 Jeff McMahan, *The Ethics of Killing*, p. 448. Such a human being is "a living but unoccupied human organism", p. 446.

139 See Edward T. Bartlett and Stuart J. Youngner, "Human Death and Destruction of Neocortex", p. 211: "We are not concerned with the death of the organism that outlives the person".

140 Tristram H. Engelhardt, *The Foundations of Bioethics*, p. 248.

141 John Lachs, "The Element of Choice in Criteria of Death", p. 251.

142 Jeff McMahan, *The Ethics of Killing*, p. 448. See also p. 451.

by the majority of philosophers who write on thanatology and bioethics. One can fault such an ethic for ignoring the existence of interests (which can be called "fundamental goods") belonging to the human being as human being, independently of the fact of being conscious of oneself or of having expressed and manifested an empirically verifiable interest, or even of the fact that one is capable of sensing pain and pleasure. Thus, for example, the death of an individual can be considered as an evil for him independently of the fact that he is in "the state of death" or that he experiences it, and regardless of his consciously expressed, actual, or past interest in continuing to live. The evil of an event does not necessarily result from the experience of pain. One can very well understand it in terms of a privation of goods, potentials, and hopes that the individual by his very nature could have possessed, realized, and fulfilled if he had not been thrust into the state of death. The evil of privation denotes the privation of a good or of a so-called personal property – such as self-consciousness – that an individual has exercised but no longer exercises, or that he has not yet exercised, or even that he will never exercise. For example, it is easy to understand that an evil has befallen someone who is deaf from birth, independently of the fact that he is or is not conscious of himself and experiences it. The evil constituted by a state of affairs does not necessarily depend on the experience that an individual has of it, but rather on the privation of a good that ought to be, that is, relative to the very nature of the personal human being. The same is true for betrayal, for example, which can be considered as an evil independently of the actual or possible experience of it that an individual – whether responsive or unresponsive, conscious or unconscious of himself – may have of it.

The shift by certain authors of the criterion for determining the death of a human being to the ethical level is based on an epistemological error. Let us assume, hypothetically, that the life of "N." is irreversibly deprived of self-consciousness as a result of an accident, or else deprived of meaning and futile from a subjective point of view.[143] This does not allow us to conclude that "N." is dead. Nor does conceptual reflection on the nature of the death of a human being imply *per se* an ethical judgment that would determine, for example, to what extent the life of "N." who has lost self-consciousness is or is not worth living. We

[143] From the perspective of "N.", who was conscious before the accident, or else of "P.", who is conscious of himself, but not from the perspective of "N.", who is not conscious of himself and may very well be "happy" to be treated as a newborn.

are looking at two arguments that are quite distinct: the quality of life to which Hoffman explicitly refers and that is based on a consequentialist, utilitarian ethic could not possibly be a pertinent analytical criterion in an inquiry into the nature of death, any more than it allows us to know whether life is still present in a particular individual, that is, whether he is definitively dead. An ethical inquiry concerning what one should or should not do with a human individual in a particular state cannot pretend to answer the question of how to define death conceptually. Quite the contrary: a conceptual definition of death, which is definitively based on a philosophical anthropology, is the point of departure from which one can develop an ethical reflection on how to deal with particular situations. The statement that "N." is dead certainly allows us to deduce a number of consequences pertaining to our ethical behavior relative to the body-corpse, but this by no means proves that the definition of death is a statement of an ethical sort.

6. DIVERSITY OF DEFINITIONS OF DEATH IN A SECULAR ETHIC

Aware of the difficulty of gaining acceptance for the neocortical definition of death in the field of health care policy, some philosophers relocate the thanatological debate within the framework of a secular ethic. This ethic asserts that it is impossible to establish, by means of philosophical reason, a universal discourse concerning moral matters, while maintaining that reason does achieve objectivity at the level of usefulness and experience. It resorts to an ethic of consent and negotiation, emptied of all substantial moral content (which does not matter provided that the procedures are followed), in order to post park rules for humanity. It sets up a general framework without moral content concerning the principles of consensus, tolerance, permissiveness, and benevolence toward particular ethics.[144] Every moral subject and each community of moral subjects lives according to its own ethical principles, without imposing its own point of view on other moral persons. As Engelhardt explains, such a secular ethic is necessarily permissive. "Perpetual peace in the absence of repression will likely come, if ever, when we are willing to endure the choices persons make with themselves, [with] their private

[144] See Tristram H. Engelhardt, *The Foundations of Bioethics*. See Bernard N. Schumacher, "Le défi d'une définition séculière de la personne pour l'éthique" and "La dictature de la conscience".

resources, [with] consenting others, and in their communities however deviant, even when those choices are profoundly wrong".[145] According to Onfray, the secular ethic maintains that everything is optional, in other words, that everyone is free to commit himself (*s'engager*) on his own turf, that is, within the domain of his own decision and his own responsibility, where everything is done willingly and where absolutes vanish. The French philosopher notes that "in the area of these new possibilities, nothing is obligatory and everything is optional.[...] The possibility of obtaining an abortion does not compel me to do so and obliges no one, nor does the possibility of having recourse to cloning or euthanasia. Increasing the number of possibilities forces no one to make a choice that is contrary to his morality".[146]

This ethic implies the impossibility of establishing rationally and *a priori* a hierarchy among the different concepts of good, which depend exclusively on the subjective or intersubjective sphere. A disagreement could not be resolved by means of reasonable arguments.[147] Inasmuch as a person had freely decided on a moral action, one could not take up a position with regard to that choice, that is, make a value judgment, at the risk of being paternalistic and intolerant. This results in a relativism among different ethical concepts of good and, more particularly, for a number of philosophers who discuss the conceptual definition of death, a relativism among definitions of death that vary according to the preferences of moral persons who are grouped in diverse moral communities. Hence the definition of personal death is no longer established by means of philosophical reason on the anthropological and ontological level, but rather is conceived as the result of a subjective or, rather, an intersubjective choice. Engelhardt proposes that "different definitions of death could be established for different communities".[148]

[145] *Ibid.*, p. 15.

[146] Michel Onfray, *Féeries anatomique*, p. 82: *"Dans le champ de ces nouveaux possibles, rien n'est obligatoire et tout facultative. [...] La possibilité d'avorter n'y contraint pas et n'oblige personne, celle de recourir au clonage ou à l'euthanasie non plus. Augmenter les possibilités ne force personne à effectuer un choix qui heurte sa morale"*. See pp. 96 ff. See also Gilbert Hottois, *Essais de philosophie bioéthique et biopolitique.*

[147] Tristram H. Engelhardt, *The Foundations of Bioethics*, p. 81: "There are real differences among moral visions. They ground substantially different understandings of bioethics. These differences flow from the availability of different premises and rules of evidence for participants in a moral controversy, so that such disputes cannot be resolved by sound rational argument or by an appeal to a commonly acknowledged moral authority. [...] Only contentless general secular morality can reach across such gulfs and allow collaboration in the absence of content-full moral concurrence".

[148] *Ibid.*, p. 252. "By making permanent loss of consciousness the point at which humans are declared dead, one would be able to establish a practice that would provide

Citing respect for individual conscience, Veatch had already proposed several years earlier that different persons ought to be allowed to choose their own definition of death on the basis of their personal philosophical conviction.[149] DeGrazia concurs, proposing that persons can decide to reject the definition of human death as the permanent cessation of circulatory-respiratory function and prefer, in the name of individual conscience, other definitions of death, such as whole-brain death, brain stem death, or neocortical death. Inconsistently, however, he rejects the possibility of relying on his moral conscience to consider as dead a human being who is still conscious but demented, because that would involve much too great a distance from the original concept of death.[150] Lizza also suggests that every moral person should be able to choose the definition of death that suits him best, given that it is impossible to define the notion of person, which in his opinion is not a univocal term. "Whether anencephalics, individuals in PermVS, and the artificially sustained, whole-brain dead are persons may thus vary according to one's moral theory".[151] Lachs explains that "since death is paradigmatically a private matter, it follows that its determination should be left open to individual control to the greatest extent possible".[152]

One of the problems with this proposal to have a diversity of definitions of death lies in its inadequacy. Indeed, if philosophical reason were capable of establishing as true the necessity of such a secular ethic without universal moral content (accompanied by the assertion, as Engelhardt maintains, that the person is defined by the exercise of self-consciousness and moral action), then it should also be capable, on principle, of establishing a conceptual definition of personal death. We are confronted with a *petitio principi*: an instance of begging the question, which rejects *a priori* the possibility that philosophical reason could inform our discourse about the definitions of human personal death, or the ethical thanatological discourse of health care policy.

uniformity in general secular moral contexts for the declaration of death for infants, the retarded, adults, and the senile [and, one could add, human beings in a so-called irreversible vegetative state]. Particular communities with their own understandings of death might exempt themselves" (p. 250). See also "Redefining Death", pp. 330–1.

149 See Robert Veatch, *Death, Dying and the Biological Revolution* (revised edition 1989), pp. 54 ff. and "The Impending Collapse of the Whole-Brain Definition of Death".

150 See David DeGrazia, *Human Identity and Bioethics*, pp. 156–7.

151 John P. Lizza, *Persons, Humanity, and the Definition of Death*, p. 98. He also maintains that what is essential to the nature of the person depends on various metaphysical, ethical, or cultural beliefs. See pp. 32, 99, 179–80.

152 John Lachs, "The Element of Choice in Criteria of Death", p. 249. See p. 250.

7. CONCLUSION

The conceptual definition of death is not on the order of an ethical discourse that could judge as to the moment when a personal human life would or would no longer be worth the trouble of living, or that would be listed as a component of a secular ethic; instead it depends primarily on a philosophical anthropology that is based on a concrete reality of being and that recognizes that the human person is essentially corporeal. This does not mean that the person can be reduced to the dimension of the body alone. The latter, in its individual specificity, is nevertheless essential to the functioning of the mind, which is to say that without the presence of his or her organism, the person is deprived of the capacity to think in this world, and thus of his or her conscious and cultural biographical dimension. On the other hand, the temporal person who is identified with his particular body cannot be reduced to his empirically verifiable actions, either, which in reality only reveal the person. A human being who is irreversibly deprived of the exercise of the so-called personal properties is fundamentally a person by the same title as someone whose personal action can be observed empirically. Personal death occurs with the destruction of the capacity of the human organism to function as a whole, and not just with the inability of one or another of its parts to function. In other words, death deprives someone of all ability to preserve his unity and to keep together the constitutive elements that make him a personal human organism. The distinction between a personal human body and a corpse lies in the organization and functioning of the vital parts, taken as a whole. Death "kills" the interior universe of the human person and returns its various parts to the physical universe. The irreversible failure (*dysfonctionnement*) of the organism's unity entails the disappearance of the person from this world.

PART TWO

THEORY OF KNOWLEDGE ABOUT DEATH

2

Scheler's Intuitive Knowledge of Mortality

1. INTRODUCTION

There is something paradoxical about the human being. On the one hand, he is not content merely with simply being "carried along by [life's] impetus", to borrow Bergson's expression,[1] but rather seems to have a consciousness of his mortality and of the fact that he *must* and *can* die, that he "knows that it must die"[2], the fact that his death could occur at any moment – *"Mors certa, hora incerta"* (Death is a sure thing; the hour – uncertain).[3] But on the other hand, to use one of Kierkegaard's expressions, he lives by a deception, "a false flatterer" (he flatters himself in his thoughts by complacently preferring the security of the moment, procrastination, and postponement), and in the conscious or unconscious refusal to face death, a confrontation that is, according to Kierkegaard, the result of serious thought.[4] I do not want to dwell on the reasons for

[1] Henri Bergson, *The Two Sources of Morality and Religion*, p. 120 [p. 1085: *"adoptant l'élan de la vie"*].

[2] Voltaire, *Dictionnaire philosophique*, vol. 4, p. 63 (at the beginning of his treatise on man); cited by Paul-Louis Landsberg, *The Experience of Death*, p. 1 [p. 71: *"sache qu'elle doit mourir"*].

[3] See Hans Jonas, "The Burden and Blessing of Mortality", p. 87. Death is "the only certainty, and the only thing about which nothing is certain" (Søren Kierkegaard, "At a Graveside", p. 91); "It is an absent presence", Paul Louis Landsberg, *The Experience of Death*, p. 6 [p. 23: *"présence absente"*]. Vladimir Jankélévitch, *La mort* and *Penser la mort?*, p. 30. Georg Simmel, *Lebensanschauung*, p. 103. From the moment of conception, "a ticket has be issued me on which a sentence of death is inscribed; the place, date, the how of the execution are blanks" (Gabriel Marcel, *Creative Fidelity*, p. 140 [p. 183: *"un billet m'a été délivré sur lequel figure une sentence de mort; le lieu, la date, le comment de l'exécution sont en blanc"*]).

[4] See Søren Kierkegaard, "At a Graveside", pp. 79 ff.

this repression of death, but rather to discuss the way in which a human being arrives at the consciousness of his death. How does a human being arrive at the certitude that he must die, and what arguments form the basis for the statement that "death is the only certainty"?[5] Heidegger goes so far as to describe death as the foundation for all certitudes. Contemporary philosophy proposes several answers: the intuitive, ontological, or innate knowledge of my death; knowledge obtained by inductive reasoning or interpersonal contact. In the following chapters I will examine these proposed explanations and give a detailed analysis of their supporting arguments.

Scheler is one of those "philosophers of life" who rejected certain currents in scientific thinking that took mechanism and finalism to the extreme of considering death as a more or less catastrophic event external to the individual and comparable to a mechanical, artificial accident.[6] In the first section of his posthumous work entitled *Death and Afterlife,* written between 1914 and 1919, he defends the notion of *natural death* (I will return to this concept) and thus distances himself also from German idealism, which maintains that death does not affect a human being. According to Scheler, every living being is essentially characterized by "the internal exhaustion of the vital agents that guide the development of the species".[7] Death is a phenomenon "that is connected with the essence of the living thing";[8] it is part of "the form and structure"[9] of all life. Life is inconceivable without death. Scheler, along with Simmel, prepares the way for Heidegger's thought:[10] death does not occur as an accident or a catastrophe, as Sartre and Levinas maintain, but rather as a natural event, since human life is directed toward death. In order to

[5] *Ibid.*, p. 75.

[6] See Henri Bergson, *Creative Evolution*, p. 57 [p. 537], as well as the works of Wilhelm Dilthey, Ludwig Klages, Friedrich Nietzsche, and Georg Simmel. For a survey of writers on thanatology who are proponents of the *Lebensphilosophie*, see Alexander Lohner, *Der Tod im Existentialismus*, pp. 23–95; Karl Albert, *Lebensphilosophie.*

[7] Max Scheler, *Tod und Fortleben*, p. 35: *"innere Erschöpfung der die Art leitenden Lebensagentien".*

[8] *Ibid.*, p. 35: *"das an das Wesen des Lebendigen geknüpft ist".*

[9] *Ibid.*, p. 22: *"zur Form und zur Struktur".*

[10] Besides the fact that Martin Heidegger owes much to Georg Simmel and Max Scheler – the Freiburg philosopher acknowledges them only in a short footnote – there are fundamental similarities between his work and Søren Kierkegaard's philosophy of death, for example in the latter's essay "At a Graveside". See Harrison Hall, "Love and Death: Kierkegaard and Heidegger on Authentic and Inauthentic Human Existence". In his reflections on death, Martin Heidegger fails to give sufficient credit to his sources of inspiration.

prove his thesis, Scheler does not use the experimental method that is dear to classical empiricism but adopts an innovative approach by referring to an intuitive knowledge of mortality.

2. MODERN MAN'S ATTITUDE TOWARD DEATH ITSELF

Scheler's thanatological reflection has a very precise origin. Its point of departure is not a discussion of Cartesian or Kantian theses, or a physiological or psychological analysis of the body-soul relationship, but rather the empirical fact that belief in immortality has progressively weakened in the West. Some view this decline as the result of theoretical and speculative arguments. Others say that the reason is to be found in scientific progress, which is supposed to bring with it the destruction of all systems of religious belief. In opposition to such an interpretation, Scheler first maintains that "the goals and methods of modern science" are not neutral, "but are in fact only religious presuppositions of another sort [...] from which the goals and methods of modern science have arisen".[11] Immortality is not scientifically or rationally "demonstrable" by means of philosophical "proofs". Scheler thinks that the many advances made by the sciences will never be able to prove the data of religion as true or false: scientific progress only goes to show "the helplessness of science against religion".[12] As history has proved on countless occasions, the existence of a personal afterlife is the object of an "immediate intuition", of "unthinking, lived experience", of a "natural world-view".[13] Like Bergson and Blondel, our author assigns to intuitive intelligence a certain preeminence over discursive intelligence.

[11] Max Scheler, *Tod und Fortleben*, p. 11: *"Tatsächlich sind es aber nur religiösen Voraussetzungen anderer Art [...] aus denen die Ziele und Methoden der modernen Wissenschaft [...] entsprungen sind"*. Recent epistemological doctrine points out that scientific facts themselves are laden with values and that the sciences cannot abstract or prescind from values. See Evandro Agazzi, *Right, Wrong and Science*, pp. 41 f, 103 ff. [pp. 48 f., 138 ff.]; Larry Laudan, *Science and Values*.

[12] Max Scheler, *Tod und Fortleben*, p. 12: *"Ohnmacht der Wissenschaft gegen die Religion"*.

[13] *Ibid.*, p. 13: *"unmittelbare Intuition"*; *"unreflektierter Lebenserfahrung"*; *"natürlichen Weltanschauung"*. "This is not a 'belief' in something, a credulous acceptance of something 'that you don't see', but rather a putative seeing, a feeling and sensing of the existence and the effectiveness of the deceased, a [...] *vivid presence* and action of the dead in the midst of our real duties and everyday business", p. 14 [*"Das ist nicht ein 'Glauben' an etwas, ein gläubiges Annehmen dessen, 'was man nicht sieht', sondern es ist ein vermeintliches Sehen, ein Fühlen und Spüren des Daseins und der Wirksamkeit der Verstorbenen, eine [...] anschauliche Gegenwart und Wirksamkeit der Toten mitten in der Erledigung der realen Aufgaben, die der Tag und die Geschäfte stellen"*]. Scheler refers to the argument that the

The reason for the decline in belief in life after death is not to be found, in Scheler's opinion, in the rational deconstruction of the "proofs" of immortality. It should be sought, rather, in *"the attitude of modern man* [which the philosopher describes as the man of *"the European West"*, whom he considers as a "collective type"][14] *toward death itself"*[15], that is, in the way "in which modern man intuitively pictures and experiences his life and his death [...] since he basically denies the core and the essence of death".[16] He flees from the intuitive certainty of his death and has ceased living in the "presence of death". He represses it from his consciousness and is content to consider it as a simple fact that will befall him someday.

3. THE CERTAINTY OF MORTALITY BASED ON OBSERVATION AND INDUCTION OR ON INTUITION

It is commonly thought that the certainty about "my death" someday is acquired from external experience, based on observation of the death of other people and from induction, that is, that it is deduced empirically from a series of specific cases. "Decidedly"[17] opposed to common notion, Scheler sets out (as Heidegger would do later) to find a reason that would allow an individual who had never experienced the death of someone else – that is, the transformation of a living human being

human person possesses activities that are independent of the body (repeating an argument that can be found, for example, in Thomas Aquinas, but without citing him) and concludes, contrary to the inference that Aquinas draw from it, that this is not enough to "prove" the immortality of the soul. "And so I don't know the first thing about *whether* a person exists after death, much less *how* he exists. [...] If he does *not* continue to exist, I will never be able to know that. If he does continue to exist, I will never be able to know that. [...] But I *believe* that the person *continues to exist* – since I have no reason to assume the contrary and the essential conditions for what I believe are evidently fulfilled", p. 47 [*"Ich weiß also kein Wort, daß die Person nach dem Tode existiere; kein Wort erst recht, wie sie existiere. [...] Existiert sie nicht fort – ich werde es nie wissen können. Existiert sie fort – ich werde es nie wissen können. [...] Aber ich glaube es, daß sie fortexistiert – da ich keinen Grund habe, das Gegenteil anzunehmen und die Wesensbedingungen für das, was ich glaube, evident erfüllt sind"*]. Scheler distances himself from the concept of a personal afterlife that was developed during the Christian-theist period and embraces a pantheistic view (*Das Wesen des Todes* and "Zur Unsterblichkeit").

14 Max Scheler, *Tod und Fortleben*, p. 28: *"modernen westeuropäischen Menschen – als Massentypus betrachtet"*.

15 *Ibid.*, p. 15: *"das Verhältnis des modernen Menschen zum Tode selbst"*.

16 *Ibid.*, p. 15: *"wie gerade der moderne Mensch sein Leben und seinen Tod sich selbst zur Anschauung and zur Erfahrung bringt [...] da er den Kern and das Wesen des Todes im Grunde leugnet"*.

17 *Ibid.*, p. 16: *"entschieden"*. Scheler describes the famous syllogism about death as "childish", p. 30.

into a corpse – to have absolutely certain knowledge of his own mortal condition. A hermit would have a presentiment of his end if he compared the various phases of his life or reflected on his experiences, such as aging, sleep, and sickness. Extrapolating from these experiences, he could conclude that there is a possibility of no-longer-being, of no longer awakening someday. These experiences, however, would not lead to an absolutely sure knowledge of his mortality, but at most to the possibility of such an end. Indeed, Scheler rightly asks (and, as we will see, this is a question that will have a boomerang effect on his own thesis) how the solitary subject could know that the curve plotting his experiences would not continue beyond all bounds, that his life was not really open to infinite possibilities, that it would not be endless, "a process that by nature goes on and on without limits".[18]

Observation of and induction from the death of others, or the memories of the hermit when he compares the phases of his life, might eventually allow one to affirm the (indeed great) "likelihood" that an individual is mortal, but not an absolute certainty about the necessity of death. To achieve that, Scheler proposes a final example: a solitary human being who would not perceive the external signs of his aging, who would not feel the weakness and fatigue and would not suffer from any illness. Scheler maintains that "in the sense that he [such a hypothetical individual] has of his life",[19] in the lived experience of the structure of each phase of life, he would have certainty about his mortality. In his opinion, the idea of death is one of "the *constitutive* elements of our consciousness".[20] It constitutes an "*eidetic* truth"[21] based on the thesis that death is an essential part of life, of its form and structure. Death is fundamentally "present already in *every* 'phase of life', however insignificant, and in its experiential structure".[22]

[18] *Ibid.*, p. 22: *"unser eigenes Leben vor uns sehen wie einen immer weiter und weiter gehenden, seiner Natur nach ungeschlossenen Prozess"*. See *ibid.*, pp. 16, 30.

[19] *Ibid.*, p. 22: *"im Gefühl von seinem Leben"*.

[20] *Ibid.*, p. 17: *"dass diese Idee zu den* konstitutiven *Elementen nicht nur unseres, ja alles vitalen Bewusstseins selbst gehört"*. "Being directed toward death is an *essential* part of the experience of every life form, and of our own as well", p. 22 [*"[...] es gehört zum Wesen der Erfahrung jedes Lebens, und auch unseres eigenen, daß sie die Richtung auf den Tod hat"*]. "Insofar as we must attribute in general a form of consciousness to every living thing – and I agree with Jennings that this is necessary – we must also attribute to it some sort of intuitive certainty about death", p. 26 [*"Soweit wir allem Lebendigen überhaupt eine Bewußtseinsform zuschreiben müssen – und ich glaube mit Jennings, daß dies notwendig sei –, soweit müssen wir ihm auch irgendeine Art der intuitiven Todesgewißheit zuschreiben"*].

[21] *Ibid.*, p. 30: *"Wesenswahrheit"*.

[22] *Ibid.*, p. 16: *"sie liegt schon in jeder noch so kleinen 'Lebensphase' und ihrer Erfahrungsstruktur"*.

Limiting his analysis of death to the biological perspective, Scheler states that life manifests itself in two different ways: on the one hand, as "a group of singular morphological and kinetic phenomena in man's external experience"[23] and, on the other hand, as the given *process* of a particular consciousness that unfolds on a bodily basis. This process possesses at any given moment (indivisible instant) of its course its proper *form* and *structure* which it shares with all living things. The study of this "disindividualized" structure of the living being, in Scheler's opinion, allows us to experience the death that is present in each phase of life, to grasp intuitively the essence of death, and thereby to know with certainty the mortality of the human condition. Death is an "*a priori* for all observation and inductive experience of the changing content of every real life process".[24] The death "encountered" at the conclusion of "being on the way" consists of "the more or less accidental *realization*"[25] of the essence of death that is present in life. This knowledge of death must not be confused with the sense of the nearness of death or the presentiment that life must end, nor with the fear of or desire for death. It is not a matter of the emotions but is lodged at a deeper level.

The structure of the vital process at an indivisible instant T (the total content of a moment) can be discerned in three qualitatively distinct dimensions that are correlative to that instant: the immediate present (pr) + the immediate past (p) + the immediate future (f) of something. Three extensions (of the vital process) can be assigned to these dimensions: perception (which relates to the present), memory (which relates to the past), and expectation (which relates to the future). These are to be distinguished from *mediate* extensions (of the vital process) through the instrumentality of reason or association or reproduction. The total content (T) lived at each indivisible instant "increases in volume with the development of the individual". The consciousness of the living being intuitively perceives, at any moment of the vital process, not only these three immediate dimensions, but also and above all the totality (T) – and that is the heart of Scheler's argument. Now this totality "*is divided anew* with the objective progress of the vital process in a characteristic direction, which direction in turn represents a specific datum of experience. The scope of the contents in the dimension of

[23] *Ibid.*, p. 18: *"als eine Gruppe eigenartiger Form- und Bewegungsphänomene in der äusseren Wahrnehmung von Menschen".*

[24] *Ibid.*, p. 18: *"Der Tod ist ein* a priori *für alle beobachtende, induktive Erfahrung von dem wechselnden Gehalt eines jeden realen Lebensprozesses".*

[25] *Ibid.*: *"die mehr oder weniger zufällige* Realisierung*".*

the past (p) and the experienced aftereffects of these past contents continue to grow, while the scope of the contents in the dimension of the immediate future (f) and the anticipatory effects of these contents decrease and diminish. Between these two scopes, however, the scope of the present becomes increasingly "compressed", so to speak. Therefore, as the amount of life that has been lived at any moment increases, along with its aftereffects, there is a corresponding decrease in the potential for experience, as found in the immediate vital expectancy".[26] Scheler maintains that although the past increases, the two other dimensions (the present and the future) necessarily decrease, given that the totality (T) is constant. He assumes *a priori* that the existence of a living being has a limited content. This experience of the diminution of the future and the augmentation of the past, according to Scheler, is tantamount to an "experience of our orientation toward death".[27] The experience of the structure of an instant of life is the basis for certitude about our mortal condition and thus reveals the reality of *natural death.*

[26] *Ibid.*, pp. 19–20: *"Dieser Gesamtumfang aber ist es, der mit dem objektiven Fortschreiten des Lebensprozesses in einer charakteristischen* Richtung *sich* neu verteilt, *welche Richtung wiederum ein spezifisches Erlebnisdatum darstellt. Der Umfang des Gehalts in der Erstreckung der Vergangenheit V und die erlebte, unmittelbare Nachwirksamkeit dieses Vergangenheitsgehalts* wächst *und wächst, während zugleich der Umfang des Gehalts in der Erstreckung der unmittelbaren Zukunft Z und die Vorwirksamkeit dieses Gehalts* abnimmt *und abnimmt. Der Umfang des Gegenwärtigseins aber zwischen beiden Umfängen wird immer stärker sozusagen 'zusammengepresst'. Mit der Menge des in jedem Augenblick als gelebt gegebenen Lebens und seiner Nachwirksamkeit* vermindert sich *also die Menge des Erlebenkönnens, wie es in der unmittelbaren Lebenserwartung vorliegt".* See *ibid.*, p. 39. Scheler repeats this argument about fifteen years later in "Idealism and Realism" (p. 342): "Even the experience of growing old and dying as a passage toward a state in which one cannot and can-no-longer live is already evident to man on the particular variations in the experienced time-structure of present, past and future. Even if we exclude all the possible experiences a man could have of other men's growing old and dying, together with all the expriences he would have through his organic feelings and states of a growing feebleness and growing inability to act in certain ways, the variations in his experienced time-structure *alone* could give him the insight that he is advancing toward a "no-longer-being-able-to-live", toward death". [p. 309: *"Auch das Erlebnis des Alterns und Sterbens als eines Hingehens auf ein Nicht- und Nichtmehrlebenkönnen ist dem Menschen schon in dem eigenartigen Wechsel der je erlebten Zeitstruktur von Gegenwart, Vergangenheit und Zukunft gewiss. Auch wenn wir alle möglichen Erfahrungen, die ein Mensch von Altern und Tod an anderen Menschen oder Lebewesen gewinnen könnte, ausgeschlossen denken; ferner alle Erfahrungen, die der Mensch durch den Ablauf seiner Organgefühle und Zustände machen würde, als da sind steigende Mattigkeit und steigendes Unvermögen zu gewissen Verhaltensweisen, so würde einzig der Wechsel seiner erlebten Zeitstruktur selbst ihm die Einsicht geben können, dass er einem 'Nichtmehrlebenkönnen' überhaupt, also dem Tode entgegenschreitet"*].

[27] Max Scheler, *Tod und Fortleben*, p. 20: *"Erlebnis der Todesrichtung".*

4. PROBLEMATIC QUESTIONS RAISED BY SCHELER'S THESIS OF AN INTUITIVE KNOWLEDGE OF MORTALITY

The intuitive knowledge of mortality is problematic, raising several questions that are not always noticed by authors who discuss Scheler's position.[28] It seems to me, in the first place, that our philosopher attempts to make an unjustifiable leap from his analysis of the *instant* of a vital phase – consisting of a total content (T) "divided" into three dimensions and limited by a beginning and especially by an end – and the application of an identical structure to organic life in its *totality*. As I see it, one cannot legitimately equate *a priori* the structure of the instant as experienced with the structure of biological life as a whole, that is, without making a detour by way of the "ontical" experience of another's death. When the subject experiences the form and structure of the instant that is perceived immediately, he certainly does arrive at a concept of the end of the vital process, which is implied by the beginning of an instant of the vital phase, because he finds himself outside the structure in question. In order to grasp by way of analogy the end of the structure of human existence, the subject would have to be positioned "outside" life and assume a perspective external to life. In my opinion, the experience of the structure of an instant does not allow us to conclude that the general tendency of a human being toward *what is to come*, toward what is possible, actually has an end and that the human being is a "Being-towards-death". In the absence of observation (of others) and induction – as in the case of Scheler's hermit – man may well have reason to think that his present trajectory toward what is yet to come, toward what is possible, is a seemingly permanent state, that his ontological openness to the future does not, in and of itself, imply an end. Nothing guarantees that his future diminishes over the course of his living process. He has no *a priori* knowledge of the fact that the scope of his possibilities is narrowing, that the margin of his (remaining) life

[28] Various authors seem to accept Scheler's argument and are content to present his position uncritically (Parvis Emad, "Person, Death and World"; Manfred Frings, *Person und Dasein*, pp. 17–23; Alois Hahn, "L'idée de la mort chez Max Scheler"; Alexander Lohner, *Der Tod im Existentialismus*, pp. 105 f.) or even maintain that this position can be proved ("nevertheless the fact that I *will* die and why seems to be proved" [*"Begründet erscheint zwar, dass und weshalb ich sterben* werde"]): Elisabeth Ströker, "Der Tod im Denken Schelers", p. 209; "This knowledge of death is inherent to finite consciousness – we must admit that Max Scheler is right" [*"Ce savoir de la mort est inhérent à la conscience finie – il faut donner raison à Max Scheler"*]: Xavier Tilliette, "Le moi et la mort", p. 193).

in decreasing.[29] Ultimately, Scheler's position rests on an unproven *a priori* assumption that we find again in Heidegger's "Being-towards-death", which I will discuss at greater length in the next chapter. More specifically, Scheler thinks that "instead, our life presents itself to us interiorly at every moment as a *circumscribed totality*, against the background of which all particular experiences and destinies appear".[30] After assuming the contingency and finitude of the human being as givens, Scheler deduces from them that every living thing is so constituted as to be mortal. In order to render plausible his thesis of an intuitive knowledge of mortality, he would have to prove, without proceeding by way of observation and induction, that human time is limited, that is, that every temporal being has an end. Like Heidegger, Scheler envisages death in connection with finite temporality, whereby he thinks of time in terms of death. Could we not, as Levinas suggests, "think of time independent of the death [...], [and] [...] think death as a function of time, without seeing in death the very project of time"?[31]

Of course death represents the natural end of the living being, including the human being. It is proper to his present biological constitution. The living being is propelled irreversibly in a direction that leads to its end: its death. The human being, however, has a consciousness of

[29] Max Scheler agrees with Nagel's statement ("A man's sense of his own experience, on the other hand, does not embody this idea of a natural limit. His existence defines for him an essentially open-ended possible future [...]. He finds himself the subject of a *life*, with an indeterminate and not essentially limited future", Thomas Nagel, "Death", pp. 9–10), inasmuch as he correctly notes that if the intuitive certainty of death were eliminated, we would "see our own life before us as an ongoing and, by nature, never-ending process", Max Scheler, *Tod und Fortleben*, p. 22 [*"unser eigenes Leben vor uns sehen wie einen immer weiter und weiter gehenden, seiner Natur nach ungeschlossenen Prozeß"*].

[30] *Ibid.*, p. 23: *"Unser Leben ist uns vielmehr innerlich in jedem Zeitpunkt als eine* geschlossene Totalität *gegenwärtig, auf deren Hintergrund alle besonderen Erlebnisse und Schicksale erscheinen"*. "Thus every first-hand life experience appears to us against the backdrop of a vital unit, temporally circumscribed before and after, which is present to us as such in every experience", p. 23 [*"So erscheint uns jede Lebenserfahrung, die wir an uns selbst machen, auf dem Hintergrund einer zeitlich nach vorn und hinten geschlossenen Lebenseinheit, die uns als solche in jedem Erlebnis gegenwärtig ist"*]. "The dying of a natural death [...] is essentially and necessarily a component of every possible experience in one's own life [...] quite independently of the experiencing subject's organization and of all content and of any other division of this process into phases [...]". p. 20 [*"Das Sterben des natürlichen Todes [...] liegt wesensnotwendig in jeder möglichen Erfahrung vom eigenen Leben [...] ganz unabhängig von der Organisation des Erlebenden und von allem Inhalt und von aller sonstigen Gleiderung dieses Prozesses in Phasen [...]"*].

[31] Emmanuel Levinas, *God, Death, and Time*, p. 113 [p. 130: *"décrire le temps indépendamment de la mort [...], penser la mort en fonction du temps, sans voir en elle le projet même du temps"*].

his mortality, of the inscription of death *in* life, only by way of a detour, by experiencing the death of another. Someone else is indispensable, not only for me to discover my identity, but also for me to understand that I am mortal. Although this induction does not allow me to attain absolute certainty about my mortality, it nevertheless contributes toward establishing some degree of probability, which gives rise to thanatological inquiry. For my part, I reject the possibility that a consciousness that is defined as a windowless monad, closed off from others, could know with absolute certainty that it is mortal. Scheler's attempt, like Heidegger's, to establish the certainty of human mortality while bracketing off ontical experience is, to my mind, unconvincing. The arguments that he proposes rest upon the unproven assumption that temporality is marked off between a precise past and a precise future. Thus, according to these two authors, an endless existence is excluded *a priori*.

3

Heidegger's Being-Towards-Death

Heidegger's notion of Being-towards-death, the possibility of the impossibility of being, has left a profound mark on the reflections on death in contemporary Western philosophy. Heidegger is a decisive figure in the contemporary movement to turn philosophical thanatology on its head: on the one hand, by the methodology of radically separating, on principle, the analysis of death from the question about possible immortality (which it consigns to the ontical realm, beyond the scope of its investigation), and, on the other hand, by "interiorizing", so to speak, death within the series of phenomena that make up life. His originality lies in having developed speculation on death at the ontological level, which he carefully distinguishes from the ontical approach used by his predecessors, Simmel and Scheler. Heidegger is not interested in the modalities of perishing and decease; instead he sets forth an interpretation in which death, that is, "authentic dying" [*das eigentliche Sterben*] constitutes *Dasein* [being-there, existence] in its essential "potentiality-for-Being" [*Sein-können*]. He deduces this interpretation from his ontology of temporality, which is characterized by the categories of end, possibility, and future.

I will not examine the historical development of Heideggerian thanatology, from his early writings to the final seminars; nor will I analyze his sources or the influences on his work.[1] I will limit myself to

[1] See Gennaro Cicchese, "L'essere mortale dei mortali: Un'analisi sul problema della morte nel pensiero del secondo Heidegger"; James M. Demske, *Sein, Mensch und Tod*; Guido Knörzer, *Tod ist Sein?*; Ingrid Leman-Stefanovic, *The Event of Death*; Werner Marx, "Die Sterblichen"; Ugo Maria Ugazio, *Il problema della morte nella filosofia di Heidegger.* See also the excellent studies by John von Buren, *The Young Heidegger*; Jean Greisch, *Ontologie et temporalité*; and Theodore Kisiel, *The Genesis of Heidegger's Being and Time.*

his definition of death as the possibility of the impossibility of Being, as he developed it in *Being and Time*. To do this, I will introduce, first, the distinction between the ontical and the ontological levels; second, I will show that Heidegger maintains, along with Epicurus, that it is impossible to experience "my death" in the sense of "the state of death". In the third place, I will describe how the philosopher of Freiburg affirms that one cannot know with certainty one's "authentic dying" through an analysis of someone else's death. Fourth, I will discuss the solution that he proposes for obtaining such certainty by referring to the notion of Being-towards-death. This notion is based on his ontology of temporality, which is characterized by the concepts of potentiality-for-Being (*Sein-können*), possibility (*Möglichkeit*), Being-ahead-of-itself (*Sich-vorweg-sein*), and Being-towards-the-end (*Sein-zum-Ende*). I will conclude with a critique of the proposed solution: I will ask, among other questions, whether Heidegger really succeeds in deducing Being-towards-death and the certainty of existential "dying", which he posits as fundamental principles of the *ego*, from the sole basis of his ontology of temporality, without having recourse to a provincial (narrow) ontical analysis of death.

1. THE DISTINCTION BETWEEN ONTICAL AND ONTOLOGICAL

Heidegger's point of departure for his thanatological speculation is the capital distinction between the sciences that he elaborates in *Being and Time*, based on the principle of the ontological difference between the entity (*das Seiende*) and Being (*das Sein*). We find on the one hand the *ontical sciences*, such as biology and medicine, anthropology and history, sociology and theology. Their object is the particular entity that moves within a specific region and is, in a sense, already unveiled before the science in question comes to unveil it, since the science prolongs the prescientific attitude that already exists with regard to this entity. On the other hand we find an *ontological science*, philosophy, the science *par excellence*, which is characterized by its universality and neutrality toward every view of the world. It transcends the "provincialism" of the ontical sciences. It has no presuppositions. Its object is Being, which is the foundation of entities and the *a priori* condition for their possibility, without however being the same as that essence of entity (*Seiendheit*). Being does not appear as such in the world, but it determines what does appear there. Since they are independent of any "province" or "realm" (*Region*), the ontological science proposes to draw out the precomprehension of the concepts belonging to the ontical sciences. The question of Being is prior to and underlies the question of a particular entity. "The question of Being aims therefore at ascertaining the *a priori* conditions not only for the possibility of the sciences which examine entities as entities of such and such a type, and, in so doing, already operate with an understanding of Being, but also for the possibility of those ontologies themselves which are prior to the ontical sciences and which provide their foundations".[2]

Heidegger posits an impassable, impermeable boundary between the two levels of knowledge. The ontological science is the foundation for the ontical science, while being completely distinct and separate from it.[3] Our author breaks with philosophical tradition in *Being and Time* by undertaking a deconstruction of the history of ontology. He no longer seeks the primary causality of entities in their origin, because entities, according to Heidegger, are irrelevant to the question of the meaning of Being. Instead he looks exclusively for the primary causality itself, which

[2] Martin Heidegger, *Being and Time*, p. 31 [p. 11: *"Die Seinsfrage zielt daher auf eine apriorische Bedingung der Möglichkeit nicht nur der Wissenschaften, die Seiendes als so und so Seiendes durchforschen und sich dabei je schon in einem Seinsverständnis bewegen, sondern auf die Bedingung der Möglichkeit der vor den ontischen Wissenschaften liegenden und sie fundierenden Ontologien selbst"*]. "*The auto-foundation of the sciences has need in turn of a foundation*, because it involves a pre-ontological understanding of Being, which the sciences of the entity [ontical sciences] are fundamentally incapable of clarifying. *The foundation for the auto-foundation* of the sciences of the entity is accomplished in provincial [regional] ontologies. The re-founding of an ontical science is accomplished first and foremost by ontology. *Re-founding a science of the entity means founding and elaborating the ontology that underlies it.* These ontologies, in turn, are based on fundamental ontology, which constitutes the *center of philosophy*. Every science of the entity necessarily harbors within it the latent, more or less elaborated ontology that upholds and founds it" ["Die Selbstbegründung der Wissenschaften bedarf ihrerseits der Begründung, *weil zu ihr ein vorontologisches Seinsverständnis gehört, zu dessen Aufhellung die Wissenschaften des Seienden grundsätzlich ausserstande sind.* Die Begründung der Selbstbegründung *der Wissenschaften des Seienden vollzieht sich in den regionalen Ontologien. Die Ontologie vollzieht allererst die Grundlegung einer ontischen Wissenschaft.* Grundlegung einer Wissenschaft vom Seienden heisst: Begründung und Ausbildung der ihr zugrunde liegenden Ontologie. *Diese Ontologien gründen ihrerseits in der Fundamentalontologie, die das* Zentrum der Philosophie *ausmacht. Jede Wissenschaft vom Seienden birgt in sich notwendig die latente mehr oder minder ausgebildete und sie tragende und begründende Ontologie"* Martin Heidegger, *Phänomenologische Interpretation von Kants Kritik der reinen Vernunft*, p. 39].

[3] In his famous lecture "Phenomenology and Theology", given in Marburg the same year as the publication of *Being and Time*, Heidegger nevertheless attributes to the ontical science of theology a greater independence with respect to the first philosophy. The latter no longer founds it but only plays a coregulating role [*un rôle de co-rection/eine korrektive Funktion*]. See Bernard N. Schumacher, "Deux ennemies irréductibles: la philosophie et la théologie selon Heidegger".

is the principal question of all philosophical inquiry. We go beyond, so to speak, the entity in order to arrive at Being, which is the foundation of the phenomenon of the world and determines what appears therein. "Being and the structure of Being lie beyond every entity and every possible character which an entity may possess. *Being is the transcendent, pure and simple*".[4] This transcendence does not end in the real transcendence of a creator, but in the Being that appears in the phenomenon of the world. Being is not God[5] but rather is always the Being of the entity, having no *Dasein* apart from the entity.

Heidegger restricts his thanatological analysis by excluding *a priori*, in the name of methodological purity (i.e., separating the ontological and the ontical levels), an ontical investigation of death, which would concentrate on a particular entity moving within a precise "realm" or "province" and would deal, for example, with the various modes of "passage", forms of dying, modalities of experiencing death. An ontical study presupposes a certain definition of death, a prior, "more or less clarified"[6] understanding of the concepts of death and life. Heidegger wishes to draw out this precomprehension that underlies the ontical sciences, insofar as it must be sketched out (*vorgezeichnet*) by means of an ontology of the *Dasein*. This ontology, nevertheless, omits a whole series of metaphysical, ethical, anthropological, and political questions about death, which are the province of the ontical sciences.

2. THE IMPOSSIBILITY OF EXPERIENCING MY OWN DEATH

After differentiating between the ontical and ontological levels, Heidegger distinguishes among several understandings of death. At the existential (ontological) level of his analysis, we find the *authentic dying*

[4] Martin Heidegger, *Being and Time*, p. 62 [p. 38: *"Sein und Seinsstruktur liegen über jedes Seiende und jede mögliche seiende Bestimmtheit eines Seienden hinaus.* Sein ist das transcendens schlechthin"].

[5] "Being is neither God nor the foundation of the world" (Martin Heidegger, *Über den Humanismus*, p. 19: *"Das 'Sein' – das ist nicht Gott und nicht der Weltgrund".*). Heidegger rejects the neo-Scholastic tradition that conceives of God's essence in terms of Being. The category of Being can have no place, according to Heidegger, in a genuine theology that is defined primarily by faith.

[6] Martin Heidegger, *Being and Time*, p. 291 [p. 247: *"mehr oder minder geklärte"*]. See *ibid.*, pp. 292 f. [pp. 248 f.]. Current findings about death provided by biology, comparative anthropology (Thomas, Morin), sociology (Ziegler, Fuchs), history (Ariès), ethics, metaphysics (Fischer, McMahan, Nagel, Scherer), and theology (Rahner, Jüngel) are excluded from ontological inquiry into death.

that is part of the *Dasein*'s potentiality-for-Being and that is stamped upon it from its birth. At the ontical level we encounter two sorts of ending that are the object of analyses by the "regional" or particular sciences: (a) *perishing* (*das Verenden*), which is proper to an animal, since it is incapable of relating to death as such, and (b) the momentary event of departing from life or *decease* (*das Ableben*), which Heidegger describes as an "intermediate" phenomenon between "authentic dying" and "perishing". This *decease*, which amounts to the final phase of the *Dasein*, is proper to human existence (*Dasein*); only man has access to death as death.[7] The *Dasein* never "perishes". It can only depart from life, provided however that it is already dying ontologically. Indeed, only a Being-towards-death, capable of "authentic dying", is able to depart from life.

Although the philosopher from Freiburg normally uses distinct terms to express realities situated on the ontical and ontological levels, he uses the same term in speaking about death. This can lead to misunderstandings.[8] The term "death" signifies either "authentic dying" or else the state of death, which in Heidegger's vocabulary designates the suppression of all possibilities and is external to life. The distinction is of capital importance. Whereas the human *Dasein* cannot be its own death (understood as "state of death", which in principle eludes any possible experience on the part of the subject), it is nevertheless capable of being its own "authentic dying". The human *Dasein* does not possess its end in the ontical sense (which is distinguished from *Being-towards-the-end* in the ontological sense), because as soon as it "possessed" that end, it would no longer be, having lost its Being-in-the-world, its Being-there [*Da-sein*]. The passage to no-longer-Being-there (*Nicht-mehr-da-sein*) implies the impossibility of sensing this no-longer-Being, that is, of experiencing it.[9] Death, as the state of death, is not capable of being

[7] See *ibid.*, p. 291 [p. 247]. Heidegger seems to connect the ability to relate to death with the faculty of speech, thus distinguishing the human being from animals: "Mortals are they who can experience death as death. Animals cannot do so. But animals cannot speak either. The essential relation between death and language flashes up before us, but still remains unthought". Martin Heidegger, *On the Way to Langage*, p. 107 [p. 215: *"Die Sterblichen sind jene, die den Tod als Tod erfahren können. Das Tier vermag dies nicht. Das Tier kann aber auch nicht sprechen. Das Wesensverhältnis zwischen Tod und Sprache blitzt auf, ist aber noch ungedacht"*].

[8] "I myself am this possibility, where death is my death. There is no such thing as death in general". Martin Heidegger, *History of the Concept of Time*, p. 313 [p. 433: *"Diese Möglichkeit – der Tod als mein Tod – bin ich selbst. Den Tod überhaupt gibt es nicht"*].

[9] See Martin Heidegger, *Being and Time*, pp. 279 f. [pp. 236 f.]

integrated into the very structure of *Dasein*. The latter lives and experiences only ontological death (the "authentic dying").

Heidegger agrees to some extent with the Epicurean position – I will return to this in more detail in Part Three of this work when I discuss death as evil – that as long as the human *Dasein* exists, the state of death is not yet really present to it, and when that state has arrived, the human *Dasein* no longer exists. In his famous *Letter to Menoeceus*, Epicurus is not referring to decease or to the state of a dying person, which occurs during the process of living and therefore can be the object of sensations and experiences. Although he admits that death can be perceived by the survivor as an evil, or as a relief and a deliverance, the Greek philosopher focuses his attention exclusively on the state of death in which the departed "finds himself" and that he defines as the state of no-longer-Being, that is, as the total and irreversible destruction of the human individual. This state lies outside the subject. It is beyond all experience, both for the survivor and for the dead person.[10] Therefore, the philosopher from Freiburg is not, as some have believed,[11] standing the Epicurean thesis on its head by claiming that as long as we are, death is, and that when we no longer are, death no longer is either. In reality, Epicurus would not have been opposed to such a statement, if we understand death as Heidegger's "authentically dying", which is different from the state of death. Epicurus and Heidegger postulate that death, understood as the state of death, is something outside the subject. Indeed, the state of death can be compared to a rendezvous that the human *Dasein* keeps missing. This human *Dasein* – I will return to this in more detail in discussing a phenomenology of death – is characterized by an "impossible simultaneity",[12] by a game of "hide-and-seek",[13] by a lack of contact with the state of death. The presence of one signifies the absence of the other, and *vice versa*. Wittgenstein remarks that "death is not an event in life: we do not live to experience death".[14] The same holds, analogously, for the state of preconception, which is beyond my experience as a living being. I grasp myself only inasmuch as I am already conceived or still

[10] See Epicurus, *Letter to Menoeceus*, § 124–5, p. 30.

[11] See Wolfgang Müller-Lauter, *Möglichkeit und Wirklichkeit bei Martin Heidegger*, p. 21; Eberhardt Jüngel, *Der Tod*, p. 24.

[12] Jacques Derrida, *Aporias*, pp. 65 [pp. 117–18: *"simultanéité impossible"*].

[13] Vladimir Jankélévitch, *La mort*, p. 34: *"cache-cache"*.

[14] Ludwig Wittgenstein, *Tractatus logico-philosophicus*, no. 6.4311, p. 147 [p. 81: *"Der Tod ist kein Ereignis des Lebens. Den Tod erlebt man nicht"*]. See Karl Jaspers, *Philosophie*, pp. 222 f.; Arnold Metzger, *Freiheit und Tod*, pp. 168 f., 182 f.; Jean-Paul Sartre, *Being and Nothingness*, p. 697 [p. 630].

living.[15] Moreover, during my lifetime my state of death will constantly be in the future. The verb "to be dead" – in the sense of a concrete actualization signifying the complete disappearance of the subject – is conjugated in the first person in the future tense only; the verb "to die", only in the future and present tenses.[16] The conjugation in the past tense makes sense only if there is an afterlife that involved, furthermore, the continuous identity of the subject. By analogy with the state of death, the conception of a (particular) human being is always in the past and the verb cannot be conjugated in the first person in the future tense.

The Epicurean statement that the state of death eludes experience on the part of the dead person implies another statement that Heidegger presupposes as proven: death means the total and irreversible disappearance of the subject, the return of the human *Dasein* to nothingness. It is the possible impossibility of its existence,[17] that is, the eternal impossibility of having any plans or of realizing what is possible. The existence of the human *Dasein*, which is an accident between two abysses of nothingness, namely, preconception and death, is conceived in relation to nothingness, the object of the emotional disposition of fundamental anxiety (*Urangst*). One would arrive (theoretically, at least, as we will see) at an experience of "my death" if there were a personal afterlife and if the subject's identity were not altered by the eventual "passage" into the state of death. The same would hold true if the deceased (who would be living) communicated to the "survivors" what difference it makes to be dead. Heidegger rejects such analyses bearing on the *postmortem* condition of the human *Dasein*, strictly limiting his ontological analysis to the this-worldly region of "this side". The point of departure for his analytical method is the "here", although someone could eventually address the *postmortem* "hereafter" in ontical speculations.[18]

[15] See Maurice Merleau-Ponty, *Phenomenology of Perception*, pp. 250–1 [pp. 249–50].

[16] See William H. Poteat, "'I Will Die': An Analysis"; Vladimir Jankélévitch, *La mort*, pp. 32 f. For a discussion of Poteat's position, see Roy W. Perrett, *Death and Immortality*, pp. 29 f.

[17] See Martin Heidegger, *Being and Time*, p. 310 [p. 266].

[18] See *ibid.*, pp. 291–2 [pp. 247–8]. Martin Heidegger, *History of the Concept of Time*, p. 314 [p. 434]. To my way of thinking, a phenomenology of death would also have to address, even if only negatively, the hidden, enigmatic face of the hereafter, a face that is turned toward nothingness, toward a continuation, or else toward a new existence. Heidegger's statement that the ontology of death is limited to this world is based on the fundamental principle that an existential analysis of death precedes, methodologically, the questions raised by biology, psychology, theodicy, and the theology of death. In my opinion, one can rightly call into question the thesis of the absolute priority and neutrality of ontology with respect to the other sciences. In his *Aporias*,

But this "eventually" will never take shape. Heidegger's statement that the analysis of the mortal human *Dasein* can take only the "here" (i.e., this world) as its point of departure presupposes a choice: the decision to think of death within the framework of an ontology that implies the radical finitude of temporality. It posits as an absolutely first principle the original finitude that defines the human *Dasein*, that Being-towards-death that has its end ontologically included in the very structure of its *Dasein* (existence).

3. THE DEATH OF ANOTHER AS A POSSIBLE OBJECT OF THANATOLOGICAL KNOWLEDGE

Having concluded that a phenomenological, existential analysis of the state of death is impossible for a deceased person, Heidegger asks whether it might not be conceivable to arrive at such an analysis by means of the experience of another's death. The survivor perceives several things: first, the phenomenon of the ontical process or event of dying, and also of departing from life (decease); second, the external phenomenon of the corpse, which momentarily preserves its human appearance, that is, its presence in the form of a bodily representation of the person who, just an instant before, was alive; finally, the consequences that such a death has on him and on the human community. The human corpse, as Heidegger correctly explains, is not a simple material thing but rather is in a state that he calls *"Nur-noch-Vorhandensein"*, or "Being-just-present-at-hand-and-no-more".[19] The departed is not abandoned but is the object of care of the survivors, who accompany it in the funeral rituals and thus pay their respects.

pp. 52 f., 78 f. [pp. 98 f., 137 f.], Derrida has shown that this existential analysis subtly reintroduces theorems that originate in ontical realms, for example, from certain forms of anthropology or from Judeo-Christian theology. "Neither the language nor the process of this analysis of death is possible without the Christian experience, indeed, the Judeo-Christian-Islamic experience of death to which the analysis testifies. Without this event and the irreducible historicity to which it testifies", p. 79 [p. 139: *"Ni le langage ni la demarche de cette analyse de la mort ne sont possibles sans l'expérience chrétienne, voire judéo-christiano-islamique, de la mort dont elle témoigne. Sans cet événement et l'irréductible historicité dont il témoigne"*]. The ontology of death and the various other ontical sciences dealing with it are characterized by an "irreducibly double inclusion", inasmuch as "the including and the included regularly exchange places in this strange topography of edges" [*"inclusion irréductiblement double"; "l'incluant et l'inclus échangent régulièrement leurs places dans cette étrange topographie des bords"*].

19 Martin Heidegger, *Being and Time*, p. 282 [p. 238: *"Nur-noch-Vorhandensein"*].

These different experiences of the death of another do not allow us, in Heidegger's view, to grasp the state of death in which the departed "finds himself", nor the nature of the transformation that he has "undergone" in his death. The survivor-spectator is not capable of living it from within, that is, of assuming the deceased person's point of view. He constantly remains outside the death or decease of someone else. At most he can be present at it. "Such Being-with the dead does not allow the experience of the authentic Being-come-to-an-end [*Zuendegekommensein*] of the deceased. Death does indeed reveal itself as a loss, but a loss such as is experienced by those who remain. In suffering this loss, however, we have no way of access to the loss-of-Being as such which the dead person 'has suffered'. The dying of Others is not something which we experience in a genuine sense; at most we are always just 'there alongside'".[20] The verb "has suffered" in the preceding passage is deliberately placed within quotation marks, because a dying person cannot, strictly speaking, suffer his death – not even in a completely passive manner – given the fact that he is still alive; the departed cannot undergo it in the present tense, either, because he is no more. The dying person and the spectator are capable of undergoing only the signs, the phenomena that herald the state of death, or afterward, for the survivor, the consequences of the loss of the loved one or even of a stranger. The fact that the survivor "suffers" such a loss does not imply that it is possible for him to experience the total loss-of-Being, the radical "non-possibility" that the departed has "suffered".

Although Heidegger rightly emphasizes in his analysis of another's death that the loss experienced by the survivors consists of a loss of certain possibilities of being with the dead person, he mentions neither the "existential" loss suffered by the survivor following the decease of a dear one, nor the value of mourning. This loss can lead the survivor to call his worldview into question, resulting in an "existential upheaval",[21] as experienced, for example, by the young Augustine. It allows one to

[20] *Ibid.*, p. 282 (English translation slightly modified) [p. 239: *"dass solches Mitsein mit dem Toten gerade* nicht *das eigentliche Zuendegekommensein des Verstorbenen erfährt. Der Tod enthüllt sich zwar als Verlust, aber mehr als solcher, den die Verbleibenden erfahren. Im Erleiden des Verlustes wird jedoch nicht der Seinsverlust als solcher zugänglich, den der Sterbende 'erleidet'. Wir erfahren nicht im genuinen Sinne das Sterben der Anderen, sondern sind höchstens immer nur 'dabei'"*].

[21] See Karl Jaspers, *Philosophie*, pp. 221–2. The personal drama involving the death of a friend, which he describes in his *Confessions* (IV, 5–10), prompts Augustine to question himself radically and to conclude that he himself is mortal.

grasp death as a "present absence", a "tragic infidelity",[22] a definitive disappearance of real dialogue, an adieu.[23] It profoundly affects the survivor, who experiences a certain "loss-of-Being" in his identity, insofar as he constituted a "we" with the departed by the bonds of love and friendship.[24] An act of love and friendship binding two persons reveals to the survivor that death is essentially a loss of Being and of earthly life. This experience of the survivor with regard to the departed, who has definitively taken leave of the world, who has gone away without leaving a forwarding address, allows him to deduce, by analogy, that a day will come when he, in turn, will take leave of life. Excluding death of a loved one from his thanatological speculation, Heidegger considers death primarily (as mentioned earlier) under the impersonal aspect corresponding to its everyday character: "everybody", understood as "they", will have to die some day.[25] This "they" is not personified, but it is invariably perceived as being someone else. It is always someone else who dies, never me. Hence the "me" seems to elude death, as though it were in a certain way "immortal". This attitude toward death, which Heidegger calls "improper", renders the survivor insensible to his own death. This attitude has been described by both Tolstoy and Scheler and taken up again in the theory of the repression of death: it is an attitude that does not allow the survivor to discover, by analogy, with certainty, the fact that he will "actually die". Heidegger concludes from this that another's death does not lead one to discover and understand death as "my own most authentic possibility", a knowledge that would allow one, among other things, to attain the state of freedom and of totality of Being.

Furthermore Heidegger fails to ask whether the dying person is, to some extent,[26] capable of experiencing his own ontical dying, his

[22] Paul-Louis Landsberg, *The Experience of Death*, pp. 12, 16 [pp. 34, 38: *"absence présente; infidélité tragique"*].

[23] See Michael Theunissen, "Die Gegenwart des Todes im Leben", pp. 211 f.

[24] See Robert Nozick, *The Examined Life*, pp. 68 ff. Although Nozick does not refer directly to death here, he concludes that "the intention in love is to form a *we* and to identify with it as an extended self, to identify one's fortunes in large part with its fortunes. A willingness to trade up, to destroy the very *we* you largely identify with, would then be a willingness to destroy your self in the form of your own extended self", p. 78. See Gabriel Marcel, *Mystery of Being*, vol. 2, p. 146 [vol. 2, pp. 147 f.]; *Homo viator*, pp. 135 ff. [pp. 189 f.]. I will discuss this thesis again in more detail in the chapter "Death as the Object of Experience".

[25] See Martin Heidegger, *Being and Time*, pp. 296 f. [pp. 252 f.].

[26] I write "to a certain extent" because the experience of dying, in its extremities, could be beyond the dying person. Here I am thinking more specifically about the moments preceding the "leap" into death, a "leap" that can be interpreted as an event, an

"decease". There is no denying that he is, *per se*, capable of it, just like the survivor who refers to the external phenomena of ontical dying and to his empathy (in the case of compassion and love). The survivor's experience, however, is not total, because for it to be total he would have to be able to experience dying from the dying person's perspective, in other words, to assume someone else's point of view. A human being, nevertheless, because of his ontological structure, cannot completely assume someone else's point of view, nor a perspective from "nowhere".[27]

Nevertheless, Heidegger maintains – correctly, in my opinion – that ontical dying (decease) and ontological dying ("authentically dying") are essentially mine, that is, that no one unburdens me of my death. Of course it is conceivable to give one's life for another, to die in his place so that he may continue to live, for example, but it is impossible to die someone else's dying, that is, his death. "By its very essence, death is in every case mine, in so far as it 'is' at all. And indeed death signifies a peculiar possibility of Being, in which the very Being of one's own *Dasein* is an issue".[28] In his course based on his *History of the Concept of Time: Prolegomena,* he specifies that "only in dying can I to some extent say absolutely 'I am'",[29] or that "death is constitutive of the being of the *Dasein*".[30] "My death" in this context does not mean, as we will see, an

instant, or a process. (I will return to this subject; see Fred Feldman, "On Dying as a Process"; Anthony C. Genova, "Death as a Terminus ad Quem"; Jay F. Rosenberg, *Thinking Clearly about Death*; James Van Evra, "On Death as a Limit"). This final phase of life remains incomprehensible to the dying person, it seems to me, as is also the case, analogously, with the passage from waking to sleeping.

27 On this subject-object relation, see Thomas Nagel, *The View from Nowhere* and *Mortal Questions.*

28 Martin Heidegger, *Being and Time*, p. 284 [p. 240: *"Der Tod ist, sofern er 'ist', wesensmässig je der meine. Und zwar bedeutet er eine eigentümliche Seinsmöglichkeit, darin es um das Sein des je eigenen Daseins schlechthin geht"*].

29 Martin Heidegger, *History of the Concept of Time,* § 34, p. 318 [p. 440: *"Erst im Sterben kann ich gewissermassen absolut sagen 'ich bin'"*].

30 *Ibid.*, § 34, p. 315 [p. 435: *"der Tod für das Sein des Daseins konstitutiv ist"*]. "With death, which at its time is only *my* dying, *my ownmost Being* stands before me, is imminent: I stand before my can-be at every moment. The Being that I will be in the 'last' of my *Dasein,* that I can be at any moment, this possibility is that of my ownmost 'I am,' which means that I will be my ownmost I. I myself am this possibility, where death is my death. There is no such thing as death in general [...]. 'I can,' or more accurately, I am this 'I can' in a superlative sense. For I am this 'I can die at any moment.' This possibility is a possibility of Being in which I always already am. It is a superlative possibility, for *I myself am this constant and utmost possibility of myself,* namely, to be no more. Care, which is essentially care about the Being of *Dasein,* at its innermost is nothing but this being-ahead-of-itself in the uttermost possibility of its own can-be. Therefore *Dasein* is essentially its death. With death, the impending is not something worldly, but

appropriation of death as a state or a possible subjective experience of my death,[31] but rather a type of particular relation, the most proper relation of the human *Dasein* with death. We find here again the notion of mineness-in-each-case (*Jemeinigkeit*) that is developed in the ninth paragraph of *Being and Time.* Heidegger refers to the category of nondelegability (*Unvertretbarkeit*) applied to death – to dying – that comes and disrupts the Being-with-one-another (*Miteinandersein*).[32] Death consists of a nonrelational possibility: ontologically speaking, I always die alone, even if ontically I have company as I "undertake" this leap into nonreturn. The "mineness" of death and its "nontransferability" constitute the essential characteristic of subjectivity.

4. BEING-TOWARDS-DEATH

Despite the impossibility of experiencing death vicariously, Heidegger does not abandon his objective of grasping death as such. His fundamental problem consists of grasping the totality of the *Dasein* by reconciling it with its constant incompleteness: (a) as soon as the *Dasein* no longer has anything outstanding (*nichts mehr aussteht*), it no longer is, and (b) as long as it is, it is fundamentally open and incomplete, never having

Dasein itself. *Dasein* stands before itself, not in a possibility of Being of its choosing, but in its no-longer-*Dasein*. Insofar as *Dasein qua* Being-possible is essentially already its death, it is as *Dasein* always already a whole", *ibid.*, pp. 313 f. [*"Mit dem Tode, der jeweilig nur als* mein *Sterben ist, steht mir* mein eigenstes Sein, *mein jeden Augenblick Seinkönnen, bevor. Das Sein, das ich im 'Zuletzt' meines Daseins sein werde, das ich jeden Augenblick sein kann, diese Möglichkeit ist die meines eigensten 'Ich bin', d.h. ich werde mein eigenstes Ich sein. Diese Möglichkeit – der Tod als mein Tod – bin ich selbst. Den Tod überhaupt gibt es nicht [...]. 'Ich kann,' genauer gesprochen, ich bin dieses 'Ich kann' in einem ausgezeichneten Sinne. Ich bin nämlich dieses 'Ich kann jeden Augenblick sterben.' Diese Möglichkeit ist eine Seinsmöglichkeit, in der ich immer schon bin. Sie ist eine ausgezeichnete, denn* ich bin selbst diese ständige, äusserste Möglichkeit meiner selbst, *nämlich nicht mehr zu sein. Sorge, die wesenhaft Sorge um das Sein des Daseins ist, ist im innersten nichts anderes als dieses Sich-selbst-vorweg-sein in der äussersten Möglichkeit des eigenen Seinkönnens. Dasein ist so wesensmässig sein Tod. Mit ihm steht nicht etwas Weltliches bevor, sondern es selbst steht sich selbst bevor, nicht in einer beliebigen Seinsmöglichkeit, sondern in der seines Nicht-mehr-daseins. Sofern Dasein qua Möglichsein wesensmässig sein Tod schon ist, ist es als Dasein immer schon Ganzes"*, p. 433].

31 As Régis Jolivet interprets it in *Le problème de la mort chez M. Heidegger et J.-P. Sartre*, p. 30.

32 "If *Dasein* stands before itself as this possibility, it has been *fully* assigned to its ownmost potentiality-for-Being. When it stands before itself in this way, all its relations to any other *Dasein* have been undone" (Martin Heidegger, *Being and Time*, p. 294) [p. 250: *"Wenn das Dasein als diese Möglichkeit seiner selbst sich bevorsteht, ist es* völlig *auf sein eigenstes Seinkönnen verwiesen. So sich bevorstehend sind in ihm alle Bezüge zu anderem Dasein gelöst"*].

attained its totality or else being unable to experience it. To resolve this problem of the radical noncoexistence of incompleteness and totality, the philosopher of Freiburg cites, from an ontological point of view, the notions of *not-yet-Being* and *end.*

Heidegger asks whether an ontological analysis of the *Dasein* and temporality allows us to arrive at a phenomenology of death. This ontological death, which he also calls "authentically dying", is understood on the basis of "thrownness" (*Geworfenheit*), the "projective" ontological structure of *Dasein* itself. Ontologically speaking, *Dasein* is not presence-at-hand (*Vorhandenheit*) or a "given", but rather it *ek-sists* insofar as it is in relation to its possibility and stands outside *Vorhandenheit.* Heidegger posits the category of possibility as an ontologically constitutive element of *Dasein,* which means that *Dasein* is "primarily Being-possible",[33] open to an infinite multiplicity of possibilities of existence. Inasmuch as it is, there is always something impending, something that it can be and that it will be. As long as it exists, it behaves toward its end as potentiality-for-Being, which expresses its anticipatory character. It tends toward its possibilities, toward its actual willing-to-be, its own potentiality-for-Being. This "thrown" character of the *Dasein* indicates its tending toward the future: it is "possible only as *something futural*".[34] As soon as it "finds itself" in a situation where the future is radically lacking,[35] it ceases to be. The future does not signify a "now" that does not yet really exist and that will only be realized after a more or less long delay but rather means "the coming in which *Dasein,* in its ownmost potentiality-for-Being, comes towards itself".[36]

Heidegger maintains that the future presses upon the present and the past, that is, that temporality is realized originally from the future, the locus of possible actualization of possibilities. His view is in marked contrast to "vulgar" conceptions of time, both Husserl's theory of retention and protention and that of Augustine, for whom the present is primary: the present of the past (memory), the present of the present (vision), and the present of the future (expectation).[37] In

[33] *Ibid.*, p. 183 [p. 143: *"primär Möglichkeit"*]; see p. 276 [p. 233].

[34] *Ibid.*, p. 373 [p. 325: *"nur möglich als* zukünftiges*"*].

[35] This is not the case, for Heidegger, with despair, for that is only one of the *Dasein*'s modes of Being toward its possibilities. See *ibid.*, pp. 279 f. [p. 236].

[36] *Ibid.*, p. 373 [p. 325: *"die Kunft, in der das Dasein in seinem eigensten Seinkönnen auf sich zukommt"*].

[37] See *ibid.*, pp. 478 ff. [pp. 426 f.]; Paul Ricoeur, *Time and Narrative,* vol. 1, pp. 5–30 [vol. 1, pp. 19–53] and vol. 3, pp. 60–96 [vol. 3, pp. 90–144]; Margot Fleischer, *Die Zeitanalyse in Heideggers Sein und Zeit.*

Heidegger, conversely, the first meaning of existentiality is in the future, from which all *existentialia* derive their origin. "But ontologically, Being towards one's ownmost potentiality-for-Being means that in each case *Dasein* is already *ahead* of itself in its Being. *Dasein* is always [already] 'beyond itself', not as a way of behaving towards other entities which it is *not*, but as Being towards the potentiality-for-Being, which it is itself".[38] Since it is primordially projection toward its own potentiality-for-Being, which is stretched out toward the future as coming-toward (*Zu-kunft*), the *Dasein* is fundamentally a Being-ahead-of-itself (*Sich-vorweg-sein*).[39] It is characterized by the fact that "there is constantly something still to be settled"[40] indicating the fact that the potentiality-for-Being of its self has not yet been "realized".

The extremity of what is yet to come, of what the *Dasein* can be, corresponds to its end. To clarify his proposition, Heidegger distinguishes two ways of understanding the end. Applied to the *Dasein*, on the one hand, it signifies the fact of really arriving at the end, a Being-at-the-end (*Zu-Ende-Sein*), a completion or the terminus of a development that actualizes potentialities. From such a concept of the end, connected with the category of (ontical) possibility, one could conclude that death constitutes the *completion* of the *Dasein*. This statement, nevertheless, would not take everyday reality into account. Indeed, death very often takes the human being by surprise and robs him of possible futures, of promising projects. The end of the *Dasein*, therefore, does not necessarily coincide with its completion. That is why, on the other hand, the end also signifies the fact of being in relation with the terminus: a Being-towards-the-end (*Sein-zum-Ende*). The *not-yet* of the end does not indicate the anticipation of a future completion, nor of something that will be realized in the future. The *not-yet-Being* is not outside Being but already belongs formally to the present inasmuch as it forms a "constitutive element" of any *Dasein*, which *"is already its 'not-yet'"*.[41] If the potentiality-for-Being makes up the *Dasein*'s essence, the former, as long as it exists, must "in each

38 Martin Heidegger, *Being and Time*, p. 236 [pp. 191–2: *"Das Sein zum eigensten Seinkönnen besagt aber ontologisch: das Dasein ist ihm selbst in seinem Sein je schon* vorweg. *Dasein ist immer schon 'über sich hinaus', nicht als Verhalten zu anderem Seienden, das es* nicht *ist, sondern als Sein zum Seinkönnen, das es selbst ist"*].

39 Heidegger describes *Dasein* by means of the concepts Being-ahead-of-itself (*Sich-vorweg-sein*), Being-already-in-the-world (*Schon-in-der-Welt-sein*, which expresses facticity and the past), and Being-with (*Mit-sein*, which denotes the present).

40 See Martin Heidegger, *Being and Time*, pp. 279, 286 [pp. 236, 242: *"eine ständige Unabgeschlossenheit"*].

41 *Ibid.*, p. 288 [p. 244: *"Konstitutivum [. . .].* je schon sein Noch-nicht"].

case, as such a potentiality, *not yet be* something".[42] As long as it exists, it is already its not-yet, which is "its death" in the sense in which it is a Being-towards-the-end and not a Being-at-the-end.[43]

This tension is proper to *Dasein*, and death is introduced in this tension toward its end (which does not necessarily coincide with its completion). The proper end of the *Dasein* is not external to it and does not happen to it in a distant future but rather is intrinsic to its Being. The *Dasein* "is already its end", to wit, "its death". It is oriented toward the realization of its entirety, which it does not reach at the moment when it is dead, when it departs from life, but rather in a movement of relation toward the extreme possibility of death, of "reaching-the-end". *Dasein*'s most authentic potentiality-for-Being, which consists of its death, is unsurpassable: that is, "*Dasein* exists as thrown Being *toward* its end".[44] "Authentically dying" indicates a relation of the *Dasein* toward its certain end, which imbues it from the moment of its projection into worldliness. Heidegger summarizes by quoting *Der Ackermann aus Böhmen*: "As soon as man comes to life, he is at once old enough to die".[45] In this he agrees with Seneca, Augustine, and Simmel, among others. The last-mentioned maintains that the *Dasein* dies at every instant of its existence, which is to say that dying (which he does not clearly distinguish from death) consists of a "formal moment of our life".[46] Heidegger's statement, nevertheless, diverges from this position, as well as from the position of *Lebensphilosophie* (life-philosophy, vitalism).[47] Death belongs in a distinctive sense to *Dasein*, since it is ontologically immanent to it through the relation of a constant possibility. "Death is a possibility-of-Being which *Dasein* itself has to take over in every case. With death, *Dasein* stands before itself in its *ownmost* potentiality-for-Being. This is a possibility in which the issue is nothing less than *Dasein*'s Being-in-the-world, pure and simple. Its death is the possibility of no-longer-being-able-to-be-there [*Nicht-mehr-dasein-können*] [...]. This ownmost, nonrelational possibility is at the same time the uttermost one. As potentiality-for-Being,

[42] *Ibid.*, p. 276 [p. 233: *"seinkönnend je etwas* noch nicht sein"].

[43] See *ibid.*, p. 289 [p. 245].

[44] *Ibid.*, p. 295 [p. 251:*"da Dasein als geworfenes Sein* zu *seinem Ende existiert"*].

[45] *Ibid.*, p. 289 [p. 245: *"Sobald ein Mensch zum Leben kommt, sogleich ist er alt genug zu sterben"*].

[46] See Georg Simmel, *Lebensanschauung*, pp. 102, 106, 109 f. See Augustine, *The City of God*, XIII, 10 f. Seneca notes in his *Letters to Lucilius* that the human being "is dying daily" (letter I, vol. 1, p. 3).

[47] *Ibid.*

Dasein cannot outstrip the possibility of death. Death is the possibility of the impossibility of *Dasein*, pure and simple. Thus death reveals itself as that *possibility that is one's ownmost, that is non-relational, and that is not to be outstripped.* As such, death is something *distinctively* impending".[48]

Heidegger bases existential solipsism, the principle of individuating the *Dasein* in the *sum moribundum*, the "I am dying", or the *moribundus*, the "one destined to die" (as distinct from ontical dying), which gives the *sum* its meaning.[49] Our philosopher manages here to reverse the Cartesian *cogito ergo sum*.[50] "Authentic dying" is the object of an absolute certainty, providing a foundation for the other certainties. The *Dasein* is "its death" by the very fact of being a *Dasein*; in other words, the "authentic dying" allows us to affirm the *ergo sum*. The possibility of the impossibility of Being constitutes the proper and constitutional structure of the *Dasein*, the foundation of its Being. Thus the "authentic dying" precedes the *sum* and gives it meaning. The ipseity of the *Dasein* consists in "authentically dying", in "my death"; ontological dying is a constitutive element, a foundation of the *Dasein*. The *Dasein's* Being is the Being-possible with regard to the extremely possible that is death. It cannot be anything other than a Being-towards-death.

This absolute certainty of "authentic dying", which Heidegger arrives at independently of ontical experiences and which he bases upon his ontology of temporality (with its characteristic categories of possibility, future, and end), is accompanied by an uncertainty as to the moment of decease, which eludes all determination. Hence death is the most certain

48 Martin Heidegger, *Being and Time*, p. 294 [p. 250: *"Der Tod ist eine Seinsmöglichkeit, die je das Dasein selbst zu übernehmen hat. Mit dem Tod steht sich das Dasein selbst in seinem* eigensten *Seinkönnen bevor. In dieser Möglichkeit geht es dem Dasein um sein In-der-Welt-sein schlechthin. Sein Tod ist die Möglichkeit des Nicht-mehr-dasein-könnens [...]. Diese eigenste, unbezügliche Möglichkeit ist zugleich die äusserste. Als Seinkönnen vermag das Dasein die Möglichkeit des Todes nicht zu überholen. Der Tod ist die Möglichkeit der schlechthinnigen Daseinunmöglichkeit. So enthüllt sich der* Tod *als die* eigenste, unbezügliche, unüberholbare Möglichkeit. *Als solcher ist er ein* ausgezeichneter *Bevorstand"*].

49 "This certainty, that 'I myself am in that I will die,' is *the basic certainty of Dasein itself.* It is a genuine statement of *Dasein*, while *cogito sum* [I think, therefore I am] is only the semblance of such a statement [...]. insofar as I am, I am *moribundus*. The *moribundus first gives the sum its sense"*, Martin Heidegger, *History of the Concept of Time*, pp. 316–17 [pp. 437–8: *"Die Gewissheit, dass ich es selbst bin in meinem Sterbenwerden, ist die* Grundgewissheit des Daseins selbst *und ist echte Daseinsaussage, während das cogito sum nur der Schein einer solchen ist. [...] sofern ich bin,* bin ich moribundus – das moribundus gibt dem sum allererst einen Sinn"].

50 See Jean-Luc Marion, "L'*ego* et le *Dasein*"; Jean-François Courtine, *Heidegger et la phénoménologie*, pp. 305 f.

thing (ontological dying) while remaining indeterminate (decease). This uncertain certainty takes up again the ancient idea, mentioned earlier, of *mors certa, hora incerta.* It can be summarized in the statement *"Death, as the end of* Dasein, *is* Dasein*'s ownmost possibility, non-relational, certain and as such indefinite, not to be outstripped. Death is,* as Dasein's end, in the Being of this entity *towards* its end".[51]

Heidegger refers to the notion of "possibility' in order to define "authentic dying": the latter is "a distinctive possibility of *Dasein*",[52] a "possibility-of-Being",[53] "the possibility of the absolute impossibility of *Dasein*",[54] "that *possibility which is one's ownmost, which is non-relational, and which is not to be outstripped*".[55] This term "possibility", which has been described by some philosophers as "altogether superfluous", "redundant", "[a] fantastically misleading [...] use of the word 'possibility'",[56] should not be understood from the ontical perspective of either logic (as non-contradictory) or metaphysics (as though in contrast to necessity or to the reality that is understood as being prior to the possibility). The possibility in question here is ontological. This kind cannot be actualized; it is not realized, unlike ontical possibility (decease). Ontological possibility forms "the most primordial and ultimate positive way in which *Dasein* is characterized ontologically";[57] it expresses the fact that the *Dasein* is oriented toward the realization of its totality, which it reaches not at the moment when it is dead – when it departs from life – but rather in a relational movement toward the extreme possibility of death. The *Dasein*'s authentic potentiality-for-Being, which consists of death, is not to be outstripped; in other words, "*Dasein* exists as thrown Being *toward* its end".[58] Ontologically speaking, the verb "to end" does not signify a *Being-at-the-end* but rather a *Being-towards-the-end.* Thus the expression

[51] Martin Heidegger, *Being and Time*, p. 303 [pp. 258–9: "Der Tod ist als Ende des Daseins die eigentlichste, unbezügliche, gewisse und als solche unbestimmte, unüberholbare Möglichkeit des Daseins. *Der* Tod *ist als Ende des* Daseins *im Sein dieses Seienden* zu *seinem Ende"*].

[52] *Ibid.*, p. 292 [p. 248: *"eine ausgezeichnete Möglichkeit des Daseins"*].

[53] *Ibid.*, p. 294 [p. 250: *"eine Seinsmöglichkeit"*].

[54] *Ibid.*, p. 294 [p. 250: *"die Möglichkeit des schlechthinnigen Daseinsunmöglichkeit"*].

[55] *Ibid.*, p. 294 [p. 250: *"als die* eigenste, unbezügliche, unüberholbare Möglichkeit"].

[56] See Paul Edwards, *Heidegger on Death*, pp. 33 ff. The definition of death as the possibility of the impossibility of all existence has also been described as a tautology (Theodor W. Adorno, *Jargon der Eigentlichkeit*, p. 506) or as an *aporia* [an internal contradiction, a dead end] (Jacques Derrida, *Aporias*, p. 72 [p. 127]).

[57] Martin Heidegger, *Being and Time*, p. 183 [pp. 143–4: *"die ursprünglichste und letzte positive ontologische Bestimmtheit des Daseins"*].

[58] *Ibid.*, p. 295 [p. 251: *"dass das Dasein als geworfenes Sein* zu *seinem Ende existiert"*].

"authentic dying" denotes, for the *Dasein*, a manner of being in relation to its certain end with which it is endowed from the moment when it is thrown into existence. The intrinsic end of Being-ahead-of-itself, which is deduced from its very finitude, is death, that radical impossibility that negates all possibilities. The "ability"/"potentiality" of the *Dasein* signifies "that *way of Being* in which *Dasein is towards* its death",[59] to the state of death that constitutes its end. "Death, as possibility, gives *Dasein* nothing to be 'actualized', nothing which *Dasein*, as actual, could itself *be.* It is the possibility of the impossibility of every way of comporting oneself-towards anything, of every way of existing".[60] Death remains a certain possibility insofar as the *Dasein* is essentially a Being-towards-death, and a possible possibility by dint of the indeterminacy that characterizes the moment of decease, the coming of which is factual.

According to Heidegger, the attitudes such as the *expectation* of or *rumination* on death in a certain way deprive death of the category of possibility, insofar as they actualize in their own manner the possibility of decease. Meditation on the instant and the manner in which ontical dying will be realized results in a weakening of death by a calculating will to have it at one's disposal. Expectation anticipates the realization of the possible and no longer considers the possible as possible.[61] Only the attitude of an *anticipation* (*Vorlaufen*) of the possibility of death (again, according to our philosopher) leaves the possibility intact as possibility. This attitude alone allows us to understand death as an existential possibility of the *Dasein*, in other words, as the Being-towards-the-end of existence. Thanks to this *'anticipation'*, which does not reify a concrete realization of death, it becomes possible to experience anguish by taking upon oneself the anguish of nothingness[62] – unlike the unauthentic life that rejects the expression of anguish and flees death, which is thereby desubjectivized; most importantly, the *'anticipation'* allows one to grasp as pure possibility the extreme and authentic possibility of the *Dasein's* Being, which is the impossibility of existence, the return to nothingness, even though the moment of the (ontical) possibility of the impossibility

59 *Ibid.*, p. 291 [p. 247: *"die* Seinsweise, *in der das Dasein* zu *seinem Tode* ist"].

60 *Ibid.*, p. 307 [p. 262: *"Der Tod als Möglichkeit gibt dem Dasein nichts zu 'Verwirklichendes' und nichts, was es als Wirkliches selbst* sein *könnte. Es ist die Möglichkeit der Unmöglichkeit jeglichen Verhaltens zu [...], jedes Existierens"*].

61 See *ibid.*, p. 364 [pp. 316–17].

62 Heidegger interprets fear and anguish in the face of death in terms of the single dimension of nothingness. Wouldn't anguish be a consequence of the radical uncertainty as to what will happen to the *Dasein* once it is dead? Moreover there would be

is indeterminate. This *'anticipation'* provides the certainty of having to die and reveals to the *Dasein* the "actually" of Being-towards-death. The forward projection of the extreme possibility is not done within the framework of a temporality marked by tension between the present and the future: it does not place itself at the terminus of the *Dasein*'s path. It is not a matter of an intellectual transposition, by the imagination, into the future of the moment of decease, as is the case with thought, expectation, or suicide.[63] The *'anticipation'* is a movement of the *Dasein* toward its ownmost possibility. It attains a proximity to death outside time, thus allowing possibility to keep its character of possibility. The *'anticipation'* of Being-towards-death makes it possible to assume death as possibility. In this way the *Dasein* attains its authenticity and freedom.

The *Dasein* receives an urgent call to free itself from being lost in an impersonal "they" so as to find its ownmost potentiality-for-Being and assume its ownmost Being, in other words, to choose itself: this call is exteriorized by means of the indeterminate ("'it' does the calling"[64]) and foreign voice of conscience, which drowns out all everyday voices.

good reasons for anguish to exist if there were a continuation of individual identity *post mortem*. Anguished fear of death could perhaps also have its origin in the fear of an infinite confrontation, of a face-to-face encounter with oneself *post mortem*. Pastimes [*divertissements*], in Pascal's sense, and the workaholic's illness could be interpreted as attempts to escape: the individual does not want to find himself face-to-face with himself or to discover what he is really like. The desire to sleep, beyond what is biologically necessary, could also have its origin in this desire to lose consciousness of Being an *ego* and in this fear of discovering oneself as one is. In this connection one could also ask why we rarely experience fear with regard to our non-Being before conception. Shouldn't the human *Dasein* have symmetrical attitudes toward nonexistence before conception and *post mortem*? According to Titus Lucretius, the past in which the *Dasein* did not yet exist is the mirror of the future in which the *Dasein* no longer exists. The past eternity is the perfect mirror image of the future eternity. Schopenhauer explains, following Titus Lucretius, that "the eternity *a parte post* without me can be just as little fearful as the eternity *a parte ante* without me, since the two are distinguished by nothing except by the interposition of an ephemeral dream of life [...]. Ceasing to be ought to disturb us as little as not having been" (*The World as Will and Idea*, vol. 3, pp. 254 f. [vol. 2, pp. 596–7]). See Titus Lucretius, *De rerum natura*, III, 830 ff., 851 ff., 972 ff. (pp. 227, 229, 237); Plato-pseudo, *Axiochus*, 365d, 369c, 370a (pp. 31, 43). I will discuss these last questions in detail in Part Three of this study.

63 In his central analysis of death, Heidegger does not address the problem of suicide, because that would deprive death of its principal characteristic, indeterminacy. The possibility of or the desire for suicide does not imply knowledge of the ontological finitude of the *Dasein*, but rather the possibility for it to stop the vital process into which it has been thrown. Suicide reveals the (ontical) possibility and not the ontological necessity of death. The experience of another's suicide is not necessary to arrive at this consciousness.

64 Martin Heidegger, *Being and Time*, p. 321 [p. 276: " *'es' ruft*"].

The *Dasein* lives authentically by responding to this call and detaching itself from the realm of "they" – a veritable nonchoice of oneself – so as to understand itself and thus to rediscover itself face-to-face with itself in an attitude of silence and truth.

5. CRITIQUE

Heidegger's attempt to establish the certainty of "authentically dying", which constitutes the foundation for the *ego*, solely upon his ontological analysis and his understanding of temporality, that is, without making a detour by way of the ontical experience of another's death, is in my view unconvincing. Only a detour by way of experiencing another's death and, more particularly, the death of a dear one – which involves mourning, inner strife (*Zerrissenheit*), and even a certain loss of identity (insofar as the *ego* is "part" of a *we*) – reveals to me the end of Being-ahead-of-itself, my "authentic dying", and my distinctive condition of mortality. In my opinion, the fact that the *Dasein* is constituted as a Being essentially ahead-of-itself does not logically imply that it is a Being-towards-the-end, a Being-mortal: it only makes it a Being radically open to the indeterminate future of possibilities. Its future is uncertain to it. It does not know what it will be like and what it will become. From the ontological point of view, nothing allows us to conclude that the tendency of the *Dasein* toward the future implies an end. An end is not ontologically included in the not-yet-Being, nor in the Being-ahead-of-itself. In other words, we cannot know the condition of Being-towards-death by relating to Being solely as something possible that is stretched out toward the future. I am not saying that an ontological analysis would prove that the *Dasein* is characterized by a tendency toward and an openness to the infinite, that is, that it would be a Being continually in possibility to which, *a priori*, no possibility could put an end. Although one could suppose this, ontical experience would prove the contrary. I am content to affirm the impossibility of deducing Being-towards-the-end solely from an ontological analysis of Being-ahead-of-itself, and I maintain that this Being-towards-the-end is conceivable only starting from the experience of the *Dasein*'s finitude, that is, from the experience of another's death. The fundamental openness of Being-ahead-of-itself does not imply its end. Its future is not necessarily limited in an essential way.[65]

65 Radical ontological openness to the future of possibilities reappears as a foundational principle within the framework of the current debate about death in the field

Heidegger's notion of Being-towards-death is based on an *a priori* decision to think of death in terms of an ontology of a radically finite temporality and to take the *here* as the point of departure for the analysis. One could contrast such an ontology with the ontological possibility of a transtemporal immortality of the *Dasein*; in that case the *Dasein* would have an endless existence within temporality and would experience an openness to infinite possibilities in which no end was ontologically inscribed. Such an existence, embodied by the character of Emilia Makropoulos[66] in the play by Karel Capek or by the immortals in *Gulliver's Travels* by Jonathan Swift,[67] would be absurd and inconceivable along the lines of Heidegger's thinking. Such an ontology, which is quite different from the one proposed by the philosopher of Freiburg, is characterized by a temporal structure stretched out toward the future, and also by an open process of noncompletion, of continual gestation, of infinite possibilities in which the future is not determined.

The human *Dasein* is understood as a "possibility-in-advance". That which is not yet is not yet really present. This ontology of utopia and of radical openness, imbued with the *principle of hope*,[68] has been elaborated

of analytical philosophy. Nagel, one of the leaders of this trend, comments in his discussion of the status of death as an evil (without mentioning existentialism or vitalism at all): "A man's sense of his own experience, on the other hand, does not embody this idea of a natural limit. His existence defines for him an essentially open-ended possible future [...]. He finds himself the subject of a *life*, with an indeterminate and not essentially limited future", Thomas Nagel, "Death", pp. 9–10. See also *The View from Nowhere*, pp. 226 f.

66 See Bernard Williams, "The Makropulos Case", pp. 82–100.

67 See the commentary by Hans Jonas, "The Burden and Blessing of Mortality", pp. 96 ff. See also Bernard N. Schumacher, "Philosophische Interpretationen der Endlichkeit des Menschen".

68 Bloch's ontology, which maintains that Being exists only in the mode of *not-yet*, is characterized not only by the fundamental categories of becoming and possibility, but also and especially by four concepts: *Not, Not-yet, Nothing* and *All*. The That [*Dass*] of the present of the human being, which he is not yet capable of living and which consequently is "*the darkness of the experienced moment*" (Ernst Bloch, *The Principle of Hope*, p. 290 [p. 338: das Dunkel des gelebten Augenblicks"]), is not yet determined; it is empty, it is a *Not* that is nonetheless necessary for the possibility of a Being, i.e., for the fullness of the as-yet indeterminate *Dass*. This *Not*, understood as *Not-yet*, is not simply nothing at all, but rather, Being a *Not-having*, it is characterized by a lack. An entity, on principle, tends toward that which it lacks and hopes to enter into possession of it someday. This tension acquires a dynamism through the instinct of hunger. Whereas the *Not* in the *Da des Jetzt* (there-of-now) is at the origin of the tension that impels Being from emptiness to fullness, *Nothing* is the negation of something, i.e., the opposite of the *All* (see *ibid.*, pp. 306 f., esp. pp. 312–13 [p. 357]). The human being, which can be defined as a Being in want [*Sein im Mangel*], who hungers, always finds himself en route toward the *All*, which indicates satisfaction, and the *Nothing*, which signifies catastrophe. Man,

by Bloch, who thus shatters the finitude of Heidegger's temporality. The not-yet-Being of Bloch does not yet exist in the present. Being does not yet exist, not even in the disguised form of a projection (*Entwurf*). The end does not consist of a limit that is already present in Being and predetermined therein but assumes the form of utopia. The category of hope makes it possible to surpass this nonpresence insofar as it anticipates the future, the end of the revelation of the homeland. In a way hope makes it possible to find oneself already at the conclusion, although it does not mean the real coming of that end.

Moreover Heidegger's thesis of death as the possibility of the impossibility of Being could just as easily be turned on its head by Levinas's thesis, which understands death as "the impossibility of every possibility".[69] The

like all entities, is not yet identical with himself; he enters into a dynamic process, starting from *Nothing*, toward a state that does not yet exist, a *Novum* that arises from the darkness of the experienced moment. This tending toward the *Novum* is only possible insofar as the category of the really possible exists. From the moment when the *Novum* is transformed into an *Ultimum*, the dynamic process stops, the possibilities vanish. This ontology of becoming, of *not-yet-Being*, assigns absolute primacy to the category of possibility (understood as "the fact-based object-suited Possible" [*"das sachhaft-objektgemäss Mögliche"*] or as "the objectively real Possible" [*"das objektiv-real Mögliche"*]; see pp. 229 f. [pp. 264 f.], pp. 235 f. [pp. 271 f.], and *Tübinger Einleitung in die Philosophie*, pp. 216 f. and "Der Mensch als Möglichkeit", p. 361) over the category of the real: it can be summarized in a logical formula corresponding to the Archimedean point (at which to place the fulcrum for the lever that will move the world). Inverting the formula of Hegel, who states that the subject must develop according to the idea that is enclosed within it, Bloch declares that the essence of the subject develops only in the dynamic and utopian historicotemporal process. "*S. is not yet P.*; Subject is not yet Predicate" (*Tübinger Einleitung in die Philosophie*, p. 219: "S ist noch nicht P, *Subjekt ist noch nicht Prädikat*"), which is to say that there is a fixed, static subject (S.) that is attributed to a concrete predicate (P.). Applied to the human being, this formula means that man's potential humanity is not yet (fully) realized, that the world as a whole and nature itself have not yet found their genuine essence. "Essential being is not Been-ness; on the contrary: the essential being of the world lies itself on the Front" (*The Principle of Hope*, p. 18 [p. 18: "*Wesen ist nicht Ge-Wesenheit; konträr: das Wesen der Welt liegt selber an der Front*"]; see *ibid.* pp. 235 [p. 271], p. 300 [p. 349]; *Experimentum Mundi*, p. 172; *Tübinger Einleitung in die Philosophie*, p. 217). Therefore a human being is not a human being from the first moment of his existence; he does not yet possess that which makes him precisely a man, but rather he gradually becomes himself. This *not-yet* implies a negation (*Not*), which, however, is provisional (*yet*); in other words, the nature of the human being (not to be confused with the perfection of his nature with respect to its inherent potential) is no longer found at the origin but rather in the future, at the conclusion of the path of the entity. S. is not yet P., but S. will become P. It must become P. if it wants to be fully S. Thus, as long as S. is not yet P., it is not yet really itself. Within this inherent tendency of S. toward P. lies the driving force of this journey: hope. See Bernard N. Schumacher, *A Philosophy of Hope*.

69 Emmanuel Levinas, *Totality and Infinity*, p. 235 [p. 262: *"l'impossibilité de toute possibilité"*]; *En découvrant l'existence avec Husserl et Heidegger*, p. 104.

first statement stipulates that nothingness testifies to the ability to be-there (*Da-sein*), whereas the second expresses the boundary that human freedom runs up against. Death means that it is impossible for the subject to have plans. The individual is no longer capable of the potentiality-for-Being, even if he has not exhausted all his possibilities. Death comes to rob the human *Dasein* of the foundation of its Being: its subjectivity. As we will see in Part Three of this study, Levinas compares death to a "pure being seized"[70] that deprives the subject of the actualization of his possibilities, of the realization of his works. Death is constitutive of the life of the *Dasein* (as Simmel, Scheler, and Jonas[71] have maintained from a biological perspective and Heidegger – on the ontological level), yet at the same time death is the utmost contradiction of life. Indeed, the human *Dasein* is likewise constituted by an ontological principle that is radically opposed to death and assumes various names, such as Bloch's "hope principle", Bergson's *"élan vital"*, or Williams's "categorical desire".

Bergson's "impetus of life" is not deduced from an ontology of temporality; in other words, it is not inscribed within the structure of time, but rather, according to Bergson, inherent to the dwindling of energy. Thus the human *Dasein* is fundamentally a not-Being-towards-death. While knowing full well that the battle against death is lost from the start, the subject – like the bull in the arena[72] – hopes that he will one day manage to overcome that enemy; the same thing is implied by Bloch's hope principle. Hope, an ontological characteristic of the human *Dasein*, is found again in what Williams calls the "categorical desire", which he distinguishes from conditional desire. To satisfy a desire is something good in itself. A human being is constantly projecting himself toward the future, desiring to possess the object of his desire. Death is the obstacle that makes it impossible to possess the object of conditional desire, which is subordinate to the fact of living, because the subject desires something while presuming that he will continue to live. Conditional desire gives the subject no reason to continue to exist, but he desires various specific "things" (e.g., food, work, family life) provided that he can continue to live. The subject could, however, prefer not to continue living. The categorical desire constitutes the driving force of human existence, which

70 Emmanuel Levinas, *God, Death, and Time*, p. 117 [p. 135: *"pur rapt"*].

71 See Hans Jonas, "The Burden and Blessing of Mortality" and *The Phenomenon of Life*.

72 See the description entitled *"Intermezzo* in the Bull Ring" by Paul-Louis Landsberg, *The Experience of Death*, pp. 45–50 [pp. 77–83].

wants to continue to live so as to accomplish and realize its plans. Indeed, it is reasonable to prefer a future in which one's plans and desires will be satisfied to a future in which that will not be the case.[73] This categorical desire does not expect that the future will "become a present in which there is no longer anything to desire",[74] which would imply, at least in a certain way, its own death. Instead, it expresses an ontological tendency that is constitutive of the human *Dasein* and allows it to continue making plans in the future. This existential desire comes into conflict with Being-towards-death.

Although there is good reason to say that the human *Dasein* essentially tends toward death – since the possibility of death always accompanies it – it is at the same time substantially "desiring". It is characterized by an existential (ontological) desire that is inherent to its Being-ahead-of-itself, which tends toward the infinity of possibilities.[75] This dialectical encounter between life and death at the very heart of human existence is revealed in exemplary fashion in the constant reaffirmation of the value of being expressed by the metabolism, a veritable process of self-preservation against the threat of its possible negation posed by death. This ontical biological fact, together with the biographical and cultural dimensions of a self-consciousness that is open to the actualization of its possibilities (whether predetermined or freely chosen), is at the source of the conflict between the two ontological constitutions (Being-towards-death and not-Being-towards-death) that make up the human being.

73 See Bernard Williams, "The Markopulos Case".

74 Nicolas Grimaldi, *Le désir et le temps*, p. 137: *"devienne un présent où il n'y ait plus rien à désirer".*

75 Heidegger's ontology (Martin Heidegger, *Being and Time*, p. 238 ff. [pp. 194 f.]) is opposed to a principle such as Bergson's impetus of life or categorical desire and ascribes the force that propels life to facticity. The spontaneity of the life principle presupposes, in Heidegger's opinion, the possibility of the impossibility of Being, which is deduced from the first horizon of the temporal constitution of the *Dasein.* According to our philosopher, Being-towards-death is prior to an ontology of life.

4

Is Mortality the Object of Foreknowledge?

We have discussed the thesis that there is an intuitive knowledge of death, as well as the ontological approach that posits *a priori* an intrinsic end to the straining forward of *Dasein*. Let us consider for a moment the philosophers who propose a "*constitutive* knowledge"[1] or a "foreknowledge"[2] of mortality. In his book entitled *Death and Thought*, Conche emphasizes that the statement "I shall die" contains an absolute certainty, a "deep-seated conviction" ("*conviction foncière*") that is not based on certain knowledge and is not something proved by deductive reasoning but depends on the "general or widely held opinions" of the average human being, on "accepted ideas (*endoxa*)".[3] It constitutes a "primary truth" that is "bound up with a feeling of *insurmountable* [and irremediable] helplessness", which is in turn connected with "the sense of being a part of nature and of sharing a common lot". The knowledge of my mortality – that universal and "all-powerful" law of nature – lies especially in what Conche calls a "consciousness of materiality", meaning that I, as a material being, am profoundly affected by the principle of dissolution. The origin of the fact that I know that I am mortal cannot be found in knowledge that is understood in the sense of objective knowledge that has been acquired. At issue here is a knowledge that Conche calls "constitutive", that is, "which has always been there, that is one with [one]self". I could not conceive of

[1] Marcel Conche, *La mort et la pensée*, p. 14: "*un savoir* constitutif".
[2] Hans Georg Gadamer, "La mort comme question", p. 20: "*une pré-connaissance*".
[3] Marcel Conche, *La mort et la pensée*, pp. 9–10: "*conviction foncière*"; "*des opinions communes ou fortement accréditées*"; "*idées admises* (endoxa)".

myself *not* knowing that. For Conche the fact of being conscious of oneself implies the fact of thinking about oneself as mortal. 'I think of myself, therefore I am mortal,' one could say; or rather, to be more precise, 'I think of myself' is identical to 'I think of myself as being mortal'. "From the moment that I am conscious – and this is what distinguishes me from an animal or an infant that cannot yet speak –, for example, from the moment that I wake up in the morning, I think *myself*, and that means: I think myself *mortal.* I cannot think without being conscious of it, and I cannot be conscious without thinking of myself. Now to think of myself and to think of myself as mortal are one and the same thing. Consequently every thought develops against the background of a knowledge of death. Death, as such, is the horizon of thought. We return to a sort of *cogito*, but such that the body, instead of being excluded from knowledge, is included in it. There is no such thing as a thought about myself that is not at the same time a thought about myself as mortal".[4]

From this we can conclude that the moment I stop thinking about death *ipso facto* I stop thinking. For thought, therefore, death is not something different, the absolute otherness of Levinas and Sartre: thought – and not just philosophy, as Schopenhauer claimed – is in itself profoundly concerned with death. Death, according to Conche, is "posited at the same time as thought, and all thought is as such thought about death".[5] Conche pursues his argument to the point where he equates the fact of thinking of oneself not only with that of thinking of oneself as mortal, but also with the fact of thinking of oneself as a corporeal being. A human being who had never had a notion of his own body or even of someone else's body "would nevertheless know that he lays himself open [*donne prise*] to death, and by understanding the principle whereby he lays himself open to death, he would understand precisely the body. An irrefutable experience teaches us that we are dependent upon a principle of death, and this is prior to all sensory notion of the body. We have here a sort of proto-experience,

[4] *Ibid.*, p. 14: *"Dès lors que je suis conscient – et c'est ce qui me différencie de l'animal et de l'enfant avant le langage –, par exemple dès que je me réveille le matin, je me pense, et cela veut dire: je me pense mortel. Je ne puis penser sans en avoir conscience et je ne puis être conscient sans me penser. Or me penser et me penser mortel, c'est la même chose. Par conséquent toute pensée se développe sur le fond d'un savoir de la mort. La mort est, comme telle, l'horizon de la pensée. Nous revenons à une sorte de Cogito, mais tel que le corps, au lieu d'être exclu du savoir, s'y trouve inclus. Il n'y a pas de pensée de moi-même qui ne soit pensée de moi-même comme mortel".*

[5] *Ibid.*, p. 9: *"posée en même temps que la pensée, et toute pensée est, comme telle, pensée (de) la mort".*

a primordial experience from which we derive the downright primitive certainty of our mortality".[6]

Conche rejects pure thought, sometimes called Cartesian thought, and maintains that the thought of a human being is always a human thought, that is, a thought of a mortal being. I constantly think, he explains, as though I had my body. My corporeality continually intervenes in the manner in which I think and in the extent to which thought carries within itself a "relation to what negates it". So it is that in the very experience of thinking one encounters the experience of what is opposed to it, namely, the body, matter. Our author concludes from this that the knowledge possessed by a human being – due to his deep-seated dependence on a principle of dissolution and death – is "inherent to the very act of thinking"; in other words, knowledge of death is not the result of an objective, inductive knowledge that "comes later". We have here a *"constitutive"* knowledge: "For every human being, the very act of *thinking* [...] is bound up with the absolute certainty of his death".[7]

Before evaluating Conche's position, I would like to turn for a moment to Gadamer, who states (as I have already mentioned) that consciousness of mortality constitutes the ontological honor of the human being. He rejects the common explanation that the human being arrives at a certainty that he must die only through the direct or mediate experience of someone else's death, and he asks whether the continual questioning about death might not be a way of hiding what we already know in our heart of hearts. Referring to his understanding of philosophy as *anamnesis* – meaning that, in order to arrive at a consciousness of what he already knows without knowing that he does, the philosopher draws from the depths of an inner well – Gadamer maintains that the knowledge of my mortality is not something acquired by my reflection but something given, an intuition granted to me at birth. "Everyone already has intuitively a knowledge of the death that he will undergo".[8] Gadamer

[6] *Ibid.*, pp. 14–15: *"saurait néanmoins qu'il donne prise à la mort, et en concevant le principe par lequel il donne prise à la mort, il concevrait précisément le corps. Une expérience irréfragable nous enseigne que nous sommes dans la dépendance d'un principe de mort, et cela avant même toute représentation sensorielle du corps. Il y a là une sorte de proto-expérience, une expérience primordiale de laquelle nous tirons la conviction tout à fait primitive de notre mortalité".*

[7] *Ibid.*, pp. 15–16: *"c'est au fait même de* [p. 16] penser [...] *qu'est liée, pour chaque homme, l'absolue conviction de sa mort".* He continues by repeating "The knowledge that man has of himself as a thinking being doomed to death is one and the same thing as man's self-constitution" [*"Le savoir que l'homme a de lui-même comme d'un être pensant voué à la mort ne fait qu'un avec l'auto-constitution de l'homme"*].

[8] Hans-Georg Gadamer, "La mort comme question", p. 20: *"Chacun a déjà intuitivement un savoir de la mort à subir".* See *ibid.*, p. 12. Josef Pieper likewise emphasizes, of course,

seems to echo the statement made by Levinas in *Totality and Infinity*. The latter remarks that "my death is not deduced from the death of the others by analogy; it is inscribed in the fear I can have for my being. The 'knowledge' of the threatening precedes every experience reasoned in terms of the death of the Other; in naturalist language this is termed an instinctive knowledge of death".[9]

that the consciousness of my mortality is capable of being deduced from the experience of someone else's death, but he seems to acknowledge also the possibility of such a certainty without making a detour by way of another's death. "And we can very well ask whether the existential certainty that we must die would not come to us even if we did not observe dying all around us. There is in fact much reason to think that this certainty of our own death is completely independent of all external experience". *Death and Immortality*, pp. 8–9 [p. 290: *"Und man kann sogar mit Fug die Frage stellen, ob wir nicht vielleicht, auch ohne die Erfahrung des Sterbens rundum, die existentielle Gewissheit haben, dass wir sterben müssen. Es spricht in der Tat vieles dafür, dass diese Gewissheit des eigenen Todes völlig unabhängig ist von jeder äusseren Erfahrung"*]. Eberhardt Jüngel declares that this knowledge of my mortality is given to me immediately, together with my existence: "And this knowledge [about the inevitability of our death] comes to us from some other source than inductive reasoning. For we are always asking about death as well if we want to understand ourselves. We know about the inevitability of our death in the form of a *question* that no one has posed to us yet exists with us: What is death? This question is given at the same time as our existence. One can of course repress it, but it is there. And in this question death itself is there in a very indefinite manner. In its inevitability it addresses us, so to speak, from our inmost being, inasmuch as it makes us ask about it: Why? What then? How much time yet? and What is it in the first place, our death?" [*"Und dieses Wissen (um die Unvermeidbarkeit unseres Todes) kommt uns anderswoher als aus Induktion. Denn wir fragen immer auch nach dem Tod, wenn wir uns selber verstehen wollen. Wir wissen um die Unvermeidbarkeit unseres Todes in der Form einer uns von niemanden gestellten, wohl aber mit uns existierenden* Frage*: Was ist der Tod? Diese Frage ist mit unserer Existenz zugleich gegeben. Man kann sie zwar verdrängen, aber sie ist da. Und in ihr ist der Tod in einer sehr unbestimmten Weise selber da. In seiner Unvermeidbarkeit geht er uns sozusagen aus unserem Innersten her an, indem er uns nach ihm fragen lässt: Warum? Was dann? Wie lange noch? Und was ist das überhaupt: unser Tod?"*]. *Der Tod*, p. 16.

9 Emmanuel Levinas, *Totality and Infinity*, p. 233 [p. 259: *"ma mort ne se déduit pas, par analogie, de la mort des autres, elle s'inscrit dans la peur que je peux avoir pour mon être. La 'connaissance' du menaçant précède toute expérience raisonnée sur la mort d'autrui – ce qui, en langage naturaliste, se dit comme connaissance instinctive de la mort"*]. He continues, "It is not the knowledge of death that defines menace; it is in the imminence of death, in its irreducible oncoming movement, that menace originally consists, that the 'knowledge of death' is (if one may put it so) uttered and articulated" [*"Ce n'est pas le savoir de la mort qui définit la menace, c'est dans l'imminence de la mort, dans son irréductible mouvement d'approche, que consiste la menace originellement, que se profère et s'articule, si l'on peut s'exprimer ainsi, le 'savoir de la mort'"*]. This position is not incompatible with the one that Levinas would defend some years later in his lectures entitled *God, Death, and Time.* He puts his argument in perspective by saying that he is not discussing the knowledge of "my death" and of my consciousness of being mortal, but rather the knowledge of death in general and of dying. "It seems to us that all that we can say or think about death and dying, and their inevitability, comes to us secondhand. We know it by hearsay or by empirical knowledge. [...] This knowledge comes to us from the experience

The claim that there is an "instinctive knowledge of death" that emerges when I am confronted with an immediate danger takes us back to the discussion of an animal's perception of death. The reactions in the face of danger of a human being who has no previous experiential knowledge of death are in my opinion simple reflexes of self-defense and self-preservation: they are instinctive, belong to the species, and do not yet imply a consciousness of man's mortality and his impending death[10]. Levinas does not explain, moreover, the nature of such an instinctive knowledge: is it rational or is it situated at the level of the reflexes? Furthermore how can one justify the connection between the feeling of fear and menace in a particular dangerous situation and the consciousness of my mortality? Is an experience of a threat sufficient to reveal to me my mortal condition? I doubt it very much. A human being who had never experienced another's death nor heard that all men are mortal would not necessarily be able to deduce that he was mortal from a threat that he was fleeing. As for Gadamer's statement that every human being "already has intuitively a knowledge of the death that he will undergo" (herein Gadamer distinguishes himself from Scheler, who attributes to every living thing this intuitive ability to grasp death), it is not supported by any argument. Although the thesis is assumed *a priori*, it is nevertheless based on a particular concept of philosophy as *anamnesis* that can be criticized, and rightly, it seems to me. In stipulating that "being conscious", "thinking of oneself", and "thinking of oneself as mortal" (which also implies a consciousness of the body, which is subject to change and corruption) are identical, Conche raises more problems than he solves. First of all, it seems problematic to equate "thinking about myself" with "thinking about myself as mortal" and to postulate that "thinking about myself" and "being conscious" (which could also be rendered as "self-consciousness") are inseparable, not to mention the even greater difficulties caused by the notion of including in the

and observation of other men, of their behavior as dying and as mortals aware of [*connaissant*] their death and forgetful of their death (which does not here mean a diversion: there is a forgetting of death that is not a diversion). Is death separable from the relation with the other [*autrui*]?", p. 8 [p. 9: *"Tout ce que nous pouvons dire et penser de la mort et du mourir et de leur inévitable échéance, il nous semble de prime abord que nous le tenions de seconde main. Nous le savons par ouï-dire ou par savoir empirique. [...] Ce savoir nous vient de l'expérience et de l'observation des autres hommes, de leur comportement de mourants et de mortels connaissant leur mort et oublieux de leur mort (ce qui ne veut pas dire ici divertissement: il y a un oubli de la mort qui n'est pas divertissement). La mort est-elle séparable de la relation avec autrui?"*].

10 See Bernard N. Schumacher, *Confrontations avec la mort*, pp. 54–65.

act of "thinking about myself" that of "thinking about myself as corporeal". But aside from all that, I think that the fundamental obstacle lies in his statement that such a consciousness of my mortality consists of a "proto-experience" that is given to me independently of my experience of someone else's death. The fact that I think of myself as mortal can only be deduced, in my opinion, from my experience of another's death. Specifically, this experience can be gained either through the real death of another person or through the trust that I place in older persons who assure me that human beings are mortal. Without having had such an experience, I could not affirm that my tending toward the future would have an end, that this end was included therein teleologically from the moment when I was thrown into worldliness. Nor am I capable of laying claim to the principle of dissolution due to my bodily constitution. Indeed, without experiencing the passage of a living body to the inert state of a corpse, it is hardly possible for me to maintain with certainty that my body is doomed to death. Even if I saw my body age, I would not yet be certain that I would die, as we have seen in our discussion of Scheler's position.

5

Inductive Knowledge of Death and Jean-Paul Sartre

After the critiques of Heidegger's solution ("Being-towards-death") formulated by Sternberger and Landsberg in the 1930s, and before those developed in recent years by Levinas, Derrida, and Macho, to cite only a few,[1] Sartre is the first well-known philosopher who, while proposing an ontology different from Heidegger's, elaborates his own concept of death in contrast to Being-towards-death – which he describes in *Being and Nothingness*[2] as a "sleight of hand".[3] His principal aim is not to conduct an "exhaustive" and "detailed"[4] investigation of death but to clarify Being-in-situation. He constructs his thanatology on the foundation of his ontology of freedom and his anthropology of Being-for-others, in which one for-itself (*pour-soi*) stands in a relation of conflict with another for-itself: the goal of Being-for-others is to reduce the other to an in-itself (*en-soi*). According to Sartre, I am not capable of expecting "my death"; death is not a conspicuous (*insigne*) possibility that is intrinsic to the for-itself, and it does not give meaning to the existence of the free for-itself. Death is extrinsic to life. It annihilates the meaning of the free projection of the possibilities of the for-itself, which, once it is dead, is definitively reduced to an in-itself, and the meaning of its past actions

[1] See Dolf Sternberger, *Der verstandene Tod*; Paul-Louis Landsberg, *The Experience of Death*; Emmanuel Levinas, *God, Death, and Time*; Jacques Derrida, *Aporias*; Thomas Macho, *Todesmetaphern*.

[2] Jean-Paul Sartre, *Being and Nothingness*. For a more thorough reading of this work, see Bernard N. Schumacher, ed., *Jean-Paul Sartre*.

[3] See Jean-Paul Sartre, *Being and Nothingness*, p. 683 [p. 617: *"tour de passe-passe"*].

[4] *Ibid.*, p. 700 [p. 633: *"exhaustive", "détaillée"*]. Concerning Sartre's experiences of death during his childhood and youth, see also *The Words*.

is henceforth conferred by the surviving for-itself. Other people, moreover, are indispensable if I am to arrive at a consciousness of my mortality. Recognizing, of course, with Heidegger along the lines of Epicurus's argument that there is, strictly speaking, no such thing as an experience of death (understood as the state of death), Sartre maintains, contrary to Heidegger and Scheler, that only a detour by way of the experience of another's death and by way of mourning leads to a recognition of one's own mortality. Sartre's reflection is a cornerstone in the debate on death and the meaning of life that left its mark the first part of the twentieth century; it seems to herald the present discussion, within the analytic tradition, of the meaning of life and the status of death as an evil (inasmuch as it deprives the subject of possibilities, interrupting the projection of his free plans for the future). Sartre's position is one of the most original contributions to thanatology in the twentieth century, but it has not received the credit that it deserves, and it has too often been presented in outline form.[5] In this chapter I will analyze step by step the train of thought developed by Sartre in *Being and Nothingness*, while questioning in particular the accuracy of his interpretation of Heidegger's Being-towards-death. In this way I will discuss, first, the realist and idealist concepts of death; second, the possibility of expecting "my death"; third, death in relation to Sartre's theory of meaning; and finally the concept of death as a victory of the other and as a situation limit.

1. THE REALIST AND IDEALIST CONCEPTS OF DEATH

In *Being and Nothingness*, Sartre distinguishes two concepts of death with the help of the double meaning of the word "term". Death can be understood, first, as a term (in the sense of "terminus, boundary") "adhering to the nothingness of being which limits the process considered".[6] Because death is what is "on the other side of the 'wall'", it is an event that is situated outside life. It is considered "pre-eminently non-human",[7] something that opens onto the nothingness of the living being. This so-called *realist* concept views death as the *state* of death that excludes all simultaneity with life, as a "transcendent to life".[8] It is "the great

5 See, for example, James P. Carse, *Death and Existence*, pp. 361 f.; Jacques Choron, *Death and Western Thought*; Alexander Lohner, *Der Tod im Existentialismus*, pp. 186 f.; Georg Scherer, *Das Problem des Todes in der Philosophie*, pp. 170 f.

6 Jean-Paul Sartre, *Being and Nothingness*, p. 680 [p. 615: *"adhérent au néant d'être qui limite le processus considéré"*].

7 *Ibid.*: *"l'inhumain par excellence"*.

8 *Ibid.*, p. 697 [p. 629: *"transcendant à la vie"*].

unknowable"[9] that limits what is human; it is the "open door" or the "window"[10] opening onto the absolute that makes possible a direct contact with the nonhuman absolute. The French philosopher rejects this first concept, for death reveals what is human only from the perspective of what is human: what is nonhuman completely eludes us. Despite his opposition to the absolute transcendence of death with respect to life, Sartre nevertheless claims that death does not exist for the living: in order to do this he refers, as we shall see, to the "situation-limit" and to his ontology of freedom. To a certain extent his position agrees with the Epicurian "nothingness of death", according to which it is impossible to experience my own being dead as death. At no point does death encroach upon the for-itself. The latter does not encounter death, although it is capable of ascertaining the consequences thereof externally by observing another's death.

A thanatology that inscribes death *within* life – I will return to this notion – arose as early as the nineteenth century in reaction to a realist conception of death. This inclusion or "incorporation" of death in the heart of life takes place first at the biological level (Klages, Scheler, Eucken, Simmel), and later occurs at the ontological level, with Heidegger being the representative *par excellence* of this position. Sartre discusses at length this second concept of death, which he calls *idealist*; according to this concept death is the final term in a series of phenomena; in other words, it belongs to that series and, in his view, goes so far as to endow it with its meaning. Death, like a final cord at the end (*terme*) of a melody, would be immanent to the existence of the human *Dasein*. Sartre notes that the purpose of this "recovery" (*"récupération"*) and, one might add, of this taming of death is not just to interiorize death, but also and above all to "humanize" what he describes as the preeminently nonhuman thing that is death. "There is no longer any *other side* of life, and death is a human phenomenon; it is the final phenomenon of life and is still life".[11] Death becomes "the meaning of life"[12] by influencing retrospectively the whole life of the subject-consciousness, just as, by analogy, the (concluding) harmonic resolution constitutes the meaning of a melody. This humanization of death also implies the "mineness" (*la "mienneté"*, Heidegger's *Jemeinigkeit*) of

9 *Ibid.*, p. 682 [p. 616: *"grand inconnaissable"*].

10 *Ibid.*, pp. 681 f. [pp. 615, 617: *"porte ouverte"*, *"lucarne"*].

11 *Ibid.*, p. 681 [p. 616: *"Il n'y a plus d'*autre côté *de la vie, et la mort est un phénomène humain, c'est le phénomène ultime de la vie, vie encore"*].

12 *Ibid.*: *"le sens de la vie"*.

death, which becomes a phenomenon of my personal life and thus renders it unique.

Sartre declares that such a recovery of death must be "sternly rejected".[13] (He fathers this notion on Rilke, Malraux, and especially Heidegger, although the latter neglects to mention his own precursors such as Scheler and Simmel.)[14] The French philosopher sees death as an antiutopia, an antiproject, and the enemy *par excellence* that strips the life of the for-itself of all meaning and brings to light the absurdity of all expectation, because the problems of the subject "receive no solution and because the very meaning of the problems remains undetermined".[15] Without digressing to discuss the positions of the German poet and the French novelist, Sartre focuses his critique on the thesis of Being-towards-death and describes it, in a few short sentences, as an attempt to recover the *Dasein*'s freedom despite the apparent limit imposed on it by death. He analyzes Heidegger's concept of "freedom-to-die"[16] (*Freiheit zum Sterben*) and of death as "my ownmost possibility" – a thesis implying the interiorization of death – and interprets it as a "sleight of hand"[17] that transforms death into an "expected death",[18] which would constitute the meaning of the life of the human *Dasein*. Sartre's critique is centered primarily on a twofold objection: on the one hand, it is impossible that death *per se* (*la mort*) could be expected (as opposed to the real possibility of expecting a particular death), and, on the other hand, it is impossible that death should confer a meaning on the existence of the for-itself.

[13] *Ibid.*, p. 683 [p. 617: *"rigoureusement"*].

[14] See Rainer Maria Rilke, *Von der Armut und vom Tode*; Serge Gaulupeau, "André Malraux et la mort"; Max Scheler, *Tod und Fortleben*; Georg Simmel, *Lebensanschauungen* and "Zur Metaphysik des Todes".

[15] Jean-Paul Sartre, *Being and Nothingness*, p. 690 [p. 624: *"ne reçoivent aucune solution et parce que la signification même des problèmes demeure indéterminée"*].

[16] *Ibid.*, p. 682 [p. 616: *"liberté pour mourir"*].

[17] *Ibid.*, p. 683 [p. 617: *"tour de passe-passe"*]. In his posthumous work *Notebooks for an Ethics*, Sartre seems to assign a more positive value to this Heideggerian definition of death: "But it is furthermore *my* death as the possibility of having no more possibility, the possibility of impossibility, otherness in my project at the very heart of this project [...] the relationship to death exists only as the possibility of the death of a certain existing thing, and since this existing thing defines itself through its projects, the possibility of the impossibility of certain projects", p. 416 [p. 432: *"Mais c'est en outre ma mort comme possibilité de n'avoir plus de possibilité, possibilité d'impossibilité, altérité dans mon projet au coeur même de ce projet [...] le rapport avec la mort n'existe que comme possibilité de la mort d'un certain existant, et comme l'existant se définit par ses projets, possibilité de l'impossibilité de certains projets"*].

[18] Jean-Paul Sartre, *Being and Nothingness*, p. 683 [p. 617: *"mort attendue"*].

2. THE EXPECTATION OF MY DEATH

To begin with, Sartre remarks, in my opinion correctly, that it is impossible to base the proper and irreplaceable selfness (*ipséité*) of the human *Dasein*, the existential "solipsism", upon the *sum moribundum*, "I am dying", or on the *moribundus*, the "one destined to die" (as distinct from ontical dying). As we have seen, Heidegger undertakes to reverse the Cartesian *cogito ergo sum*, which he describes as a mere appearance, and in his *History of the Concept of Time: Prolegomena*, he supposes that "my death" is foundational for all certainties. A human being is "his death" by the very fact that he is a human being: that is, it is "my death" that allows me to affirm the *ergo sum*. The "ability-to-die" at every moment of its existence is the proper structure of the *Dasein*, the foundation of its being, its selfness. It precedes the *sum* and gives it meaning. The human *Dasein* cannot be anything other than a Being-towards-death. Heidegger's starting point, in Sartre's view, is to individualize human death by maintaining that "to die is the only thing which nobody can do for me".[19] As we have seen, no one is capable of relieving someone else of his death. Sartre describes this Heideggerian statement as "gratuitous" and attributes it to "evident bad faith in the reasoning". To die is not the "only" thing that nobody is capable of doing for me. There are other possibilities – such as to love or to take an oath – that my subjectivity alone is in a position to project. If we examine human acts from the perspective of their utility, their function, their efficiency, or their result, Sartre explains, we see that someone else can very well take my place and realize "my" possibilities: anyone is able to die in my place or die for our country or love a particular person.

By referring to the existential solipsism of death, Heidegger individualizes the human *Dasein*: in other words, Sartre notes, "it is by projecting itself freely toward its final possibility that the *Dasein* will attain authentic existence [...] in order to attain the irreplaceable uniqueness of the person".[20] Sartre accuses the philosopher from Freiburg of circular reasoning. Indeed, how can such an individuation of death be proved? Is the death that will befall me one fine day really *my* death? Sartre rejects Heidegger's existential solipsism, arguing that "there is no personalizing virtue which is peculiar to *my* death. Quite the contrary, it becomes *my*

[19] *Ibid.*, p. 683 [p. 618: *"mourir est la seule chose que personne ne puisse faire pour moi"*].

[20] *Ibid.*, p. 683 [p. 617: *"projetant librement vers sa possibilité ultime que le Dasein accédera à l'existence authentique [...] pour atteindre à l'unicité irremplaçable de la personne"*].

death only if I place myself already in the perspective of subjectivity; it is my subjectivity defined by the pre-reflective *cogito* which makes of my death a subjective irreplaceable, and not death which would give an irreplaceable selfness to my for-itself. In this case death can not be characterized; *for it is death* as *my* death, and consequently its essential structure as death is not sufficient to make of it that personalized and qualified event which one can *wait* for".[21]

Sartre's critique of Heidegger's attempt to base selfness on the *sum moribundum* is surely pertinent, but it fails to draw attention to the *a priori* foundation that underlies Being-towards-death. As I have already mentioned, the constitution of *Dasein* as a being essentially in-advance-of-itself does not logically imply that it is a Being-toward-the-end, a mortal being; it only supposes that it is a being radically open to the future (as coming-toward (*l'à-venir*; German, *Zu-kunft*)) of possibilities, toward the indeterminate. From the ontological point of view, nothing allows us to conclude that this tending toward the future (as coming-toward) implies an end. An end is not contained ontologically in Not-yet-being nor in Being-in-advance-of-itself. In other words, as I have already emphasized, one can not know the condition of Being-towards-death by referring exclusively to the possible being that is stretched out toward the future (as coming-toward). Sartre refuses to think of death within the framework of an ontology that presupposes the radical finitude of temporality. He develops an ontology of the radical openness of the free for-itself in which death is not included ontologically in the free tending of the for-itself toward the future as coming-toward. Death comes from outside subjectivity. The ontological structure of finitude does not reveal the condition of the for-itself as Being-towards-death; rather, it merely "determines" its freedom, which, although absolute in itself, makes itself limited when it acts. The irreversible character of the freedom of the for-itself is due to its contingency and to its situation in time (*temporalisation*). "Even if one is temporally indefinite – that is, without limits – one's 'life' will be nevertheless finite in its very being because it makes itself unique. Death has nothing to do with this. Death

[21] *Ibid.*, pp. 683–4 [pp. 618–19: *"aucune vertu personnalisante qui soit particulière à* ma *mort. Bien au contraire, elle ne devient* ma *mort que si je me place déjà dans la perspective de la subjectivité; c'est ma subjectivité, définie par le Cogito préréflexif, qui fait de ma mort un irremplaçable subjectif et non la mort qui donnerait l'ipséité irremplaçable à mon pour-soi. En ce cas la mort ne saurait se caractériser* parce qu'elle est mort *comme ma mort et, par suite, sa structure essentielle de mort ne suffit pas à faire d'elle cet événement personnalisé et qualifié qu'on peut* attendre"].

occurs 'within time', and human-reality, by revealing to itself its unique finitude, does not thereby discover its mortality".[22] To summarize, the finitude of the for-itself is not established by death, according to Sartre, but by the act of freedom. Even if the for-itself were immortal, it would be finite. Death is a simple contingent fact coming from outside the structure of the finite for-itself, which is to say that the mere discovery of its own finitude does not imply that its condition is Being-towards-death. Only the "experience" of another's death allows me to discover my "authentic dying", when I become responsible for the meaning of the existence of someone else who has died.

Sartre continues his critique of Being-towards-death by focusing his attention on the problematic aspect of waiting for "my death". He does this by distinguishing two ways of waiting: "expecting death" (*s'attendre à la mort*) does not mean "waiting for death" (*attendre la mort*). To illustrate this difference, he takes the example of the waiting that precedes the arrival of a train at the station. I am waiting in the Paris station for the arrival of Peter on the train from Chartres, while considering the possibility that external factors might act upon this predetermined mechanical course of events and slow or stop the train. Because of their indetermination, I cannot keep track of these various factors that cause the train to arrive at the Paris station with more or less of a delay; they are unforeseeable. I am in a position to *wait for* Peter and at the same time to *expect* that his train will be delayed. The same goes for "my death".

The object of the wait is a definite event brought about by various (likewise definite) processes, the occurrence of which is foreseeable. The same is true for the mortal condition of the for-itself. The latter is, from the biological perspective, a relatively self-enclosed and isolated system. Hence I am capable of waiting for "my death" – the natural death that is "actualized" at the natural end (*terme*) of the biological process of the for-itself – in the sense that I am essentially a mortal: "my death" that is to come is a sure thing – *mors certa*.

"The actualization" of "my concrete death", the coming of the "moment" of "my death", eludes determination because it is due, according to Sartre, to chance, the result of biological processes and external factors. Given that "my death" can arise at any moment after I have been

[22] *Ibid.*, p. 699 [p. 631: *"Pour être temporellement indéfinie, c'est-à-dire sans bornes, sa 'vie' n'en sera pas moins finie dans son être même parce qu'il se fait unique. La mort n'a rien à y voir; elle survient 'entre temps', et la réalité-humaine, en se révélant sa propre finitude, ne découvre pas, pour autant, sa mortalité"*].

thrown into worldliness – *hora incerta* – I am incapable of waiting for my death. I can only expect it.

The expression "waiting for my death" applies to the consciousness of the necessity that I *must* die someday, whereas "expecting my death" refers to the fact that I *can* die from one moment to the next. Sartre remarks that there is only a qualitative difference between the two sorts of death expressed in the two attitudes toward life: waiting for so-called natural death means accepting the *limited* undertaking of life, and waiting for so-called accidental or sudden death (due to an accident, illness, etc.) is tantamount to accepting the fact that life is "an enterprise which is *lacking*".[23]

Given that death, according to Sartre, is constantly lying in wait for the for-itself and can appear at any moment, before the for-itself has finished or fulfilled its task, before it has realized its possibilities, he concludes that one can only wait for a natural death by resorting to blindness or dishonesty. Every death "falls" into our lives by chance. Death always falls in the category of the indeterminate; this is true even for the death that appears to be the most natural, like the last note of a melody. The element of chance that "decides" the precise moment for the "actualization" of death, even "natural death", deprives it of every attribute of a harmonious end. "This perpetual appearance of chance at the heart of my projects can not be apprehended as *my* possibility but, on the contrary, as the nihilation [*néantisation*] of all my possibilities, a nihilation which *itself is no longer a part of my possibilities.* Thus death is not *my* possibility of no longer realizing a presence in the world but rather *an always possible nihilation of my possibles which is outside my possibilities*".[24] Several pages further on, Sartre concludes: "Therefore I can not wait for it; that is, I can not thrust myself toward it as toward one of my possibilities. Death can not therefore belong to the ontological structure of the for-itself".[25]

Heidegger would most certainly agree with Sartre about making a distinction between waiting for "my death" and expecting "my death",

[23] *Ibid.*, p. 686 [p. 620: "*une entreprise* manquée"].

[24] *Ibid.*, p. 687 [p. 621: "*Cette perpétuelle apparition du hasard au sein de mes projets ne peut être saisie comme* ma *possibilité, mais, au contraire, comme la néantisation de toutes mes possibilités, néantisation qui* elle-même ne fait plus partie de mes possibilités. *Ainsi, la mort n'est pas* ma *possibilité de ne plus réaliser de présence dans le monde,* mais une néantisation toujours possible de mes possibles, qui est hors de mes possibilités"].

[25] *Ibid.*, p. 697 [p. 629: "*Je ne saurais donc l'attendre, c'est-à-dire me jeter vers elle comme vers une de mes possibilités. Elle ne saurait donc appartenir à la structure ontologique du pour-soi*"].

in the sense in which the French philosopher understands it. It seems to me that in this context we are dealing with a misunderstanding on Sartre's part: he has not understood Being-towards-death as the possibility of the impossibility and, more specifically, [Heidegger's] use of the expression "to wait for my death".

Indeed, in the first place, Heidegger does not explicitly reject an understanding of death as the nihilation of the many projects and ontical possibilities of the human *Dasein* (death is not identical to the accomplishment of *Dasein*; on the contrary, it very often takes it by surprise and deprives it of future possibilities). Of course, death is its most extreme and ownmost (ontological) possibility. Death is part of the ontological structure of human nature, and, paradoxically, at the same time it involves the suppression of this same structure and of its possibilities. Second, Heidegger does not claim, even implicitly, that the *Dasein* waits for death: we have seen that he rejects the attitudes of waiting and rumination with respect to death, which remove death from the very category of possibility. The Heideggerian understanding of death as ontological possibility does not translate its physical presence into the heart of life, but it does express an end that is inherent to Being-in-advance-of-itself, namely, that it belongs to the very structure of the *Dasein*. When Sartre says that Being-towards-death belongs to a so-called idealist concept of death – in other words, death as "a human phenomenon" or "the final phenomenon of life, [which] is still life"[26] – his description proves to be inconsistent with a close reading of the pertinent passages from *Being and Time*.

3. DEATH AS ANOTHER'S VICTORY

Sartre is not content to denounce Heidegger's thanatological theory; he develops an original way of understanding human death by integrating it into the ontological structure of the Being-for-others and into his ontology of freedom, as well as into his theory of meaning.

The human being, as described in *Being and Nothingness*, is fundamentally free with relation to all ends, all values, all natural determinations, and any determination whatsoever of another (*hétérodétermination*). Freedom itself posits the value and the rules of its acts. This free, autonomous consciousness is constantly entering into relation with like beings. Sartre analyzes the rapport among these for-itselfs from the

[26] *Ibid.*, p. 681 [p. 616: *"un phénomène humain", "le phénomène ultime de la vie, vie encore"*].

perspective of the look. He starts with an insignificant scenario: "I am in a public park. Not far away there is a lawn and along the edge of that lawn there are benches. A man passes by those benches. I see this man; I apprehend him as an object and at the same time as a man".[27] The apparent calm is suddenly interrupted when the other's look rests upon me: this other for-itself in turn grasps me as a phenomenon, dispossesses me of myself, reducing me to the status of an object, that is, an *artifact*, an in-itself. Such a reduction even runs counter to the original determination of the for-itself, which "is perpetually determining itself *not to be* the in-itself. This means that it can establish itself only in terms of the in-itself and against the in-itself".[28] Otherness reveals itself as a curse that throws the subject being looked at into the midst of things, thereby causing its alienation, the disintegration of its universe, of its values. The appearance of another in the world corresponds to a decentralization of the original for-itself: his look strikes me in my being, reveals my slavery and thus my shame. The other objectifies me, therefore, before becoming in turn an object to me as I try to "recover" my subjectivity, my "being", for my being can be realized only insofar as I seize another's freedom, subjecting it to my freedom. The for-itself, which is outstretched toward the impossible ideal synthesis of the in-itself-for-itself, is imprisoned in the circle of look-looker-looked-at, that struggle of objectifying and recovering his subjectivity. In this bitter rivalry that pits one for-itself against another, there is neither victor nor vanquished. This state constitutes the permanent structure of the Being-for-others. There is no room for a non-objectifying reception of my being by another.

The Sartrean type of relationship between one for-itself and another that is presented in *Being and Nothingness* is dominated by a negative intersubjective ontology that is characterized by a perpetual conflict. From Sartre's perspective, the other's look is a continual executioner for the self: "Hell is other people".[29] The relation between two for-itselfs

[27] *Ibid.*, p. 341 [p. 311: *"Je suis dans un jardin public. Non loin de moi, voici une pelouse et, le long de cette pelouse, des chaises. Un homme passe près des chaises. Je vois cet homme, je le saisis comme un objet à la fois et comme un homme"*]. See also *ibid.*, pp. 331 f., 473 f., 527 f. [pp. 300 f., 430 f., 478 f.].

[28] *Ibid.*, p. 134 [p. 128: *"se détermine perpétuellement lui-même à n'être pas l'en-soi. Cela signifie qu'il ne peut se fonder lui-même qu'à partir de l'en-soi et contre l'en-soi"*].

[29] Jean-Paul Sartre, *No Exit*, pp. 45 and 23 [pp. 93, 42: "l'enfer, c'est les Autres"]. "My original fall is the existence of the Other" – *Being and Nothingness*, p. 352 [p. 321:*"Ma chute originelle, c'est l'existence de l'autre"*]. "Thus original sin is my upsurge in a world where there are others" – *ibid.*, p. 531 [p. 481: *"Le péché originel, c'est mon surgissement dans un monde où il y a l'autre"*]. In his *Notebooks for an Ethics*, Sartre describes this

is not one of respect and love for the other in his being and his individuality, but rather a war without armistice and without a winner. Being-for-others is a reciprocal internal negation of the other. Even the attitudes of indifference and hatred toward the other, attitudes that consist of building my subjectivity on the ruins of another's, do not make this ontological reciprocity with the other disappear. Indifference, by a perpetual sense of lack and unease, reminds me of the other's existence. Hatred, in turn, also implies a recognition of the other's freedom.[30]

hellish situation very precisely: "Every attempt of the For-itself to be In-itself is by definition doomed to fail. From this we can fully account for the existence of Hell; that is, that region of existence where existing means using every trick in order to be, and to fail at all these tricks, and to be conscious of this failure. It is the world of madness that Spinoza and the Stoics talk about", p. 472 [p. 488: *"Tout effort du Pour-soi pour être En-soi est par définition voué à l'échec. Ainsi peut-on rendre compte universellement du règne de l'Enfer, c'est-à-dire de cette région d'existence où exister c'est user de toutes les ruses pour être et c'est échouer au coeur de ces ruses et avoir conscience de l'échec. C'est le monde de la folie dont parlent Spinoza et les Stoïciens"*].

30 The theory of negative intersubjectivity developed in *Being and Nothingness*, which takes as its point of departure an ontology of the for-itself-in-itself, contains certain weaknesses that Sartre explicitly acknowledged in his writings subsequent to *Being and Nothingness* by proposing a slight modification of his anthropology. He supposes that the for-itself is *per se* capable of breaking up the hellish circle of relations between one consciousness and another, by means of a conversion that he does not explain precisely. To be sure, in his *Critique of Dialectical Reason* (vol. 1, pp. 79 ff.) [vol. 1, pp. 193 ff.] he continues to speak about an intersubjectivity of the subject-object, whose original situation is still one of conflict; because of this intersubjectivity, the initial attitude of the individual lies in violence, which can erupt in an overt war for power. The danger that each poses to each reduces the other to an inhuman human being or a foreign race. Sartre transposes the law of mutual integration among for-itselfs, as developed in *Being and Nothingness*, to the level of relations among groups. Each group treats the other group from a perspective of utility. With a view to mitigating his thesis of conflict, our author introduces the dimension of exchange and mutual service or of work toward a common goal. This sort of intersubjective relation, which is more positive than the one developed in *Being and Nothingness*, nevertheless does not involve considering the other as an end in itself and as a being deserving respect. Only in his posthumously published work, *Notebooks for an Ethics*, does Sartre distance himself from *Being and Nothingness* and introduce respect and the recognition of each other's freedom. He admits that there is an attitude in which the subject goes so far as to rejoice in the other without trying to appropriate him or her. Such is love. "I love if I *create* the contingent finitude of the Other as being-within-the-world in assuming my own subjective finitude and in *willing* this subjective finitude, and if through the same movement that makes me assume my finitude/subject, I assume his finitude/object as being the necessary condition for the free goal that it projects and that it present to me as an unconditional end" (*Notebooks for an Ethics*, p. 501) [p. 516: *"J'aime si je* crée *la finitude contingente de l'Autre comme être-au-milieu-du-monde en assumant ma propre finitude subjective et en* voulant *cette finitude subjective, et si par le même mouvement qui me fait assumer ma finitude-sujet, j'assume sa finitude-objet comme étant condition nécessaire du libre but qu'elle projette et qui se présente à moi comme fin inconditionnelle"*]. See *ibid.*, pp. 415 f.,

Sartre thoroughly integrates death into the ontological structure of Being-for-others. Contrary to the Heideggerian thesis that death is a nonrelational state disrupting Being-with-one-another (*Miteinandersein*), the French philosopher declares that death is essentially inseparable from relating to others and understands it as the definitive victory, the triumph of the surviving for-itself over the dead for-itself, who is thus reduced to an in-itself, a thing devoid of self-consciousness. At its death, the for-itself brutally ceases to be "in a state of postponement" (*en "sursis"*). It is suddenly thrown into an inability to change or to give meaning to its past actions or to change their meaning. Henceforth its existence is forever fixed. Its consciousness of itself has been abolished. Slipping away entirely into the past, its consciousness congeals into an in-itself, without any upsurge of a new consciousness. The meaning of its life and of its past actions is hereafter dependent – I will return to this idea shortly – on the goodwill and the freedom of the surviving for-itself. The latter freely decides the fate of the former, whether by allowing his existence to fall into the oblivion of the masses or by reconstituting his life. The dead for-itself – in other words, the in-itself – continues to enter into the fundamental ontological structure of Being-for-others, but it is at the mercy of the surviving-other and can undergo important changes externally without being responsible for them.

Death is the outcome of the struggle that pits the freedom of one for-itself against that of another, because it awards the victory to the surviving for-itself. In this specific context, death is an "alienation", "a total *dispossession*"[31] of the person of the for-itself to the advantage of the Other; this dispossession should be understood to occur not only at the

418 f., 507 f. [pp. 430, 434, 523 f.]. A similar tone can be found also in his book-length interview, *Hope Now,* in which Sartre emphasizes that the presence of the other and the me-for-the-other [*le moi-pour-autrui*] take on priority with respect to the for-itself, which is to say that what I do is carried out in relation to and with an consciousness of the other. We recognize in this the concept of moral conscience. Sartre confesses: "In *Being and Nothingness* my theory of others left the individual too independent. [...] Nonetheless, I did consider that each consciousness in itself, and each individual in himself, was relatively independent of the other. I hadn't determined what I am trying to determine today: the dependence of each individual on all other individuals", pp. 71–2 [p. 40: *"[j'avais] laissé chaque individu trop indépendant dans ma théorie d'autrui de* L'Être et le Néant. *[...] je considérais malgré tout que chaque conscience en elle-même, chaque individu en lui-même était relativement indépendant de l'autre. Je n'avais pas déterminé ce que j'essaie de déterminer aujourd'hui: la dépendance de chaque individu par rapport à tous les individus"*]. See also "Interview with Jean-Paul Sartre", p. 13.

31 Jean-Paul Sartre, *Being and Nothingness,* p. 695 [p. 628: *"aliénation", "une totale* dépossession*"*].

level of material goods but above all at the level of self-determination. Once dead, the for-itself is "a prey for the living".[32] Being in complete submission to them, it is no longer able to defend itself. It is condemned to exist only through the surviving for-itself. This is the scandal of death, its absurdity. It "is presented as the permanent alienation of my being-possibility which is no longer *my* possibility but that of the Other".[33]

The statement that death is absurd is in contrast to Heidegger, who, according to Sartre, would claim that Being-towards-death confers meaning upon human existence. I will not explain in detail here why Sartre's interpretation is wrong in this regard, because I have already indicated that Heidegger excludes from his ontological analysis the question of the meaning of life and of the evil of death, which is the province of an ontical analysis. The ontological study of Being-towards-death includes no judgment as to the possible absurdity of death, or of life.[34] Sartre's critique with regard to Heidegger is based on the theory of meaning that the French philosopher relates to his presentation of the for-itself and the threat posed by the other.[35]

What does this theory imply for our perception of death? It stipulates that the past derives its meaning from the present and the present from the future. The future (as coming-toward, *l'à-venir*) lends meaning to the free action, whether present or past, of the for-itself. Hence the latter is "[yet] *to come* to itself" (*"à venir à soi-même"*).[36] "To be oneself is to come to oneself".[37] This is the structure of selfness. The end illuminates what is, or, to put it the other way around, past and present actions receive their meaning from future actions. The former are continually in a state of postponement (*en sursis*), waiting for the meaning that the latter will confer upon them. "What-is, therefore, takes on its meaning only when

[32] *Ibid.* [*"en proie aux vivants"*].

[33] *Ibid.*, p. 699 [pp. 631 f.: *"se présente comme l'aliénation permanente de mon être-possible qui n'est plus* ma *possibilité, mais celle de l'autre"*].

[34] See Martin Heidegger, *Being and Time*, pp. 290 ff. [pp. 246 ff.]. Within the context of Sartre's reflections on the necessary connection between death and freedom, one might ask whether an immortal or endless life, which according to Sartre would not leave any room for freedom, for possible choices, would not be absurd and wearisome and diminish the value of present life. I will return to this question in Part Three.

[35] It is worth explaining that Sartre's theory of meaning is not limited to the meaning that the for-itself freely gives to its actions – my discussion moves at this level – but also involves dimensions that are beyond the meaning bestowed by the for-itself and that are in some way imposed from outside its subjectivity. See Jean-Paul Sartre, *Being and Nothingness*, p. 654 [pp. 591 f.].

[36] *Ibid.*, p. 687 [p. 621: "à venir *à soi-même"*].

[37] *Ibid.*, p. 688 [p. 622: *"Être soi, c'est venir à soi"*].

it is *surpassed* toward the future".[38] The meaning of a free action of the for-itself is not given by someone else,[39] nor by nature, but by the for-itself, which alone freely chooses the meaning that it wants to attribute to his past. Similarly, its future free actions will determine the meaning of its present. The actual free conduct of a for-itself in the present appears to him paradoxically to be fully conscious and pellucid (the prereflexive *cogito*) and at the same time totally masked by a free determination that it still must wait for until its future (as coming-toward) confers a meaning on its present action. Hence the for-itself is essentially *waiting*, manifesting itself by means of a series "of waitings which themselves wait for waitings".[40] These waitings tend toward an ultimate rest, which is impossible, in which a solution would be provided for all these problems: the fullness of the in-itself-for-itself that would offer a complete overview of its past life and would fix forever the plotted curve of its existence.

As long as the for-itself is alive, it is capable of changing the meaning of its free past actions and of continually starting over. Death's entrance upon the scene, which is due to chance and beyond the freedom of the for-itself, definitively paralyzes, in an immutable present, the projection of the freedom of the for-itself toward the future (as coming-toward). The dead for-itself is no longer capable of conferring meaning retrospectively upon its actions; that is henceforth the province of the survivors. Hence, for Sartre, death wears the mantle of absurdity, for not only does it destroy every project and contradict the fundamental aspiration of the for-itself to become a being in-itself-for-itself, but it also and most importantly takes away from the dead for-itself the ability to give a meaning – which comes from the future – to its past free actions. The absurdity of death does not lie primarily in the return to nothingness of the for-itself, or in the suppression of its self-consciousness, but above all in the alienation (transfer of ownership) of its being-possible: the latter is at the mercy of the surviving-other who decides on what meaning to attribute to the life of the deceased and to his past actions. The absurdity of death, like that of life, lies in the nonrealization of the waiting,[41] in the indetermination of the problems: "Death is never that which gives life

[38] *Ibid.*, p. 638 [p. 578: *"Ce qui est ne prend donc son sens que lorsqu'il est* dépassé *vers l'avenir"*].

[39] Sartre explains, of course, that someone else can give a meaning to my past and even define a person in bad faith.

[40] *Ibid.*, p. 688 [p. 622: *"d'attente d'attentes qui attendent elles-mêmes des attentes"*].

[41] "If I am a waiting for waitings for waiting and if suddenly the object of my final waiting and the one who awaits it are suppressed, the waiting takes on retrospectively the

its meanings; it is, on the contrary, that which on principle removes all meaning from life. If we must die, then our life has no meaning because its problems receive no solution and because the very meaning of the problems remains undetermined".[42] Of course, we must also mention that Sartre proposes another reason for the absurdity of death: he makes use of the concept of absurdity to characterize facticity as opposed to freedom. Life and death are absurd, for whereas I am condemned to be free, I am compelled to be born and to die: that is, I did not choose to be born or to be a mortal. Death is "*a contingent fact* which as such on principle escapes me and originally belongs to my facticity".[43] And a few pages further on, Sartre writes, "I am a free mortal".[44]

The theory of meaning with regard to the free for-itself rests, in the final analysis, on the famous Sartrean theory that existence precedes essence. If the latter is not a present given but is made through free projection into the future (as coming-toward) – the for-itself shapes itself as it pleases – then it is correct to maintain that death leaves "in indetermination the realization of the ends which make known to me what I am".[45] I maintain, without going into detail, since this has been debated at length, that the essence of the for-itself is a given that is beyond the liberty of the conscious-subject, that is, that it precedes existence. What I am with regard to my essence – and not what I could be in terms of my self-realization by developing my many capabilities and possibilities – does not depend on the future: so I am from the moment that I am thrown into worldliness. Moreover, an event or an action is likely, in my opinion, to receive a meaning not only retroactively, by being incorporated into a larger unit (for instance, one's personal life, history, values, or faith), but also in the very presentness (*présentéité*) of its actualization and in the intentionality of the acting consciousness. It is certainly correct to say that death leaves the realization of ends and

character of *absurdity*", *ibid.*, p. 689 [p. 623: *"Si je suis attente d'attentes d'attente et si, d'un coup, l'objet de mon attente dernière et celui qui attend sont supprimés, l'attente en reçoit rétrospectivement le caractère* d'absurdité"].

42 *Ibid.*, p. 690 [p. 624: *"la mort n'est jamais ce qui donne son sens à la vie: c'est au contraire ce qui lui ôte par principe toute signification. Si nous devons mourir, notre vie n'a pas de sens parce que ses problèmes ne reçoivent aucune solution et parce que la signification même des problèmes demeure indéterminée"*].

43 *Ibid.*, p. 697 [p. 630: "un fait contingent *qui, en tant que tel, m'échappe par principe et ressortit originellement à ma facticité"*].

44 *Ibid.*, p. 700 [p. 632: *"je suis un libre mortel"*].

45 *Ibid.*, p. 696 [p. 629: *"dans l'indéterminé la réalisation des fins qui m'annoncent ce que je suis"*].

projects in indetermination, but these ends do not indicate what I am. Rather, they signify what I could be under the aspect of the realization of my possibilities. I am what I am, with respect to my essence, already at the very moment in which I project myself into the future.

Sartre conceives of death as an enemy, for it interrupts the projection of the possibilities of the for-itself; death can be perceived, as has been noted by many analytical philosophers whom I will discuss in detail in Part Three, as an evil insofar as it is a privation of possibilities. The French philosopher, nevertheless, makes a leap of logic when he connects this break in the projection of my possibilities with the absurdity of my whole life. Indeed, I am capable of working out and giving a meaning to many actions of my life, even if I must finally die, which implies the nonrealization of a multitude of my possibilities. The return to nothingness does not *per se* remove the meaning from my past actions. On the other hand, as Sartre maintains, it can render absurd the ontological tending toward "being", toward integration for-itself-in-itself, or, to put it differently, toward complete happiness and the fulfillment of the person's very being.

The Sartrean demand for an "afterward", with a view to conferring a meaning on present and past free actions, can be interpreted in two different ways, within the context of his perception of death as an absurdity. On the one hand, the absurdity originates in the inability of the dead for-itself to give a meaning to its past life, so that the concession of meaning to the departed for-itself henceforth depends on the goodwill of the surviving-other. On the other hand, death is absurd because by radically suppressing the projection of possibilities, it blocks the realization of the most profound tendency of the for-itself, which is none other than the unity of the for-itself-in-itself. Death definitively eliminates the very nucleus of the for-itself, which is autonomous freedom, and reduces the for-itself to an in-itself. The Sartrean position seems to imply that life would have a meaning if, on the one hand, the for-itself continued to exist *postmortem* while preserving its personal identity and continuing to project itself freely toward the future (as coming-toward) – which would also suppose a resurrection of the body so that the for-itself could continue to be-in-situation – or, on the other hand, if the for-itself managed to attain the identity of the for-itself-in-itself, which consists in the totality of meaning.[46] But since death signifies *a priori* the complete

[46] In his *Notebooks for an Ethics* (p. 326), Sartre considers the possibility of an unending temporal life in which the for-itself could realize all its possibilities. Sartre indirectly

destruction of the subject, since by definition freedom requires death and since the for-itself-in-itself cannot be realized, death reveals, in Sartre's opinion, the absurdity of life and the victory of the other's freedom over that of the dead for-itself.

4. DEATH AS A SITUATION-LIMIT

Sartre blazes for himself a trail that runs midway between the idealist concept, which considers death as an intrinsic part of the biological or ontological structure of the for-itself, and the realist concept, which sees it as extraterritorial to life. To do this he transposes the problem of the relation between life and death to the level of his ontology of freedom. As we saw earlier, the look of the other is a real limit to the absolute freedom of the for-itself, a limit that does not belong to the freedom of the for-itself but is something external to its subjectivity. Its vain attempt to arrogate to itself the other's freedom is expressed in the "unrealizable thing to be realized", which Sartre describes as "the exteriority which remains exteriority even in and through the attempt on the part of the For-itself to interiorize it".[47] This unrealizable represents the extraterritorial limit to the for-itself, but only as the limit to its freedom. By choosing itself freely, the freedom of the for-itself elects its own limits. Finitude is external to the for-itself.[48]

characterizes such a life as absurd, because insofar as the for-itself realized all its possibilities, it "would disappear as an individuality and as freedom. But for this choice not to have the pure gratuitousness of a divine choice, it is necessary that its limitation not come from itself. It is not a matter of choosing one's limits on the basis of an available infinity but of choosing within limits. These limits, therefore, are necessarily given. [...] Hence the choice of possible implies death and death as contingency. It also implies that these possibles *may always* not be realized. [...] To be free is to run the perpetual risk of seeing one's enterprises fail and death cut off the project. Also discuss the finitude of death. Freedom does not conceive of itself apart from death" [*Le pour-soi "disparaîtrait en tant qu'individualité et en tant que liberté. Mais pour que ce choix n'ait pas la pure gratuité du choix divin, il ne faut pas que sa limitation lui vienne de lui-même. Il ne s'agit pas de choisir ses limites à partir d'une infinie possibilité mais de choisir dans des limites. Ces limites sont donc nécessairement données. [...] Ainsi le choix des possibles implique la mort et la mort comme contingence. Il implique aussi que les possibles* puissent toujours *ne pas être réalisés. [...] Être libre c'est courir le risque perpétuel de voir ses entreprises échouer et la mort briser le projet. Parler aussi de la finitude de la mort. La liberté ne se conçoit pas en dehors de la mort"*, p. 339].

47 Jean-Paul Sartre, *Being and Nothingness*, p. 678 [p. 613: *"l'irréalisable à réaliser"* as *"l'extériorité qui demeure extériorité jusque dans et par la tentative du Pour-soi pour l'intérioriser"*].

48 See *ibid.*, p. 679 [pp. 613–14].

In the same way that he understands the other's freedom as a limit to my freedom, Sartre shifts the interpretive parameters for the notion of "meaning" and describes death as a "situation-limit" external to the freedom of the for-itself, as a pure "contingent fact".[49] It is a question of a "given"[50] coming from outside the subjectivity of the for-itself by the very fact that the other exists. Death lies in the future meaning that my actual for-itself will have for the other: once dead, as we have just seen, my being-possible eludes my possibility and henceforth belongs to the possibility of the other. Death, of course, is external to the for-itself: that is, the latter is never capable of encountering death. Death does not constitute the possibility of the for-itself, as Heidegger maintains, but rather "the indefinite permanence of its being-for-others".[51] It does not exist for the living for-itself and eludes its direct experience. It only intervenes unexpectedly (*entre-temps*) and reveals itself as "indiscoverable".[52]

In this shift of thanatological speculation to the level of the ontology of the for-itself, Sartre changes the meaning commonly attributed to the concepts of mortal and death: the former represents "the present being which I am for the Other", and the latter represents "the future meaning of my actual for-itself for the Other".[53] Death limits not only the future projects of the for-itself, but also and most importantly the meaning of the past actions of the dead for-itself by leaving them at the mercy of the interpretation of the surviving-other. Although death never touches the for-itself, and although the latter never encounters its death as a living for-itself, it is nevertheless capable of experiencing it in the sense that death haunts it in the middle of each of its projects as its 'unavoidable reverse side'. "The freedom that is *my freedom* remains total and infinite. Death is not an obstacle to my projects; it is only a destiny *of these projects elsewhere.* And this is not because death does not limit my freedom but because freedom never encounters this limit. I am not 'free to die', but I am a free mortal. Since death escapes my projects because it is unrealizable, I myself escape death in my very project".[54]

49 *Ibid.*, p. 697 [p. 630: *"situation-limite"*, "fait contingent"].

50 *Ibid.*, p. 699 [p. 631: *"donné"*].

51 *Ibid.*, p. 699 [p. 632: *"la permanence indéfinie de son être-pour-l'autre"*].

52 *Ibid.*, p. 698 [p. 630: *"l'indécouvrable"*].

53 *Ibid.*, p. 699 [p. 632: *"l'être présent que je suis pour l'autre"; "le sens futur de mon pour-soi actuel pour l'autre"*].

54 *Ibid.*, p. 700 [p. 632: *"La liberté qui est* ma liberté *demeure totale et infinie; non que la mort ne la limite pas, mais parce que la liberté ne rencontre jamais cette limite, la mort n'est aucunement un obstacle à mes projets; elle est seulement un destin* ailleurs de ces projets. *Je ne suis pas*

5. CONCLUSION

Although we must emphasize the pertinence of some of Sartre's objections to the position proposed by Heidegger, I doubt that Sartre's critique, taken as a whole, is "irrefutable", as Jolivet maintains.[55] Indeed, several of his attacks against the philosopher of Freiburg prove to be inadequate: for example, his arguments against the notion of death as my possibility and as the meaning of my existence, or those aimed against the idea of waiting for my death. Sartre's speculation, however, is not content with a simple critique of Being-towards-death and of the so-called realist concept. It proposes an innovative way of understanding death, in the very precise context of his ontology-anthropology of Being-for-others and of freedom as the foundation for being, at the same time that it addresses the problem of the meaning of life and the absurdity of death.

Even before Bloch undertook to demolish the Heideggerian ontology of finitude in his work *The Principle of Hope* by developing an ontology of radical openness, Sartre rejected, from the ontological point of view, the presentness of being (namely, the end) in not-yet-being. The foundation for the finitude of the Sartrean for-itself does not lie in death but rather in freedom, which, although absolute, makes itself limited. The experience of the death of another impels me to be responsible for the meaning that I will give to the existence of the dead for-itself. Death does not reveal itself through Heideggerian existential anguish, but rather through the intervention of the freedom of the other and, ultimately, by the death of another. Sartre does not view death as *my* possibility, but rather as the end of my possibilities so as to become finally *the possibility of the other.* The originality of his position consists of shifting the interpretive parameters: from my death as something that separates me from others we move to my death as something intrinsically bound up with my relation to others, a relation that is nevertheless deeply imbued with a merciless struggle for total domination of the freedom of the other. Hence death is perceived within this particular context as the tragic outcome of the combat that one for-itself wages upon the other (and vice versa) from the moment when they are thrown into worldliness.

'libre pour mourir', mais je suis un libre mortel. La mort échappant à mes projets parce qu'elle est irréalisable, j'échappe moi-même à la mort dans mon projet même"].

[55] Régis Jolivet, *Le problème de la mort chez M. Heidegger et Jean-Paul Sartre*, p. 44: *"irréfutables"*.

An interesting question, which I will examine in Part Three, is, to what extent can death be an evil for the dead for-itself? To what degree can it harm him (within the context where the surviving-other confers or denies a meaning to the actions of the dead for-itself and decides on the latter's fate), if the dead individual is no more? We find here again the challenge of Epicurus, namely, that death cannot be an evil; it cannot do me any harm, given that when I am dead I am no more; similarly, in the case of Sartre's argument one could object that the other can do me no harm by changing the meaning of the actions of my life, because I am no longer there to suffer from it or be affected by it. The reduction of the dead for-itself to an in-itself, in which the meaning of its past actions is irreversibly subordinated to the freedom and good pleasure of the surviving for-itself, the total, unalterable victory of the latter over the dead for-itself is for Sartre an expression of the absurdity of death. This absurdity, therefore, does not lie principally in the fact that the subject-consciousness returns to nothingness, nor in the fact that it is impossible for the for-itself *in se* to project itself freely toward the future, toward future possibilities, that is, continually to create its own essence and to allot significance to its present and past actions. Hence the absurdity of death (and, we might add, the evil thereof) lies only secondarily in that instantaneous reduction to nothingness of its possibilities and projects.

Sartre's thanatology is based first and foremost on his ontology of freedom and on the concept of facticity, as well as on his thesis of the negative relation between one for-itself and the next. Once this foundation is called into question, the concept of death within the framework of the relation to the other should be corrected as well. One can no longer maintain that death is absurd, or an "evil", starting from the premise of a merciless struggle pitting one for-itself against the next – although one might affirm both propositions by taking up a position at the level of facticity and freedom. One would have to support this absurd and "evil" character on the basis of the fact that death deprives the for-itself of its ability to project its possibilities and its projects, and that it interrupts – sometimes brutally – the fundamental tendency of the for-itself to accomplish and realize personal projects. This is how certain analytical philosophers have reasoned, as we will see in Part Three. Moreover, within the framework of an ontology that promotes positive intersubjectivity, in which the other would no longer be perceived as an enemy but rather as an indispensable help toward the full realization of the free for-itself – and not just as something necessary to the discovery of the free for-itself – and in which the bond between one for-itself and the next is characterized by a modicum of friendship or love: in this context, I say, another's death, and more particularly the death of a dear one, could no longer be understood as the final victory that subjugates his freedom, but rather as the possibility, albeit sorrowful, for the survivor to be pushed out into deep waters, to allow his equilibrium to be upset, and to call himself into question. The death of another, which Jaspers has described as a "situation limit",[56] could take on, despite its negative quality, a certain positive role by encouraging the survivor to discover his being, his very foundation: it would impel him to transcend his contingency and his facticity and, in the final analysis, to live better.

[56] See Karl Jaspers, *Philosophie*, pp. 220 f.: *"Grenzsituation"*.

6

Knowledge of Mortality Is Inseparable from the Relation to the Other

Sartre is not the only contemporary philosopher in the first half of the twentieth century to insist that the experience of another's death is necessary to arrive at a consciousness of the mortal condition of the human being. In his essay, *The Experience of Death*, Landsberg alludes to the axiom "The death of one's neighbor is infinitely more than just the death of another"[1] and speculates that the mere experience of the death of a person totally unrelated to me does not necessarily lead to experiential knowledge of the necessity of my death. The experience of the death of someone who is loved, rather, is what makes it possible for an "intuition of the *necessity* of death",[2] a certainty about our mortal condition, to arise; it also empowers me to transcend the generalizing dimension ("people die") that submerges my death in the unconscious. "The awareness of the necessity of death is only provoked by *participation*, by the personal love in which the whole experience is bathed. We constituted a 'we' with the dying man. And it is through this 'we', through

[1] Paul-Louis Landsberg, *The Experience of Death*, p. 11 [p. 32: *"la mort du prochain c'est infiniment plus que la mort d'autrui en général"*]. Although he professes to be absolutely certain about our mortal condition, Gabriel Marcel is silent as to the origin of that certainty. He declares instead, on the basis of his famous reply to Brunschvicg in 1937 – "What matters is neither my death, nor yours; it is the death of the one we love" (*Presence and Immortality*, p. 231 [p. 182 : "ce qui compte, ce n'est nit ma mort, ni la vôtre, c'est celle de qui nous aimons"]) – that the death of a loved one shakes an individual much more than the thought of his own death. Death appears as an ordeal of presence. Marcel insists on this connection between death and love, which he relates to the notion of fidelity.

[2] Paul-Louis Landsberg, *The Experience of Death*, p. 13 [p. 35: *"intuition de la* nécessité *de la mort"*].

the very strength of this community, which constitutes as it were a new order of persons, that we are led to an experiential knowledge of our own *mortality* [*de notre propre* devoir mourir]".[3] The necessity of death is not yet identical in meaning to the statement that every human being must die but rather relates essentially to the persons whom I love and to myself. Landsberg explains that the general necessity of having to die that is communicated by this experience is not of a logical but of a "symbolic" nature. Our author states that "*the other represents* in reality *all the others*" and goes on to say that the other "is 'Everyman' and this Everyman dies each time in the death of the man we know, who dies his own death".[4] The experience of the death of a dear friend can lead me either to the consciousness that I must die or else to a "renewed consciousness" ("*re-conscience*") of this necessity by tearing me away from the comfortable generalization "Everyone will die someday".[5] Landsberg

[3] *Ibid.*, p. 14 [p. 36: *"La conscience de la nécessité de la mort ne s'éveille que par la* participation, *que par l'amour personnel dans lequel baignait entièrement cette expérience. Nous avons constitué un* 'nous' *avec le mourant. Et c'est dans ce* 'nous', *c'est par la force propre de ce nouvel être d'ordre personnel, que nous sommes amenés à la connaissance vécue de notre propre* devoir mourir"]. See Fridolin Wiplinger, *Der personal verstandene Tod*, p. 45: "The first thing that such an experience tells me during this awakening, the first thing that dawns on me thereby, is the *certainty of my own death with that of the loved one*, because it is the experience that I am taken away from myself along with that person, and thus the experience of human death in general [. . .] with a certainty that no argumentation, however profound, and no speculative substantiation can attain, but which the most self-assured prognoses of science and technology can no longer shake either, despite their confidence that they will one day conquer death. For I have experienced the fact that *Death is separation from the one whom we love*" [*"Das erste, was solche Erfahrung mir bei diesem Erwachen sagt, mir durch sie aufgeht, ist die* Gewissheit des eigenen Todes mit dem des geliebten Menschen, *weil sie die Erfahrung ist, dass ich mir selbst mit ihm selbst entzogen werde, und darin die Erfahrung des Menschentodes überhaupt, des 'allgemeinen Todes' [. . .] in einer Gewissheit, an die keine noch so tiefsinnige Argumentation und spekulative Begründung desselben heranreicht, die aber auch die selbstsichersten Prognosen der Wissenschaft und Technik in ihrer Zuversicht, doch noch einmal den Tod zu besiegen, nicht mehr erschüttern können. Denn ich habe erfahren*: Tod ist Trennung von dem, den wir lieben"].

[4] Paul-Louis Landsberg, *The Experience of Death*, p. 15 [p. 37: *"symbolique"*; "'l'autre représente *en réalité* tous les autres"; *"[l'autre] est le* 'Jedermann' *et ce* chacun *meurt chaque fois dans le prochain qui meurt de sa mort singulière"*]. See also his *Einführung in die philosophische Anthropologie*, p. 70.

[5] "Man has by no means derived a more or less probable rule from material for inductive reasoning, but rather has attained a genuine essential knowledge from a particular case. He has further developed his sense of life and has enriched it with a sudden, intuitive and for him indubitable experiential certainty. An individual may learn a thousand times in school to parrot the sentence, 'all men are mortal,' but only through a real experience of death – whether it be the death of another human being, or else a dire threat, or especially a genuine, heroic sacrifice of one's own life – does he arrive at a real knowledge of the necessity that hangs over everyone's head" [*"Hat der Mensch*

explains that this experience allows the survivor to experience, thanks to the bond of love uniting two persons who make up a We (a theme that is developed quite well by Nozick[6]), "death within his own existence" due to his loss and the interruption of the community that the survivor formed with the deceased. "The experience of death in the solitude that follows loss", as well as the "sense of the tragic infidelity" in the departure of the deceased – Landsberg aptly describes mortality as the state of "ontological infidelity"[7] – certainly teach the bereaved "the qualitative nature of absence and separation"[8], but it says nothing whatsoever about the experience of *my death* as a state. The experience of the death of a loved one does not enable me to experience the death in which the deceased "finds himself", nor my own future death. The experience of death provided by the loneliness following a loss does not mean the experience of the state of death.

Landsberg deviates somewhat from this position in his *Einführung in die philosophische Anthropologie*, where he says that the certainty of my mortality originates in a feeling of finitude that is inherent in the living

auch keineswegs aus Induktionsmaterial eine mehr oder minder wahrscheinliche Regel aufgestellt, sondern an einem Fall eine echte Wesenserkenntnis gewonnen, sein Lebensgefühl weiter entwickelt und um eine plötzliche, gefühlsmässige und für ihn unbezweifelbare Erfahrungsgewissheit bereichert. Mag das Individuum den Satz 'alle Menschen sind sterblich' tausendmal in der Schule nachplappern lernen, nur durch ein wirkliches Erleben des Todes, sei es am Sterben eines andern Menschen, sei es auch in echter Bedrohtheit und besonders in echter heroischer Preisgabe des eigenen Lebens, gelangt es zu einer wirklichen Kenntnis von der über Allen schwebenden Notwendigkeit"], Paul-Louis Landsberg, *Einführung in die philosophische Anthropologie*, pp. 57–8.

6 "Each person in a romantic *we* wants to possess the other completely; yet each also needs the other to be an independent an nonsubservient person. Only someone who continues to possess a nonsubservient autonomy can be an apt partner in a joint identity that enlarges and enhances your individual one. And, of course, the other's well-being – something you care about – requires that nonsubservient autonomy too. Yet at the same time there is the desire to possess the other *completely*. This does not have to stem from a desire to dominate the other person, I think. What you need and want is to possess the other as completely as you do your own identity. This is an expression of the fact that you *are* forming a new joint identity with him or her. Or, perhaps, this desire just *is* the desire to form an identity with the other. Unlike Hegel's description of the unstable dialectic between the master and the slave, though, in a romantic *we* the autonomy of the other and complete possession too are reconciled in the formation of a joint and wondrous enlarged identity for both", Robert Nozick, *The Examined Life*, p. 74.

7 Paul-Louis Landsberg, *The Experience of Death*, p. 16 [p. 38: *"la mort à l'intérieur de [sa] propre expérience"*; *"L'expérience de la mort dans la solitude consécutive à la perte"*; *"ressentiment de l'infidélité"*; *"l'état d'infidélité ontologique"*].

8 *Ibid.*, p. 18 [p. 41: "qualitativement *l'absence et l'éloignement"*].

thing and that is subsequently confirmed by experience. The fact of my mortality and of the limited scope of my life is grasped, according to Landsberg, by means of an "emotional orientation" that is intentional and part of a person's affective life. Certainty about my mortal condition is found in the way in which I experience myself in time. "We cannot doubt that we are mortal. It belongs to the manner in which we experience time".[9] It seems to me that Landsberg, too, following Scheler and Heidegger, presupposes that the temporality of the human *Dasein* is finite. Experience of the fact that human beings die is not at the origin of the consciousness of mortality, but it does confirm it. "It is clear that in our self-consciousness we arrive at the knowledge of death, indeed, a knowledge of death that is entirely free of doubt, without any need whatsoever of complicated inductive reasoning. Man does not acquire knowledge of his mortality through induction; instead he actualizes this knowledge to the extent that he becomes an individual threatened by death and manages to develop a feeling of himself as an individual".[10] The death of a loved one, who is perceived in his irreplaceable individuality, awakens in the survivor not only a sense of the menace of death, but also the certainty about his own death that he already possessed. The death of the other reinforces his consciousness of his mortality.

The consciousness of my mortal condition, moreover, does not proceed from a heroic abandonment of my life,[11] for in order to do that, I would have to be conscious already of the fact that I am capable of losing my life. Initially this consciousness is generally due to the fact of having experienced the deaths of several human beings, who then, in a second moment, can of course blend into an impersonal "everyone". The real and profound attainment of consciousness on the personal level emerges from an experience of the death of a loved one with whom I have at least a bond of friendship and love or of simple compassion. This experience leads me to take death, and in particular my death, seriously; in other words, to borrow an expression from Kierkegaard,

9 Paul-Louis Landsberg, *Einführung in die philosophische Anthropologie*, p. 52: "Gefühlsrichtung"; *"Wir können nicht daran zweifeln, dass wir sterblich sind. Es gehört zu der Art, wie wir uns in der Zeit erfahren"*.

10 *Ibid.*, p. 56: *"Es ist klar, dass wir in unserem Selbstbewusstsein zum Todeswissen gelangen, und zwar zu einem durchaus zweifelsfreien Todeswissen, ganz ohne jene komplizierten Induktion nötig zu haben. Nicht durch Induktion gewinnt der Mensch das Wissen um seine Sterblichkeit, sondern er aktualisiert dies Wissen in dem Masse, als er totbedrohtes Individuum wird und zur Entfaltung eines Gefühles von sich selbst als Individuum gelangt"*.

11 See *ibid.*, pp. 58, 70.

it leads me to think of death as my lot.[12] It enables me either to discover my mortality outright or else to pass from the abstract, conceptual consciousness that I too often file in the obscure compartment labeled "everyone will die", to a vivid and "emotional" consciousness. I feel for the first time – or once again – that death concerns me personally and can "touch" me from one moment to the next. This experience awakens me from the comfortable, lethargic slumber in which I refuse "my death" and forces me to face my ontological reality as a finite, mortal being. The death of the other reveals to me that I personally belong to the category of "everyone", that I, too, am one of those "other" mortals. A child raised alone and transported to a desert island (to borrow an image from Voltaire),[13] who has never experienced the death of another, could wonder, on his experiences of the death of animals and plants, or else of the continual seasonal changes in nature, whether he was mortal and would die someday. This questioning, resulting from the observation that there is a life-and-death dialectic in the vegetable and animal kingdoms, does not allow one to attain any degree of certainty as to the mortal condition of the thinking subject "man".

[12] See Søren Kierkegaard, "At a Graveside", p. 75.
[13] Voltaire, *Dictionnaire philosophique*, vol. XIX, p. 376.

7

Death as the Object of Experience

In the preceding pages we have seen that the human being's consciousness that he *can* and *must* die has its origin in the experience of the death of another human being. One might wonder whether this consciousness is accompanied by a knowledge not only of dying, but also and especially of death as such, that is, the state of the deceased human subject. Our concern here is to determine whether a phenomenology of death is possible.

It is possible to maintain in the first place that *dying* (someone else's or one's own) can, to a certain extent, form the object of experience. A human being can "attend" the process in a way as a spectator, "share the fact of someone's dying"[1] as well as his own agony (insofar as he is conscious). The conscious person who is dying is able to intentionalize the world and the state in which he finds himself, to experience the successive stages thereof, and to communicate his experiences to those around him by speech or signs. Once he sinks into a state of unconsciousness, such as a coma, he is no longer capable of communicating to another person his experience of dying. If he could nevertheless still experience it, this would have to happen in some other manner than through intentionality and conscious experience.

In contrast to dying and the phenomenal expressions of human death – for instance, a cadaver or the gradual decomposition of the body of what was a moment ago still a person – death (that is, the state of death), despite the certainty of its "presence", seems to be beyond the experience of the living individual and to elude the intentional intellect

[1] Robert Nozick, "Dying", p. 22.

and phenomenological reduction. The phenomenological method describes what appears to the observer in the very manner in which it is manifested or describes the mode of presentation of something that presents itself. It seems that death does not present itself in the same way as the external object of perception or the lived experience of consciousness. Death would be a "nonphenomenon" for the survivor.

Before pursuing this matter further, I would like to call attention to the two fundamental options available to the thanatologian (philosopher of death) when he considers the *postmortem* state by asking whether the dead person – as opposed to the survivor – can experience the state in which he "finds himself". This question will be of capital importance when we discuss the Epicurean challenge in Part Three of this book. Death (after decease) can signify either a radical and irreversible nonexistence of the subject, his definitive annihilation, or else an individual existence that would have "crossed over" the frontier of life's end. In the first case, it is maintained that the "dead person" would be incapable of experiencing his "death", that is, his state of death, because he would no longer exist. In the second case, it is maintained that the "dead person" would be capable of experiencing, at least theoretically, the state in which he finds himself. One can also speculate as to whether the latter would be capable, theoretically, of communicating his experience to his survivors, that is, to the human beings who had not yet "passed beyond" the stage of decease. Paranormal phenomena, such as near-death experiences, apparitions of dead people, communications from beyond the grave through mediums, or reincarnation, seem to me to be scientifically unproved, at least given the present state of our knowledge.[2] The thanatologian, therefore, could not refer to the experiences of the dead. It seems that we find ourselves, as philosophers, facing a hermetically sealed barrier.[3] This is the starting point for my reflection on the subject of the possibility of a phenomenology of death.

If human death is not given as an object to the living, if it never appears to them, shouldn't we conclude that any attempt to reflect on death by means of the phenomenological method would be doomed to failure from the start? Wouldn't a phenomenology of death be tantamount to babbling, to mere verbiage, that is, speculation based on

[2] See Ronald W. K. Paterson, *Philosophy and the Belief in a Life after Death*, pp. 131 f.; Alfred Jules Ayer, "What I Saw When I Was Dead…".

[3] Here I am not interested in the question raised by Augustine in *The City of God*, book XIII, xi, p. 312, whether it is possible to be "in" death, given that "before death comes, he is not dying but is living; when death has come he is not dying but dead. The one state, then, is before death, and the other after. Just when, then, is man 'in death'?"

meaningless concepts or else on imaginary constructs? Wouldn't death be "meta-phenomenological"?[4] Having no ontological density for the philosopher, since it is a privation of selfness (*ipséité*), the absence of a for-itself, death seems to allow us to approach only as far as its threshold and only by means of metaphors and symbols. The notions or the images that we have of death depict an absence. Since the philosopher cannot adopt the dead person's perspective, he finds himself constrained to assume the perspective of the living. He does not look at death as it "is" for the dead person, but rather as it appears to the living, that is, through the phenomena associated with the cadaver: death manifests itself as the change from a living body into a corpse. Does this mean that the philosopher is forced to approach death solely from the angle of what precedes it and, in the final analysis, to speak only about life?[5] In short, everything would lead us to believe that a phenomenological reduction of death would be doomed from the start.

Taking as our point of departure the fact that my death (the state of death or being in death), like that of the other, always escapes me – because I fail to objectivize it as such – could we argue that death is a pseudoproblem? As Spinoza says,[6] shouldn't the wise man meditate on life rather than on death? Isn't the philosopher compelled to remain silent before the nonphenomenon of death and to leave thanatological discourse to the good offices of the theologian? Wouldn't the thanatologian do better to abide by Wittgenstein's maxim, "What we cannot speak about we must pass over in silence"?[7] Shouldn't he be content to think "about" death, to consider the concerns and circumstances surrounding it, but

4 Simon Critchley, *Very Little ... Almost Nothing*, p. 74.

5 On this subject Jankélévitch explains that "the philosophy of the other side arrives too late, like the firemen, and it is competent to speak only in posthumous fables regarding life after death; the philosophy of this side arrives too early and speaks only about life; as for the philosophy of the threshold or of the intermediate space, philosophizing about an almost-nothing that is much too subtle to be known, it arrives either a moment before – and then it knows about an infinitesimal life, a biography reduced to its final moments, but still a positive fullness – or else a moment afterward – and then it becomes the infinitesimal eschatology of an infinitesimal afterlife. Too early, too late!" [*"la philosophie de l'au-delà arrive trop tard, comme les pompiers, et elle n'est compétente que dans les fabulations posthumes relatives à la survie; la philosophie de l'en-deçà arrive trop tôt et ne parle que de la vie; quant à la philosophie du seuil ou de l'entre-deux, philosophant autour d'un presque-rien beaucoup trop fin pour être connu, elle survient soit l'instant d'avant – et elle connaît alors une vie infinitésimale, une biographie réduite aux derniers moments, mais toujours une plénitude positive – soit l'instant d'après – et elle devient alors l'eschatologie infinitésimale d'une survie infinitésimale. En avance, en retard!"*]: Vladimir Jankélévitch, *La Mort*, p. 38.

6 See Baruch Spinoza, *Ethics*, Part IV, proposition 67, p. 187.

7 Ludwig Wittgenstein, *Tractatus logico-philosophicus*, no. 7, p. 151 [p. 82: *"Wovon man nicht sprechen kann, darüber muss man schweigen"*].

never to think of death itself? Even more radically, as Wiplinger suggests,[8] isn't it impossible for the philosopher to speculate about death, or even to speak about it, since death is not the object of experience? Yet, on the contrary, shouldn't we maintain, with Jankélévitch, that despite its 'non-phenomenal character', death is for the philosopher "the problem *par excellence* and even, in a sense, the sole problem"?[9] Isn't death, as the phenomenologist Fink insists, the "most often interpreted moment of the *Dasein*"?[10]

Despite the importance and the significance of philosophical inquiry into death and the possibility of analyzing phenomenologically the consequences of death through the human attitudes of farewell, mourning, and internal conflict or through the change of a living body into a corpse, it is nonetheless true that, as Socrates already emphasized in the *Apologia*, no one possesses "any real knowledge of what comes after death".[11] Contemporary philosophers, on the whole, although they are from very different schools of thought, agree in saying that death is "inconceivable",[12] "unthinkable",[13] "enigmatic, indefinable",[14] "inexplicable",[15] "inconceptualizable",[16] a "*terra incognita*, a mysterious

[8] See Fridolin Wiplinger, *Der personal verstandene Tod*, pp. 26 f.

[9] Vladimir Jankélévitch, *La mort*, p. 51: *"le problème par excellence et même en un sens le seul"*. See Vladimir Jankélévitch, *Penser la mort?*, p. 9. In this he agrees with Levinas, who regards death as "the 'fullness' of the question" ("Le philosophe et la mort", p. 342).

[10] "Many can talk about death and about the dead, but never say the one thing that death actually is. Death itself is not a phenomenon; it occurs as a removal from the world of phenomena, as 'withdrawal', as disappearance from the one all-encompassing presenteism [*Anwesen*] on which 'all phenomena' are assembled on principle. Because death, strictly speaking, is not a phenomenon, yet infiltrates and overshadows all the phenomena of human life – because it is the emptiness of nothingness which disturbs us yet also fills us with fathomless confidence – it is the most often interpreted moment of *Dasein*" [*"Viele können vom Tode und vom Toten aussagen – doch nie das eine, was der Tod eigentlich ist. Er selbst ist kein Phänomen, geschieht als die Entrückung aus der Erscheinungswelt, als 'Entzug', als Wegschwinden aus dem einen, allumfangenden Anwesen, worin prinzipiell 'alle Phänomene' versammelt sind. Weil der Tod streng genommen kein Phänomen ist, doch alle Phänomene des Menschenlebens durchwirkt und überschattet – die uns ängstigende, aber auch mit abgründigem Vertrauen erfüllende Leere des Nichts ist, ist er das am meisten interpretierte Daseinsmoment"*]: Eugen Fink, *Metaphysik und Tod*, p. 56.

[11] "No one knows with regard to death whether it is not really the greatest blessing that can happen to a man, but people dread it as though they were certain that it is the greatest evil, and this ignorance, which thinks that it knows what it does not, must surely be ignorance most culpable" (Plato, *Socrates' Defense (Apology)*, 29 a-b [p. 15]).

[12] Karl Jaspers, *Psychologie der Weltanschauungen*, p. 261: *"etwas Unvorstellbares"*; Hans-Georg Gadamer, "La mort comme question", p. 10.

[13] Karl Jaspers, *Psychologie der Weltanschauungen*, p. 261: *"Undenkbares"*.

[14] Eberhardt Jüngel, *Der Tod*, p. 11: *"rätselhaft"*.

[15] Søren Kierkegaard, "At a Graveside", p. 96.

[16] Kenneth A. Bryson, "Being and Human Death", p. 346: "The Inconceptualizability of Death".

and unknown territory";[17] that it is "undiscoverable",[18] "the enigma",[19] the "most unknown of unknowns", and the "nothingness of knowing".[20] If this is the case, how can one then find a basis for a phenomenology of death, which remains veiled to our intentional intellect?

Death, as does preconception,[21] proves to be a limit that our thinking can only approach asymptotically, and it seems, at first glance, to elude the phenomenological method. While recognizing that it is impossible to have a direct experience of death, which never appears as such, one could envisage the possibility of a rational discourse on the subject, which would cite the appearing of human finitude, the relation of the *Dasein* to its future death (Heidegger), or the passivity of the *Dasein* with regard to death, understood as radical otherness (the phenomenology of the other, Levinas).

The limit point of thought about death raises the question about the relation between the phenomenal and the nonphenomenal, as well as the question about how the phenomenologist might classify phenomena such as death, which are not offered (to the observer) in the mode of intuitive donation (*Eingebung*). While it is invisible in the sense of phenomenal nonperception, death is nevertheless present somehow at every moment of human existence, and it belongs, in a certain way, to the phenomenal world. The same is true of time. An absence of knowing about death, as described by Socrates, does not imply, in Levinas's opinion, an "absence of relationship".[22] One could perhaps approach death by referring to the attitude of a living person with regard to his death, inasmuch as he is "in relation with something that does not come from him".[23] Death escapes

[17] See Jay F. Rosenberg (*Thinking Clearly about Death*, p. 191), who rejects, however, such a description of death.

[18] Jean-Paul Sartre, *Being and Nothingness*, p. 698 [p. 630: *"l'indécouvrable"*].

[19] Fred Feldman, *Confrontations with the Reaper*, pp. 56 ff.: "Enigma".

[20] Emmanuel Levinas, "Le philosophe et la mort", p. 342: *"plus inconnu des inconnus"; "néant du savoir"*.

[21] I prefer to use the term "conception", which expresses more precisely the beginning of the existence of a human being than the term "birth". Many authors use the two interchangeably. Determining when a human being is a person is not the issue here. See Part One of this book.

[22] Emmanuel Levinas, *God, Death, and Time*, p. 19 [p. 21: *"absence de relation"*].

[23] "The unknown character of death, which is not given [*qui ne se donne pas*] at first as nothingness, but is the correlative of an experience of the impossibility of nothingness, does not mean that death is a region from which no one has returned and which consequently remains, in fact, unknown; the unknown character of death means that the very relation with death cannot come about in the light, that the subject is in relation with something that does not come from him. We could say that he is in relation with the mystery" [*"L'inconnu de la mort qui ne se donne pas d'emblée comme néant, mais qui*

me, Levinas notes, not because death is nothingness, but because I cannot grasp it. A thanatological analysis should not take as its point of departure nothingness, about which we know nothing, but should start instead "from a situation in which something absolutely unknowable appears – absolutely unknowable, *i.e.*, foreign to all insight, rendering impossible any assumption of possibility – a situation, however, in which we ourselves are seized".[24] A phenomenology of death could in that way, perhaps, develop on the ground of absolute otherness and the relation of the living individual with it.

Contemporary philosophical thanatologians have advanced various arguments as to whether or not it is possible to grasp death as a phenomenal object. In this chapter, I will begin by discussing two hypotheses – the mutual exclusiveness of the states of life and death and death *in* life [i.e., as part of life] – while considering the validity of speaking about "my death" and the possibility of imagining "my death". After that I will ask whether love might not be capable of unveiling the unthinkable character of death. I will conclude with an analysis of passivity and of the boundary by examining the relation between death and sleep or between death and conception/preconception.

1. MUTUAL EXCLUSIVENESS OF THE STATES OF LIFE AND DEATH

As we noted in the preceding section, many contemporary philosophers maintain that death, understood as the state of death, eludes the direct experience of the historical living individual, of the philosopher who finds himself this side of death. Vuillemin sums it up as follows: "The only thing that we ever experience is menace, and not death".[25] Indeed, death is extraterritorial to the living. It does not enter into the life process. It is not *in* (or *part of*) life. Here I am not asking the question of whether the dead person has an experience of "what it is like to be

est corrélatif d'une expérience de l'impossibilité du néant signifie non pas que la mort est une région dont personne n'est revenu et qui par conséquent demeure, en fait, inconnue; l'inconnu de la mort signifie que la relation même avec la mort ne peut se faire dans la lumière; que le sujet est en relation avec ce qui ne vient pas de lui. Nous pourrions dire qu'il est en relation avec le mystère"]. Emmanuel Levinas, *Le Temps et l'Autre*, p. 56.

[24] *Ibid.*, p. 58: *"d'une situation où quelque chose d'absolument inconnaissable apparaît; absolument inconnaissable, c'est-à-dire étranger à toute lumière, rendant impossible toute assomption de possibilité, mais où nous-mêmes sommes saisis"*.

[25] Jules Vuillemin, *Essai sur la signification de la mort*, p. 147: *"Nous n'expérimentons jamais que la menace, et non la mort"*.

dead".[26] This hypothesis of the nonexperience of death is the point of departure for the question treated in Part Three of this book, namely, whether death is an evil *per se*, depending on the circumstances, or a good *per se*. This theory of the extraterritorial character of death and the question of whether death is an evil are said to have originated with the Greek philosopher Epicurus, whose position presents an ineluctable challenge to philosophical thanatologians of the twenty-first century, whether they be of the phenomenological, existentialist, or analytical school.

On the basis of his *a priori* assumption that the dead subject does not exist, Epicurus formulates in his *Letter to Menoeceus* his famous thesis that "death is nothing to us", the purpose of which is to diminish somewhat the fear of death. The subject does not find himself in the state of death during his existence, nor in the state of existence once he has died. "So death [...] is nothing to us, since so long as we exist, death is not with us. But when death comes, then we do not exist".[27] The Greek philosopher maintains that the states of life and death are mutually exclusive and that there is no middle ground possible, no conceivable coexistence of the two. We are faced with a radical alternative (*aut-aut*, either-or). Unlike my mortal condition and my dying, my state of death or the state of a dead person cannot be experienced directly by me as long as I live. Within this particular framework one grasps the difficulty of a phenomenological approach concerning death. On the one hand, as long as the philosopher is alive, he is incapable of experiencing the state of death, which escapes the mode of donation/giving (in the phenomenological sense of the term) and which does not appear as a phenomenon susceptible to a phenomenological reduction. On the other hand, when the philosopher is dead, either he experiences nothing, since he no longer exists, or else he experiences (his) death but is not in a position to communicate what (his) death is and what it is like to be dead to the living people who have remained on the other side of the impervious boundary.

We find this mutual exclusiveness between the states of life and death in the writings of many contemporary philosophers. In his *Tractatus logico-philosophicus*, Wittgenstein says that "death is not an event of life: we do not live to experience death".[28] Ricoeur notes that it is an "external

[26] See Thomas Nagel, "What Is It Like to Be a Bat?".

[27] Epicurus, *Letter to Menoeceus*, § 124–125 (p. 30). I will return at greater length to the basis for the Epicurean position in Part Three of this book.

[28] Ludwig Wittgenstein, *Tractatus logico-philosophicus*, no. 6.4311, p. 147 [p. 81: *"Der Tod ist kein Ereignis des Lebens. Der Tod erlebt man nicht"*].

menace, in the sense that it is not involved in life".[29] Indeed, the state of death is comparable to a rendezvous that the human being keeps on missing. As we have already noted in our discussion of Heideggerian Being-towards-death, it is characterized by an "impossible simultaneity",[30] a game of "hide and seek",[31] a lack of contact with the state of life. The presence of one indicates the absence of the other and *vice versa.* As long as a person lives, his death is futural (*à-venir*), and when it is present, the person as a living terrestrial being has disappeared: that is, death moves in the moment a person departs from earthly life. The person who is living historically in time never meets his death, so to speak. "It is impossible to be both 'in life' and 'in death' at one and the same time".[32] In his *Philosophie,* Jaspers emphasizes that "my death is not something that I can possibly experience; I can only experience in relation to it [...]. The impossibility of experiencing death is irrevocable; in dying I suffer death, but I never experience it".[33] Here he takes up a theme found not only in Husserl, who explains that "no one can experience death in himself"[34] (whereby he means no one from this side), but also in Kant, who maintains that "no one can experience his own death (for life is a condition of experience); one can only perceive it in others".[35]

Merleau-Ponty, too, referring likewise to birth (instead of conception), maintains that the state of death is strictly speaking beyond the experience of the historical living individual, that "my death" cannot be the object of my experience as a living being. "Neither my birth nor my death can appear to me as experiences of my own, since, if I thought of them thus, I should be assuming myself to be pre-existent to, or outliving, myself, in order to be able to experience them, and I should therefore not be genuinely thinking of my birth or my death. I can, then,

[29] Paul Ricoeur, "Vrai et fausse angoisse", p. 36: *"menace externe en ce sens que la vie ne l'implique pas".*

[30] Jacques Derrida, *Aporias,* p. 65 [pp. 117 f.: *"simultanéité impossible"*].

[31] Vladimir Jankélévitch, *La Mort,* p. 34: *"cache-cache"*; Fred Feldman, *Confrontations with the Reaper,* p. 111.

[32] Augustine, *The City of God,* book XIII, x (p. 311): *"Et in vita et in morte simul non potest esse".*

[33] Karl Jaspers, *Philosophie,* p. 222: *"Mein Tod ist* unerfahrbar *für mich, ich kann nur in Beziehung auf ihn erfahren. [...] Die Unerfahrbarkeit des Todes ist unaufhebbar; sterbend erleide ich den Tod, aber ich erfahre ihn nie".* See Françoise Dastur, *La mort,* pp. 7 f.

[34] Edmund Husserl, "Die anthropologische Welt", p. 332: *"Den Tod kann niemand an sich erfahren".*

[35] Immanuel Kant, *Anthropology from a Pragmatic Point of View,* §27, p. 44 [*"Das Sterben kann kein Mensch an sich selbst erfahren (denn eine Erfahrung zu machen, dazu gehört Leben), sondern nur an andern wahrnehmen"*, § 24, p. 465].

apprehend myself only as 'already born' and 'still alive' – I can apprehend my birth and my death only as prepersonal horizons: I know that people are born and die, but I cannot know my own birth and death".[36] Indeed, Merleau-Ponty is taking up the hypothesis set forth by Sartre two years earlier, in 1943, in *Being and Nothingness*, which stipulates that death is "*a contingent fact* [...], a pure fact as is birth; it comes to us from outside and it transforms us into the outside".[37] There is a similar discussion in the lectures given by Levinas in 1975–6 and published under the title *La Mort et le Temps*, in which he emphasizes "the impossibility of reducing death to an experience" – we should add, 'for the living individual' – and he speaks of a "noncontact between life and death".[38] "The relation with the death of the other", he continues, "is not a *knowledge* [*savoir*] about the death of the other, nor the experience of that death in its particular way of annihilating being (if, as is commonly thought, the event of this death is reducible to this annihilation). There is no knowledge of this ex-ceptional relation ("ex-ception" meaning here to grasp and to set outside the series). This annihilation is not phenomenal; nor does it give rise to anything like a coincidence of consciousness with it (yet those are the two dimensions of knowledge). From the death of the other, pure knowledge (i.e., lived experience [*vécu*], coincidence) retains only the external appearances of a *process* (of immobilization) whereby someone, who up until then expressed himself, comes to an end".[39] The

[36] Maurice Merleau-Ponty, *Phenomenology of Perception*, p. 250 [pp. 249–50: *"Ni ma naissance ni ma mort ne peuvent m'apparaître comme des expériences miennes, puisque, si je les pensais ainsi, je me supposerais préexistant ou survivant à moi-même pour pouvoir les éprouver, et je ne penserais donc pas ma naissance ou ma mort pour de bon. Je ne puis donc me saisir que comme 'déjà né' et 'encore vivant', – saisir ma naissance et ma mort que comme des horizons prépersonnels: je sais qu'on naît et qu'on meurt, mais je ne puis connaître ma naissance et ma mort"*].

[37] Jean-Paul Sartre, *Being and Nothingness*, pp. 697 f. [p. 630: "*un* fait contingent, *[...] un pur fait, comme la naissance; elle nous vient du dehors et elle nous transforme du dehors"*]. See Eugen Fink, *Metaphysik und Tod*, pp. 35 f.; Karl Löwith, "Die Freiheit zum Tode", p. 423.

[38] Emmanuel Levinas, *God, Death, and Time*, p. 10 [p. 11: *"l'impossibilité de réduire la mort à une expérience"; "non-contact entre vie et mort"*].

[39] *Ibid.*, p. 16 [p. 18: *"La relation avec la mort d'autrui n'est pas, continue-t-il, un savoir sur la mort d'autrui ni l'expérience de cette mort dans sa façon d'anéantir l'être (si, comme on le pense communément, l'événement de cette mort se réduit à cet anéantissement). Il n'y a pas de savoir de cette relation ex-ceptionnelle (ex-ception: saisir et mettre hors série). Cet anéantissement n'est pas phénoménal ni ne donne lieu à aucune coïncidence de la conscience avec lui (ce sont là les deux dimensions du savoir). Le pur savoir (= vécu, coïncidence) ne retient de la mort d'autrui que les apparences extérieures d'un* processus *(d'immobilisation) où finit quelqu'un qui jusqu'alors s'exprimait"*]. We find a similar description in the writings of Thomas Macho (*Todesmetaphern*, p. 195): "Death is inaccessible to our *experiences*; we

"being" of death, if we may express it in those terms, cannot be assimilated, according to Levinas: it always escapes the survivor. Death merely "constitutes" the last leg of the journey, leaving behind it the one who, a moment ago, was among the living. "One does not encounter it, properly speaking",[40] which is to say that "when death is there, we [as earthly living things], are no longer there".[41]

To sum up, most contemporary philosophers who study thanatology agree in saying that there is no experience of death for the living individual. This is true both for "my death", as we will see in a moment, and for the death of the other. Some authors, such as Fink and Bollnow,[42] make a distinction between *Eigentod* (one's own death) and *Fremdtod* (someone else's death) by specifying that the latter is a phenomenon situated within temporality and therefore subject to experience, whereas the former corresponds to a phenomenon outside time, or rather to a phenomenon that puts an end to temporality. It is certainly correct to maintain that the death of the other is a phenomenon situated within temporality, if we understand "death" as the fact of dying together with the corpse that continues to exist a moment after decease – things that

experience neither our own death nor the death of other human beings (even those we have loved). Nevertheless we experience the *transformation* of our fellow men into corpses. We cannot explain this transformation [...] and cannot *understand* it. Still, we *experience* its unconditional facticity. We experience *everything* about death that can be brought into experience through our confrontation, so to speak, with corpses. We do *not* experience *death*, but we do experience *the dead*. In our experience of *the dead*, *death* is not revealed to us; we experience only the *resistance* that the *dead* offer to us in their pure presence. There is no access to the experience of *death*; we owe the fact that we seek and ask about this experience, however, to the inexplicable experience that every encounter with *the dead* provides. In the beginning was the corpse, and afterwards came all the theory. We wanted to explain an experience that eludes all attempts at explanation" [*"Der Tod ist unserer* Erfahrungen *entzogen; wir erfahren weder den eigenen Tod noch den Tod der anderen (und selbst der geliebten) Menschen. Gleichwohl erfahren wir die* Verwandlung *von Mitmenschen in Leichen. Wir können diese Verwandlung nicht erklären [...] nicht* verstehen. *Dennoch* erfahren *wir ihre unbedingte Faktizität.* Alles, *was sich vom Tod in Erfahrung bringen lässt, erfahren wir gleichsam in der Konfrontation mit den Leichen. Wir erfahren* keinen Tod, *wohl aber erfahren wir die* Toten. *In der Erfahrung der* Toten *wird uns der* Tod *nicht offenbart; wir erfahren nur den* Widerstand, *den uns die* Toten, *in ihrer puren Anwesenheit, entgegenhalten. Es gibt keinen Zugang zur Erfahrung des* Todes; *dass wir nach dieser Erfahrung suchen und fragen, verdanken wir aber der unerklärlichen Erfahrung, die uns jede Begegnung mit* Toten *verschafft. Am Anfang war die Leiche; und danach kam alle Theorie. Erklären wollten wir eine Erfahrung, die sich allen Erklärungsversuchen entzieht"*].

40 Emmanuel Levinas, "Le philosophe et la mort", p. 343: *"On ne la rencontre pas, à proprement parler".*

41 *Ibid.*, p. 347: *"quand la mort est là, nous [en tant que vivant terrestre], on n'est plus là".*

42 See Eugen Fink, *Metaphysik und Tod*, p. 37. Otto Friedrich Bollnow, "Der Tod des andern Menschen".

are all appearances. The "death of the other", as such, is always the same as "my death" in the sense that both of them escape temporality and elude any eventual experience. Of course, the survivor experiences the consequences of the death of a loved one, which are manifested in emotional upset and intellectual confusion, or in the phenomena that indicate the transformation of the living body into a corpse. Nevertheless the state of death always transcends historical, temporal life. The living individual never encounters Death, which is not a personified entity; it assumes no external form such as a skeleton, as in the Woody Allen routine,[43] or the Grim Reaper, alluded to in the title of a book by Feldman.[44]

In conclusion, and before analyzing the meaning of the expression "my death", I would like to mention one practical consequence of this mutually exclusive relation between the states of death and life. This corollary, of course, does not deny the possibility of learning how to die, as recommended by Montaigne,[45] but rather recognizes the impossibility of training for death and, more particularly, for my death by anticipating it, by mystical trances, religious experiences, or therapies. Because "my death" is beyond all experience, I cannot practice being dead.

2. THE MEANING OF THE EXPRESSION "MY DEATH"

In thanatological literature we often encounter the expression "my death". There is, of course, no doubt about the validity of this expression in a Heideggerian context. I am capable of being "my death" already by dint of 'anticipation' (*Vorlaufen*), which is not an intellectual and imaginary transposition of my decease and my death; rather, it is a movement of the human *Dasein* toward its ownmost possibility, a tending toward its death, and a "mineness" of death. One can also say "my death" and mean the state in which I will find myself once I have died, a state that implies an afterlife and the preservation of my personal identity. The use of the phrase "my death" raises problems inasmuch as the term "death" can mean either the total and irreversible disappearance of the person or the Augustinian being in death. Let us take a closer look at this problem by examining the ability to imagine "my death".

I am capable of imagining "my death" in several ways. Being conscious that I *can* die at any moment, I can imagine "my death" in a more

[43] See Woody Allen, "Death Knocks".
[44] See Fred Feldman, *Confrontations with the Reaper.*
[45] See Michel de Montaigne, *The Complete Essays*, chap. xx, pp. 56 ff. [pp. 127 ff.].

or less distant future. Various human acts, for instance, obtaining a life insurance policy or drawing up a will, confirm this possibility. I am also capable of imagining "my death" in a more direct, tangible manner. As opposed to the "mood", to quote Kierkegaard, associated with being a witness to the death of another, matters get really earnest, according to the Danish philosopher, when one starts "to think of oneself as dead",[46] that is, "to witness his own death, to witness the closing of the casket, to witness that everything that fills the senses in a worldly and mortal way ceases in death".[47] While still alive, I live in anticipation of the hours that will follow my decease, the tears of my relatives and friends, the preparations for my burial (which I may have arranged in advance), my burial, and the days and weeks that follow my being laid to rest in the ground. I visualize the reactions of my circle of acquaintances and of my town. I "smell" "my cadaver", which already is beginning to decompose, and the fragrance of the flowers placed on my coffin; I hear the weeping, the singing, the eulogy, the procession, and so forth. By means of dreams, thoughts, and fantasies, I imagine the way in which the world will go on without my presence, and I will try perhaps to picture my reputation and my influence. In this specific context, I am capable of imagining this state of "Postself",[48] of "my death", as an event in the world. In the course of this imaginative visualization, I can be subject to certain experiences and thus experience, in a way, "my death". I can also imagine that I am a witness present at "my death". Imagining such events, nevertheless, is possible for me only insofar as I am alive, acting as my own double from the viewpoint of a spectator of "my death".

Now what about the ability to imagine "my death" from the perspective of the dead-me? It seems reasonable to me to accept the possibility of this, provided that one believes that the subject survives decease (in an afterlife). On the other hand, if one defines death as the person's return to nothingness, then I cannot imagine my burial from the perspective of the dead-me, nor even experience it. Access to "my death" "from the inside",[49] to borrow an idea from Nagel, is ruled out, it seems to me. One could argue to the contrary by maintaining that such access

46 Søren Kierkegaard, "At a Graveside", p. 75.

47 *Ibid.*, p. 76.

48 Edwin S. Shneidman, *Deaths of Man*, pp. 43 f. On the possibility of imagining "my death", see Anthony Flew, "Can a Man Witness His Own Funeral?"; Ian T. Ramsey, "Persons and Funerals: What Do Person Words Mean?"; Jay F. Rosenberg, *Thinking Clearly about Death*, pp. 194 f.; Roy W. Perrett, *Death and Immortality*, pp. 25 f.

49 Thomas Nagel, "What Is It Like to Be a Bat?", p. 87.

would be possible by way of imagining the cessation of my experiences and (the resulting) nothingness. The latter, nevertheless, does not give itself as a "thematizable event".[50] To be present as a living individual at my annihilation is self-contradictory. As a subject, it is not possible for me to abstract myself from my subjective perceptions. We find again the argument of the sixth paragraph of Kant's *Critique of Pure Reason*: "The I think must be able to accompany all my representations".[51] Whenever I attempt to imagine a state of affairs, including "my death", I am conscious of, or at least I presuppose, without necessarily being conscious of it, my presence as a spectator.[52] Imagining "my death" requires simultaneously the disappearance of the spectator-me, which is not possible. Being incapable of assuming the perspective of nothingness, I am not able to imagine what it would be like, from inside a "dead-me", to be dead in the sense of nonexistent. In *Anthropology from a Pragmatic Point of View*, Kant notes that "the thought *I am not* simply cannot exist: for if I am not, then I cannot be conscious that I am not. I can indeed say 'I am not healthy,' and think such *predicates* of myself negatively (as is the case with all *verba*); but when we are *speaking* in the first person, it is a contradiction to *negate* the subject itself, so that the subject annihilates itself".[53] "My death", in a certain sense, never exists for me. It seems to me that there is an abyss between the state of "my death" and the me to whom it "will occur". How can this event of my death, which cannot be grasped, "happen" to me? I think that we have touched here on a central point of the Epicurean doctrine of the nonencounter with death, which will have important consequences for determining whether or not death is an evil. (Indeed, how can I affirm that death is an evil for dead-me when I no longer exist and I have no more sensations?) If one opts *a priori* for nonsurvival, the possibility of experiencing "my death" entails a contradiction: I cannot simultaneously be – which is required

50 Emmanuel Levinas, *God, Death, and Time*, p. 19 [p. 21: *"événement thématisable"*].

51 Immanuel Kant, *Critique of Pure Reason*, § 16, p. 246 [p. 136: *"Das*: Ich denke, *muss alle meine Vorstellungen begleiten* können*"*].

52 On the subject of the spectator, see Sigmund Freud, "Thoughts for the Times on War and Death", p. 289 [p. 49]. Gabriel Marcel, *Creative Fidelity*, pp. 140 f. [pp. 183 f.] and *Presence and Immortality*, p. 48 [p. 40].

53 Immanuel Kant, *Anthropology from a Pragmatic Point of View*, § 27, p. 44 [*"Der Gedanke: ich bin nicht, kann gar nicht existieren; denn bin ich nicht, so kann ich mir auch nicht bewusst werden, dass ich nicht bin. Ich kann wohl sagen, ich bin nicht gesund, u.d.g. Praedicata von mir selbst verneinend denken (wie es bei allen Verbis geschieht); aber in der ersten Person sprechend das Subjekt selbst verneinen, wobei alsdann dieses sich selbst vernichtet, ist ein Widerspruch"*., § 24, pp. 465–6].

in order to experience "my death" – and not be, that is, be deprived of all experience.

This impossibility of imagining "my death" from the perspective of "me-dead" applies also – contrary to statements by Edwards and Perrett[54] – to "his death", the death of the other. Someone else cannot imagine, strictly speaking, "my death" from inside or what it is like to be dead, any more than I can. In this sense, "my death" is a fact for someone else who is present at it. The survivor does not experience my state of death, but rather my decease and my corpse. This argument is true also of my preconception: although I am able to imagine – as a spectator – the human and familial history before my projection into worldliness, what it would be like "to be" before that projection is nevertheless inaccessible to me, despite what Edwards and Perrett say.

To conclude, I would like to highlight two aspects of the debate. On the one hand, the impossibility of imagining "my death" or "my preconception" does not imply immortality, as Tilliette claims.[55] (I will not digress to refute this position, since the arguments have been made earlier.) On the other hand, so-called existentialist philosophy does not aim, as Rosenberg incorrectly states, to unveil the mystery of death or what it is like to be dead.[56] Existentialist philosophers are not the "worst offenders"[57] in contradicting the thesis defended in the preceding

54 See Paul Edwards, "My Death", p. 417. Roy W. Perrett, *Death and Immortality*, pp. 26–7: "Suppose that we concede that my death is the dissolution of my body and the cessation of my experiences. But if the fact that this other person is alive when thinking of my death doesn't disqualify him from thinking of this, then why should my being alive prevent me from thinking of this either? Moreover, if it is admitted that we can conceive of our nonexistence before our birth, why is there no problem here when there is supposed to be one about the conceiving of our own nonexistence after death?" Of course it is correct to maintain that if someone else were capable of imagining and conceiving of "my death", there would be no reason not to attribute the same ability to me. Nevertheless it seems to me that the distinction between imagining "my death" as a witness and imagining "my death" from the perspective of "me-dead" has been overlooked".

55 See Xavier Tilliette, "Le moi et la mort", pp. 197 f.

56 See Jay F. Rosenberg, *Thinking Clearly about Death*, p. 191. He refers to an article by Paul Edwards entitled "Existentialism and Death: A Survey of Some Confusions and Absurdities", which does not discuss the primary sources of existentialism but rather Anglo-Saxon commentators on them; the article, in my opinion, is based on a misunderstanding of the texts (Edwards's book, *Heidegger on Death: A Critical Evaluation*, is a case in point). This leads me to think that Jay F. Rosenberg has not spent much time poring over the works of existentialists. Douglas N. Walton has penned a critique similar to Rosenberg's: "Contrary to what seems the prevalent existentialist view, we cannot have a direct awareness of death as a positive phenomenon": *On Defining Death*, p. 54.

57 Jay F. Rosenberg, *Thinking Clearly about Death*, p. 233, note 5.

paragraphs, a thesis that Rosenberg correctly sets forth: it is impossible to imagine oneself as a witness to one's funeral, and one cannot know and experience what it is like to be dead. None of the classical existentialist or phenomenological philosophers would have denied this.

Hence "my death" and also death as such always seem to escape me. Whether alive or dead, I can never encounter it. What I do encounter is always a consequence of another's death (the corpse, for example) but never of "my death". Epicurus is precisely right on this point.

3. DEATH IN LIFE

In reaction to the thesis of the mutual exclusivity of the states of life and death, some twentieth-century philosophers such as Scheler, Simmel, and Theunissen develop the theory of death *in* life. They insist that death should no longer be seen as something inorganic and external like "the snip of the scissors with which the Fate puts an end to life",[58] but rather as a formal constituent of life. Death is inseparably joined with life; it is intimately present to it. It is at work even within life. Does the presence of death *within* life – the significance of which we will have to define more precisely – allow us to intentionalize death, to grasp it as a phenomenon, to experience it? Does it make a phenomenology of death possible? Scheler developed the thesis that the idea of death – which is "clear and evident"[59] – "is one of the *constitutive* elements of [our] consciousness";[60] does his intuitive hypothesis of death mean, as some have claimed,[61] that the essence of death is grasped? Isn't it more logical to reason that the thesis of death *in* life is situated at a different level of discourse, where death is understood as the mortality of the living individual, and hence that it does not contradict the thesis of the mutual exclusivity of life and death? In order to answer these questions I think that it will be helpful to look more closely at the theory of death *in* life.

The development of this theory was made possible by the decline of animism, as represented by Spinoza and Leibniz, and by an increasingly mechanistic understanding of the world and of the human being,

[58] Georg Simmel, "Zur Metaphysik des Todes", p. 32: *"als den lebenbeendigenden Parzenschnitt ansieht"*. See also *Lebensanschauung*, p. 110.

[59] Max Scheler, *Tod und Fortleben*, p. 30: *"klare und leuchtende Idee"*.

[60] *Ibid.*, p. 17: *"zu den* konstitutiven *Elementen [unseres] Bewusstseins"*.

[61] See Georg Scherer, *Das Problem des Todes in der Philosophie*, pp. 47 f.; Elisabeth Ströker, "Der Tod im Denken Schelers", p. 210.

accompanied by a gradual exclusion of metaphysics from the realm of rational discourse.[62] Whereas classical philosophical speculation about death moves within the larger framework of the body-soul dualism, late-nineteenth-century thanatology approaches death principally through its relation to life and begins to leave the questions of immortality and the meaning of life out of the discussion.

Despite the important contributions by poets and writers such as Hölderlin, Rilke, or Tolstoy to the theme of death *in* life, I will concentrate on a few contemporary philosophers, in particular Simmel, Scheler, Jonas, and Theunissen. I deliberately omit Heidegger, who has already been discussed at length and who was inspired by the first two thinkers just mentioned. In this school of the philosophy of life, Simmel refuses to understand death as imposing a limit upon life from outside. If that were the case, life would be suddenly interrupted in its projection toward the future of its possibilities by an "event" that is external to it: death. Viewed in this way, life would be in some sense immortal. Simmel distances himself from such a concept of death, which, he claims, is held by "most people";[63] the German philosopher proposes instead to "insert" death into the heart of biological life. Death is not only present at the moment of its realization – decease – but is already "there" from the moment when the individual is thrown into worldliness. "From the start, death is intrinsically bound up with life".[64] Life

62 See Renée Bouveresse, *Spinoza et Leibniz: L'idée d'animisme universel*; François Duchesneau, *La physiologie des Lumières*; Jacques Roger, *Les sciences de la vie dans la pensée française au XVIIIe siècle*. For some contemporary philosophical thanatologians such as Schulz, Fuchs, Ebeling or Theunissen, the end of metaphysics is a self-evident fact. Ebeling even declares that we have reached a point of no return with the famous Heideggerian thesis of Being-towards-death, as though it dealt a death blow to the traditional philosophical analysis that still considered immortality to be an essential issue. Some authors, such as Schulz, claim that only a biological philosophical thanatology is rational and capable of fully comprehending death. In my opinion, they deny the principle that there are differences among what Apel has called various "types of rationality" (*"Das Problem einer philosophischen Theorie der Rationalitätstypen"*) and of methods, among different legitimate viewpoints from which to grasp reality. For now I do not want to enter into a detailed discussion of the positions of these contemporary thanatologians, whom I personally consider dubious from a theoretical and historical perspective (think, for example, of the current revival of interest in metaphysical thanatological questions in analytical philosophy). See note 15 of the introduction of the present book.

63 Georg Simmel, "Zur Metaphysik des Todes", p. 30: *"den meisten Menschen"*. It is interesting to note here the parallel with Scheler (*Tod und Fortleben*), who speculates that the decline in the belief in an afterlife has its origins in the hypothesis that death is something external to life.

64 Georg Simmel, "Zur Metaphysik des Todes", p. 30: *"der Tod von vornherein und von innen her dem Leben verbunden"*. See also *Lebensanschauung*, p. 107.

is situated in an overall context "that is aimed towards death [...]. But at every moment of our life we *are* beings that will die, and the moment would be otherwise if this were not our innate destiny that is somehow at work in that moment".[65] Simmel describes death as a mold that imparts form to life; it shapes it; it is a "formal moment of our life".[66] He quotes Kierkegaard's remark "death minds its own business in life".[67]

Scheler, following Simmel, advocates inserting death *into* life, arguing that the existence of a *natural death* would help modern man rediscover the idea of death as well as the belief in an afterlife. He rejects Weismann's[68] thesis – adopted by Carrel but called into question in recent decades by Hayflick and Moorhead[69] – which holds that some cells are "a-mortal" and considers death as something accidental and external to the living being. In this theory death is viewed as "catastrophic",[70] an "ambush"[71] caused by factors external to the subject. The latter stumbles upon death by chance as though he were running into a "wall"[72] in the darkness. Death is the consequence of environmental wear and tear on the subject, who no longer manages to defend himself and eventually perishes; it always comes from outside. As I have already noted in passing while discussing intuitive knowledge of human mortality, Scheler declares that the living being is characterized by "a slow exhaustion of a vital force which we can assume to be self-actuating",[73] an "*internal exhaustion* of the vital agencies on which the development of the species depends".[74] Death, as Scheler states, is a phenomenon "connected with the essence of the living thing";[75] it is part of "the form and structure"[76]

[65] Georg Simmel, "Zur Metaphysik des Todes", pp. 30 f.: *"der auf den Tod angelegt ist [...]. Aber in jedem einzelnen Momente des Lebens* sind *wir solche, die sterben werden, und es wäre anders, wenn dies nicht unsere mitgegebene, in ihm irgendwie wirksame Bestimmung wäre"*. See *ibid.*, p. 32 and also *Lebensanschauung*, p. 110.

[66] Georg Simmel, *Lebensanschauung*, p. 102: *"ein formales Moment unseres Lebens"*.

[67] Søren Kierkegaard, "At a Graveside", p. 76.

[68] See August Weismann, *Über Leben und Tod*, and the studies by Maupas, Calkins, and Carrel; Louis-Vincent Thomas, *Anthropologie de la mort*, pp. 70 f.; Edgar Morin, *L'homme et la mort*, pp. 339 f.; M. Steiner, "Der Tod als biologisches Problem".

[69] See Leonard Hayflick, "The Cell Biology of Human Aging" and *How and Why We Age*; Michael Fossel, *Reversing Human Aging*.

[70] Max Scheler, *Tod und Fortleben*, pp. 23, 31: *"katastrophal"*.

[71] *Ibid.*, p. 23: *"Anrennen"*.

[72] *Ibid.*, pp. 23, 30: *"Wand"*.

[73] *Ibid.*, p. 34: *"einer langsamen Erschöpfung einer als selbständiges Agens anzunehmenden Lebenskraft"*.

[74] *Ibid.*, p. 35: "innere Erschöpfung *der die Art leitenden Lebensagentien"*.

[75] *Ibid.*, p. 35: *"das an das Wesen des Lebendigen geknüpft ist"*.

[76] *Ibid.*, p. 22: *"zur Form und zur Struktur"*.

of life. Life is unthinkable without death. The latter is a traveling companion: "It accompanies one's whole life as a component of *all* its moments".[77] Death "belongs to the substance 'life'".[78] It is "an absolute and definitive structure of the world".[79] Scheler even maintains that the coming of death "appears as the necessary fulfillment of the meaning of a life".[80] Death is "a formative, guiding force in his life; something that organized and built up his life".[81] "Death is part of the form and structure in which all life is given to us alone, our own or any other, and this is true *from within and from without.* It is not a frame that is added by chance to the picture of individual psychological or physiological processes, but rather a frame that belongs to the picture, without which it would not be the picture of a *life*".[82]

Jonas, who is later joined by Theunissen,[83] takes up the theme of the two German writers: citing contemporary developments in biology, he notes that "death is coextensive with life", which is to say that "you cannot have one without the other".[84] Death is an "essential attribute of life as such",[85] meaning that the organic constitution of life implies death. Death is "inscribed" deep within the cells of the living being; it is the inseparable companion, a constitutive "element" of biological life.

This concept of death as an indispensable element in the development and propagation of life, which Simmel, Scheler, Theunissen, and Jonas situate at the biological level – which is not to imply a sort of Manichaeism whereby death coexists as an "incarnate" being together with life – leads again by way of analogy to the Hegelian life-death dialectic. As Bernard had already noted, life is characterized by a twofold process of "creation" and "organic destruction",[86] by a twofold

77 *Ibid.*, p. 26: *"er begleitet das ganze Leben als ein Bestandteil* aller *seiner Momente".*

78 *Ibid.*, p. 30: *"zum Wesen 'Leben' gehört".*

79 *Ibid.*, p. 34: *"eine absolute und endgültige Welteinrichtung".*

80 *Ibid.*, p. 30: *"als notwendige Erfüllung eines Lebenssinnes erscheint".*

81 *Ibid.*, p. 31: *"Der Tod, das war für sein Leben eine formende, eine richtende Gewalt; etwas, was dem Leben Gliederung und Aufbau gab".*

82 *Ibid.*, p. 22: *"Der Tod gehört zur Form und zur Struktur, in der uns allein jegliches Leben gegeben ist, unser eigenes wie jedes andere, und dies* von innen und von aussen. *Er ist nicht ein Rahmen, der zufällig zu dem Bilde einzelner psychischer oder physiologischer Prozesse hinzukommt, sondern ein Rahmen, der zu dem Bilde gehört und ohne den es nicht das Bild eines* Lebens *wäre".*

83 See Michael Theunissen, "Die Gegenwart des Todes im Leben".

84 Hans Jonas, "The Burden and Blessing of Mortality", p. 87.

85 *Ibid.*, p. 87.

86 Claude Bernard, *Leçons sur les phénomènes de la vie communs aux animaux et aux végétaux*, p. 1: *"creation"* and *"destruction organique"*. Concerning the thesis that death is a condition for life, see Pierre Sprumont, "La mort comme condition de la vie".

movement of phenomena: "phenomena of vital creation or organizational synthesis, and phenomena of death or organic destruction [...]. In a living thing, everything creates itself morphologically and organizes itself, and everything dies and destroys itself".[87] We encounter this idea of a twofold movement already in the writings of Stahl, Haller, and Lamarck; it is also at the basis of the modern explanation of metabolism, which is composed of anabolism (synthesis) and catabolism (destruction).

Thus life is inconceivable without death; they are inseparable and make up "an indissoluble fusion", to borrow an expression by Simmel.[88] The last-mentioned writer explains, however, that "life, in and of itself, requires death as its opposite, as the 'Other'".[89] The German author considers them as thesis and antithesis. Death offers resistance to the vital principle. Confronted by this continual threat of death, which, according to Jonas, is perpetually lying in ambush for it,[90] life must constantly assert itself in order to continue. Bichat had already remarked that life was an "ensemble of functions that resist death".[91] Indeed, metabolism is the expression of a constant Yes to life. According to Jonas, it is a "reclaiming which ever reasserts the value of Being against its lapsing into nothingness".[92] He concludes that "being has become a task rather than a given state, a possibility ever to be realized anew in opposition to its ever-present contrary, not-being, which inevitably will engulf it in the end".[93] Even accompanying biological life, death is simultaneously the contradiction thereof.

The thesis of death *in* life underscores the fact that death is a constituent element of human biological life and that it is opposed to life while being inseparable from it. Within this particular intellectual

87 Claude Bernard, *Sur les phénomènes de la vie communs aux animaux et aux végétaux*, p. 40: *"des phénomènes de création vitale, ou synthèse organisatrice; et des phénomènes de mort, ou de destruction organique. [...] Chez un être vivant, tout se crée morphologiquement, s'organise, et tout meurt et se détruit".*

88 Georg Simmel, *Lebensanschauung*, p. 107: *"unlösbarer Verschmelzung".*

89 *Ibid.*, p. 111: *"Das Leben fordert von sich aus den Tod als seinen Gegensatz, als das 'Andere'".*

90 See Hans Jonas, "The Burden and Blessing of Mortality", p. 91.

91 Xavier Bichat, *Recherches physiologiques sur la vie et la mort*, Part I, p. 57: *"ensemble des fonctions qui résistent à la mort".*

92 Hans Jonas, "The Blessing and Burden of Mortality", p. 91.

93 *Ibid.*, p. 90. Further on the passage continues: "Only in confrontation with ever-possible not-being could Being come to feel itself, affirm itself, make itself its own purpose. Through negated not-being, 'to be' turns into a constant choosing of itself. Thus it is only an apparent paradox that it should be death and holding death it off by acts of self-preservation which set the seal upon the self-affirmation of Being", p. 91.

framework Scheler develops the notion of "natural death", which signifies the conclusion of the biological process of the living individual. The death of the living individual occurs when the "forces" of death have definitively gained the upper hand over the forces of life. This happens inevitably when the natural limit of hope for life has been reached. This natural death is preceded by what one could call an aging program, which is a synthesis between the wear and tear caused by the living individual's environment and the "chemical" wear and tear taking place within the human body. Scheler contrasts this so-called natural death with the kind of death that is termed accidental, which he describes as catastrophic and equates with the thesis of the extraterritoriality of death with respect to life. Accidental death is not necessarily connected with the aging process and can occur at any moment, even at a very early stage of biological development, that is, well before the natural biological clock has run down by itself. Without dwelling on this point, it seems to me to be quite correct to distinguish natural death from accidental death; nevertheless, I keep my distance when these two kinds of death are contrasted, as Scheler does, within the more general context of a conflict between the thesis of death *in* life and the thesis of the extraterritoriality of death with respect to life. In fact I think, on the one hand, that the latter thesis does not deny that death is inscribed at the very heart of the living individual's biological process (at the cellular level or for the living individual as a whole) but rather expresses an interruption of the projection toward the future (as coming-toward, *l'à-venir*) of the subject's possibilities. On the other hand, I think that death is always caused – regardless of the context, whether natural or accidental – by a destruction of the functioning of the metabolism, which has become incapable of repairing the damage caused by an accident or an illness.

Once the theory of death in life has been presented, one may ask whether the inclusion of death *within* life makes it possible to know and experience death. Which sort of death are we talking about here? Wouldn't such discourse about death be situated at a different level of understanding death from the level of the discourse that proponents of the thesis of death *in* life think that they are opposing, namely, the Epicurean thesis?[94] In referring to the structure of a phase of life, Scheler in effect proposes a knowledge and an experience of death. He states that the idea of death "belongs to the *constitutive* elements of

94 See Max Scheler, *Tod und Fortleben*, p. 23.

[our] consciousness".[95] Thus the essence of death does not lie in decease, which is "the more or less *accidental realization* of this 'essence'"; rather, it can already be discerned within the structure of life, "apart from all individual accessories".[96] It is the object of a direct intuitive knowledge; it is a "clear and evident idea".[97] It would seem that Scheler maintains, as some have believed,[98] that intuitive knowledge is capable of grasping the essence of death. If that were the case, the reader would have to marvel that the German philosopher has said nothing to describe or explain that essence. It seems to me that we are dealing here, instead, with an equivocation on the notion of death. In the present context Scheler is not referring to death understood as the state of death, but rather to mortality, to the individual's orientation toward his death, which is inscribed in the heart of the living individual. This is what Scheler's intuition apprehends. Hence such an understanding of death, which is the basis for the thesis of death *in* life, does not abolish the Epicurean challenge, as Scheler had intended. Nor does it make possible a phenomenology of death as such, but only a phenomenology of mortality or of the consequences of decease. The thesis of death *in* life has made a major contribution toward the understanding of death as a traveling companion in life, even when it is clarified that of course the two do not coincide: at the cellular level there is no simultaneity of life and death. This thesis does not posit a real presence of death (understood as a state) at the heart of life – which would be tantamount to saying that the living individual and the dead individual coincide – but rather a long-familiar truth: the human being is mortal; from the moment of his conception he is a Being-towards-death, the concrete actualization of whose death-decease can occur at any moment. He is nevertheless subject also – with respect to some of his biological parts – to little "deaths" (in the sense of decease). Death is, in a way, necessary for the development of the principle of organic human life; it is inseparably united with it.[99] The thesis of life *in* death does not

[95] *Ibid.*, p. 17: *"zu den* konstitutiven *Elementen [unseres] Bewusstseins"*. He goes on to ask, "in what form does the essence of death present itself in the *external* experience that we have of vital phenomena, whatever they may be?" [*"als was stellt sich das Wesen des Todes dar in der äußeren Erfahrung, die wir von irgendwelchen Lebenserscheinungen machen?"*], p. 18.

[96] *Ibid.*, p. 18: *"die mehr oder weniger* zufällige Realisierung *dieses 'Wesens' 'Tod'"; "aus allem individuallen Beiwerk richtig herauszusehen"*.

[97] *Ibid.*, p. 30: *"klare und leuchtende Idee"*.

[98] See Georg Scherer, *Das Problem des Todes in der Philosophie*, pp. 47 f.; Elisabeth Ströker, "Der Tod im Denken Schelers", p. 210.

[99] There are, however, so-called a-mortal cells (for example, the mitochondria of the germ cells of organisms and bacteria that can multiply indefinitely and for which

mean that the subject as a whole dies in small doses until the moment when he is completely dead, but rather that certain cells of the individual die and that the human person is destined to die.

This presence of death *at the heart* of life, under the twofold aspect of the mortality of the living subject and the occurrence of little deaths at the level of parts of his organism, does not allow us to grasp death as a phenomenon. The theory of death *in* life does not suppose that death is a material principle or is embodied by a force that has a physical existence within life and coexists with it. Although death is life's favorite traveling companion, it remains extraterritorial to the person's state of life. I maintain that the two theses in question – death *in* life and the extraterritoriality of death with respect to life – are situated at two different levels of understanding death. The fact that they are often contrasted in the thanatological literature seems to me to be the result of a failure to distinguish between the state of death (the subject of the Epicurean discourse) and the fact of being a mortal. The thesis of death *in* life substitutes mortality for the state of death and passes from an understanding of death as an instant to an understanding of death as a process.[100] The contrast between these two theses lies rather, to my way of thinking, in their attitudes toward death and, more particularly, toward my death; the contrast is situated within the larger context of a *meditatio mortis*. Whereas Epicurus deduces from his thesis the nonexistence of death for the individual and the baselessness of his fear with regard to it, Simmel, Scheler, and Heidegger try, each in his own way, to awaken modern man to the presence of death so that he can look it in the face.

Neither the theory of death *in* life nor the theory of the extraterritoriality of death with respect to life allows us to develop a phenomenology of death as such. That always seems to be outside life, whether life is understood at the personal or cellular level. It never appears to the philosopher as a phenomenon. The only perceptible phenomena

death is probably always accidental); some plants are potentially "immortal", such as creeping plants (although they do not survive as individuals, since what survives consists only of individual fragments from "colonies" of sprouts) or plants with running roots, and some animals, for instance coelenterates, are as well.

100 Philippe Ariès comments: "the sense of death that had formerly been concentrated on the historical reality of the moment itself was henceforth diluted and distributed over the whole of the life, and in this way lost all its intensity": *The Hour of Our Death*, p. 314 [vol. 2, p. 26: *"Le sentiment de la mort, autrefois concentré dans la réalité historique de son heure, était désormais dilué dans la masse entière de la vie, et perdait ainsi toute son intensité"*].

are those appertaining to the consequences of death: mourning, the farewell, the corpse, and so forth. If the thesis of death *in* life does not make a phenomenology of death possible, could an analysis based on love, which establishes a certain shared identity between two persons, succeed in doing so?

4. LOVE AS THE UNVEILING OF WHAT IS UNTHINKABLE ABOUT DEATH

Would the experience of the death of a dear one, with whom the survivor had ties of friendship and love and who together with him formed a "we" – as Marcel, Landsberg, Wiplinger, and Nozick have emphasized – allow the survivor not only to become aware of his own mortality but even to think the unthinkable about death? The survivor, in mourning, is deprived of the existence and the presence of the beloved other, which leaves an emotional void; does that give us reason to say that he is capable of experiencing the death of his friend and therefore of having the experience of what his own death will be? Although it is impossible to experience the same privation "undergone" by the deceased, one can nevertheless ask whether my friend's death does not lead me to experience the loss of my presence in the world.

Of course, one may venture to say that the survivor undergoes, at the death of a loved one, a loss in being – and not of being – located at the level of the shared "we". The experience of such a loss is not the same as an experience of the loss "undergone" by the deceased, but rather the experience of the loss of community that he formed with the survivor. The latter experiences the radical nonpresence of the deceased, the painful privation of the other's being, the peculiar presence of his absence.[101] The experience of the consequences of the definitive departure (*disparition*) of a dear one cannot be compared to an experience of the state of death.

Some thanatologians have used the same term "death" to designate two distinct realities, death and mortality. Sometimes this has led them to the erroneous conclusion that their theory of intersubjectivity allowed them to lift the veil of mystery that shrouds death. From the experience of the death of a loved one, they have deduced the possibility of logically

[101] In Part Three of this book I will ask whether the loss "undergone" by the deceased – who no longer exists – can be considered as an evil for him, even though he does not experience that loss.

deriving its essence. A careful reading of the texts shows that none of the authors who defend a theory of intersubjectivity holds such a position, not even Wiplinger.[102] Moreover they do not state (with the exception of Wiplinger this time) that the experience of the death of a neighbor is equivalent to the experience of "my death", but rather, as I already said, that it reveals to the survivor his mortal condition; it awakens him from the lethargic slumber in which he tells himself that "everybody" will die someday. On this point they reject Heideggerian Being-towards-death: their certainty of "authentically dying" (*"proprement mourir"*) comes about indirectly, by way of the experience of another's death, especially the death of the loved one. The opposition between the solipsistic Heideggerian thanatology and intersubjective thanatology stops there.

Except in the case of Wiplinger, the two currents of thought agree, not in their manner of attaining certainty about my mortality, but in their affirmation that death consists in a nonphenomenon *par excellence* that escapes the direct experience of the living individual. It is impossible for that individual to experience, whether by an anticipation or by love, what it is like to be dead. Heidegger is right when he declares that "in such Being-with the dead, the authentic Being-come-to-an-end of the deceased is precisely the sort of thing which we do *not* experience. Death does indeed reveal itself as a loss, but a loss such as is experienced by those who remain. In suffering this loss, however, we have no way of access to the loss-of-Being as such which the dying man 'suffers'".[103] To put it simply, the experience of the death of a loved one does not call into question again the Epicurean thesis of the "nothingness of death".

5. THE PHENOMENOLOGY OF DEATH

Taking into account these findings that the living individual never experiences the state of death, that the theories about "death *in* life" and

[102] See Fridolin Wiplinger, *Der personal verstandene Tod*, p. 43; Paul-Louis Landsberg, *The Experience of Death*, p. 19: "No one would claim that the experience of the death of one's neighbor is the same as an experience of one's death" [p. 42: *"Nul ne saurait prétendre que l'expérience de la mort du prochain soit un équivalent de l'expérience de* ma mort"]; Igor A. Caruso, *Die Trennung der Liebenden*.

[103] Martin Heidegger, *Being and Time*, p. 282 [pp. 238 f.]: *"dass solches Mitsein mit dem Toten gerade nicht das eigentliche Zuendegekommensein des Verstorbenen erfährt. Der Tod enthüllt sich zwar als Verlust, aber mehr als solcher, den die Verbleibenden erfahren. Im Erleiden des Verlustes wird jedoch nicht der Seinsverlust als solcher zugänglich, den der Sterbende 'erleidet'"*.

intersubjectivity do not make it possible to experience death (but only mortality), and that death as such escapes an intentional reduction, one might legitimately wonder whether a phenomenology of death does not, in fact, remain impossible.[104] Does this lack of direct access to death necessarily lead to silence? Is it not better, as Wittgenstein advises,[105] to pass over in silence what we cannot speak about? Shouldn't we say instead, with Jankélévitch, that to reject the "right to speculate on the nothingness of death, on the pretext that that nothingness is unthinkable, is to dispute the legitimacy of philosophical thinking in general"[106]? Aren't we identifying the phenomenon here with the thing in itself? Aren't we reducing the ultimate reality to the dimension of what can be perceived by the senses by taking as our point of departure the principle that only what is sensible can be the subject of experiences?

I agree that death escapes the experience both of the survivor and of the dead individual, who, according to the mind-set that denies an afterlife, no longer is. This does not mean, however, that death is the nothingness of thought, inasmuch as it does not nullify all thought. The "nothingness of death" and its nonphenomenal character are not sufficient reasons to remain silent on the subject of death. The issue that concerns me here is not determining whether death or the idea of death gives us food for thought by calling human life into question and by forcing man to engage in philosophical inquiry. As Schopenhauer emphasizes, "Death is the true inspiring genius, or the muse of philosophy", explaining immediately that "without death man would scarcely philosophize".[107] It is not a matter here of knowing the nature, the quiddity, or "whatness" of death, but of legitimizing a phenomenological analysis, the object of which would be death. Wouldn't such an analysis, on the contrary, have to be content with a study of dying and of the "Being-mortal" dimension of *Dasein*? To put it another way, wouldn't it

[104] "Death is not an experience because no one lives through it. Death is not something we suffer or do because it is not a state. Death does not lend itself to phenomenological investigation because it is absurd to investigate the being of non-being. Death as such is inconceptualizable", Kenneth A. Bryson, "Being and Human Death", p. 347.

[105] See Ludwig Wittgenstein, *Tractatus logico-philosophicus*, no. 7, p. 151 [p. 83].

[106] Vladimir Jankélévitch, *La mort*, p. 47: *"droit de spéculer sur le néant de la mort, sous prétexte que ce néant est impensable, c'est contester la légitimité d'une pensée philosophique en général"*.

[107] Arthur Schopenhauer, *The World as Will and Idea*, vol. 3: p. 249 [vol. 2, p. 590: *"Der Tod ist der eigentliche inspirierende Genius oder der Musaget der Philosophie [...]. Schwerlich sogar würde auch ohne den Tod philosophiert werden"*]. See Yves Ledure, "L'acte philosophique et la pensée de la mort dans la philosophie de Schopenhauer".

have to be satisfied with a discourse "on the *appearance to oneself* of the finite character of one's own existence"[108] and with a description of the manner in which the human being relates to his own death?

The recognition that there is a mysterious, unknowable dimension about death in itself, which is due to its exteriority with respect to life, is not sufficient grounds for renouncing philosophical thanatological speculation, a phenomenology of death. Certainly, death – that event without project (*Entwurf*) – is radical otherness that the living and the dying never personally encounter; certainly it is shrouded in mystery, as authors with such different opinions as Levinas and Feldman unceasingly emphasize;[109] some philosophers, however, have imagined that an approach could be made by means of the categories of passivity and nondonation (with reference to a theory of affectivity without intentionality[110]) or the categories of threshold and frontier. Other philosophers have suggested approaching death by extrapolating from a phenomenology of sleep and of conception. Let us take a closer look at this.

The philosopher cannot develop a phenomenology of death starting from the nothingness of death (since it eludes all knowledge), but rather by starting from a situation in which the absolute unknowable appears and the subject himself is grasped (*saisi*). Indeed, for a living philosopher, death is eschatological; he will never be able to possess it as a living subject; it is that nonontological possibility that will never be realized for the philosopher, strictly speaking, in that he will never be capable of experiencing it as long as he is alive. Death is never a present moment, a *now*, for the living individual. It is, as Kamlah remarks, a "sheer occurrence".[111] This absence of the living-me at the time of death's "presence" is not due, Levinas says,[112] to the nothingness of the subject, as Epicurus argues, but to the inability of the self to grasp death; on

[108] Françoise Dastur, *La mort*, p. 37: "*sur* l'apparaître à soi-même *du caractère fini de sa propre existence*".

[109] See Fred Feldman, *Confrontations with the Reaper*, pp. 55 f.

[110] See Emmanuel Levinas, *God, Death, and Time*, pp. 18–19 [p. 21]; Michel Henry, *The Essence of Manifestation*.

[111] "Death as an event is neither an action nor a behavior but rather sheer occurrence [...]. A 'sheer occurrence', in turn, is one that affects us without any additional activity whatsoever on our part, for example, an unexpected fortunate love or a heart attack or, again, death" [*"Der Tod als Ereignis ist keine Handlung, kein Sichverhalten, sondern pures Widerfahrnis. [...] Ein 'pures Widerfahrnis' hingegen ist ein solches, das uns gänzlich ohne eigenes Zutun trifft wie z.B. eine unerwartete beglückende Liebe oder ein Herzinfarkt oder nun wieder der Tod"*], Wilhelm Kamlah, *Meditatio mortis*, pp. 9–10.

[112] See Emmanuel Levinas, *Le Temps et l'Autre*, p. 59.

the contrary, death 'grasps' us. Death escapes the subject's control, and when faced with it, "the subject is no longer a subject".[113] He is incapable of exercising power over death, which is to say that he loses his control as a subject. He cannot assimilate death and take it on but finds himself cast into a radical passivity. At a given moment, the subject is in relation with something radically other, "whose very existence is made up of otherness".[114] "My death", Levinas remarks, "comes from an instant over which I cannot exercise my power in any way [...]. Death is a menace that approaches me like a mystery; [...] it approaches although it cannot be taken on, so that the time that separates me from my death simultaneously diminishes and never stops diminishing; it includes a final interval that my consciousness cannot pass beyond and over which there will somehow be a leap from death to me. The last leg of the journey will be made without me; the time of death is flowing upstream; the ego in its projection toward the future finds itself overturned by a movement of imminence, sheer menace, which comes to me from an absolute".[115] Certainly Levinas accepts the Epicurean thesis of the "nothingness of death" when it says that it is impossible for the living human being to experience the state of death. He departs from it by refusing to confine thanatological thought to the dilemma between being and nothingness. Contrary to the affirmation – which Epicurus makes *a priori* – of nothingness after death, he is content with the mystery of death and with describing it as otherness. His discourse on death is not situated on the same level as that of the Greek philosopher, for he refers not to the state of death but to Augustinian "being in death": that instant of passing, that frontier between the land of the living and the land of the dead, as the analytical philosophers Feldman and Rosenbaum describe it.[116]

How much of this "last leg of the journey" is it exactly in which my consciousness somehow fails and "my death" appears? This frontier

[113] *Ibid.*, p. 57: *"par rapport auquel le sujet n'est plus sujet".*

[114] *Ibid.*, p. 63: *"dont l'existence même est faite d'altérité".*

[115] *Ibid.*, p. 211: *"Ma mort vient d'un instant sur lequel, sous aucune forme, je ne peux exercer mon pouvoir. [...] La mort est une menace qui s'approche de moi comme un mystère; [...] elle s'approche sans pouvoir être assumée, de sorte que le temps qui me sépare de ma mort, à la fois s'amenuise et n'en finit pas de s'amenuiser, comporte un dernier intervalle que ma conscience ne peut franchir et où un saut, en quelque façon se produira de la mort à moi. Le dernier bout de chemin se fera sans moi, le temps de la mort coule en amont, le moi dans son projet vers l'avenir se trouve bouleversé par un mouvement d'imminence, pure menace et qui me vient d'une absolue".*

[116] See Fred Feldman, *Confrontations with the Reaper*, pp. 108 f.; Stephen E. Rosenbaum, "How to Be Dead and Not Care: A Defense of Epicurus", p. 121.

is the "place" of the "leap" between the conscious-living-me and the "dead-me". Do we not find a similar leap between the states of consciousness and unconsciousness, waking and sleeping, conception and the nonbeing before projection into the world?

We can interpret the mutual exclusivity of the states of life and death with the help of the image of the frontier. This image has two distinct meanings: on the one hand, an impassable boundary and, on the other hand, a free passage that is not clearly delimited, a sort of nonlimit, a permeable frontier. Just as sleep is characterized by a transparent frontier and by what Johnstone calls "gatelessness"[117] (meaning that the person who is falling asleep is suddenly in the sleeping state without having consciously crossed the threshold of the frontier), so too the subject suddenly "finds" himself in death. Since one cannot be awake and sleep,[118] live and be dead, at the same time, it would seem that we are dealing with a leap, and that the last leg of the journey immediately preceding this leap is characterized by a lack of consciousness on the subject's part and by mystery. If sleep signifies the cessation of consciousness (as in the case of dreamless sleep), or, more precisely, of alert consciousness, then the transition into the state of sleep escapes me insofar as I am conscious and alert. I can be aware of the gradual diminishment of my state of consciousness and (thus) of my falling asleep, but there comes a moment when I plunge into sleep, a moment that escapes my intentionality. This observation is made possible by my experience of reawakening and by the repetitive cycle of waking and sleeping.

At the threshold of death we are involved in a sort of possibility of the impossible. Passing over the frontier between the state of life and the state of death is similar, for Derrida,[119] to the movement of a step that crosses over an indivisible line. Because it eludes our intuition, this "step" is the cause of the problem raised by the experience, not of death as such, but of the "impossible, rejected, denied or forbidden passage"; the experience of an impracticable passage or simply of "nonpassage".[120] The last-mentioned takes on various meanings: first, the impermeability and insuperability of the frontier; second, the permeability and indefiniteness of the frontier that makes the frontier impossible; finally, the impossible is a nonpassage in which there is no longer a path, in which

117 Henry W. Johnstone, "Discussion. Toward a Phenomenology of Death", p. 396.
118 See Augustine, *The City of God*, XIII, xi (p. 312).
119 See Jacques Derrida, *Aporias*, pp. 10–11 [p. 29].
120 *Ibid.*, pp. 8, 12 [pp. 25, 32: *"passage impossible, refusé, dénié ou interdit"*; *"non-passage"*].

the "coming or the future advent would have no relation to the passage of what happens or comes to pass".[121] Derrida opts for the image of mutual waiting by the two states, characterized by the fact that "the one and the other never arrive together at this rendezvous".[122] Simultaneity is impossible here. Derrida remarks that death is "ultimately the name of impossible simultaneity and of an impossibility that we know simultaneously".[123] Human experience always stops at the threshold of the frontier of death. One cannot "cross it while remaining alive".[124]

Since no living individual is capable of experiencing the death of another or his own death, and since the philosopher finds himself obliged to turn back once he reaches the insuperable threshold of death's door, perhaps we would arrive at a better understanding of death indirectly, by way of an analysis of sleep[125] and of conception. Although it would be useless to extrapolate from the experience of sleep to the experience of death, extrapolating from a phenomenology of sleep to a phenomenology of death would no doubt be more productive. The structure of the "beginning" of death is similar to the corresponding structure in going to sleep: both involve a loss of alert consciousness. During the course of the process of falling asleep a moment comes when the subject is no longer capable of experiencing the end of his waking state. The analogy, of course, has its limits: the experience of sleep does not reveal what it is like to be dead; indeed, sleep does not suppress the subject's consciousness; it certainly suspends alert consciousness, but it makes room for the emergence of consciousness during nocturnal dreams, which by means of symbols express the unconscious life of the individual.

In a short essay entitled "The Anthropological World", which concludes with the question of immortality, Husserl acknowledges the impossibility of experiencing death. While distancing himself from Heideggerian Being-towards-death, which he describes as "the dazzling, pensive ways in which Heidegger cavorts with death",[126] the father of

[121] *Ibid.*, p. 21 [p. 47: *"venue ou l'avenir de l'événement n'aurait aucun rapport avec le passage de ce qui passe ou se passe"*].

[122] *Ibid.*, p. 65 [p. 117: *"l'un et l'autre n'y arrivent jamais ensemble, à ce rendez-vous"*].

[123] *Ibid.*, p. 65 [pp. 117 f.: *"au fond le nom de la simultanéité impossible et d'une impossibilité que nous savons simultanément"*].

[124] Jean-Pierre Vernant, *L'individu, la mort, l'amour*, p. 146: *"passer en restant vivant"*.

[125] See, for example, Jan Linschoten, "On Falling Asleep"; Henry W. Johnstone, "Discussion. Toward a Phenomenology of Death", "Toward a Philosophy of Sleep", and "Sleep and Death".

[126] He adds, "and which death will hardly agree to accept". Edmund Husserl, "Die anthropologische Welt", p. 332: *"Die blendenden, tiefsinnigen Weisen, in denen Heidegger*

phenomenology proposes getting around the obstacle of death by referring to the experience of sleep. The latter is a mode of human life and yet it is "the sister of death".[127] Whereas falling asleep, in its initial phase, is analogous to dying (the subject experiences it), the passage from life to death resembles the passage from waking to sleeping. The type of sleep that we are dealing with here, which would best approximate death, is not a sleep abounding with dreams, for the individual who dreams has a world, but rather, as Lessing already emphasized,[128] a dreamless sleep. This reflects the fact that the life of "proprioception of the human being who knows that he is living in the world"[129] ceases. As with death, the subject in the final phase of falling asleep is distinguished by his passivity; he is freed from all control; he has no more control over anything; he no longer grasps anything by clear perception; he apprehends nothing that is present. This being closed off from the world and from all clear perception that characterizes dreamless sleep does not imply that life as flux has disappeared. Here Husserl develops the question of a possible afterlife, which I do not want to dwell on and which I will mention only in passing. On the basis of the analogy between death and its sister (or brother), which is sleep, he asks whether death is not followed by life, as is the case with sleep, which flows into awakening. By analogy with sleep, wouldn't human death, "seen from within", be "an abandonment of the world"[130]? Husserl concludes that "life as it flows cannot stop, and the ego 'can' stop enduring in it in the manner of this flowing", even though "this flowing has passed over into a mode of non-waking, which no longer can lead to an awakening".[131] Husserl denies the immortality

mit dem Tode umspringt, wird sich der Tod schwerlich gefallen lassen" [The French translation of Husserl's remarks compares Heidegger's manner of dealing with death to a trapeze act].

127 *Ibid.*, p. 338: *"der Tod Bruder des Schlafes"*. Referring to the concepts of brother and sister to describe death is commonplace: see Jean-Pierre Vernant, *L'individu, la mort, l'amour*, pp. 131 f.; Arthur Schopenhauer, *The World as Will and Idea*, vol. 3, p. 256 [vol. 2, p. 598]; Søren Kierkegaard, "At a Graveside", p. 80.

128 See Ludwig Uhlig, *Der Todesgenius in der deutschen Literatur von Winckelmann bis Thomas Mann*, pp. 15 f.

129 Edmund Husserl, "Die anthropologische Welt", p. 337: *"als Leben der Selbstwahrnehmung des in der Welt lebend sich wissenden Menschen zu leben"*.

130 *Ibid.*, p. 338: *"von innen gesehen ein Fahrenlassen der Welt"*.

131 *Ibid.*, p. 338: *"das strömende Leben kann nicht aufhören, und das Ich 'kann' darin aufhören, in der Weise dieses Strömens zu dauern? Obschon dieses Strömen in einen Modus der Unwachheit übergangen ist, der nicht mehr in ein Erwachen führen kann"*. The passage continues: "Man cannot be immortal. It is necessary for man to die. Man has no worldly preexistence; in the world of time and space he was nothing before and will be nothing afterward. But the transcendental original life, the life that ultimately creates the world and

of the human being in the classical sense, as well as preexistence in this world. Man was nothing before his conception and will be nothing once he is deceased. Husserl defends an idea of immortality by referring to the original transcendental life, the life that created the world and the individual human ego.

Besides sleep, certain authors such as Schopenhauer and Landsberg[132] examine unconsciousness (e.g., a swoon) or conception (we have already considered the latter term briefly). Following Lucretius, who inquires into the asymmetric attitude toward the two extremes of human existence (namely, death and conception), one might ask whether an analysis of conception[133] might lift one swath of the mysterious veil that covers death. (In Part Three of this book I will discuss this question, which is taken up again in the modern era by Schopenhauer and especially by the analytical tradition.) Just like falling asleep and the threshold of death, conception is a "limit experience". I have no direct experience of my conception; I have no impressions of it. I have no intentional knowledge of my conception that could bring me (in thought) to the self who was being conceived and who, a moment before that, was not yet conceived. I cannot be present at my own conception. It escapes my power of possession. It is something given to me. I receive it passively. In a way I am deprived of my conception, as is also the case with the threshold of my death. It does not belong to me in the sense in which my experiences belong to me; it is foreign to what I have experienced in the mode of intentionality. Could conception be regarded, by analogy with death, as radical otherness? Despite my absolute and "apodictic" certainty that I was conceived at a precise moment and that "it happened" to me in a certain way, my conception escapes my direct experience, any

its final ego cannot come into being from nothingness and pass into nothingness, it is 'immortal', because dying has no meaning for it, etc." [*"Der Mensch kann nicht unsterblich sein. Der Mensch stirbt notwendig. Der Mensch hat keine weltliche Präexistenz, in der zeitlich-räumlichen Welt war er früher nichts, und wird er nachher nichts sein. Aber das transzendentale urtümliche Leben, das letztlich weltschaffende Leben und dessen letztes Ich kann nicht aus dem Nichts werden und ins Nichts übergehen, es ist ‚unsterblich', weil das Sterben dafür keinen Sinn hat, etc"*].

132 See Arthur Schopenhauer, *The World as Will and Idea*, vol. 3, pp. 256 f. [vol. 2, p. 598]; Paul-Louis Landsberg, *The Experience of Death*, pp. 10 f. [pp. 31 f.].

133 See for example Bernard P. Dauenhauer, "On Death and Birth"; Natalie Depraz, "Naître à soi-même"; Michel Henry, "Phénoménologie de la naissance". As I have already noted, unlike most philosophers I will use here the term "conception" instead of "birth", because a concrete individual already exists before birth, and because it is possible *per se* to experience the prenatal state of being by means of various techniques.

intuitive insight, and my memory. This certainty is based on the trust that I place in the accounts of the generation previous to mine and on any experience that I may have of the conception of a child. I cannot make my conception present. Somehow I always arrive late; it is a singular possibility that I cannot overtake and that reveals to me my radical contingency, in that I very well might not have been. As Fink remarks, not even the earliest and most detailed memories ever reach as far as "a beginning of consciousness. This chain is not endless, either, but is broken off by becoming lost in an impenetrable darkness. No subject of knowledge, however idealized it may be in the extent to which it possesses that knowledge, can reach its own limit".[134]

The territories situated upstream from my conception and my death always remain veiled; only those that are downstream of this frontier can be unveiled somewhat by a phenomenological analysis by referring to the concepts of nondonation and passivity. While he is certain of his preconception and his future death, the human being is not capable of experiencing them and finds himself in radical ignorance in their regard.

If death as such remains veiled and hermetically sealed from all sense experience, as Epicurus remarks, can one still maintain that "death is an evil"? Would such a statement have any meaning at all within the framework of a philosophy that presupposes the annihilation of the subject after his decease? Indeed, how can one claim that death is an evil for someone who no longer exists and is incapable of experiencing it?

[134] Eugen Fink, "Vergegenwärtigung und Bild", p. 38: "*[...] trifft wesensmäß nie einen 'Anfang' des Bewußsteins. Diese Kette ist auch gleichermaßen nicht unendlichen, sondern sie endet, indem sie sich in ein unwegsames, undurchdringliches Dunkel verliert. Kein noch so idealisiertes Erkenntnissubjekt, sofern es ein Wesen dieselbe Erkenntnis hat, kann hier je an seine Grenze stoßen*".

PART THREE

DOES DEATH MEAN NOTHING TO US?

8

The "Nothingness of Death"

Epicurus and His Followers

1. PRESUPPOSITIONS OF THE EPICUREAN THESIS OF THE "NOTHINGNESS OF DEATH": MATERIALISM, HEDONISM, AND EXPERIENTIALISM

In order to mitigate the fear of death, or even nip it in the bud, Epicurus demonstrates that it must not matter to the individual: it "is nothing to us", because the subject does not find himself in the state of death during his existence, nor in existence once he is deceased. "Death [...] is nothing to us, since so long as we exist, death is not with us; but when death comes, then we do not exist".[1] This thesis of the "nothingness of death" corresponds to two features of Epicurean thought: on the one hand, a hedonistic ethos of pleasure and happiness, which is itself based on his theory of sense knowledge (or "experientialism"), and, on the other hand, an atomistic and materialistic view of the world. The latter prompts the philosopher of the Garden to say that death signifies the nonexistence of the subject, despite the temporary presence of the corpse. The separation of the soul from the body at decease does not mean, for Epicurus, that the soul continues to exist in itself, as Plato and (according to some interpretations) Aristotle maintain. Being corporeal, since it is composed of atoms, and hence mortal, the soul dissolves at the moment of the subject's death. Its atoms are dispersed in all directions. Thus it is impossible for the 'dead' soul to be the subject of sensations: "death is deprivation of sensation".[2] Human death means the irreversible end of the individual and of all experience.

[1] Epicurus, *Letter to Menoeceus*, § 125 (p. 30).
[2] *Ibid.*, § 124 (p. 30).

Epicurus disagrees with Plato and Aristotle not only on the question of death and afterlife, but also on the question of happiness.[3] More specifically, Epicurus differs from them in that he does not connect the idea of good with the notion of the perfection of human nature. Distancing himself from a theory of happiness based on the virtues, he proposes the thesis that happiness is found in pleasure, which is "the beginning and end of the blessed life".[4] Cicero records in his treatise *De finibus* that the philosopher of the Garden based his ethics on the statement that "every animal, as soon as it is born, seeks for pleasure, and delights in it as the Chief Good, while it recoils from pain as the Chief Evil, and so far as possible avoids it".[5] Determining whether a state of affairs or an event is good or evil depends, for Epicurus, on the sensation that the subject may have of it.[6] Underlying Epicurean hedonism

3 See Plato, *Gorgias*, 494c-499b (pp. 276–82.); *Republic* IX, 576c-587b (pp. 803–15); *Philebus* 11a-67b (pp. 1087–1150). Aristotle, *Nicomachean Ethics*, X, 1–5, 1172a 17–1176a 30.

4 Epicurus, *Letter to Menoeceus*, § 129 (p. 31).

5 Marcus Tullius Cicero, *De finibus*, lib. I, ix, 30 (p. 33): *"Omne animal, simul atque natum sit, voluptatem appetere eaque gaudere ut summo bono, dolorem aspernari ut summum malum et, quantum possit, a se repellere"*. A concise, exact formulation of this eudaemonistic hedonism was penned by John Stuart Mill (*Utilitarianism*, p. 257): "The creed which accepts as the foundation of morals Utility, or the Greatest Happiness Principle, holds that actions are right in proportion as they tend to promote happiness, wrong as they tend to produce the reverse of happiness. By happiness is intended pleasure, and the absence of pain; by unhappiness, pain, and the privation of pleasure [...]. Pleasure, and freedom from pain, are the only things desirable as ends; and [...] all desirable things [...] are desirable either for the pleasure inherent in themselves, or as means to the promotion of pleasure and the prevention of pain". One cannot help comparing this to the Epicurean theory of pleasure recorded as follows by Marcus Tullius Cicero: "The whole teaching of Epicurus about pleasure is that pleasure is, he thinks, always to be wished and sought for in and for itself because it is pleasure, and that on the same principle pain is always to be avoided for the simple reason that it is pain". *Tusculan Disputations*, V, xxxiii, 95 (p. 521) [*"Totumque hoc de voluptate sic ille praecipit, ut voluptatem ipsam per se, quia voluptas sit, simper optandam expetendam putet, eadenque ratione dolorem ob id ipsum, quia dolor sit, simper esse fugiendum"*].

6 "What is without sensation, in his judgment [i.e., Epicurus's, as summarized by Cicero], has no concern with us". Marcus Tullius Cicero, *Tusculan Disputations*, V, xxxi, 88, p. 517 [*"quod autem sensu careat, nihil ad nos id iudicet pertinere"*]. A little further on Marcus Tullius Cicero returns to the theme of the state of death, describing it as "an eternal refuge where nothing is felt" (V, xl. 117 (p. 543)) [*"quoniam mors [ubi est] ibidem est aeternum nihil sentiendi receptaculum"*]. The Greek philosopher refrains from distinguishing among various degrees of pleasure, calling attention to the fact that even though "every pleasure [...] is good, yet not every pleasure is to be chosen" (Epicurus, *Letter to Menoeceus*, § 129 (p. 31)); it is possible that a particular pleasure – drinking too much, for example – has severe pain as its consequence: a headache the day afterward. He continues: "even as every pain also is an evil, yet not all are always of a nature to be

we find the experientialism that plays a major role in the argument about the "nothingness of death". In order for a state of affairs or an event to be described as good or evil, the subject must be capable of experiencing it, which presupposes temporal and spatial parameters. Epicurus maintains that a person can be happy or unhappy only insofar as he has experiences (in which he is subject to pleasures or pains). One classifies a state of affairs as good or evil according to the experience that it occasions. An event that could not be experienced would be indifferent.

2. "DEATH IS NOTHING TO US"

The three theses mentioned are of capital importance in reading the famous passage from the *Letter to Menoeceus* in which Epicurus describes the way that leads to happiness. This way passes through liberation from all fear, more particularly from the fear of death. The philosopher of the Garden is interested in death because of his ethical concern about finding a basis for a good life. The second of his *Principal Doctrines* – "Death is nothing to us; for what has been dissolved has no sensation, and what has no sensation is nothing to us"[7] – is repeated almost word for word in numbers 124–6 of the *Letter to Menoeceus*:

> Become accustomed to the belief that death is nothing to us. For all good and evil consists in sensation, but death is deprivation of sensation. And therefore a right understanding that death is nothing to us makes the mortality of life enjoyable, not because it adds to it an infinite span of time, but because it takes away the craving for immortality. For there is nothing terrible in life for the man who has truly comprehended that there is nothing terrible in not living. So that the man speaks but idly who says that he fears death not because it will be painful when it comes, but because it is painful in anticipation. For that which gives no trouble when it comes, is but an empty pain in anticipation. So death, the most terrifying of ills, is nothing to us, since so long as we exist, death is not with us; but when death comes, then we do not exist. It does not then concern either the living or the dead, since for the former it is not, and the latter are no more. But the many at one moment shun death as the greatest of evils, at another as [the cessation of the affairs] of life. But the wise man does not fear the cessation of life, for neither does life offend him nor does the absence of life seem to be any evil. And just as with food he does not seek simply the larger

avoided. Yet by a scale of comparison and by the consideration of advantages and disadvantages we must form our judgment on all these matters".

[7] Epicurus, *Principal Doctrines*, § 2 (p. 35); also in *La Philosophie épicurienne sur pierre: Les fragments de Diogène d'Œnoanda*, fragment 30 (p. 39).

share and nothing else, but rather the most pleasant, so he seeks to enjoy not the longest period of time, but the most pleasant.[8]

In this passage Epicurus does not deny that "my dying", like "someone else's dying", can arouse a reasonable fear and can be perceived as evils, for they occur within the context of life and are the object of sensations. Nor does he deny that another person's death and his state of death can evoke more or less vehement and disconcerting feelings in the survivor(s), in other words, that each is likely to be perceived as an evil or alternatively as a good and a deliverance. The heart of his argument consists mainly of emphasizing the following difficulty: how can the death of "N." be an evil for "N." himself, who is dead, given that he is no longer capable of experiencing anything? The Epicurean argument in the passage cited implies the following points:

1. In order for the fear of death to have a reason for being, or for "N.'s" state of death (S) to be a good or an evil for the living "N.", it is necessary for the latter to have the experience of it at a precise moment (M-1) and in a precise place (P-1), that is, that he be affected and touched by it.
2. This first point is based on the premise that a state of affairs "A" is an evil or a good for "N.", provided that "N." is capable of experiencing "A" in M-1 and P-1 (experientialism). This assertion implies, for Epicurus, a causal element in the experience. Experientialism underlies Epicurean hedonism insofar as an evil or a good exists only through the intermediary of sensation, that is, that of pain or pleasure.
3. This second point presupposes, *a priori*, the postulate that "N." would not be capable of experiencing a state of affairs "A" in M-1 and P-1 unless the latter took place during the life of "N.", and thus before "his" death. This allegation implies, negatively, that "N." cannot be affected by anything after his death (the need for a subject).
4. If "N." is incapable of experiencing S in M-1 and P-1 – given that when S is present, "N." no longer exists, that is, S is not situated during the life of "N." – then S can be neither an evil nor a good for "N." It is nothing to us.
5. It is unreasonable to fear something (here S) that is "nothing to us".

[8] Epicurus, *Letter to Menoeceus*, § 124–6 (pp. 30–1, omitting several emendations suggested in the English version).

6. Fear of death (understood in the very precise sense of the state of death) is devoid of rational foundation.

I will discuss several points of the Epicurean argument at greater length in the next chapter. The structure of the argument, it seems to me, is helpful within the framework of our study of other arguments, both ancient and modern, that refer to it (whether implicitly or explicitly). Besides the pro-Epicureans, I will mention some philosophers who are opposed to him. Among the latter we find some arguments that strangely resemble those employed by proponents of analytical philosophy, although these more recent philosophers do not cite them.

3. THE ANCIENTS

3.1. Lucretius

We turn our attention first, naturally, to a Roman philosopher, Lucretius. In the third canto of *De rerum natura*, he argues for a temporal symmetry between the eternity of the past and the future eternity and concludes from it that "therefore death is nothing to us, it matters not one jot".[9] The past, when the subject did not yet exist, is the perfect mirror image of the future, when he is no longer. And just as the subject returns to nothingness once he is deceased, so too he is nothing before his conception. A few lines further on, Lucretius repeats the argument of his master, Epicurus: "For if by chance anyone is to have misery and pain in the future, he must needs himself also exist then in that time to be miserable. Since death takes away this possibility and forbids him to exist for whom these inconveniences may be gathered together, we may be sure that there is nothing to be feared after death, that he who is not cannot be miserable".[10]

3.2. Socrates and Plato

The apocryphal work of Plato entitled *Axiochus* or *On Death* likewise defends the Epicurean thesis. Axiochus, a brave and venerable old

[9] Titus Lucretius, *De rerum natura*, III, 830 (p. 227): *"Nil igitur mors est ad nos neque pertinet hilum"*.

[10] *Ibid.*, III, 862–8 (pp. 229, 231): *"Debet enim, misere si forte aegreque futurumst, ipse quoque esse in eo tum tempore, cui male possit accidere. Id quoniam mors eximit, esseque prohibet illum cui possint incommoda conciliari, scire licet nobis nil esse in morte timendum, nec miserum fieri qui non est posse"*..

Athenian, has contracted a serious illness and suddenly becomes a prey to fear of death, that "grim reality", which torments his mind with the thought "that I am to lose this light of day and these goods".[11] Citing Epicurean experientialism, Socrates rebukes him for combining the senses with insensibility without taking the trouble to reflect. Since he no longer is, the dead person no longer is capable of feeling and experiencing. Anticipating Lucretius's argument in which death is the mirror image of preconception,[12] Socrates emphasizes that "just as in the administration of Draco and Cleisthenes there was nothing evil that concerned you – for it is elementary that you, whom the evils could have concerned, did not exist – so not even after death will there be any evil. For you, whom it would concern, will not exist".[13]

Although Socrates declares in this context that the state of death is devoid of consciousness and existence, he simultaneously – and paradoxically – mentions an afterlife so as to argue that death does not mean a "removal of the goods", but rather a "purer enjoyment of them [...] [and] of pleasures undiluted by all pains".[14] A little earlier in the dialogue, however, he restates the Epicurean thesis: "*Socrates*: I once heard even Prodicus say that death concerns neither the living nor those who have passed away. *Axiochus*: What do you mean, Socrates? *Socrates*: That death is of no concern for the living – as for the dead, they no longer are. Consequently, neither does it concern you now – for you are not dead – nor, if you should experience something [i.e., if that misfortune befalls you], will it concern you, for you will not exist. Futile is the grief to lament for Axiochus over what neither concerns nor will concern Axiochus [...]".[15] Axiochus, nevertheless, is not satisfied by the arguments presented by Socrates, which he describes, in view of his own mature years, as "fine sayings", "current chatter of the times", and "nonsense devised for the young".[16] He retorts that death is an evil,

[11] Plato-pseudo, *Axiochos*, 365c (p. 31). See Jackson P. Hershbell, *Pseudo-Plato, Axiochus*. Axiochus expresses the position defended by Frances M. Kamm (*Morality, Mortality*, pp. 13 f.) and Thomas Nagel ("Death", pp. 1 f.) concerning death as an evil for the dead "N.", because it deprives him of being and of the goods of life.

[12] See Titus Lucretius, *De rerum natura*, III, 832–42 (pp. 227, 229).

[13] Plato-pseudo, *Axiochus*, 365d-3 (p. 33).

[14] He continues: "For, released from this prison, you will come to that place where all stress, mourning, and old age are missing", *ibid.*, 370d-e (p. 45).

[15] *Ibid.*, 369b-c (pp. 41–3).

[16] *Ibid.*, 369d-e (p. 43): "For my mind pays no attention and is not seduced by the eloquence of your words. Such reasonings do not even touch the surface; rather they result in a pompous parade of verbal splendor, and fall short of the truth. Sufferings

because it deprives one "of goods for living",[17] a thesis adopted by most analytical philosophers, as we will see in Chapter 10. But Socrates does not admit defeat and replies: "Axiochus, you thoughtlessly make a connection with deprivation of the goods by introducing the awareness of evils, forgetting that you are dead. What distresses him who is deprived of the goods is the suffering of the evils in its place. But someone who does not exist is unaware even of deprivation [need for a subject]. How, then, could there be pain for what will provide no knowledge of the things that will cause pain [experientialism]?"[18] For Socrates, as for Epicurus and Lucretius,[19] the privation of the goods of life could be an evil only for a person capable of experiencing their absence. Since the state of death is identified with the nonexistence and nonsensation of the subject, the latter is not capable of experiencing the absence of the goods of life or the absence of his being.

3.3. Seneca

Seneca, too, who recommends thinking unceasingly about death "in order that you may never to fear it",[20] cites the Epicurean argument in his thirtieth *Letter to Lucilius.* In it he reports Bassus's point of view; the latter is dying and keeps trying to convince his interlocutor, "in the spirit of Epicurus", that it is wrong to fear death. "'And it is just as insane,' he adds, 'to fear what will not happen to him, as to fear what he will not

are not content with clever arguments, but are satisfied only with those things able to touch the soul".

17 *Ibid.*, 369d (p. 43).

18 *Ibid.*, 369e-370a (p. 43).

19 "No longer now will your happy home give you welcome, no longer will your best of wives and sweet children race to win the first kisses, and thrill your heart to its depths with sweetness. You will no longer be able to live in prosperity, and to protect your own. 'Poor man, poor man!' they say, 'one fatal day has robbed you of these prizes of life.' But they do not go on to add: 'No longer withal does any craving possess you for these things.' If they could see this clearly in mind and so conform their speech, they would free themselves from great fear and anguish of mind", Titus Lucretius, *De rerum natura,* 894–903 (p. 233) [*"Iam iam non domus accipiet te laeta, neque uxor // optima, nec dulces occurrent oscula nati // praeripere et tacita pectus dulcedine tangent. // Non poteris factis florentibus esse, tuisque // praesidium. Misero misere, aiunt, omnia ademit // una dies infesta tibi tot praemia vitae". // Illud in his rebus non addunt: "Nec tibi earum // iam desiderium rerum super insidet una". // Quod bene si videant animo dictisque sequantur, // dissolvant animi magno se angore metuque*].

20 Seneca, *Letters to Lucilius (Ad Lucilium Epistulae Morales)*, Letter XXX, 18 (vol. 1, p. 221): *"tu tamen mortem ut numquam timeas, semper cogita"*. See *ibid.*, Letter XXVI, 8 (vol. 1, p. 191).

feel if it does happen.' Or does anyone imagine it to be possible that the agency by which feeling is removed can itself be felt? 'Therefore,' says Bassus, 'death stands so far beyond all evil that it is beyond all fear of evils'".[21] Refusing to consider death as an evil or a good in itself, he classifies it, as Epicurus and the cynics had done,[22] as something indifferent.[23] His line of reasoning repeats the Epicurean arguments of experientialism and the nonexistence of a subject in the state of death. "Death is a release from all suffering, a boundary beyond which our ills can not pass – it restores us to that peaceful state in which we lay before we were born. If anyone pities the dead, he must also pity those who have not been born. Death is neither a good nor an evil; for that only which is something is able to be a good or an evil. But that which is itself nothing and reduces all things to nothingness consigns us to neither sphere of fortune; for evils and goods must operate upon something material".[24] "In death there is nothing harmful, for there must exist something to

[21] *Ibid.*, Letter XXX, 6 (vol. 1, p. 215): *"Tam demens autem est, qui timet, quod non est passurus, quam qui timet, quod non est sensurus. An quisquam hoc futurum credit, ut per quam nihil sentiatur, ea sentiatur? 'Ergo, inquit, mors adeo extra omne malum est, ut sit extra omnem malorum metum'"*.

[22] See John M. Rist, *Stoic Philosophy*, p. 237.

[23] See Seneca, *Letters to Lucilius*, Letter LXXXII, 10 (vol. 2, p. 247) and 13 (vol. 2, p. 249); Letter XCIX, 12 (vol. 3, p. 137).

[24] Seneca, *To Marcia on Consolation*, Letter XIX, 5 (p. 67): *"Mors dolorum omnium exsolutio est et finis ultra quem mala nostra non exeunt; quae nos in illam tranquillitatem, in qua antequam nasceremur iacuimus, reponit. Si mortuorum aliquis miseretur, et non natorum misereatur. Mors nec bonum nec malum est. Id enim potest aut bonum aut malum esse, quod aliquid est; quod vero ipsum nihil est et omnia in nihilum redigit, nulli nos fortunae tradit: mala enim bonaque circa aliquam versantur materiam"*. In his letter *To Polybius on Consolation*, Seneca proposes a choice: "For if the dead retain no feeling whatsoever, my brother has escaped from all the ills of life and has been restored to that state in which he had been before he was born, and, exempt from every ill, he fears nothing, desires nothing, suffers nothing [...]. If, however, the dead do retain some feeling, at this moment my brother's soul, released, as it were, from its long imprisonment, exults to be at last its own lord and master [...]. And so why should I pine away in yearning for him who either is happy or does not exist? But to weep for one who is happy is envy; for one who does not exist, madness", Letter IX, 2–3 (pp. 379 f.) [*"Nam, si nullus defunctis sensus superset, evasit omnia frater meus vitae incommode et in eum restitutus est locum in quo fuerat antequam nasceretur, et, expers omnis mali, nihil timet, nihil cupit, nihil patitur [...] Si est aliquis defunctis sensus, nunc animus fratris mei, velut ex diutino carcere emissus, tandem sui iuris et arbitrii [...] Quid itaque eius desiderio maceror, qui aut beatus aut nullus est? Beatum deflere inuidia est, nullum dementia"*]. See *Letters to Lucilius*, Letter XXIV, 18 (vol. 1, p. 177) and Letter LXXXII (vol. 2, pp. 241–59). "Would you not think him an utter fool who wept because he was not alive a thousand years ago? And is he not just as much a fool who weeps because he will not be alive a thousand years from now?", *ibid.*, Letter LXXVII, 11 (vol. 2, p. 175) [*"Nonne tibi videtur stultissimus omnium, qui flevit, quod ante annos mille non vixerat? aeque stultus est, qui flet, quod post annos mille non vivet*].

which it is harmful".[25] Therefore death is nothing with respect to the dead person; it is indifferent to him; it is neutral.

3.4. Cicero

In the *Tusculan Disputations*, Cicero asks whether death can be considered to be an evil. In his discussion we read arguments that are virtually identical to those already cited maintaining that death is an evil because it deprives the subjects of the goods of life. We find also the same type of counterarguments emphasizing the need for a subject: in order for a state of affairs "A" to be considered as an evil for "N.", he must be present at the moment when "A" occurs. "For they must exist if they *are* wretched: but just now you said that the dead did not exist. Now if they do not exist they cannot be anything. Therefore they cannot be wretched either".[26] His interlocutor launches a counterattack – in much the same manner as Axiochus and some analytical philosophers – by declaring that the evil of death is due to the privation of goods and of life itself, "the light of day"; it is due to "the mere fact of not existing, when one has existed"[27] and enjoyed life. The evil of death consists of "the departure from all those things that are good in life".[28] Crassus is unhappy because by dying he left behind great wealth, and Pompey is, too, because death stripped him of his glory. If that is the case, one should also admit that the fact of not having been conceived, or of not having existed at all, can be an evil for "N.", be he real or hypothetical, because he would be deprived of more numerous goods or simply of the goods of life.[29] We find again here the argument

[25] Seneca, *Letters to Lucilius*, Letter XXXVI, 9 (vol. 1, p. 251) [*"Mors nullum habet incommodum; esse enim debet aliquid cuius sit incommodum"*]. Seneca, however, does not situate his argument on the level of the subject, to determine whether the state of death is an evil or a good for the dead person, but rather on the ethical plane, by declaring that virtuous or vicious acts confer upon death its good or bad value. "Life is neither a good nor an evil; it is simply the place where good and evil exist", *ibid.*, Letter XVIX (vol. 3, p. 137) [*"Vita nec bonum nec malum est: boni ac mali locus est"*].

[26] Marcus Tullius Cicero, *Tusculan Disputations*, book I, vi, 12 (p. 17): *"Sint enim oportet, si miseri sunt; tu autem modo negabas eos esse qui mortui essent. Si igitur non sunt, nihil possunt esse; ita ne miseri quidem sunt"*. See *ibid.*, I, xxxviii, 91 (p. 109), and *De finibus*, book II, xxxi, 100 (pp. 191, 193).

[27] Marcus Tullius Cicero, *Tusculan Disputations*, book I, vi, 12 (pp. 15 f.): *"luce"*; *"Nam istuc ipsum, non esse, cum fueris, miserrimum puto"*.

[28] *Ibid.*, book I, xxxiv, 83 (p. 97): *"discessus ab omnibus iis quae sunt bona in vita"*.

[29] *Ibid.*, book I, vi, 13 (p. 17): "What? more wretched than never to have existed at all? It follows that those who are not yet born are wretched now, because they do not

proposed by Lucretius about the symmetry between death and preconception, a symmetry that has been widely discussed by analytical philosophers, as we shall see.

Cicero likewise refers to another argument by proposing several examples, for instance, Pompey: if he had died as a result of a serious illness in Naples, death would not have deprived him of goods, but of the evils that assailed him or threatened him once he recovered from the illness;[30] and even if his life had been filled with goods after his illness, how can anyone maintain that his death deprived him of a pleasant situation, implying "that the dead feel the need of the comforts of life, and that this is a condition of wretchedness?"[31] In order to maintain that death is an evil for someone, one must solve the problem, How "is it possible for the man who does not exist to 'feel the need' of anything?"[32] Since he assumes the mortality of the soul [materialism] and the need for feeling, for experience in order to be able to speak about a lack [experientialism], Cicero concludes that the dead person is deprived of neither the goods nor the evils of life.[33]

One might reply that the evil of death consists precisely of "the mere absence of sensation",[34] and this would certainly be correct, if being deprived of sensation meant a complete lack of feeling. But since the subject himself no longer exists once he is dead, how can one imagine him confronting an evil when there is no substrate to "suffer" from that evil, to sense a lack or a privation?

exist, and that we, if we are to be wretched after death, have been wretched before we were born. My recollections previous to my birth do not report me wretched" [*"Quid? miserius quam omnino numquam fuisse? Ita qui nondum nati sunt miseri iam sunt, quia non sunt, et nos, si post mortem miseri futuri sumus, miseri fuimus ante quam nati. Ego autem non commemini, ante quam sum natus, me miserum"*].

30 See *ibid.*, book I, xxxiv, 83 f. (pp. 97 f.).

31 *Ibid.*, book I, xxxvi, 87 (p. 103): "But let us go so far as to make the admission that mankind are deprived of blessings by death: must we therefore also grant that the dead feel the need of the comforts of life, and that this is a condition of wretchedness?" [*"Sed hoc ipsum concedatur, bonis rebus homines morte privari; ergo etiam carere vitae commodis, idque esse miserum?"*].

32 *Ibid.*: *"An potest is qui non est re ulla carere?"*

33 See *Ibid.*, book I, xxxvi, 88 (p. 105 f.): "But not even a living man 'feels the need of' a good, if he does not want it [...]. 'to feel the need of' is appropriate to a sentient being, and in a dead man there is no sensation: in a dead man therefore there is no possibility either of 'feeling the need of'" [*"Sed ne vivus quidem bono caret, si eo non indiget [...]. Carere enim sentientis est, nec sensus in mortuo; ne carere quidem igitur in mortuo est"*]. And a bit further on (xxxvii, 89 (p. 107)): "No one can be wretched when sensation has entirely gone" [*"Nec enim potest esse miser quisquam sensu perempto"*].

34 *Ibid.*, book I, xxxvii, 90 (p. 107): *"sine sensu esse"*.

Cicero raises another point in the discussion, which we find again in the writings of the analytical philosophers: is it a greater evil to die young than with a surfeit of years and of worldly goods, fulfilled by the realization of one's potential and one's plans? Such "old wives' fables"[35] are based on the premise that the enjoyment of more goods and the realization of more potential and beneficial plans are better than the enjoyment of fewer goods and the realization of less potential and fewer beneficial plans. It is better to have some part of life's goods than no part at all.

3.5. Plutarch

Like Cicero, Plutarch refers several times to Epicurus while raising a series of objections that we find again in the writings of some analytical philosophers. In his *Letter of Condolence to Apollonios*,[36] he keeps trying to demonstrate in various ways that death is not an evil. One sort of argument that he proposes is based on a combination of the positions of Epicurus and Lucretius. Since death is the complete and irreversible separation of soul and body, it implies the absence of all sensation. No good and no evil, no pleasure and no pain, is capable of affecting the dead person, because pleasure and pain can exist in the first place only if there is a substrate, thus a living subject (need for a subject). The dead person "finds himself" in a state comparable to the state of preconception, when for "N." – who did not exist – there was neither pleasure nor pain, no good and no evil. Just as the events preceding his conception did not concern him, so too those that will take place after his death will be of no importance to him either.

At first glance one might think that Plutarch is advocating here the Epicurean thesis of the "nothingness of death", but this impression is quickly dispelled when the passage in question is reread in context. Indeed, Plutarch means to argue that death, far from being an evil, is a good, even in the case of a premature death, which is the subject of the present consoling letter to Apollonios, whose son died at a young age.

Plutarch refers to Epicurus while he is elaborating the third of the working hypotheses proposed by Socrates in the *Apology*.[37] According

[35] *Ibid.*, book I, xxxix, 93 (p. 111): *"Pellantur ergo istae ineptiae paene aniles ante tempus mori miserum esse".*

[36] See Lucius Mestrius Plutarch, *A Letter of Condolence to Apollonios*, 15, 109E ff. (pp. 149 ff.).

[37] See Plato, *Socrates' Defense*, 40c-41b (p. 25).

to Socrates, death resembles (a) sleep or (b) a long journey to a far-off place; more specifically it can be defined as (c) an annihilation of body and soul. Although the three images help him to explain why death is not an evil, Plutarch nonetheless does not state that death is indifferent to the dead person. He argues, in effect, on two different and apparently contradictory levels: on the one hand, death is a good, because it delivers the subject from the additional evils that life would have had in store for him if he had continued to live (and this is particularly true in the case of a premature death by which the subject "is spared many evils"[38] and that delivers him "from greater ills"[39]); on the other hand, death is an evil, because it is – contrary to the Epicurean view – a loss,[40] all the more so if the life in question was a happy one.

Well before Nagel advocated the position and a whole series of analytical philosophers followed him, Plutarch proposed the thesis that death is an evil, not so much because of the insensible state in which the dead person "finds himself" – as we saw a moment ago in the lines penned by Cicero – but because it deprives him of his existence, of his life and hence of "present felicity".[41] Plutarch no longer considers here the goods *yet to come* (or the evils to come, respectively), but rather the goods that the subject possesses at the moment of his decease. Death is assuredly an evil for someone who has a fortune and is well off, who leads a happy life, because in his eyes it signifies "a most appalling issue [outcome], a point at which their present felicity will end".[42]

Besides this reference to the privation of goods (such as wealth, power, friendship, virtue) to demonstrate in what respects death is an evil, Plutarch emphasizes (as several contemporary philosophers would later propose)[43] that it consists of "the threat of non-being, which allows those once dead no return to being"[44] and in "the dissolution of the soul into what has neither thought nor feeling".[45] Plutarch seems to maintain

38 Lucius Mestrius Plutarch, *A Letter of Condolence to Apollonios*, 34, 119F (p. 201).

39 *Ibid.*, 16, 110E (p. 155). See *ibid.*, 28, 115E ff. (pp. 179 f.); 31, 117E ff. (pp. 189 f.).

40 Lucius Mestrius Plutarch, *That Epicurus Actually Makes a Pleasant Life Impossible*, 29, 1106C (p. 145): "losing good things". Concerning the theme of this work, see Klaus-Dieter Zacher, *Plutarchs Kritik an der Lustlehre Epikurs*.

41 Lucius Mestrius Plutarch, *That Epicurus Actually Makes a Pleasant Life Impossible*, 30, 1106E (p. 145).

42 *Ibid.* (pp. 145 f.).

43 See for example Frances M. Kamm, *Morality, Mortality*, pp. 19 f.; Jules Vuillemin, *Essai sur la signification de la mort*, p. 45.

44 Lucius Mestrius Plutarch, *That Epicurus Actually Makes a Pleasant Life Impossible*, 30, 1106F (p. 147).

45 *Ibid.*, 27, 1105A (pp. 135 f.).

that every death – whether the untimely ("accidental") death of a young man or the "timely" ("natural") death of an old man – is always an evil in itself for the subject, because it deprives him of his existence and constitutes the "[total] privation of life",[46] even if that life is filled with evils.[47] Every human being, regardless of his state in life, fears his nonbeing, that is, the definitive loss of his person. This is just as true for those who have possessions and enjoy a good life as it is for those whose life is filled with evils; the difference between these two categories of persons lies in the degree of privation. The happy subject is deprived of his life and furthermore of the goods and pleasures that he enjoyed, whereas the one whose existence is filled with evils will be deprived "only" of his life.

Following Cicero, Plutarch also replies to the Epicurean objection (the need for a subject who would undergo the evil of death) in terms similar to those of certain analytical philosophers such as Feinberg and Pitcher.[48] Certainly, someone who is dead cannot be subject to the evil of death, because he is deprived of sensations and experiences: "Lack of sensation is no hardship to those who when the time comes no longer are". The evil of death, however, affects "those that are, when they think of the damage they shall sustain by it in the loss of their beings".[49] In the

[46] *Ibid.* (p. 137).

[47] "If then relief from expecting infinite woe is highly pleasant, how can it not be painful to be deprived of hope of everlasting weal and to lose a felicity beyond compare? For not to be is a boon to neither class of men: it is unnatural and inimical to everything that is" (*ibid.*, 30, 1106D (p. 145)). The continuation of the passage seems to refute what Lucius Mestrius Plutarch has just affirmed: it says that insofar as the living person is surrounded by evils, death can be considered as a good, since it delivers him from those evils.

[48] See Joel Feinberg, *Harm to Others*; George Pitcher, "The Misfortunes of the Dead".

[49] Lucius Mestrius Plutarch, *That Epicurus Actually Makes a Pleasant Life Impossible*, 30, 1106E (p. 147). (The second part of the quotation is cited here from *Plutarch's Morals*, vol. 2, p. 202, which is much closer to the French version cited by Schumacher.) We find a similar critique written by Bayle ("Lucrèce", pp. 827 f.): "Epicurus and Lucretius suppose [...] that man fears death only because he imagines that it is followed by a great positive unhappiness. They are wrong, and they offer no remedy to those who regard the simple loss of life as a great evil. Love of life is so firmly rooted in the heart of man that this indicates that life is considered a very great good; hence it follows that, for the sole reason that death takes away this good, it is feared as a very great evil. What good is it to say against this fear, '*you will not feel anything after your death*'? Won't you immediately hear the reply, '*It is quite enough for me to be deprived of the life that I love so much; and if the union of my body and my soul is a state that belongs to me and that I ardently wish to preserve, you cannot claim that my death, which destroys that union, is something that does not concern me.*' Let us conclude that the argument of Epicurus and Lucretius was not well framed and that it can be useful only against the fear of pains in the next world. There is another sort of fear that they ought to fight against: the fear of the privation of the pleasures of this life" [*"Epicure et Lucrèce supposent [...] que*

final analysis, this evil is due, in Plutarch's opinion, to the fact that "not to be [...] is unnatural and inimical to everything that is".[50]

The dissolution into nothingness of a subject that has had a taste of life, pleasures, and goods (without, of course, denying the sorrows and evils) seems worse than the horrible Epicurean descriptions of Hades. Plutarch rebukes the philosopher of the Garden, and his follower Lucretius as well, for not having taken into consideration the fear of Hades and omitting from his speculation other sorts of fear of death, which Cicero had enumerated in his treatise *De finibus*:[51] the fear of no longer being, of no longer existing; the fear of losing one's "self", of the disappearance of the subject; the fear, for someone who is happy, of being deprived of the goods that he enjoys.

3.6. Augustine

We find certain features of the Epicurean argument in the writings of Augustine, who shifts the focus of the discussion from the state of death to decease, which he calls "being-in-death".[52] After arguing in

l'homme ne craint la mort que parce qu'il se figure qu'elle est suivie d'un grand malheur positif. Ils se trompent, et ils n'apportent aucun remède à ceux qui regardent comme un grand mal la simple perte de vie. L'amour de la vie est tellement enraciné dans le cœur de l'homme, que c'est un signe qu'elle est considérée comme un très grand bien; d'où il s'ensuit que de cela seul que la mort enlève ce bien, elle est redoutée comme un très grand mal. A quoi sert de dire contre cette crainte: vous ne sentirez rien après votre mort? *Ne vous répondra-t-on pas aussitôt,* c'est bien assez que je sois privé de la vie que j'aime tant; et si l'union de mon corps et de mon âme est un état qui m'appartient, et que je souhaite ardemment conserver, vous ne pouvez pas prétendre que la mort qui rompt cette union est une chose qui ne me regarde pas. *Concluons que l'argument d'Epicure et de Lucrèce n'était pas bien arrangé, et qu'il ne pouvait servir que contre la peur des peines de l'autre monde. Il y a une autre sorte de peur qu'ils devaient combattre; c'est celle de la privation des douceurs de cette vie"*].

50 Lucius Mestrius Plutarch, *That Epicurus Actually Makes a Pleasant Life Impossible*, 30, 1106D (p. 145). "No doubt it is wrong to contemplate with such horror the dissolution of nature [...]. But the fact that almost everyone is subject to this impression is sufficient proof that nature has a horror of annihilation" (Marcus Tullius Cicero, *De finibus*, book V, xi, 31 (pp. 425, 427)) [*"Etsi hoc quidem est in vitio, dissolutionem naturae tam valde perhorrescere [...], sed quia fere sic afficiuntur omnes, satis argumenti est ab interitu naturam abhorrere"*].

51 See Marcus Tullius Cicero, *De finibus*, book V, xi, 31 (pp. 425, 427). Concerning Titus Lucretius, see Charles Segal, *Lucretius on Death and Anxiety*, pp. 12 f.

52 Augustine, *The City of God*, XIII, xi, I (pp. 312 f.). He describes decease as being *"in morte"*, which is distinguished from the state of being alive, that is, before dying in the first sense of the word, and from the state of being dead, which is to say, after death occurs. Augustine attempts to determine "when can we ever say that a man is dead [i.e., 'in death'] except while he is dying [i.e., passing away]?" (XIII, x, (p. 311)); *"quando, nisi cum detrahitur, erit in morte?"*

favor of a personal afterlife in the state of death, he asks whether it is possible for the subject to be, and thus to experience, once he has died. Transposing the mutual exclusion of the states of life and death, as formulated by Epicurus, to the states of life and decease, he asks in *The City of God*, "just when, then, is a man 'in death'?"[53] How is it possible, given this mutual exclusion, to consider decease to be an evil? Should we not instead, like Epicurus (although he situates his discussion on another level), understand it as something indifferent? "Being-in-death" seems to be neither an evil nor a good, considering that there is no underlying subject who could sense that state of decease. It is evident that this state resembles the Epicurean state of death, in which the subject is deprived of all sensations.[54]

4. MODERN THINKERS: MONTAIGNE, FEUERBACH, SCHOPENHAUER, AND OTHERS

The thesis of the philosopher of the Garden is found also in the writings of Montaigne. Death "does not concern you dead or alive: alive, because you are; dead, because you are no more".[55] For the French essayist, death is not an evil; nor is it the privation of life.[56] He takes issue with the idea that life has a value in itself, emphasizing that "life is neither good nor evil in itself".[57] He repeats the "mirror image" argument of Lucretius and reasons as follows: since we do not worry about the fact that we did not exist before our conception, we shouldn't worry either about our future death.[58]

The French thinker is joined by Feuerbach, who likewise repeats the Epicurean declaration that the states of life and death are mutually exclusive. He uses it to develop his thesis that death is a mere appearance, which is to say that it has reality only insofar as it is a comparison and a relation. The effective end of a subject, and therefore his death, does not exist for him, strictly speaking; rather, it has reality only for the survivor. "Death is death and painful only before death, but not in death; thus death is a spectral being that is only when it is not, and is

[53] Augustine, *The City of God*, XIII, ix (p. 310): *"quando sit in morte?"*
[54] See *ibid.*, XIII, ix (pp. 309).
[55] Michel de Montaigne, *The Complete Essays*, book I, chap. xx, p. 66 [p. 108: *"ne vous concerne ni mort ni vif: vif, parce que vous êtes; mort, parce que vous n'êtes plus"*].
[56] See *ibid.*, I, xx, p. 61 [p. 99].
[57] *Ibid.*, I, xx, p. 65 [p. 106: *"la vie n'est de soi ni bien ni mal"*].
[58] See *ibid.*, I, xx, p. 65 [p. 105].

not when it is [...]. The end or non-being of the individual, then, has no reality for the individual himself, because it is not for that self; only something that is the object of his feeling, of his consciousness has reality for the individual. The individual ceases to be only for others, not for himself".[59]

Schopenhauer, for his part, repeats almost word for word the mirror image of Lucretius. I will discuss this in the chapter on the challenge to philosophy posed by the peaceful state of preconception. Anyone who declares that death is an evil, because it deprives the subject of the goods of life and of his being, ought to maintain that the state preceding conception is an evil and something to be feared, but that is not the case. "For the eternity *a parte post* [after my life] without me can be just as little fearful as the eternity *a parte ante* [before my life] without me, since the two are distinguished by nothing except the interposition of an ephemeral dream of life [...], it is in and for itself absurd to look upon not being as an evil; for every evil, as every good, presupposes existence, nay, even consciousness [need for a subject], but the latter ceases with life".[60] Citing Epicurus explicitly, the German philosopher concludes that "to have lost what cannot be missed [experientialism] is clearly no evil. Therefore ceasing to be ought to disturb us as little as not having been. Accordingly, from the standpoint of knowledge there appears absolutely no reason to fear death. But consciousness consists in knowing; therefore, for consciousness, death is no evil".[61]

The thesis of the "nothingness of death" has been defended recently by several analytical philosophers, for example, Glannon,[62]

59 Ludwig Feuerbach, *Todesgedanken*, p. 84: *"Nur vor dem Tode, aber nicht im Tode ist der Tod Tod und schmerzlich; der Tod ist so ein gespenstisches Wesen, dass er nur ist, wenn er nicht ist, und nicht ist, wenn er ist. [...] Das Ende oder Nichtsein des Individuums also, da es nicht für dieses selbst ist, hat keine Realität für es selbst; denn für das Individuum hat nur das Realität, was Gegenstand seiner Empfindung, seines Bewusstseins ist. Das Individuum ist nicht mehr nur Anderen, nicht für sich selbst"*.

60 Arthur Schopenhauer, *The World as Will and Idea*, vol. 3, p. 254 f. [vol. 2, chapter 41, p. 596: *"Denn die Unendlichkeit 'a parte post' ohne mich kann sowenig schrecklich sein als die Unendlichkeit 'a parte ante' ohne mich; indem beide durch nichts sich unterscheiden als durch die Dazwischenkunft eines ephemeren Lebenstraums [...] ist es an und für sich absurd, das Nichtsein für ein Übel zu halten; da jedes Übel wie jedes Gut das Dasein zur Voraussetzung hat, ja sogar das Bewusstsein; dieses aber mit dem Leben aufhört"*].

61 *Ibid.*, vol. 3, p. 254 [vol. 2, p. 597: *"Verloren zu haben, was nicht vermisst werden kann, ist offenbar kein Übel: also darf das Nicht-Sein-Werden uns so wenig aufrechten wie das Nicht-Gewesen-Sein. Vom Standpunkt der Erkenntnis aus erscheint demnach durchaus kein Grund, den Tod zu fürchten: im Erkennen aber besteht das Bewusstsein; daher für dieses der Tod kein Übel ist"*].

62 See Walter Glannon, "Temporal Asymmetry, Life, and Death".

Green,[63] Rosenberg,[64] Rosenbaum,[65] Suits,[66] and Soll,[67] whose arguments I will discuss in the next chapter. As we shall see, many other philosophers implicitly or explicitly refer to it for the sole purpose of refuting it. In this regard we might mention Feinberg, Feldman, Fischer, Nagel, Perrett, Williams, and others.

63 See O. H. Green, "Fear of Death".
64 See Jay F. Rosenberg, *Thinking Clearly about Death*, pp. 189 f.
65 See Stephen E. Rosenbaum, "How to Be Dead and Not Care: A Defense of Epicurus", "The Harm of Killing: An Epicurean Perspective", and "Epicurus and Annihilation".
66 See David Suits, "Why Death Is Not Bad for the One Who Died".
67 See Ivan Soll, "On the Purported Insignificance of Death".

9

Discussion of Experientialism and the Need for a Subject

1. THE *A PRIORI* CHARACTER OF THE EPICUREAN ASSERTION THAT DEATH IS NOTHING TO US

The Epicurean thesis of the "nothingness of death" has not always met with great interest among philosophers. Many of them consider it as "preposterous and stupid", "the most absurd thing",[1] a "vacuity",[2] "fine sayings," and "nonsense devised for the young [i.e., babblings]",[3] a "jest",[4] "extremely implausible," and "an ancient sophism that purports to justify indifference to death".[5] According to Mothersill, the Greek philosopher's point of view on the subject of death "will hardly bear looking into, but may have been intended as little more than an eristic flourish".[6] Such a rejection of the Epicurean "nothingness of death", which is dismissed out of hand by describing it as a sophism, shows, in my opinion, that the gauntlet thrown down by the philosopher of the Garden is not taken seriously: this important challenge is opposed to the commonsense notion that death is an evil, perhaps even the worst of evils. Surprisingly, terms similar to those cited (against the Epicurean thesis) are sometimes used to describe the thesis that death is an evil.

1 Steven Luper, "Annihilation", p. 270.
2 Richard Rorty, "The Contingency of Selfhood", p. 11.
3 Plato-pseudo, *Axiochus*, 369d-e (p. 43).
4 Søren Kierkegaard, "At a Graveside", p. 73.
5 Mary Mothersill, "Death", p. 88. See Paul-Louis Landsberg, *The Experience of Death*, pp. 39 f. [pp. 68 f.]; Eberhardt Jüngel, *Der Tod*, p. 18; Josef Pieper, *Death and Immortality*, p. 20 [p. 301]; Fridolin Wiplinger, *Der personal verstandene Tod*, p. 26.
6 Mary Mothersill, "Death", p. 88.

This thesis betrays insufficient reflection,[7] in Rosenberg's opinion, or "naïveté", according to Fagot-Largeault;[8] Rosenbaum calls it a "myth".[9] Is it really without any rational basis whatsoever? Are we dealing with the transformation of a peculiar psychological phenomenon into a disputed theoretical point, as Mothersill asserts?[10] Should we not rather maintain, like Feldman, that "there is nothing incoherent about the naïve view that death can be an evil for the deceased"?[11]

The Epicurean thesis of the "nothingness of death" implies basic assumptions, explained in the preceding chapter, that are worth examining critically. An initial premise – that of *experientialism* – states that every evil and every good lies in sensation, in other words, in the experience of pleasure (in the case of good) or of pain (in the case of evil). In order for a state of affairs to be described as a good or an evil for a subject, he must be capable of experiencing it (of being the subject of pleasures or pains), which presupposes parameters in time and space. A state of affairs that remained detached from experience – such as death – would be indifferent. A second premise – *the need for a subject* – states

[7] "It is typically held, I suppose, without much reflection on the matter, that death is a bad thing, an evil", Jay F. Rosenberg, *Thinking Clearly about Death*, p. 189; see *ibid.*, p. 197.

[8] "It is astonishing, nevertheless: the naïveté with which some authors in the utilitarian tradition (who are probably rich and in good health rather than poor and sick) accept as self-evident that life is a good, that more life is better, and that death is an evil, if not the greatest of evils (Nagel, 1979; Kohl, 1992)" [*"On s'étonne néanmoins de la naïveté avec laquelle quelques auteurs appartenant à la tradition utilitariste (probablement riches et en bonne santé plutôt que pauvres et malades) admettent comme une évidence que la vie est un bien, que plus de vie c'est mieux; et que la mort est un mal, sinon le plus grand des maux (Nagel, 1979; Kohl, 1992)"*], Anne Fagot-Largeault, "Vie et mort", p. 1585. It seems to me that the author has not read closely the texts concerning the debate over "the evil of death" within the context of analytical philosophy; furthermore, she cites scarcely any arguments for positions contrary to her own.

[9] Stephen E. Rosenbaum, "How to Be Dead and Not Care: A Defense of Epicurus", p. 134. He presents excellent, well-founded counterarguments.

[10] "What I think has happened is that Nagel has tried to transform a peculiar and interesting psychological phenomenon into a disputed point of theory", Mary Mothersill, "Death", p. 86. To the question of "whether it is a bad thing to die" there can be, in his opinion, no "interesting general answer". "[It] makes me doubt that Nagel's question could ever have any interesting general answer. Indeed, for us who believe that the death of others is sometimes good, sometimes bad, and anyway inevitable while at the same time believing that our own death, no matter what the circumstances, would be an unthinkable, unparallelled disaster, there can be no general *question* 'whether it is a bad thing to die'", *ibid.*, p. 87.

[11] Fred Feldman, *Confrontations with the Reaper*, p. 156. See also Thomas Nagel, "Death", pp. 1 f.; Roy W. Perrett, *Death and Immortality*, pp. 46 f.

that the death of "N." cannot constitute an evil for him, because he no longer exists. Indeed, in order for a state of affairs "A" to be described as an evil for "N.", the "existential" presence of the latter is required. This thesis is equivalent to the third point that I emphasized in the preceding chapter, within the framework of my analysis of the Epicurean "nothingness of death": "N." would not be capable of experiencing a state of affairs "A" in T-1 and P-1 unless "A" took place during the life of "N.", and therefore before "his" death. In other words, "N." cannot be affected by "A" after he has died, given that he no longer is; he can be affected only insofar as he is alive. Hence death cannot be an evil for the dead "N.", since when the death of "N." is present, "N." is no more. Lucretius could not be more explicit on this subject: "For if by chance anyone is to have misery and pain in the future, he must needs himself also exist then in that time to be miserable. Since death takes away this possibility and forbids him to exist for whom these inconveniences may be gathered together, we may be sure that there is nothing to be feared after death, that he who is not cannot be miserable".[12] In his defense of the Epicurean thesis of the "nothingness of death" and his critique of the possibility of posthumous evils, Rosenbaum adopts this second principle: "It is impossible for a loss to be bad for a person at a time when that person is dead. This is because nothing can be bad for a person unless it can have some effect on the person, and nothing can have some effect on a person unless the person is not dead. Thus, if harms are losses which are bad, then posthumous harms are not possible".[13] Epicurus raises an axiological question by asking whether death is an evil and, more particularly, whether it is an evil for the one who is dead. It is not a question of determining whether death is an evil for the survivors – especially for those who loved the deceased – but whether is an evil for the subject himself, not when he is still living (i.e., dying),

[12] Titus Lucretius, *De rerum natura*, III, 862–8 (pp. 229, 231): *"Debet enim, misere si forte aegreque futurumst, ipse quoque esse in eo tum tempore, cui male possit accidere. Id quoniam mors eximit, esseque prohibet illum cui possint incommoda conciliari, scire licet nobis nil esse in morte timendum, nec miserum fieri qui non est posse"*.

[13] Stephen E. Rosenbaum, "The Harm of Killing: An Epicurean Perspective", p. 221. Several pages earlier, he remarks that "for there to be posthumous harm on a harm-as-interest-invasion theory, it must be true not that a person's interests survive her death (in Feinberg's sense), but that a person's *having* her interests survives her death. One's interests may survive one's death in some sense, but one's having those interests cannot", *ibid.*, p. 217. See also "How to Be Dead and Not Care: A Defense of Epicurus", p. 125; Walter Glannon, "Temporal Asymmetry, Life, and Death", pp. 237–9; Jeff McMahan, "Death and the Value of Life", pp. 234 f., 240 f.; Mary Mothersill, "Death", p. 86; Richard W. Momeyer, *Confronting Death*, p. 19.

but from the moment when he is deceased, when he "finds himself" in the state of death. The question becomes even more interesting for the philosopher, from the methodological perspective, if we take the same point of departure as Epicurus and equate *a priori* death (the state of death, that is) with the state of nonsurvival.

Certainly, one could reject the Epicurean thesis of the "nothingness of death" by assuming, on a reasonable basis, that the individual survives.[14] Thus one would maintain that the survivor – despite the impossibility of feedback – manages to judge whether his state is an evil or a good. As I have already emphasized,[15] the philosopher nevertheless cannot, for lack of scientific foundation, rely on alleged experiences of death or on visions of dead subjects who have appeared to survivors, which are said to provide a response to the question of whether death is an evil or a good for the dead person. For my part I prefer to assume, by way of a methodological hypothesis – and not as something "proven" – the nonexistence of the deceased, so as to situate myself at the same point of departure as Epicurus.[16] In doing so, I am nevertheless not endorsing the postmetaphysical thanatology propounded by Schulz, Fuchs, and Ebeling,[17] for example, who characterize the question of an eventual personal afterlife as meaningless for a post-Heideggerian philosophy.

2. FIRST SERIES OF EXAMPLES AGAINST EXPERIENTIALISM: COMPARISONS BETWEEN TWO STATES OF LIFE

As an initial attempt to illustrate the weakness of Epicurean experientialism, we present a series of examples in order to demonstrate that

[14] On this topic see Bernard N. Schumacher, "Philosophische Interpretationen der Endlichkeit des Menschen".

[15] See Part Two, Chapter 7.

[16] A definition of death as "state of death" does not logically imply the nonbeing of its subject, as certain philosophers would maintain when they declare that for death really to be death, it must imply the denial of any sort of personal afterlife. See for example Leonard W. Sumner, "A Matter of Life and Death", pp. 153 f.; Peter C. Dalton, "Death and Evil", p. 202. Feinberg indirectly supports such a thesis (*Harm to Others*, p. 79): "but death (real total death of the person, not the mere 'apparent death' of theological teachings) is the cessation of one's existence, the first moment of a state of nonbeing". Some philosophers try to prove that death is total: see Jay F. Rosenberg, *Thinking Clearly about Death*, who devotes a large part of his book to the question of an eventual afterlife, and Fred Feldman, *Confrontations with the Reaper*, who argues for an immortality after decease that lasts as long as the body does not decompose.

[17] I presented their position in the Introduction.

certain events can be described as evils although the subject has no experience of them at a given place and time (P-1 and T-1) and even though they are not unpleasant to him. Let us take the case of "N." – Ms. or Mr. Everyman – who has had a serious accident at P-1 and T-1. As a result of massive injuries, he irreversibly loses his higher brain functions and remembers neither the accident nor his life before the accident. According to the doctors, he will never be able to recover, and his mental state is comparable to that of a little child. We can imagine that this person is completely happy, since all his desires are satisfied. Although he does not experience what has happened to him – namely, the loss of his higher brain functions – it is nevertheless commonly assumed that an evil has "befallen" him. The subject of the evil is not "N." in an infantile state, but rather "N." before the terrible accident. The state of the former is characterized as an evil in relation to another state, that of "N." before the accident, or the state of "N." if the accident had not taken place. The brutal interruption of his natural adult development, of the plans and the realization of the hopes connected with his higher mental faculties, is readily understood to be an evil. We can take as our second example the case of a subject who suddenly falls into a coma. Although he is incapable of sensations, and therefore of bad experiences, his state is nevertheless commonly considered to be an evil. A third illustration would be the case of a subject whose partner has been unfaithful or who has been betrayed, mocked, despised, and disdained by his family, friends, and acquaintances; or else a subject whose reputation has been destroyed by slander, without his being aware of it.[18] It has also been remarked that an individual exposed to a heavy dose of radioactivity has suffered harm, an evil, without experiencing it (consciously).

This first series of examples reveals that one can describe as an evil the state in which a particular subject finds himself, independent of his experience thereof. The evil in question is on the order of privation. The privation is evident when we compare two states of things occurring *within* the life of a subject: on the one hand, the state of the infantile

[18] See Thomas Nagel, "Death", pp. 5–7; James Rachels, *The End of Life*, pp. 46–7; Joel Feinberg, *Harm to Others*, p. 87. Intending to make plausible the thesis that evil can be done to a dead person, Feinberg tries to show that some interests of human beings can be violated without their realizing it. See also Robert Nozick, "On the Randian Argument", pp. 220 f. The latter's approach begins with a comparison between two states of a subject's life. His primary intention is not to show that death is an evil for the dead "N." but rather to denounce an experiential ethic in which the moral evaluation of actions is determined solely by the manner in which they really or intentionally touch and affect persons.

"N.", the comatose "N.", the betrayed and despised "N.", the "N." whose personal life has been made public, or the "N." who has been exposed to radioactivity; and, on the other hand, the state of "N." before his accident, of "N." before the coma, of the "N." who is respected, of the "N." whose personal affairs remain private, or of "N." who has not been exposed to radioactivity. In these examples, the evil is not due to the experience of a pain, but to the privation of goods, possibilities, and hopes that the subject would have been able to possess, realize, and enjoy if he had not been thrown into another state, for example, infantile or comatose. From this finding some have deduced, by analogy – by comparing the two states of life and death – that the evil of death for the dead "N." lies in the privation of the goods, possibilities, and hopes that he would have been able to possess or realize and that he would have been able to enjoy if he had continued to live.[19]

I do not think, however, that this first series of arguments is sufficiently convincing to demonstrate that the death of "N." is an evil for "N." Indeed, all the examples of this series are located within a dialectic of life, which is to say that they compare two states in the life of "N." They remain at the level of present experience (presenteity), of a state of affairs "A", and they overlook the category of possibility: there is still the possibility that the ignominious, infantile, or comatose state in which the living "N." happens to be after a certain event might not be definitive and that "N." could, in a more or less near future, experience the evil that has happened to him. Indeed, it seems to me that Epicurus would have little difficulty in accepting the thesis that underlies this initial series of examples, namely, that what "N." does not experience now can be perceived by him, in a more or less distant future, as an evil. The philosopher of the Garden would reject, however, a thesis that maintains that those states of affairs that "N." cannot experience either now or in the future – which is precisely the case with death – could be considered as evils for "N." A second series of examples, comparing

[19] "If he had not died, he would have continued to live it [his life], and to possess whatever good there is in living" (Thomas Nagel, "Death", p. 7). In his response to experientialism, Nagel presents death as "an abrupt cancellation of indefinitely extensive possible goods" (p. 10), as an evil of privation. He adds, however – as we will see later when we examine what that privation consists of – that the ultimate reason for the evil of death consists in no longer being able to live as a subject, i.e., the disappearance of the "ego", the subject of possibilities, experiences, and hopes. We might add, following Sartre, that this evil lies in the very impossibility of giving an ultimate meaning to my life and my actions, a meaning which, after my decease, will be subject to the good pleasure of the survivors.

the state of life with the state of death, is therefore required in order to respond to him.

3. SECOND SERIES OF EXAMPLES AGAINST EXPERIENTIALISM: COMPARISONS BETWEEN A STATE OF LIFE AND A STATE OF DEATH

Citing Nagel's example of an "N." who has (unwittingly) been despised and betrayed, Nozick considers "N." once he has died: in this (second) example, we find out what happened to him by reading a biography composed after his death. We find in it, on the one hand, a true account of his life with all the misfortunes that he did not experience and, on the other hand, the joy and the happiness that he claimed to have experienced throughout his life. Nonetheless the reader would not wish to lead such a life; everyone agrees in thinking that it was fraught with evils, even though "N." had never experienced them and declared quite honestly that he had led a happy life.[20] Another example, proposed by McMahan, concerns "N." who is spending his vacation on a desert island without any means of communication. Two days before the end of his stay, the masterpiece of his lifeswork is destroyed. Unable to reach him, his friends decide to wait for his return to announce the bad news to him. But the day before his departure, he is attacked by a shark while he is swimming and dies from the injuries. One could say that he dies "a happy man" in a certain sense, because he knows nothing about the destruction of his masterpiece. Despite his ignorance and nonexperience of the calamity, it is nevertheless generally admitted that an evil had befallen him.[21] We are confronted here with situations analogous to the state of death, in the sense that there is no future possibility of experiencing the evil: a state of affairs "A" is perceived as an evil happening to "N." without the latter's having experienced it during his life. There is certainty that he will never experience this evil – and thus the elimination of the "possibility" – only after his decease.

[20] See Robert Nozick, "On the Randian Argument", p. 221. We find an almost identical example in the writings of James Rachels, *The End of Life*, pp. 46–8.

[21] See Jeff McMahan, "Death and the Value of Life", p. 235. These examples seem to me more realistic and more convincing than the one proposed by John Martin Fischer: the case involves "N.", who is despised, and a Mr. White, whose mission is to see to it that "N." will never have the possibility of experiencing the evil that has befallen him (John Martin Fischer, "Death, Badness, and the Impossibility of Experience", p. 345).

This second series of examples still does not prove, however, that Epicurean experientialism is false; it simply calls attention to the commonsense thesis that one can reasonably maintain that an evil has befallen "N." even though he has not had – and may never have – any experience of it. By analogy, it would seem that death could be considered as an evil for "N." even though he does not experience that state (no longer being a subject). To demonstrate that death is an evil, it is indispensable, as we shall see, to refer to the specific characteristics of certain evils that are on the order of privation and that do not necessarily have to be experienced by the subject. Without dwelling further on the notion of the evil of death as the privation of something – I will return to this topic in the next chapter – I would like to call attention now to a third set of possible arguments against the Epicurean presupposition of experientialism: posthumous evils.

4. THIRD SET OF POSSIBLE ARGUMENTS AGAINST EXPERIENTIALISM: POSTHUMOUS EVILS

The plausible existence of posthumous evils was suggested by the Ancients in response to the question posed by Solon: can one say about a human being before his death that he is happy? Pointing out the fact that, as long as he is alive, a person is capable of being subject to many evils, Solon proposes that one can safely maintain that the person has been happy only after he has died. Nevertheless Aristotle is not convinced: in the first chapter of the *Nicomachaean Ethics*, he considers it debatable that the dead "N." is "beyond evils and misfortunes". "For both evil and good are thought to exist for a dead man, as much as for one who is alive but not aware of them, honours and dishonours and the good or bad fortunes of children and in general of descendants".[22] Aristotle, however, assigns little weight to his own proposition, because he considers happiness to be the activity of the *psyche* that is in keeping with human virtues. As a general rule, the vicissitudes in the life of a virtuous human being do not have much of an effect on him. Such a subject is motivated interiorly and not exteriorly. The philosopher is certainly not denying that the posthumous events described as evils have some effect on the individual's happiness, but these effects are, he hastens to

[22] Aristotle, *Nicomachean Ethics*, I, 10, 1100a14 f. Nagel ("Death", p. 4) also proposes two examples of posthumous evils (failure to respect the wishes and last will of the deceased; slander of a deceased author).

explain, "weak and negligible,"[23] so that ultimately they will have only a small impact on the happiness in which he finds himself.

This passage seems to contain a paradox: Aristotle appears to maintain simultaneously that the happiness of "N.", on the one hand, cannot be affected once he has ceased living, since happiness is an activity of the living *psyche*, and, on the other hand, that it can be affected, but in a "trifling" manner, as he puts it. One way of resolving this apparent dilemma would be to distinguish between two senses of *eudaimonia*, which Aristotle[24] does not differentiate in the passage in question. *Eudaimonia* can mean a function of the individual *psyche*, and thus everything that happens to me – with the exception of relational properties – must happen to me within the limited span of time between my conception and my death; the other meaning is what is achieved in my life as a whole, which can then be affected by relational properties that do not necessarily have to arise within the parameters of my life. This second way of speaking about *eudaimonia* is similar to Feinberg's attempt to argue for the existence of posthumous evils and to name the subject of them. In his book *Harm to Others*, in which he presents a considerably revised defense of his earlier positions,[25] Feinberg rejects the Epicurean thesis of experientialism by maintaining that an evil can befall the dead "N." insofar as the interests of the living "N." are affected by events occurring after his death: for example, failure to respect his wishes as expressed in his last will and testament, the posthumous breaking of a promise made to him or of a contract that had been entered into with him during his lifetime, the destruction of his artistic works, or the loss of his reputation.

Citing the close connection between interests and wants, our author, like Ross,[26] distinguishes between two categories of wants: the desire

[23] Aristotle, *Nicomachean Ethics*, I, 10, 1101b1 f. (p. 949): "Even if anything whether good or evil penetrates to them, it must be something weak and negligible, either in itself or for them, or if not, at least it must be such in degree and kind as not to make happy those who are not happy nor to take away their blessedness from those who are".

[24] See David Furley, "Nothing to Us?", p. 87. For another interpretation of this passage from Aristotle, see Kurt Pritzl, "Aristotle and Happiness after Death".

[25] See Joel Feinberg, "Harm and Self-Interest" and "The Rights of Animals and Unborn Generation(s)". For critiques of his positions, see Barbara Baum Levenbook, "Harming Someone after His Death" and "Harming the Dead, Once Again"; Don Marquis, "Harming the Dead"; Ernest Partridge, "Posthumous Interests and Posthumous Respect".

[26] See William D. Ross, *Foundations of Ethics*, p. 300. [Translator's note: In his French text, Schumacher translates the English noun "want" by *désir*.]

to accomplish and the desire for satisfaction. The accomplishment of a want requires that the object wanted by "N." be realized; the satisfaction of a want corresponds to the pleasant, agreeable experience that takes place in the mind of "N." when he thinks that the wanted object has been realized. If it is not realized, we can say that the want is followed by defeat. What harms someone's interest is the defeat that represents the nonaccomplishment of the want, and not "N.'s" frustration at the nonrealization of the wanted object. Hence death can be regarded, according to Feinberg, as the defeat of certain interests that "N." had during his lifetime, even though, as a dead subject, he is not capable of feeling the least pain.[27]

Still intent on pointing out the weaknesses of experientialism, Feinberg next remarks that the range of goods and evils for a human being is necessarily wider than his subjective experience and longer than his biological life. This is a result of the fact that the objects of his interests normally correspond to events that occur outside his immediate experience and in a future time. Examples of such interests would be the preservation of his artistic, musical, or literary works after his death; the victory of the social or political cause for which he fought during his lifetime; and so forth. Acknowledging with Epicurus that the dead person can be affected, from the perspective of sensation, neither by defamation nor by disdain, nor by the praise of a surviving-other, Feinberg nevertheless claims that defamation can be considered as an evil, because it harms the interests that were vital to "N." while he was alive. "None of these events will embarrass or distress me, since dead men can have no feelings; but all of them can harm my interests by forcing non-fulfillment of goals in which I had placed a great stake".[28] Death is an evil for "N.", because it prevents him from accomplishing the goals that he had set for himself.

5. THE SUBJECT OF POSTHUMOUS EVILS

After disqualifying the Epicurean presupposition of experientialism, Feinberg concentrates on the difficult problem of designating the subject

[27] "Harm to an interest is better defined in terms of the objective blocking of goals and thwarting of desires than in subjective terms [...]. The object of a focal aim that is the basis of an interest, then, like the object of any want, is not simply satisfaction or contentment, and the defeat of an interest is not to be identified with disappointment or frustration", Joel Feinberg, *Harm to Others*, p. 85.

[28] *Ibid.*, p. 87.

of his posthumous evils. He begins by stating that there can be no "harm without a subject to be harmed"[29] and that "the surviving interests [...] must be the interests of someone or other".[30] Our author rejects the possibility that there may be interests separate from the subject, for then these would be nobody's interests, or else those of the "social contract",[31] or of an absolute mind – a metaphysical assertion that does not seem very economical in his estimation. He admits, however, that the subject in question cannot be the dead person, since the latter no longer exists, strictly speaking. A dead person could not devise interests and project wants. Citing the distinction introduced by Pitcher[32] between the individual before his decease and the individual after his decease, he asserts that the subject of posthumous evils is none other than the human being who used to be alive, the person before his death: "I would like to suggest that we can think of some of a person's interests as surviving his death [...] and that in virtue of the defeat of these interests, either by death itself or by subsequent events, we can think of the person who was, as harmed".[33] "Posthumous harm occurs when one of the deceased's surviving interests is thwarted after his death. The subject of a surviving interest and of the harm or benefit that can accrue to it after a person's death is the living person *antemortem* whose interest it was".[34]

This solution to the problem of the subject, however, is not very convincing. Indeed, one can make a distinction, as Rosenbaum does, between the personal interests that survive death and a person's having interests that survive his death. His own interests can certainly continue to exist after his death; this is not the case with the self that has such interests.[35] To clarify his position, Rosenbaum proposes the example of

29 He continues: "and when death occurs it obliterates the subject, and thus excludes the possibility of harm", *Ibid.*, p. 80. "If the absence of a subject precludes our speaking of posthumous harms, then equally it precludes our speaking of death as a harm (a rather harder pill to swallow) since both death and posthumous events are postpersonal. Either death and posthumous events both alike can be harms or neither can", p. 82.

30 *Ibid.*, p. 89.

31 See Ernest Partridge, "Posthumous Interests and Posthumous Respect", pp. 255 f.

32 See George Pitcher, "The Misfortune of the Dead", pp. 161 f. This idea is adopted by Barbara Baum Levenbook ("Harming the Dead, Once Again", p. 162) in his response to Marquis, which appeared one year after Feinberg's second proposition: "the subject who is harmed is the living-person-who-was".

33 Joel Feinberg, *Harm to Others*, p. 83.

34 *Ibid.*, p. 93. See *ibid.*, p. 89.

35 See Stephen E. Rosenbaum, "The Harm of Killing: An Epicurean Perspective", p. 217. See also John Donnelly, "The Misfortunate Dead: A Problem for Materialism", p. 164.

"N." whose interest is to become a millionaire by T-1. If, for the interval from T-2 to T-5, this interest turns into an interest in becoming an artist, a law passed at T-2 forbidding citizens to become millionaires cannot therefore be considered as an evil for "N.": at the moment when the law goes into effect, "N." no longer has an interest in becoming a millionaire. The law can be considered as an evil only for someone who presently has such an interest.

This objection can also be understood as the refutation of a "retroactive" causality that stipulated, for example, that a state of affairs "A" occurring in "N.'s" future could change in some way the living conditions of "N." Hence there would be events after the death of "N." that would alter his life and his past. Both Feinberg and Pitcher take care to emphasize that their position does not imply a causality understood along the lines of physical causality. They argue, rather, from a nontemporal perspective, in which "the occurrence of the event makes it true that during the time before the person's death, he was harmed – harmed in that the unfortunate event was going to happen. If the event should not occur, the *antemortem* person would not have been so harmed. So the occurrence of the *postmortem* event is responsible for the *antemortem* harm".[36] Hence, if the world were completely destroyed by a nuclear catastrophe during the presidency of Obama's successor, it would still be true that the former today would be the next-to-last president of the United States.[37]

This solution is not far removed from that of Silverstein, who proposes as the "key to the resolution of the Epicurean dilemma" the introduction of a fourth dimension combining temporality with timeless eternity.[38] It is commonly accepted that there can be evils independent of the geographical presence (P) of "N."; given this fact, one could likewise agree that "N." could be affected by an evil independently of its existence at a particular moment in time (T). Silverstein denounces

[36] Joel Feinberg, *Harm to Others*, p. 168.

[37] See *ibid.*, p. 91: "An event occurs after Smith's death that causes something to happen at that time. So far, so good; no paradox. Now, in virtue of the thing that was caused to happen at that time it is true that Smith was in a harmed condition before he died. It does not suddenly 'become true' that the *ante-mortem* Smith was harmed. Rather it becomes apparent to us for the first time that it was true all along – that from the time Smith invested enough in his cause to make it one of his interests, he was playing a losing game".

[38] He introduces this dimension following Quine, whom he cites as the voice of authority. See Willard Van Orman Quine, "Physical Objects", a typewritten manuscript quoted in Harry S. Silverstein, "The Evil of Death", p. 111.

the preferential treatment granted to place when a state of affairs is being characterized as an "evil". A fourth dimension would allow us to consider posthumous events, "in Quine's words [...] 'as coexisting in an eternal or timeless sense of the word'".[39] On this basis, Silverstein concludes that the Epicurean challenge has been resolved: "[N.'s] death coexists with [N.] ('in an eternal or timeless sense of the word') and is therefore a possible object of [N.'s] suffering, and is therefore an intelligible [N.]-relative evil".[40] This solution seems to solve the problem of the need for a subject, but at "excessive metaphysical cost",[41] as Yourgrau has underscored.

A third attempt to describe the subject with relation to the evil of death is found in Perrett,[42] who remarks, as Feinberg and Pitcher also have done, that the need for a subject does not necessarily imply that he be alive; a logical subject would be sufficient. Such a "logical person" exists, for example, in the memory of the family or of the friends of the deceased, as well as in the memory of the community or of humanity. Thus, despite the disappearance of "N." once he has died, Perrett insists that one can still attribute properties to him, which imply interests. This solution is equally and symmetrically valid for future persons and generations: they, too, have interests, even if today they are concretely deprived of them because they do not yet exist in physical reality. Environmental ethics, for example, is based on the fact that it is possible for human beings living today to encroach on the interests of logical persons belonging to a future generation – who are not yet born. In other words, it is possible to do them harm, despite their present nonexistence.[43]

This last solution entails a metaphysical difficulty: how to show the connection between the logical person and the living person "N." Although the question about the subject's locality is very interesting, it seems to me nevertheless that it distracts us from solving the problem discussed in this chapter. It is based on the presupposition that a subject must necessarily exist in order for it to be possible to attribute evils to him. In my opinion, the real question is not *who* is the subject or object of the evil of

39 Harry S. Silverstein, "The Evil of Death", p. 111.

40 *Ibid.*, p. 112. See *ibid.*, p. 116.

41 Palle Yourgrau, "The Dead", p. 141. See Stephen E. Rosenbaum, "How to Be Dead and Not Care: A Defense of Epicurus", pp. 129–34.

42 See Roy W. Perrett, *Death and Immortality*, pp. 53 f.

43 See Barbara Baum Levenbook, "Harming the Dead, Once Again", p. 163; Roy W. Perrett, *Death and Immortality*, p. 54.

death, but rather whether the existence of a subject is necessary in order for evils to exist. We could reformulate the question by asking what is the nature of evil. If we define evil – as I will do in the next chapter – as a privation of the goods or the interests of a subject, we resolve, to my way of thinking, both the problem of experientialism and that of the need for a subject. The privation solution makes discourse about evil possible without presupposing either experience or a subject.

10

Death

An Evil of Privation

It is assuredly correct to assume that someone who is deaf from birth is unable – and, we may suppose, never will be able – to experience personally that a Mozart symphony is performed badly, for such an experience implies the faculty of hearing. Let us suppose, furthermore, that nothing in his immediate surroundings allows him to deduce that the performance is bad. Rosenbaum, who accepts experientialism, concludes that the performance therefore could not be perceived as an evil for "N.": it does not affect him at all; he does not experience it in any way. Generalizing from this example, Rosenbaum makes a logical leap to conclude: "If a person cannot experience a state of affairs at some time, then the state of affairs is not bad for the person. Dead persons cannot experience any states of affairs."[1]

Let's look again at the example of the deaf person, focusing our attention on his condition as a state. We can certainly admit that if no one drew the deaf person's attention to the fact that he is deaf, he would not know that he is affected by an evil. Nevertheless his ignorance does not prevent us from having good reason to speak of an evil in this context – that is, where "N." experiences his state neither directly nor indirectly through the consequences brought about by his state. We are dealing with an evil of privation,[2] since being deaf is the privation of an ability

[1] Stephen E. Rosenbaum, "How to Be Dead and Not Care: A Defense of Epicurus", p. 123. See O. H. Green, "Fear of Death", p. 100: "A condition for the occurrence of good and evil will be that they be experienced by a sentient being [...]. Consciousness of a state or event which is a subjective good or evil is necessary for its being so".

[2] An evil of privation is not regarded as something in itself, as something concrete that can be experienced as such, but is situated at the level of what is not, or of what no longer

that "N." ought to have possessed as a member of the human species. This example shows that the evil of a state of affairs does not necessarily depend on the experience that a subject has of it, but rather on the privation of a good that ought to be his.

Similarly, the scorn and betrayal of "N." mentioned in the preceding chapter are evils independent of the actual experience (as in the first series of examples against experientialism) or the possible experience (as in the second series of examples) that "N." might have of them. They are not necessarily situated within the context of a precisely defined time and place. As Nagel has emphasized, "a man's life includes much that does not take place within the boundaries of his body and his mind, and what happens to him can include much that does not take place within the boundaries of his life. These boundaries are commonly crossed by the misfortunes of being deceived, or despised, or betrayed".[3] The fact that "N." experiences or does not experience – now, later, or ever – the state of affairs "A" in no way changes the fact that "A" is an evil *per se.* The evil does not lie in the possibility that the discovery thereof would make him unhappy, as Soll supposes.[4] We can say, for example, that "the discovery of betrayal makes us unhappy because it is bad to be betrayed – not that betrayal is bad because it makes us unhappy".[5] The evil of betrayal consists of the privation of a good that is due to the human subject as one possessing an intrinsic dignity: namely, treatment in keeping with his human dignity.

The assertion that death is an evil of privation raises two questions: on the one hand, of *what* does death deprive the subject? Are we talking about a privation of the pleasures that accompany life, of the person's future projects (hopes, possibilities, interests, desires, goals), of his faculties for devising projects (his will, intelligence, etc.), or, indeed, of the

is. It is understood as a relational property that appears between two states: between a pleasure or a good and its disappearance, between being and the absence of being, between a possibility and the lack of that possibility, etc.

3 Thomas Nagel, "Death", p. 6. "It therefore seems to me worth exploring the position that most good and ill fortune has as its subject a person identified by his history and his possibilities, rather than merely by his categorical state of the moment – and that while this subject can be exactly located in a sequence of places and times, the same is not necessarily true of the goods and ills that befall him", *ibid.*, p. 5.

4 See Ivan Soll, "On the Purported Insignificance of Death", pp. 27 f. Nor is it a question, in the present case, of considering instances where ignorance of "A" is better than consciousness of "A" for "N.", as in the discussion by André Gombay, "What You Don't Know Doesn't Hurt You".

5 Thomas Nagel, "Death", p. 5.

subject's very existence? On the other hand, is death an evil in all cases? Wouldn't some deaths be considered as an evil or a good depending on the circumstances, that is, depending on the sort of life that such and such an individual would have led, had he not died at T-1?

1. OF WHAT DOES DEATH DEPRIVE THE SUBJECT?

A first attempt at an answer would be that death deprives the individual of the pleasures and goods of life (such as wealth, power, friendship, or virtue) that he would have been able to possess or enjoy if he had continued to live. The evil of "N.'s" death can be measured by the quantity of pleasures and goods that "N." is said to have possessed during his life. To the extent that "N." possesses pleasures and goods, his death will be considered an evil; if, on the contrary, his life contains more evils than pleasures, his death will be regarded as a good.

To this suggestion Epicurus objects (rightly, it seems to me) that happiness, which he identifies with pleasures, does not consist in the mere accumulation of them. The philosopher of the Garden classifies pleasures according to a hierarchy of desires. He makes a distinction between vain desires (for glory and wealth) and the desires that proceed from human nature, among which he differentiates between necessary desires (to alleviate hunger, for example) and those that are not necessary (to eat well or too much). Whereas one must never seek to satisfy *vain desires*, this is not the case with *natural desires*. According to Epicurus, the gratification of natural, nonnecessary desires, which do not seek to take away pain or compensate for what is lacking, results in *kinetic pleasures*, that is, in states of pleasure caused by the very process of the pleasures (eating well, for example, or psychical joy). The satisfaction of natural, necessary desires, on the contrary, which brings about the absence of physical and spiritual pain, suffering, and want, produces *static pleasures*. This second state of pleasure is described as *ataraxia*, or the absence of psychical disturbance: the soul's static pleasure, which is achieved once the subject has eliminated all pains, all unease (vain desires that cannot be realized), and every interior imbalance, including the fear of the gods and the fear of death, which cause imbalance.

The Greek philosopher does not conceive of happiness as a quantity of joy, nor as the sum total of partial pleasures or as the achievement of good by the practice of virtue; happiness consists, rather, in an absence of troubles (*ataraxia*). Since it is not connected with time or duration, such happiness does not fit into a teleological system, inasmuch as it does not lie in the future but in the moment being experienced; this allows the wise man to transcend the immanence of time so as to be transposed beyond time into a quasi-eternal mode of being. Therefore once the individual has attained *ataraxia*, he finds himself at the pinnacle of life – his existence is accomplished. He has lived a complete human life from which he is capable of departing without regret, without any feeling whatsoever of want. Nothing new is able to increase the value of his life and of his happiness. Having arrived at happiness, he becomes indifferent to its duration. Referring to his concept of time as a series of instants, Epicurus declares that every pleasure is already the expression of happiness – which is found in the present moment. There is, therefore, the same sum total of pleasure in a finite time as in an unlimited time. Increasing the duration of a human life by several years or even to infinity would therefore not change the attitude of pursuing pleasure. The wise man, free of all fear, already lives the fullness of happiness in the tranquility of the present and does not aspire to more happiness; he does not care about the duration of happiness: "He seeks to enjoy not the longest period of time, but the most pleasant".[6] "Time that is unlimited and time that is limited afford equal pleasure, if one measures pleasure's extent by reason".[7] And Lucretius follows in his footsteps when he remarks that "by living [more] we cannot forge for ourselves any new pleasure".[8]

This argument of the Greek philosopher, nevertheless, is valid only for the wise man who has attained happiness, and not for the common mortal who strives for this state of *ataraxia* without ever attaining it; hence the death of an ordinary person could be regarded as a privation of the pleasures and goods of life and, therefore, in the final analysis, as an evil. Certainly, in the particular case of the Epicurean wise man, one may concede that a surplus of pleasures and goods is not in itself necessarily better than a reduction thereof; this is true also of enjoying them for a longer time. The "greatness" of a pleasure does not necessarily depend on its duration. The Epicurean wise man would not be happier if he could remain longer in that state. Death, therefore, would not deprive him of more happiness, given that he has already arrived at the pinnacle of happiness before his decease. Still, one can wonder whether

[6] Epicurus, *Letter of Menoeceus*, § 126 (p. 31).

[7] Epicurus, *Principal Doctrines*, § 19 (p. 36).

[8] Titus Lucretius, *De rerum natura*, book III, 1081–2 (p. 245): *"nec nova vivendo procuditur ulla voluptas"*. See *Idem*, book III, 944 f. (p. 235).

it would not be preferable – even for the wise man – to choose a new activity that is valuable in his estimation: if a life offered such an option, would it not be superior to a life that was doomed to be interrupted by death, in which such a choice would be impossible? Doesn't death deprive the wise man of his ability to choose an action that he regards as having great value? Doesn't it take away something precious in itself that would have allowed the subject to carry on an activity dear to him?

A second attempt at an answer is to propose that death robs the subject of his desires, interests, and projects, in other words, of the goals that he has set for himself in life. "A person's full appreciation of his own mortality tends to produce a feeling of despair, an attitude that his life is futile and meaningless because any of his desires may be empty and vain. Death cuts off our projects. It leaves us unfulfilled and incomplete. What meaning can we find in life by pursuing pleasure, if death always leaves us with unfulfilled aspirations?"[9] Of course, not all desires are so important that death could be described as an evil because it interrupts their possible fulfillment. To apply Williams's distinction again, we can maintain, on the one hand, like Epicurus, that there are desires and interests that are limited to the duration of human life and depend on it. The desires in question are *hypothetical* or *conditional* desires, which assume that the subject will continue to live. On the other hand, *categorical* desires do not depend on the fact that the subject continues to live, but they do presuppose that "N." desires to continue living so as to conceive and fulfill those same desires. The evil of death is situated within the context of this second category of desires: it interrupts the fulfillment of categorical desires. "It is rational to aim for states of affairs in which his want is satisfied, and hence to regard death as something to be avoided; that is, to regard it as an evil".[10] Indeed, "to want something [...] is [...] to have reason for resisting what excludes having that thing: and death certainly does that, for a very large range of things that one wants".[11] The evil of death consists in "non-satisfaction",[12] in the

9 Fred D. Miller, "Epicurus on the Art of Dying", pp. 171 f.

10 Bernard Williams, "The Makropulos Case", p. 85.

11 *Ibid.*

12 *Ibid.*, p. 88: "non-satisfaction of his desires. Thus, granted categorical desires, death has a disutility for an agent, although that disutility does not, of course, consist in unsatisfactory experiences involved in its occurrence". Steven Luper ("Annihilation", p. 271) takes a position similar to that of Williams, although he cites Nagel: "It seems reasonable to say, then, that whatever prevents me from getting what I want is a misfortune for me. But if something that thwarts my desire is an evil for me, then dying is an evil for me [...] since it thwarts my desires [...]. An event can prevent me from

thwarting of categorical desires, a frustration that does not necessarily have to be experienced and felt.

This position prompts two remarks. To begin with, once again we are confronted with the problem of the subject. More precisely, Williams's thesis and that of Luper stipulate that an evil befalls "N." at a time when "N." no longer exists and therefore no longer has categorical desires. Can we understand death as an evil for "N.", when death prevents the fulfillment of a desire and eliminates the desire itself by eliminating the person? The individual no longer exists so as to have desires.[13] Second, the proposition that "death deprives the subject of the realization of his desires and interests" does not take into consideration those desires or goals that transcend, so to speak, individual contingency. A person can desire an object that goes beyond his personal good while still including it (e.g., the common good). At this level, the death of "N." is an evil inasmuch as it destroys his ability to work personally for the realization of one of those transcendent goals or desires. Although the death of Gandhi or Martin Luther King, Jr., did not destroy their hopes for world peace and for a world without racism, it nevertheless deprived them of their efforts to bring about what they hoped for, efforts that were certainly effective. Moreover there are, on the one hand, personal desires, the satisfaction of which depends on being alive, and, on the other hand, transcendent desires, which can be satisfied independently of the subject's state. The (objective) fulfillment of a desire is not necessarily identical to the (subjective) satisfaction thereof.

Death prevents us not so much from realizing our hopes (just like our possibilities, projects, interests, and desires) as from forming and projecting them into the *future*, and from working for their realization. Death cannot destroy our transcendent hopes, which continue after

fulfilling my desires not just by frustrating my attempts to fulfill them, but also by *removing* my desires. If an event pulls one of my desires out by the roots, it certainly does prevent me from fulfilling it. It is in this sense that dying thwarts my desires". On page 276 he enumerates several categories of desires that are never thwarted by the arrival of death: desires to flee, independent desires, and conditional desires (if I were alive at T-1, "A" would be the case at T-1). "Dying is a constant threat to those of us who are unable or unwilling to abandon our concern for projects and lives whose welfare depends crucially on us, and so for us death is an evil". See Robert C. Solomon, "Is There Happiness after Death?", pp. 190–3. See also Joel Feinberg, *Harm to Others*, pp. 79 f.

[13] See Rosenbaum's critique of the article by Luper: Stephen E. Rosenbaum, "Epicurus and Annihilation", p. 298. As an answer to this difficulty it has been proposed (as noted earlier) that the subject of the evil of death is not the dead "N." but rather the living "N.", more specifically at the moment when he forms his desires.

our death, but it can destroy our ability to form such hopes and to be involved in realizing them. Death, therefore, is an evil inasmuch as it deprives the subject of what Nagel calls the constitutive goods of human life, goods that are "formidable benefits in themselves"[14] (as opposed to the good and bad experiences that they occasion), such as the ability to experience, to think, to be conscious and self-conscious, to act, to perceive, to desire. Indeed, one cannot do justice to the human person by concentrating exclusively on his ability to experience pleasures and pains; it is also necessary to insist more particularly on his possibilities and his hopes, as well as on his self-determination. This second category of abilities figures prominently in the ontology of Not-yet-being that is advocated in contemporary philosophy by Heidegger and Sartre as well as by Bloch, Marcel, and Pieper. These authors describe the person as tending toward the *future*, the locus of the realization of his projects. Continually in gestation, the person moves within an open system and is characterized by the mode of forward-looking-possibility, to use one of Bloch's expressions (*Möglichkeit-nach-vorwärts*). Far from being a static living being that may already have attained its fullness, the person is dynamic, constantly realizing itself and remaining by nature open to transformation. Imbued with an anticipating consciousness from which it cannot escape, it is above all "under way", a *Homo viator* whose mind is set on the future.[15]

The category of possibility is, according to Heidegger,[16] the ultimate and original determination of the human being. He is not a living being to which *abilities* could be added, but one who is – starting from an already of the reality of "being able" – turned toward the future in which he is actualized. *Dasein* is projected into the temporal world, knowing neither whence it comes nor whether it is going, but knowing only this "there" (*da*); it is open to an infinite range of possible ways of existing. "*Dasein* [...] is primarily Being-possible".[17] Understood ontologically as a projection toward its possibilities, toward authentic will-for-Being (*Seinwollen*), *Dasein* is fundamentally a potentiality-for-Being (*Seinkönnen*), which expresses its anticipatory character.

On the basis of such an understanding of the person, we can form a concept of death as the irreversible interruption of the projection toward

[14] Thomas Nagel, "Death", p. 2.

[15] See Bernard N. Schumacher, *A Philosophy of Hope.*

[16] I discussed this at length in Part Two, chapter 3.

[17] Martin Heidegger, *Being and Time*, p. 183 [p. 143: *"Das* Dasein [...] *ist primär Möglichkeit"*].

the future of the subject's projects and possibles. Death is the antipossibility and constitutes the limit of all ability, of all possibility; strictly speaking, it is not, as Heidegger claimed, the possibility of impossibility, but rather, as Sartre discerned, the impossibility of possibility, that is, "an always possible nihilation of my possibles which is outside my possibilities".[18]

If the evil of death consists of the fact that a certain range of the subject's possibilities will remain unrealized, Nagel formulates this more precisely: "But more fundamental is the fact that they will then cease even to be possibilities – when I as a subject of possibilities as well as of actualities cease to exist".[19] "Now the various possibilities, some of which make up my life, and many of which I will never realize, are contingent on my existence. My existence is the actuality on which all these possibilities depend".[20]

However, Nagel also declares, contrary to Kamm's interpretation,[21] that the evil of death comes from the fact that "my world will come to an end [...]. One day this consciousness will black out for good and subjective time will simply stop".[22] Death is an evil because it deprives the subject of all possibilities, and more particularly of the very possibility of being an "ego", a "self".[23] To a great extent this idea is adopted by

[18] Jean-Paul Sartre, *Being and Nothingness*, p. 687 [p. 621: *"néantisation toujours possible de mes possibles, qui est hors de mes possibilités"*]. It seems appropriate to emphasize here that the evil of death, in Sartre's view, does not lie primarily in the impossibility *in se* for the dead for-itself to project itself freely toward the future, toward future possibles: i.e., for it to create its essence continually and to accord meaning to its past and present actions. The principal cause of the evil and absurdity of death lies, as we have seen, in the reduction of the dead for-itself to an in-itself in which the meaning of its past actions is irreversibly subjected to the freedom and good pleasure of the surviving for-itself, who enjoys a total victory over the dead for-itself. Death is an evil because it irreversibly robs the subject of the possibility of conferring meaning on his past actions and on his life; it fixes the subject for all eternity in the moment in which he found himself at his decease.

[19] Thomas Nagel, *The View from Nowhere*, p. 226.

[20] *Ibid.*, p. 227.

[21] "It [Nagel's position] does not consider that our attitudes toward death are connected to the significance of the destruction of a certain type of entity or interference with a certain process, per se, rather than with the loss of more goods", Frances M. Kamm, *Morality, Mortality*, p. 22.

[22] Thomas Nagel, *The View from Nowhere*, p. 225.

[23] Richard Wollheim, for his part, insists on the fact that the evil of death lies primarily in the loss of the phenomenological attitude of the subject. Death does not deprive us of some particular pleasure, nor even of pleasure. "What it deprives us of is something more fundamental than pleasure: it deprives us of that thing which we gain access to when, as persisting creatures, we enter into our present mental states and which,

such different authors as Sartre, Scherer, Unamuno,[24] Vuillemin, Nagel, Kamm, and Jankélévitch: the last-mentioned maintains that "death is a void that suddenly gapes in the full continuum of being; the entity, suddenly rendered invisible, as though by the effect of a prodigious black-out, is engulfed in a twinkling of the eye in the trap of non-being".[25] For the subject himself, death is above all a privation of his existence, the necessary substrate for his ability to realize possibilities, projects, hopes, interests, and desires and to project them into the future. "What frightens the individual", Vuillemin remarks, "is not at all the fact that the atoms of which he is made could feel the dissolution of the aggregate, but rather that the aggregate itself disappears".[26] In the same way, Cicero's interlocutor in the first book of the *Tusculan Disputations* notes that the evil of death lies precisely in "the mere fact of not existing, when one has existed",[27] namely, in the destruction of the person himself, the subject of the goods of life. "A Radical Limbo Man", Kamm remarks, "who took the Extinction Factor to an extreme, might actually have no interest in the goods of life except as a vehicle for consciousness of

from then onwards, we associate in some special way with our past mental states and our future mental states. It deprives us of phenomenology, and, having once tasted phenomenology, we develop a longing for it which we cannot give up: not even when the desire for the cessation of pain, for extinction, grows stronger", *The Thread of Life*, p. 269.

24 See Jean-Paul Sartre, *Being and Nothingness*, pp. 687 f. [pp. 621 f.]. "In death, however, every possibility is cut off [...]. In it not only does an entity cease to be, but also – if death is man's ultimate fate – an ego that knows of itself and wills itself, inasmuch as it knows about being, is extinguished" [*"Im Tod aber wird jede Möglichkeit abgeschnitten [...]. In ihm hört nicht nur ein Seiendes auf zu sein, sondern wird, falls der Tod das letzte Schicksal des Menschen ist, ein Ich, das um sich selbst weiss und sich will, indem es um Sein weiss, ausgelöscht"*]: Georg Scherer, *Sinnerfahrung und Unsterblichkeit*, p. 56. "What terrifies me is annihilation, annulment, the nothingness beyond the grave. What more could hell do?, I used to say to myself. And that idea tormented me. In hell, I would say, one suffers but one is alive; and what matters is to live, to be, even if it is while suffering", Miguel de Unamuno, *Diario intimo*, p. 40; see also pp. 122–3.

25 Vladimir Jankélévitch, *La mort*, p. 7: *"la mort est un vide qui se creuse brusquement en pleine continuation d'être; l'existant, rendu soudain invisible comme par l'effet d'une prodigieuse occultation, s'abîme en un clin d'oeil dans la trappe du non-être"*. "Death is simultaneously the pure and simple negation of the essence of essence and the pure and simple negation of being [...] the pure and simple non-being of being". [*"La mort est à la fois la négation pure et simple de l'essence de l'essence et la négation pure et simple de l'être [...] le pur et simple non-être de l'être"*], p. 69.

26 Jules Vuillemin, *Essai sur la signification de la mort*, p. 45: *"Ce qui effraie l'individu ce n'est point que les atomes qui le composent puissent ressentir la dissolution de l'agrégat, mais que l'agrégat lui-même disparaisse"*.

27 Marcus Tullius Cicero, *Tusculan Disputations*, I, vi, 12 (p. 17): *"Nam istuc ipsum, non esse, cum fueris, miserrimum puto"*.

himself, seeing his conscious life as a worthy means of avoiding permanent nonexistence. Such a person would take what is bad to be not loss of opportunity for the goods of life, but lack of possibility of conscious existing *per se* [...]. It is concern with the total absence of possibility of more conscious life for us, I believe, that lies behind the claim that the nothingness of death is bad in itself, not merely bad instrumentally. Death is bad because it is final".[28] Death is an evil because it interrupts the process that maintains in being the already-present person and thus interferes with the process of his life. Kamm could not be any more blunt when she says: "death is bad because it means everything for oneself is *all over*. Since we could prefer to postpone things being all over, even if this did not increase the total amount of goods we had in our life, we must be trying to avoid something about death other than that it diminishes the amount of goods of life we have".[29] It seems that a human being, *by his very nature*, would prefer to postpone the end of his life, and that the contents of one life or another, and more particularly the prospects of increasing the totality of goods therein, do not affect this preference. For this purpose he would even be willing to be submerged in an unconscious, comatose state from which he could "awaken" unharmed in a more or less distant future, without any change in his being, so as to live out the rest of his life. Such an individual, whom Kamm calls "Limbo Man", is more concerned about "the absence of the possibility of any significant future for himself"[30] than about supplementary goods.

[28] Frances M. Kamm, *Morality, Mortality*, p. 65. "Staying alive could be good not because it involves things that are intrinsically good (and by comparison with which nothingness is bad), but because it compares favorably with the intrinsic (noncomparative), albeit nonexperiential, badness of the nothingness of death. People may want to stay alive only because the alternative is posthumous nothingness. It may be that something – even without any intrinsically positive features – is preferable to post-something nothingness, and yet, if something has intrinsically negative features (such as torture), these can override the negative of nothingness", *ibid.*, p. 19.

[29] *Ibid.*, p. 19. She continues: "The condition that things not be all over for us is not necessarily connected with our having *more* goods than we would otherwise have if we died. For example, someone might prefer putting off a fixed quantity of goods of life by going into a coma and returning to consciousness at a latter point to have them. Such a person (call him the *Limbo Man*) would be concerned with his not being all over, in a way that was independent of wanting *more* goods of life [...]. Furthermore, an extreme version of his attitude could help explain the 'nothingness' proponent's claim that life is good only relative to the badness of nothingness: this person could care little for the goods of life per se and could see living as a means of avoiding his being 'all over'. As evidence for this, he would not object to living completely in an unconscious state, so long as this was a coma from which it would be possible for him to return to life", *ibid.*, pp. 21–2.

[30] *Ibid.*, p. 49.

His primary interest is not to enjoy more goods and to realize more possibilities, but simply to live and thus to put off, in a way, the moment of his decease, that is, the moment of his disappearance into nothingness, the moment when everything will be over, when the meaning of his actions will be fixed forever, and he will no longer exist as a subject.

2. IS DEATH ALWAYS AN EVIL?

2.1. Death as an Evil Depending on the Circumstances

2.1.1. *An Evil Determined by a Calculation of the Subjective Value of the Life*

Once it has been admitted that death is an evil of privation, the question of whether it constitutes an evil in itself or depending on the circumstances becomes urgent. If one situates the privation solely at the level of the goods of life, that is, external material goods or goods within the individual (excluding those goods that are constitutive of human life), or at the level of possibilities and hopes, the conclusion is generally that only some deaths are capable of being characterized as an evil. Indeed, death is understood as an evil *in the measure* in which it deprives an individual of pleasures, goods, hopes, possibilities, interests, and desires that he might yet have formed and realized and that he would have been able to enjoy if he had not died at T-1. The concept of measure here indicates a utilitarian sort of calculation that presupposes hedonism, applied to the kind of life that the individual would have led if he had continued to live after T-1. Hence the death of a physically and psychologically healthy person who is more or less young is regarded, generally speaking, as an evil (because it deprives him of many possibilities, hopes, accomplishments, interests, and desires), as opposed to the death of a person in the terminal phase of a painful physical illness or of a person who is dying a so-called natural death; this second kind of death is regarded, generally speaking, as a good, because it delivers the subject from a situation that has become insufferable. The death of "N." can therefore be understood either as an evil or as a good, depending on the circumstances, that is, according to the concrete situation. Feldman summarizes this viewpoint well in his book *Confrontations with the Reaper*: "When the life as a whole I would have led if I had continued to live is worse for me than the life as a whole I would have led if I die now, then it is best for me to die now. My death, in this sort of case, is a blessing for me".[31] Similarly, McMahan notes that "death is bad for a person (or developing person) at any point in his life, provided that the life that is thereby lost would on balance have been worth living. Other things being equal, the badness of death is proportional to the quality and quantity of the goods of which the victim is deprived".[32] As a way of deciding whether death is a good or an evil, Feldman, for example, proposes calculating the difference between the subjective value of the life in the case where the individual dies at T-1 and its value in the situation in which he continues to live and does not die until T-2. If the calculation indicates that the first situation is favorable, the death is considered as a good. If it appears, on the contrary, that the individual would have enjoyed more goods and realized more possibilities and hopes, one could consider his death as an evil.[33]

Nevertheless I have some difficulty imagining how such a calculation would be put into practice. One might perhaps envisage the possibility of such a calculation in extreme cases, such as the terminally ill patient who is suffering intense pain or the old man who is awaiting his so-called natural death, because their future can be determined with more or less certainty. Perhaps it is possible to estimate, in these specific cases, the approximate number of possibilities and hopes (by defining them clearly, that is, excluding those that are beyond the limits of our thought and imagination) that they can still realize concretely and to foresee that the rest of their life would contain a preponderance of ills and very few pleasures. I question, however, the criteria that would allow us to

[31] Fred Feldman, *Confrontations with the Reaper*, p. 226. See *ibid.*, pp. 140 f.

[32] Jeff McMahan, "Death and the Value of Life", p. 262. See also Peter C. Dalton, "Death and Evil", p. 203; Dorothy L. Grover, "Death and Life"; Mary Mothersill, "Death", p. 92; Leonard W. Sumner, "A Matter of Life and Death", pp. 157 f.

[33] "So the general principle says that to find the extrinsic value for a person [P] of a state of affairs [S], subtract the value for him of the life he would lead if it is false from the value for him of the life he would lead if it is true [...]. The extrinsic value of a state of affairs for a person is the result of subtracting the value-for-him of the life he leads if it does not occur from the value-for-him of the life he leads if it does occur. In other words: D: The extrinsic value for P of S = the difference between the intrinsic value for S of the life S would lead if P is true and the intrinsic value for S of the life S would lead if P is false [...]. To find the answer, we must ask about the value for him [a boy who died while unconscious on the operating table] of the life he leads if he dies when he in fact dies; and we must compare that value to the value for him of the life he would have led if he had not died then. If the life terminated by that death is worse for the boy than the life not terminated by that death, then his death on that operating table was extrinsically bad for him; otherwise, not", Fred Feldman, *Confrontations with the Reaper*, pp. 150 f.

attribute to a state of affairs, "A", one or another sum total of pleasure, or of pain; I also question the method of calculating a sum of goods and evils in the future. Doesn't the future elude knowledge and certainty in calculation? Isn't all that hypothetical? It is possible, indeed, that a state in which the sum of pains exceeds the sum of pleasures may still lead an individual, in a completely unforeseeable way, to a dimension of being that had been hidden to him before, a dimension of which he becomes aware only a short time before his death and from which he obtains a great benefit. Such a calculus cannot be applied subjectively but forces one to take the objective point of view, in which the "ego" steps outside time, so to speak. My actions, as a whole, receive their meaning only in the future, and ultimately after my death; the sum of the pleasures and ills in a slice of my life or, in this case, in my whole life will not be calculable until such time as I find myself outside that slice of my life, that is, until I have died. It should be noted, finally, that not one of the authors who advocate such an arithmetic approach actually presents concrete cases and detailed calculations.

The definition of death as an evil depending on the circumstances applies above all to the sort of death that is described as violent, to "accidental" or "premature" death, which is "not natural". The calculus considers the interval between T-1 and T-5, where T-5 is understood as the natural limit of a human life, that is, so-called natural death. If an individual died such a death, one would not consider it as an evil, because it is the ultimate and natural term of human life, which in itself cannot be prolonged; one would not try to calculate the quantity and quality of pleasures that the individual would have enjoyed if he had continued to live. We have here the "critical theory", which declares that the only death that is to be feared and considered an evil is premature, so-called accidental death. As for "natural" death, it is likened to a good. A shorter-than-normal duration of life – the quality of life remaining equal – is considered an evil.

2.1.2. *An Evil Determined According to the Categories of Accidental and Natural*

2.1.2.1. THE IDEA OF NATURAL DEATH. Twentieth-century thanatology developed the ideal of "natural" death,[34] which is characterized by

[34] Jean Baudrillard (*L'échange symbolique et la mort*, p. 248) remarks that "corresponding to the biological definition of death and the logical will of reason is an ideal form and standard of death, which is 'natural' death [...]. Natural death is that death which

a scientizing, technological approach[35] to death. It proposes a universal explanation of death as the end of the biological process of an organism, as a simple, observable fact that is detached from all values. Scientific rationality requires – within the framework of this reductionistic interpretation of science – that human death be an exclusively biological phenomenon, in which biology is understood in the mechanical sense. Scientific reason, supposedly, is capable of measuring, quantifying, and grasping this phenomenon, to the point of discovering its causes someday and controlling it.

Scientists of this school set themselves the goal of conquering "accidental" (i.e., "nonnatural") death resulting from an accident, strictly speaking, or from an illness. This sort of death is described as violent because it interrupts the surge toward the future. It is perceived as a "social scandal"[36] resulting from personal or communal negligence, as "a failure, a 'business lost' [...]. When death arrives, it is regarded as an accident, a sign of helplessness or clumsiness that must be put out of mind".[37] According to Aristotle and Bichat,[38] it is distinguished from "natural" death, which "is actualized" at the conclusion of the biological

comes under the jurisdiction of science, and which is destined to be wiped out by science. Clearly this means that death is inhuman, irrational, senseless, like nature when it is not domesticated (the Western concept of 'nature' is always that of a subdued, tamed nature). The only good death is a conquered death, one subject to the law: this is the ideal of natural death" [*"A la définition biologique de la mort et à la volonté logique de la raison correspond une forme idéale et standard de la mort, qui est la mort 'naturelle'. [...] La mort naturelle est celle qui est justiciable de la science, et qui a vocation d'être exterminée par la science. Ceci signifie en clair: la mort est inhumaine, irrationnelle, insensée, comme la nature lorsqu'elle n'est pas domestiquée (le concept occidental de 'nature' est toujours celui d'une nature refoulée et domestiquée). Il n'y a de bonne mort que vaincue, et soumise à la loi: tel est l'idéal de la mort naturelle"*].

35 See Walter Schulz, *Subjektivität im nachmetaphysischen Zeitalter*, p. 142.

36 Jean Baudrillard, *L'échange symbolique et la mort*, p. 248: *"scandale social"*.

37 Philippe Ariès, *The Hour of Our Death*, p. 586 [vol. 2, p. 297: *"un échec, un* business lost. *[...] Quand la mort arrive, elle est considérée comme un accident, un signe d'impuissance ou de maladresse, qu'il faut oublier"*]. Death is understood as an intrusion into the scientific and medical quest for a life without end: "I myself tend to adhere to the concept of death as an accident, and therefore find it difficult to reconcile myself to it for myself or for others [...]. People do not forgive themselves easily for having failed to save their own or others' lives", Alvin I. Goldfarb, "Discussion".

38 "There is violent death and again natural death, and the former occurs when the cause of death is external, the latter when it is internal, and involved from the beginning in the constitution of the organ, and is not an affection derived from a foreign source. In the case of plants the name given to this is withering, in animals, senility", Aristotle, *On life and death*, 478 b 25–8. Xavier Bichat, *Recherches physiologiques sur la vie et la mort*, Part One, article 10, pp. 200 f.

process of the living thing and results from the natural debilitation of the organism's intrinsic forces. In the writings of Feuerbach[39] and of those who understand death as an evil *depending on the circumstances*,[40] this "natural" death is described as good, tranquil, easy, and nonviolent, so that it does not engender fear. Hence society regards itself as having the responsibility and even the obligation to do everything in its power, with the help of science, to abolish "accidental" death and thus to allow every citizen to die a "natural" death. Hence the phenomenon of death is integrated into the heart of a "new social contract"[41] together with a particular concept of social justice and egalitarianism in which each individual has a fundamental right to life and to a "natural" death. According to the critical theory of death, this should eliminate both the

39 "Death in and of itself is not dreadful, no! A healthy death in accordance with nature – death that occurs at an advanced age, occurs when a man has had enough of life, as was the case in the Old Testament with the patriarchs and other men blessed by God [...]. The only dreadful death is an unnatural, violent, horrible death" [*"Schrecklich ist nicht der Tod an und für sich; nein! Der naturgemässe, gesunde Tod – der Tod, der im hohen Alter erfolgt, dann erfolgt, wann der Mensch das Leben satt hat, wie es im Alten Testament von den Erzvätern und anderen gottgesegneten Männern heisst [...]. Schrecklich ist nur der unnatürliche, gewaltsame, grausame Tod"*], Ludwig Feuerbach, *Die Unsterblichkeitsfrage vom Standpunkt der Anthropologie*, pp. 236 f.

40 Whereas the proponents of the "critical theory" base their discussion solely on the distinction between accidental death and natural death, those analytical philosophers who defend the thesis of death as an evil depending on the circumstances shift their discussion from the biological to the ethical level: one decides, by a personal choice, whether or not a life is worth the trouble of continuing, i.e., whether it has somehow attained its so-called natural limit. In such a situation the decease of "N." does not deprive him of possibilities and hopes but delivers him from a physical state of life that is no longer worth the trouble of living, more precisely, from a state of life marked by many pains and complications. Thus, it could very well be that the accidental death of "N." is in reality not an evil, as the adherents to the "theory of natural death" would maintain, but rather a good. Despite their differences, the two camps agree in characterizing so-called natural death as a good.

41 Jean Baudrillard, *L'échange symbolique et la mort*, p. 248: *"nouveau contrat social"*. See Ivan Illich, "The Political Uses of Natural Death", pp. 36 f. and *Medical Nemesis*, pp. 142 ff. [pp. 192 f.]. Herbert Marcuse ("The Ideology of Death", p. 69) remarks that "the gradually increasing duration of life may change the substance and character not only of life but also of death. The latter would lose its ontological and moral sanctions; men would experience death primarily as a technical limit of human freedom whose surpassing would become the recognized goal of the individual and social endeavor". See Werner Fuchs, *Todesbilder in der modernen Gesellschaft*, pp. 67 f., pp. 181 f. Now, at the dawn of the third millennium, claiming such a right is particularly relevant, since there are great inequities in the way in which individuals are treated by the medical community and insurance companies: for example, someone who is rich is treated differently from someone living in poverty. See Ivan Illich, *Medical Nemesis*, pp. 139 f. [pp. 189 f.]; Jean Ziegler, *Les vivants et les morts*, pp. 74 f., 102 f., 124 f.

existential shock of death[42] and the fear of it.[43] This fear would arise only in the case of a sudden and unexpected accidental, violent death that occurred before the subject had completed the natural duration of his life.[44] "Accidental" death is depicted as an evil that must be eradicated as quickly as possible from the face of the earth.[45]

2.1.2.2. OBJECTIONS TO THE 'CRITICAL THEORY OF DEATH'. The philosophical speculation of the "critical theory of death"[46] – which maintains that only accidental death should be feared – is part of the postmetaphysical current of thought in which only the biological concept of death is valid. Every other type of philosophical thanatology is perceived as irrational. The thesis of 'natural' death – as affirmed by Fuchs, for example – supposes that only a biological thanatology is capable of fully comprehending the phenomenon of death, that it alone is rational. This same thesis claims to provide a total explanation of death: on the one hand, by refusing to grant the color of rationality to any discourse that is not modeled on that of the natural sciences, it denies what Apel has called the various "types of rationality"[47] and of methodology, that is, different legitimate points of view from which to grasp reality; on the other

[42] I question this idea, because every death, even if it was strictly speaking "natural" in the sense used by the proponents of the 'critical theory of death', has the power to destabilize the world of the survivor. This is manifested especially in the case of the death of a loved one.

[43] The fear of 'death or my death' can consist in a fear of dying (accidentally or naturally) and of the pains that may accompany it, a fear of 'experiencing' nothingness (Epicurus) or hell (Plato and many religions) once one has died, a fear of the unknown, of my personal disappearance, of being deprived of my goods and possibilities. From this perspective it is characterized by a certain violence.

[44] See Werner Fuchs, *Todesbilder in der modernen Gesellschaft*, p. 76.

[45] See *ibid.*, pp. 67, 72, 76, 82, 181 f.

[46] Johannes Schwartländer, "Der Tod und die Würde des Menschen", p. 25. The author refers to the theory developed by Werner Fuchs, *Todesbilder in der modernen Gesellschaft*.

[47] See Karl-Otto Apel, "Das Problem einer philosophischen Theorie der Rationalitätstypen". The ideal of 'natural' death presupposes *a priori* that one must exclude from the domain of rationality any discussion of the meaning and the 'why' of death, that is, in reality, philosophical discourse, the specific purpose of which is to raise of question of the 'why' by taking a comprehensive point of view. Moreover rationality cannot be reduced, in my opinion, to the sort of knowledge obtained by the mathematical and biological sciences (ontological and methodological reductionism), but rather characterizes all discourse that is distinguished by a certain rigor (the search for reasons and logical correlations) and a certain objectivity (which is defined as a independent discourse of the subject, along with reference to some objects). See Evandro Agazzi, "Reductionism as Negation of the Scientific Spirit" and *Right, Wrong and Science*, pp. 25 ff. [pp. 25 ff.].

hand, it excludes the dimensions of the existential limit situation, of the person and of the symbol that characterize the various Western cultures. Although the biological approach allows one to explain and bring to light certain constitutive processes of the phenomenon of death, it is incapable of answering the questions that have unceasingly troubled the human mind on this subject, or of quieting them. Although the ideal of 'natural' death claims to be comprehensive, it is actually, in my opinion, a disguised flight from death, a repression of human death, which is dehumanized by that idealization.

While constituting an event that is natural to the biological structure of the human being and that interrupts his projection into the future, death at the same time destroys the biographical dimension of a subject who is open to the free realization of possibilities. Human death also involves personal, cultural, existential, and spiritual dimensions. Although there is no denying that he can survive only in a biological context, the human person in his *conditio humana*, in which he acts and lives culturally, historically, and freely, is defined by the surpassing (without the negation or exploitation) of his natural environment and his physical form. Arendt notes that "the mortality of man lies in the fact that individual life, with a recognizable life-story from birth to death, rises out of biological life. This individual life is distinguished from all other things by the rectilinear course of its movement, which, so to speak, cuts through the circular movement of biological life".[48]

Reducing death to the biological level alone so as to attain 'absolute' scientific objectivity and certainty, while excluding metaphysical questions and thanatological philosophical speculation, is tantamount to denying an important and essential dimension of the human person: the possession of a moral and cultural conscience,[49] as well as the character of a *res cogitans* (thinking thing) having intentionality and freedom. Indeed, the human subject is distinguished by actions that are both immanent (e.g., the manifestations of psychical life) and transcendent (e.g., the intentionality that is capable of making for itself representations of reality without itself becoming that reality, that is,

[48] Hannah Arendt, *The Human Condition*, p. 19. See Georg Scherer, *Das Problem des Todes in der Philosophie*, pp. 21 f.

[49] This 'biocultural' or 'biological-spiritual' character is manifested also in the human attitude toward death and the corpse, which is not treated as a mere thing (see Werner Fuchs, *Todesbilder in der modernen Gesellschaft*, p. 71 and Martin Heidegger, *Being and Time*, pp. 281 f. [pp. 238 f.]). Humanity displays profound respect for the corpse in the act of burying it, while fully aware that the corpse is not the same as a person.

substantially). The human person distances and frees himself, to a certain extent, from his biological determination and causes a new world to spring up by means of culture and speech. Besides this opening toward the universal, the human person is endowed with a moral conscience, that is, with the ability to express moral judgments. Whereas the purely biological dimension is content with rules that are constitutive of its nature, the human dimension adds the dimension of 'what ought to be', together with the dimension of freedom, which cannot be reduced to freedom of action yet is rooted in free will.

Therefore, since the human person is distinguished by his body, his mind (*esprit*) and by his moral and cultural conscience, a comprehensive analysis of death cannot bracket off such realities, which are essential to his nature. If the person transcends in a certain way the *bios*, his environment (*Umwelt*), we can grasp him, as Gadamer remarks,[50] not only with the help of the natural sciences and by means of their conceptual tools, but also and especially with the help of the human sciences, which are also based on forms of rational discourse.

2.1.2.3. CLARIFICATION OF THE TERMS 'NATURAL' AND 'ACCIDENTAL' AS APPLIED TO DEATH. Before continuing our discussion of the ideal of natural death, it will be helpful, I think, to clarify the terms 'natural' and 'accidental' as applied to death, given that they are likely to be misinterpreted.

1. The human being has, in himself, a limited duration of life ('natural death'), although at any moment he may leave this world, against his will or freely, even before his internal biological clock has ceased functioning 'naturally' (which would be the equivalent of an 'accidental' death).
2. Every human death is 'natural' because it is inscribed within the biological human constitution: the human being is essentially a "Being-towards-death" (the thesis of death in life); so-called accidental death is, from this perspective, 'natural'; it is, furthermore, necessary to the development of life and of evolution.
3. Every death is 'accidental' in the sense that it robs the subject of his future and personal biological existence and deprives him of his goods, his possibilities, and his freedom. From this perspective, there is fundamentally no difference whatsoever between the 'accidental' death of a young (or not-so-young) person and the 'natural' death of an elderly person (defined in 1).

[50] See Hans Georg Gadamer, "Schlussbericht", p. 377.

Refusing to consider that natural death is in fact an accidental death (as would be the case if one adopted the third point of view), the proponents of the 'critical theory' and some analytical philosophers affirm that 'natural' death is welcome and they describe it as a good. Their argument starts from the unproven underlying presupposition that someone who died a natural death (which does not arouse fear) would have completed his task and accomplished everything in his life that he deemed important.[51] They implicitly maintain that 'natural' death would not deprive the subject of his possibilities and his freedom, of projects still unrealized, of the goods of life; on the contrary, 'accidental' death would be an evil for the subject, because it prevents him from eventually realizing a multitude of projects and possibilities, while taking the goods of life away from him. It seems to me, nevertheless, that the proponents of the critical theory of death show signs of a certain inconsistency when they describe death sometimes as an evil and sometimes as a good. In effect, they maintain, at first, that every accidental death must be eliminated with the help of science: the result of this would be that human beings would die a 'natural' death only, about which they have no fear. Yet science has as its implicit goal the elimination of death itself, and this perspective implies a second thesis in the background, that natural death – the only kind that would remain, since accidental death would have been conquered – would be considered as an evil to be overcome.

2.1.2.4. THE PROBLEM OF NATURAL DEATH. So-called natural death is, as Nagel rightly describes it, "the most serious difficulty with the view that death is always an evil".[52] Indeed, the issue is knowing "whether the nonrealization of this possibility [of continuing to live] is in every case a misfortune, or whether it depends on what can naturally be hoped for"; in other words, "we still have to set some limits on *how* possible a possibility must be for its nonrealization to be a misfortune".[53] The fundamental question presents itself in these terms: is it possible to "regard as a misfortune any limitation, like mortality, that is normal to the species"?[54] Certainly, one can reasonably argue that the death of an individual at age twenty (an 'accidental' death) would be a greater evil than his death at the age of one hundred ('natural' death), inasmuch as he would have

[51] See, for example, Bertrand Russell, *Portraits from Memory*, p. 52; Robert Nozick, "Dying", p. 27.

[52] Thomas Nagel, "Death", p. 9.

[53] *Ibid.*

[54] *Ibid.*

been able to enjoy the goods of life for a hundred years and he would have had much more time at his disposal to realize his potential and his hopes.[55] This does not allow us, however, to deduce that natural death is a good insofar as the subject has realized his hopes and potential, or even if he has achieved a full and complete life. Indeed, every death is an evil, for it means, according to Nagel, "an abrupt cancellation of indefinitely extensive possible goods".[56]

A human being can "clearly conceive"[57] of an uninterrupted, unending existence. He can very well imagine himself having the ability to project himself "indefinitely" into the future, continually devising and realizing new possibilities and never having "had *enough*".[58] Death "can be said to deprive its victim of what is in the relevant sense a possible continuation of life",[59] which would allow him to realize his potential. Rachels emphasizes that "if there was anything bad about the death, it is because we are able to view a life as in principle open-ended, as always having further possibilities that still might be realized, if only it could go on".[60] Death brings to light the divergence, or even the contradiction,

55 "But if the *praemia vitae* are valuable; even if we include as necessary to that value consciousness that one possesses them; then surely getting to the point of possessing them is better than not getting to that point, longer enjoyment of them is better than shorter, and more of them, other things being equal, is better than less of them [...]. If the *praemia vitae* and consciousness of them are good things, then longer consciousness of more *praemia* is better than a shorter consciousness of fewer *praemia*", Bernard Williams, "The Makropulos Case", pp. 84 f.

56 Thomas Nagel, "Death", p. 10.

57 *Ibid.*, p. 8: "we can clearly conceive of what it would be for him to go on existing indefinitely".

58 Robert Nozick, "Dying", p. 27: "Is there no point when we will have had *enough*?" On the subject of the boredom of an endless life, see Bernard N. Schumacher, "Philosophische Interpretationen der Unsterblichkeit des Menschen".

59 Thomas Nagel, "Death", p. 9.

60 James Rachels, *The End of Life*, p. 51. Scherer is even more explicit, while referring obliquely to Sartre: "[...] the fact that man opens himself to ways of his own being, discovers and projects himself, and in projecting such possibilities opens for himself Being-in-the-world in its significance [...]. Death, in contrast, robs him of all such possibilities. It is precisely the end of all positive possibilities for being, the end of all of man's behavior with regard to himself and thus to Being [...]. Possibly death means precisely that I am swallowed up by nothingness, because it puts an irrevocable end to my ability to dispose, to my seizing of possibilities, to my free conduct of myself. In other words, death causes me to stop being a subject and a person; it makes me an object, a thing that others dispose of and which can no longer dispose of itself" [*"dass der Mensch sich Weisen seines eigenen Seins erschliesst, sich entdeckt und entwirft, sich im Entwerfen solcher Möglichkeiten das innerweltlich Seiende in seiner Bedeutsamkeit aufschliesst [...]. Der Tod dagegen raubt alle solche Möglichkeiten. Er ist gerade das Ende aller positiven Seinsmöglichkeiten, allen Verhaltens des Menschen zu sich selbst und darin zum Sein*

between the reality of a physically limited life and the surreal possibility of an unending life. No longer being able to project oneself into the future, to form possibilities, to have hopes, or to enjoy goods constitutes from such a perspective an evil in itself, regardless of the circumstances or of the fact that one day every person reaches his natural physical limit.

To justify these assertions, Nagel relies principally on his distinction between the subjective viewpoint and the objective viewpoint. The latter envisages the future of "N." according to the limits set by the (natural) present hope for life. The subjective and biographical viewpoint (what Nagel defines as "the internal awareness of my own existence"[61]) regards the future of "N." as "indeterminate and not essentially limited".[62] According to this viewpoint, the human being is characterized by a future that is open to the realization of infinite possibilities. The sense that he has of his own existence does not contain the idea of a limit: "his existence defines for him an essentially open-ended possible future".[63] This subjective viewpoint is radically opposed to the Heideggerian presentation of death as the possibility of impossibility and, more specifically, as "my ownmost possibility of impossibility", for death means a rupture of possibilities and hopes that itself is not a possibility for the subject. Nagel remarks, "the thought of the annihilation of this universe of possibilities cannot then be thought of as the realization of yet another possibility already given by an underlying subjective actuality. The subjective view does not allow for its own annihilation, for it does not conceive of its existence as the realization of a possibility".[64] From the subjective viewpoint, "there seems to be nothing still more basic which reveals the actuality of my existence as in turn the realization of

[...]. Der Tod bedeutet möglicherweise gerade mein Verschlungenwerden vom Nichts, weil er meinem Verfügenkönnen, meinem Ergreifen von Möglichkeiten, meinem freien Michverhalten ein unwiderrufliches Ende setzt. Anders ausgedrückt: Der Tod lässt mich aufhören, ein Subjekt und eine Person zu sein, er macht mich zu einem Objekt und Ding, über das verfügt wird und das selber nicht mehr verfügen kann"], Georg Scherer, *Der Tod als Frage an die Freiheit*, p. 60. "The possibility of losing our being in death, of being annihilated, of no longer being at all, makes death such a dire threat to us". [*"Die Möglichkeit, im Tode das Sein zu verlieren, zunichte zu werden, schlechthin nicht mehr zu sein, macht den Tod für uns zu jener äussersten Bedrohung"*], *ibid.*, pp. 58–9.

61 Thomas Nagel, *The View from Nowhere*, p. 226: "the internal awareness of my own existence carries with it a particularly strong sense of its own future, and of its possible continuation beyond any future that may actually be reached".

62 Thomas Nagel, "Death", p. 10.

63 *Ibid.*

64 Thomas Nagel, *The View from Nowhere*, p. 227.

a possibility of existence which is correlative with a possibility of non-existence based on the same foundation".[65] It is only through the experience of another's death, as we saw in Part Two of this book, that the subject becomes aware that he must die. The death of the other can produce in him that brutal shock that provokes a consciousness of the possible definitive loss of his interior world, a loss that he had thought of until then as "a set of ungrounded possibilities as opposed to a set of possibilities grounded in a contingent actuality".[66]

Being mortal in no way changes the parameters of the problem, for, as Nagel explains, "the fact that we will all inevitably die in a few score years cannot in itself imply that it would not be good to live longer".[67] He concludes that "if there is no limit to the amount of life that it would be good to have, then it may be that a bad end is in store for us all".[68]

Certainly, one can maintain that when a person no longer has the ability to complete his task or, on the contrary, when he has accomplished everything that he deemed important, he should no longer rebel so much against the idea of dying. It seems to me, however, that one can rightly ask, along with Nozick: "if nothing important is possible or left, mightn't being someone who continues even so be one of the important ways to be? And having done everything you considered important, mightn't you set yourself a *new* goal"?[69] A subject's possibilities always surpass what he has effectively realized; he is capable of realizing effectively only a few of his projected possibilities, of the infinite possibilities, and that means that the natural physical limit of life does not necessarily correspond to the subjective (biographical) limit.

According to such a perspective, a human being always dies prematurely; in other words, as Kojève emphasizes in his *Introduction to Reading Hegel*, "before exhausting all the possibilities of his being (or better: of his denying or creative activity)". A human being "always dies a 'violent' death, if you will, for his death is what prevents him from doing something else that he has not done. Every man who is dead could have prolonged his activity or denied it: therefore he has not completely exhausted his human existential possibilities".[70] Death brings to light

65 *Ibid.*

66 *Ibid.*, p. 228.

67 Thomas Nagel, "Death", p. 10.

68 *Ibid.*

69 Robert Nozick, "Dying", p. 21.

70 Alexandre Kojève, *Introduction à la lecture de Hegel*, p. 523: *"avant d'avoir épuisé toutes les possibilités de son être (ou mieux: de son action négatrice ou créatrice)"; "meurt toujours, si l'on*

the tension between the reality of a life that has been lived and the possibility of a life that could still be lived.

2.2. Death as an Evil in Itself

If we consider death as depriving the subject "of life"[71] (and thereby of the constitutive goods of human life), we can conclude from this, according to Nagel, that "death is in itself an evil",[72] that it is so "in every case",[73] that is, even when life would be filled with negative experiences and would have no more future, time being "closed off" (*clos*), to cite an image used by Marcel.[74] Nagel could not be clearer on this subject in his book *The View from Nowhere*: "Life can be wonderful, but even if it isn't, death is usually much worse. If it cuts off the possibility of more future goods than future evils for the victim, it is a loss no matter how long he has lived when it happens. And in truth, as Richard Wollheim says, death is a misfortune even when life is no longer worth living".[75] Nagel bases his argument on a twofold *a priori*: on the one hand, the ability to experience is a good in itself – to have any sort of experience whatsoever is better than not to have any experience at all; on the other hand, bad experiences (therefore the contents of the ability to experience) that make life less good do not allow us to say that life is an evil and death a good – even if they seem to outweigh the good experiences. Setting out from this point of departure, our author concludes that death is always an evil in itself, for "it is good simply to be alive, even if one is undergoing terrible experiences".[76] Nagel does not fail to point out that the value attributed to a life has nothing to do with mere organic survival. Indeed, "almost everyone would be indifferent (other things [being] equal) between immediate death and immediate coma followed by death twenty years later without reawakening".[77]

If death is intrinsically an evil, the principal reason is that it involves the loss of life, which is a good in itself and always "is worth living even

veut, d'une mort 'violente', car c'est sa mort qui l'empêche de faire autre chose encore qu'il n'a pas fait. Tout homme qui est mort aurait pu prolonger son activité ou la nier: il n'a donc pas épuisé complètement ses possibilités existentielles humaines".

71 Thomas Nagel, "Death", p. 3.

72 *Ibid.*, p. 1.

73 *Ibid.*, p. 9.

74 See Gabriel Marcel, *Mystery of Being*, vol. 2, p. 161–2 [vol. 2, p. 162].

75 Thomas Nagel, *The View from Nowhere*, pp. 224 f.

76 Thomas Nagel, "Death", p. 2.

77 *Ibid.*

when the bad elements of experience are plentiful, and the good ones too meager to outweigh the bad ones on their own. The additional positive weight is supplied by experience itself, rather than by any of its contents".[78] What is desirable about life, according to Nagel, is not primarily having good experiences – that remains secondary. In the first place one desires "certain states, conditions, or types of activity. It is *being* alive, *doing* certain things, having certain experiences, that we consider good".[79]

When Nagel speaks about death as an evil in itself, he is not discussing the contents or the quality of the life that "N." would have had if he had not died; his discourse is situated, rather, in my opinion, on a more fundamental or ontological level, namely, on the level of the ability (considered as a good) to have experiences, hopes, and possibilities. One can nevertheless assert that death is an evil in an even more fundamental sense: it signifies the absolute end of the existence of a particular individual; it deprives him of his very being. Such discourse applies to every death, even "natural" death. In my opinion, the difference between an accidental death and a natural death does not correspond to an opposition between an evil and a good, but rather to a distinction between two evils. It certainly seems reasonable to maintain that, for the same individual, it is a greater evil to die at the age of twenty than at the age of ninety, if we suppose that the additional seventy years would have allowed him to enjoy many other goods and to realize countless other possibilities. However, there is no real difference between these two deaths, which are both privations of the subject. Although death irreversibly interrupts the possibilities of such and such a subject and destroys his ability to project himself into the future, it deprives him above all of his existence. In annihilating him, it forever destroys also every possibility of actualization. Death is an evil because it deprives the individual of something that he profoundly desires: to be, to exist, to live.

This assertion nevertheless does not exclude the possibility that "N.", from his particular viewpoint, at a given moment and in the particular circumstances of his life, might prefer death to the continuation of his life – even though the price to be paid would be very high, namely, the loss of his very being, as a conscious, free subject. Whatever the motives for it may be (heroism, loss of meaning in life, unbearable sufferings

78 *Ibid.* See *ibid.*, p. 3.

79 *Ibid.*, p. 3.

from a physical or psychological illness, etc.), such a preference for death does not indicate, in my opinion, that it is an evil or a good according to the circumstances. It seems to indicate, rather, that death can appear to the subject himself as a lesser evil compared to the continuation of his life in certain conditions. It is quite possible that subjectively and in certain circumstances one might prefer death, a state of nonbeing without sensations, to life, a state filled with sensations, when those of pain and suffering reach an intolerable degree. The issue here is not a choice between a good and an evil, but rather a subjective preference: better a greater loss that would be easier to endure (death itself, which is without sensation and free of physical and/or psychological sufferings) than a smaller loss that is more difficult to endure (the painful sensations accompanying such a life). This subjective preference of death over present life is not so much a choice between life and death as a choice between "my death now" and "my future death". The first delivers me from the intolerable situation in which I presently find myself, and the second leaves me in the state of suffering of longer or shorter duration that my life will have to offer. Therefore, it is not so much life *per se* that I have renounced, but rather the physical and/or psychological sufferings that accompany my present life. Therefore, I can very well prefer death while regarding it as an evil, for the evil of death is not dependent on the circumstances; it is an evil in itself, even if at a particular moment I subjectively judge that my life is or is not worth the trouble of living.

3. DEFENSE OF THE CHARACTERIZATION OF DEATH AS AN EVIL IN VIEW OF THE PEACEFUL STATE OF PRENATAL NONEXISTENCE

The thesis that death is a "privation" is faced with a challenge: the state before conception is likewise regarded as a privation. Indeed, (1) if the state of death (a state of nonexistence) is an evil of privation, it would seem that prenatal nonexistence ("preconception") must also be an evil of privation; (2) common sense, however, does not regard prenatal nonexistence as an evil of privation on the basis of our attitude toward it, contrary to our attitude toward death; (3) hence we must conclude that death is not an evil of privation.

In order to defend death as an evil of privation, we must, it seems, take a step backward and call into question again the first premise, which is accepted in this argument as true. In particular, we can ask how it follows, from the fact that death is an evil of privation, that the state of prenatal nonexistence ("preconception") is also an evil of privation. Indeed, to conclude this is tantamount to assuming that there is a symmetry between the period of nonexistence before conception and the one after decease. This is the position of Lucretius, who maintains that the past, in which the subject did not yet exist, is the mirror of the future, in which the subject is no more. The past eternity is the perfect image of the future eternity. Being nothing before conception, the subject is nothing after his decease. Someone who experienced nothing of the war against the Carthaginians because he was not yet conceived will not experience pain after his death, either, that is, once he no longer exists.

> Therefore death is nothing to us, it matters not one jot, since the nature of the mind is understood to be mortal: and as in time past we felt no distress, while from all quarters the Carthaginians were coming to the conflict, when the whole world, shaken by the terrifying tumult of war, shivered and quaked under the high heaven, and men were in doubt under which domination all men were destined to fall by land and sea; so when we shall no longer be, when the parting shall have come about between body and spirit, from which we are compacted into one whole, then sure enough nothing at all will be able to happen to us who will then no longer be, or to make us feel, not if earth be commingled with sea, and sea with sky.[80]

A few verses later, Lucretius mentions the idea of symmetry between the prenatal and *postmortem* states by referring to the famous image of the mirror. According to some commentators,[81] his purpose is not to demonstrate that only someone who presently exists can be the subject of evils, but rather to show the irrationality of fears about the past and future nonexistence of the subject. "Look back also and see how the ages of everlasting time past before we were born have been to us nothing. This therefore is a mirror which nature holds up to us, showing the time

80 Titus Lucretius, *De rerum natura*, III, 830–42 (pp. 227, 229): *"Nil igitur mors est ad nos neque pertinet hilum quandoquidem natura animi mortalis habetur. Et velut ante acto nil tempore sensimus aegri, ad confligendum venientibus undique Poenis, omnia cum belli trepido concussa tumultu horrida contremuere sub altis aetheris oris in dubioque fuere utrorum ad regna cadendum omnibus humanis esset terraque marique, sic, ubi non erimus, cum corporis atque animae discidium fuerit quibus e sumus uniter apti, scilicet haut nobis quicquam, qui non erimus tum, accidere omnino poterit sensumque movere, non si terra mari miscebitur et mare caelo"*. A similar example is found in the apocryphal dialogue by Plato-pseudo, *Axiochus*, 365d-e (p. 33). See Marcus Tullius Cicero, *Tusculan Disputations*, book I, vi, 13 (p. 17) and xxxvii, 90 (p. 107); Seneca, *Letters to Lucilius*, vol. 6, letter 54, 4 (pp. 361, 363); Lucius Mestrius Plutarch, *A Letter of Condolence to Apollonios*, 15, 109F (pp. 149 f.).

81 Because of different interpretations, this point is debated. See Philip Mitsis, "Epicurus on Death and the Duration of Life", pp. 305 f.

to come after we at length shall die. Is there anything horrible in that? Is there anything gloomy? Is it not more peaceful than any sleep?"[82] Since a person is indifferent to what happens before his conception, he should also view the state after decease calmly and not regard it as an evil. For – as Epicurus had already emphasized – in order that an evil may befall a subject, "he must needs himself also exist then in that time to be miserable".[83]

However, common sense rightly has difficulty imagining such a symmetry; it maintains, instead, that an asymmetrical attitude toward the two states in question is reasonable. Thus one may ask whether there is not a connection between this first premise and the second, that is, whether there is not in fact a connection between the attitude (of fear) toward the state of death and the attitude (of serenity) toward the state of preconception, on the one hand, and their value, on the other (whether or not they are designated an evil of privation). Of course, one cannot deduce an evil from a fear (Nagel is right in maintaining that the fear that it arouses in us is not the reason why death is an evil; rather, because it is an evil, we fear it[84]). However, a fear can be an indicator of an evil:[85] this means that the difference between our attitudes with

82 Titus Lucretius, *De rerum natura*, III, 972–8 (p. 237): *"Respice item quam nil ad nos anteacta vetustas temporis aeterni fuerit, quam nascimur ante. Hoc igitur speculum nobis natura futuri tempori exponit post mortem denique nostram. Numquid ibi horribile apparet, num triste videtur quicquam, non omni somno securius extat?"* For a more in-depth study of Titus Lucretius, see Pierre Boyancé, *Lucrèce et l'Épicurisme*; Diskin Clay, *Lucretius and Epicurus*; Edward John Kenney, *Lucretius*; Jean Salem, *La mort n'est rien pour nous*; Traudel Stork, *Nil igitur mors est ad nos*; Barbara Price Wallach, *Lucretius and the Diatribe against the Fear of Death*.

83 Titus Lucretius, *De rerum natura*, III, 863–4 (p. 229): *"ipse quoque esse in eo tum tempore, cui male possit accidere"*. See also Arthur Schopenhauer, *The World as Will and Idea*, vol. 3, pp. 253–5 [vol. 2, pp. 594–6].

84 I do not concede the proposition that a state of affairs is an evil because it is feared or regretted by the subject, but I maintain that it is feared or regretted because it is an evil.

85 It is reasonable to suppose that a state described as an evil must cause pain, i.e., a reaction of regret and fear, and that a state described as a good must cause pleasure, i.e., a reaction of joy, free of all fear. Parfit attempts to defend the reasonableness of our asymmetrical attitudes toward prenatal and postmortem nonexistence, not on the basis of a difference between the states themselves (which is what I will try to do), but rather based on the fact that the human being has "sided with the future". He argues, with the help of several examples, that "N." is indifferent about past pains (or that he assigns them little importance) but is not indifferent to future pains. If "N." had to choose between experiencing pains in the past or in the future, he would always prefer having had the experience already rather to being subjected to it in the

regard to prenatal nonexistence and *postmortem* nonexistence justifies calling into question again the first premise of the counterargument. It is precisely the (alleged) symmetry between these two states that the difference in attitudes invites us to examine more closely.

As we have seen, Nagel defends the thesis that death constitutes in itself an evil of privation; he explains, for example, that the same thesis cannot be defended *à propos* the state of preconception. In the latter case, there is no privation because the subject "N." could not be conceived substantially any earlier (T, -1) than he was conceived in reality (T-0). Moreover, "N." could not have been born before T-1, except perhaps for the small margin allowed by premature birth. If "N." had been conceived and born much earlier than these events took place in reality, he would have been a different person. To cite Nagel again, the time preceding the conception of "N." was therefore "not time in which his subsequent birth prevents him from living. His birth,

future. The same goes, *vice versa*, for pleasures: one prefers enjoying pleasures in the future to having enjoyed them in the past. However, the examples offered by Derek Parfit (*Reasons and Persons*, pp. 165 f.) and repeated by Robert Nozick (*Philosophical Explanations*, pp. 744 f.), do not demonstrate, as Roy W. Perrett thinks (*Death and Immortality*, p. 61), that our asymmetrical attitude toward past and future nonexistence is as reasonable as our attitude toward past and future pains and pleasures. Indeed, there are evils that most persons would prefer to suffer in the future – and, if possible, as close as possible to their decease – rather than in the past, such as the loss of a reputation, of honors, of wealth; or the loss of family and friendship; or mourning. The actualization of such evils can give rise to other evils. Moreover, these examples apply mainly, as Parfit himself admits, to the evils that a subject is capable of experiencing, which is not the case for the nonexistence characteristic of death and preconception. The attempt to establish the reasonableness of our asymmetrical attitudes upon the basis of an argument concerning past or future goods is no more convincing. Anthony L. Brueckner and John Martin Fischer ("Why Is Death Bad?") remark that prenatal nonexistence deprives "N." of goods to which he is indifferent, whereas the nonexistence after his decease would deprive him of goods that he desires and deeply hopes to possess. It is possible, however, to remember some past goods that do not necessarily leave him indifferent; one is indifferent to past goods only if one has forgotten them or if they do not influence the present moment in which one finds oneself. Hence I could enjoy the memory of the beautiful moments of my life, such as meeting my wife, Michele, or the birth of my daughters, Myriam, Sophia, and Teresa, and of my son, Nicolas. Would the asymmetry be valid only for the past goods that "N." had forgotten and that would have no influence on the present? I find it regrettable that Nagel ("Death", p. 8) limits himself, in the article in question, to examining death as a privation of possibilities – without discussing the privation of existence itself – and seems bewildered when he is asked to explain our asymmetric attitudes toward the sorts of nonexistence before conception and after death.

when it occurs, does not entail the loss to him of any life whatever".[86] Conception is defined here as a constitutive property of the personal identity of "N." Nagel concludes that, from a logical perspective,[87] the subject could not be conceived earlier than he actually was, whereas he could die later. This is an argument that Kaufman repeats while referring to the person as a psychological identity.[88] In the final analysis, this first attempt at a response is founded on Kripke's thesis concerning the necessary connection between origin and personal identity; this theory stipulates that if "N." resulted from a different sperm and ovum than those from which he actually came, "N." would no longer be the same person.[89] Of course, one could imagine the possibility of postponing – even by a considerable interval – the conception of "N." by freezing an ovum and a sperm that are responsible for the biological personal identity of "N." That identity would not be changed by the fact that he would be born much later. It would also be possible to freeze the fertilized ovum some time after its union with the sperm and to decide to thaw it twenty years later and to allow it then to continue its natural development. The biological personal identity

86 Thomas Nagel, "Death", p. 8: "The time prior to a man's birth is time in which he would have lived had he been born not then but earlier. For aside from the brief margin permitted by premature labor, he *could* not have been born earlier: anyone born substantially earlier than he was would have been someone else. Therefore the time prior to his birth is not time in which his subsequent birth prevents him from living. His birth, when it occurs, does not entail the loss to him of any life whatever".

87 Derek Parfit (*Reasons and Persons*, p. 175) criticizes Nagel, pointing out that even if it is logically impossible to be conceived earlier, it is nevertheless possible even to regret truths. When the Pythagoreans learned that "the square root of two was not a rational number", they regretted it. However, Nagel does not say that it is impossible to regret one's past nonexistence; his purpose is to show why regretting one's past nonexistence is irrational.

88 Kaufman's argument is based on memory as the central criterion of personal identity. See Frederik Kaufman, "An Answer to Lucretius' Symmetry Argument against the Fear of Death" and "Death and Deprivation; Or, Why Lucretius' Symmetry Argument Fails". In the latter article he explains (pp. 309–10) that "no, it is not possible for a person in the psychological sense to exist earlier than in fact he or she did, because a psychological continuum which, by hypothesis, starts earlier, would be a sufficiently different set of memories and experiences, and hence be a different psychological self [...]. Imaginatively moving a person 'back' disrupts the psychological self with which we are concerned. There are not, however, similar problems with imaginatively projecting the life of a person 'forward', that is, past the actual time of death. In imaginatively extending a psychological continuum beyond the point at which it was in fact extinguished, we do not have to disrupt the previous contents of the continuum; we simply make additions to it".

89 See Saul Kripke, *Naming and Necessity*, pp. 111 f.; Derek Parfit, *Reasons and Persons*, pp. 351 f.

of that individual would not be changed, either. Thus one could maintain that he could be born later than he was born in reality; however, one could not assert that "N." could be conceived earlier than he was in fact.

A reference to logical (hypothetical) worlds as a counterargument to the necessity of the origin is hardly convincing. According to this line of reasoning, the personal identity of "N." would not be determined by a physical or psychological continuity that was valid for "N." within the framework of just one possible world, but would be instead a "metaphysical personal identity"[90] in an imagined possible world distinct from the present world. Similarly, the argument that the moment of decease is essential to "N." because his conception is essential to him is not very convincing. Different possible lives of "N." can diverge from a common point of departure, but according to Nagel they cannot tend toward a common conclusion from different starting points. These would not be different possible lives of one and the same person, but rather a set of different possible persons whose lives would have equivalent conclusions. "Given an identifiable individual, countless possibilities for his continued existence are imaginable, and we can clearly conceive of what it would be for him to go on existing indefinitely".[91] This argument does not even satisfy its author, to whom it seems "too sophisticated to explain the simple difference between our attitudes to prenatal [preconceptional] and posthumous nonexistence".[92]

However, even if "N." could have been conceived and born earlier, as presupposed in Nozick's example (which is mentioned by Nagel in a footnote to his article "Death"),[93] we could not conclude from this that a nonexistent subject would be able to be deprived of something, even of his existence. Nagel seems to prove the asymmetry between death and preconception on the basis of the fact that death is the definitive and irreversible end of "N.'s" possibilities and plans for his life, unlike preconception, which constitutes the very "possibility" of his possibilities. In the aforementioned article, however, Nagel neglects to consider that death deprives an existing subject of his existence, whereas a nonexistent subject cannot be deprived of his existence. The difference between the state of preconception (or prenatal nonexistence) and the state of

90 Anthony L. Brueckner and John Martin Fischer, "Being Born Earlier", p. 113; "Why is Death Bad?", p. 223. See also "Death's Badness", pp. 43–4, note 2.
91 Thomas Nagel, "Death", p. 8.
92 *Ibid.*, p. 8, note 3.
93 *Ibid.*

death lies, in the final analysis, in the fact that the second constitutes a real privation of the subject, unlike the first; this difference is on the order of the loss and destruction of an already existing human being. Unlike death, in which the subject is no more and the possibility of life belongs definitively to the past, the state of preconception is characterized by a "possibility" that a subject may come into existence.

Conclusion

> A good way of testing the calibre of a philosophy is to ask what it thinks of death.[1]

Death is not a topic that the philosopher should treat in passing or on which we should not waste our time. On the contrary, it is one of the most important philosophical questions. Raising a whole series of inquiries, it stimulates philosophical speculation; for some it is at the very origin of the philosophical act. This consists, in part, of discovering what prevents a human being from knowing himself as he is in reality, that is, as Heidegger has rightly emphasized, a Being-towards-death, and (subsequently) of bringing him to live in authenticity. The confrontation with death leads to a meditation on life and human nature.

A philosophical reflection on death requires above all that one clarify the term, which implies an anthropological definition of the person, a definition that will have ethical repercussions on problems concerning the end of life. The definition of so-called personal death, which is based on Lockean anthropology, involves several important problems, and proponents of this position do not always apply it consistently, either on the anthropological, theoretical level or with regard to its ethical implications. Furthermore, the notion of person underlying the definition of so-called personal death and the ethics of interests are both based on the presuppositions of the Epicurean thesis of "the nothingness of death", which are very problematic. I have opted for a definition of personal death that is at variance with the anthropological dualism

[1] Santayan, quoted by Jaroslav Jan Pelikan, *The Shape of Death*, p. 5.

of Lockean origin that has been adopted by many philosophers in the bioethical debate, who would define person by the empirically verifiable exercise of self-consciousness and by activity as a moral subject. Personal human death occurs, rather, when the organism is irreversibly incapable of functioning as a whole, a condition that itself implies the person's departure from this world.

The Heideggerian thesis of Being-towards-death, which relies on the intuitions of Simmel and Scheler, as well as the critique thereof by Sternberger, Landsberg, and Sartre, are attempts in the first half of the twentieth century to answer the question about the knowledge of death (or mortality) and about the possibility of a thanatological phenomenology. After addressing Scheler's intuition, Heidegger's ontology, and Sartre's deduction, as well as the theses concerning a foreknowledge of death or an ontology of love, I concluded that one cannot deduce from a purely ontological analysis the necessity of the *Dasein*'s Being-towards-death. In order to do that, it is necessary to pass by way of the experience of someone else's death. My critique of Heidegger's and Scheler's theses is based on a concept of the human being as essentially open to the future, as a free projection toward the future. This projection is not limited ontologically, nor in an *a priori* manner, nor from the subjective viewpoint – as both Nagel and Sartre have emphasized – by an end, which is to say that the subject does not have an *a priori* consciousness of the fact that the field of his possibilities is narrowing. Human life is not perceived as a closed totality, as Scheler and Heidegger maintain; for them death is envisaged in its connection with a finite temporality, to the point where time itself is thought of in terms of death. I maintain that it is not possible, starting from an ontological analysis of Being-ahead-of-itself, to deduce Being-towards-the-end. The latter is unthinkable without an experience of the human being's finitude, in other words, unless one experiences the decease and the corpse of the other. The essential openness of the Being-ahead-of-itself does not ontologically imply an end. Death is the impossibility of possibles, because it interrupts the subject's projection of his possibles. This ontology resurfaces in the debate about whether or not death is an evil.

Phenomenological reflection on death in recent decades is still heavily influenced by the discussion resulting from the Heideggerian analysis of Being-towards-death. It systematically disregards, however, the very important and fruitful contributions of recent analytical speculation that proposes theses and arguments on the theoretical and ethical levels. This speculation, for its part, is generally characterized by a systematic bracketing off of the thanatological debate of the first half of the twentieth century, to which it refers "in passing", at most. It likewise overlooks more recent phenomenological approaches, such as that of Levinas or the postmodern approach proposed by Derrida in his discussion of Heidegger. In his preface to *Other Minds*, for example, Nagel cites what he considers to be a lack of originality and/or of argumentative support in most philosophical works of the past as his pretext for maintaining that it is not necessary or not worth the trouble to study them.

The present study deals with the knowledge of death and of our mortal condition and with the question of whether death is an evil. Its objective, besides a systematic and analytical reflection on death, is to start a dialogue among authors representing various currents in contemporary Western philosophy who discuss death from a theoretical perspective. Phenomenologists and existentialists have been presented along with proponents of the recent analytical tradition, as well as the postmodernists, in passing. The reader who is acquainted with the positions developed during the first part of the twentieth century, or with those of the more recent phenomenological and postmodernist trends, can only marvel at how similar they are – which is not in itself a criticism – to several essential theses proposed by the analytical philosophers (for example, the thesis of death as an evil that deprives the subject of his possibilities), and at the fact that these authors limit themselves to the field of Anglo-Saxon philosophy. Generally speaking, they consider only recent publications in English and disregard a whole series of interesting thanatological works in other languages that were written recently or else two or three generations ago. A careful reading of the texts produced by the analytical trend gives the impression that the majority of these philosophers have not taken the trouble to read the contemporary "classics" of the philosophy of death but have limited their study to discussions of them in secondary literature that often contains errors.

To give a specific example, Rosenberg, in his study on death, intentionally omits Heidegger's phenomenological analysis, which he considers "dramatic and metaphorical",[2] without having read his writings firsthand, it seems to me.[3] Thus he affirms superficially, in my opinion,

[2] Jay F. Rosenberg, *Thinking Clearly about Death*, p. 207. "The dark obscurities of Heidegger's phenomenological ruminations", *ibid.*, p. 213.

[3] As evidence for his statement he cites an article by Paul Edwards ("Existentialism and Death") that does not discuss Heidegger's positions directly but rather his Anglo-Saxon commentators.

that the so-called existentialists – he mentions Heidegger and Sartre – are "the worst offenders" with respect to his own thesis, namely, that no person knows or can know what it is like to be dead.[4] According to him, the philosopher from Freiburg maintained that there is an intuitive knowledge of mortality – which is in reality Scheler's position – as well as a possibility of experiencing one's own death, which is simply false. Another typical example appears in the very first lines of Williams's article about the case of Makropulos and the boredom associated with immortality: he is careful to warn his reader that he distances himself from the work of "some existentialists" who "seem to have said that death was what gave meaning to life, if anything did, just because it was the fear of death that gave meaning to life".[5] It is certainly possible that "some existentialists" – who are they? – might have held such a position, but if we refer to the classical texts of that philosophical current, I doubt very much that Williams is correct. Clearly, Heidegger refused to discuss the question of the meaning of death, because that would be on the order of an ontical reflection. As for Sartre, he declares precisely the opposite, that is, that death robs life of its meaning. The same goes for Camus. Marcel, for his part, introduces the notion of hope in order to overcome death, which he considers the antiutopia. Moreover, despite his professed desire to oppose the existentialist philosophers, Williams actually adopts part of their heritage by declaring that death is an evil – a thesis that Sartre had already defended by referring to the notion of possibility.

All contemporary philosophical thanatologians, to varying degrees, have noted the importance of the Epicurean thesis of the "nothingness of death" in speculating about death. However, many philosophers have too often dealt with it "in passing", content to denounce it as a "sophism" without having read carefully, it seems to me, the passages in which the philosopher of the Garden presents and develops his thesis, and without presenting a detailed analysis of his arguments. Kierkegaard, for example, describes it as a "jest".[6] More recently, it has been described as preposterous and "absurd",[7] a "vacuity"[8] that "may have been intended

4 See Jay F. Rosenberg, *Thinking Clearly about Death*, p. 191 and footnote 5 on p. 233. We find a similar critique penned by Douglas N. Walton, *On Defining Death*, p. 54. Neither Heidegger nor Sartre ever made such a statement (contradicting Rosenberg's thesis).

5 Bernard Williams, "The Makropulos Case", p. 82.

6 Søren Kierkegaard, "At a Graveside", p. 73.

7 "Epicurus's famous argument, for example, is about as absurd as any I have seen", Steven Luper, "Annihilation", p. 270. "Epicurus's absurd claim", *ibid.*, p. 272.

8 Richard Rorty, "The Contingency of Selfhood", p. 11.

as little more than an eristic flourish".[9] Should we waste time, therefore, discussing this "extremely implausible" thesis that, according to Mothersill, is nothing but "an ancient sophism that purports to justify indifference to death"?[10]

Despite these negative judgments with regard to the Epicurean challenge, I remain convinced of its capital importance. We see it reemerging constantly, in various forms, in contemporary philosophical thanatology. We find it, in the first place, whenever the very possibility of a phenomenology of death is called into question. Indeed, death, in the sense of the state of death, escapes the direct experience of the living subject and appears as a limit point of thought, a final frontier, something external to the subject's existence. The perceptible phenomena are on the order of consequences of death – mourning, farewell, the corpse, the emotional and/or intellectual shock – or else the beginnings of death – the dying process – and do not actually reveal its nature. Direct access to the nature of death is forbidden to the phenomenologist philosopher, who cannot apprehend what it is like to be dead. A phenomenological approach could be made by means of the categories of passivity and nondonation, with reference to the theory of affectivity without intentionality, or just as well through the notions of threshold and frontier, and finally by extrapolating from a phenomenology of sleep and of conception. Such an analysis is always situated below the boundary separating the states of life and death.

A second instance of the Epicurean challenge appears in the difficulty of imagining "my death" from the perspective of the dead-me. If one postulates an afterlife, one admits that it is possible to experience "one's own death". On the contrary, if one follows the philosopher of the Garden in postulating that death causes the subject to return to nothingness, one cannot strictly speaking either imagine or experience one's state of death, that is, "one's own death". Indeed, I cannot be present at my annihilation, for I am not capable of abstracting myself as a subject from my subjective perception. Imagining "my death" would involve at the same time the disappearance of the spectator-me, which is impossible. Hence it seems, from this very specific point of view, that "my death" never exists for me, that it does not affect me and in a way never arrives for me, either living or dead, given the postulate that there is no afterlife. This nonencounter with death, correctly enunciated by Epicurus and repeated by Wittgenstein, raises the following question,

9 Mary Mothersill, "Death", p. 88.
10 *Ibid.*

among others: how can death be an evil for the dead-me when my ego no longer exists and has no more sensations?

The challenge of Epicurus emerges a third time at the heart of the controversy between, on the one hand, the thesis of the mutual exclusion of the states of life and death and, on the other hand, the thesis of death *in* life. By noting correctly that death is somehow inscribed already in the program of the living being, adherents of the second thesis situate their discourse – without explicitly saying so – on the level of a particular interpretation of the concept of death: they equate it with mortality when they maintain that the living being is destined to die from the moment of his conception and that the unfolding of life requires death. Nevertheless they do not thereby abolish the Epicurean challenge, as many interpreters have believed. Philosophers commonly contrast the extraterritoriality of death with respect to life and the interiority of death *in* life. In my opinion there is no real opposition between these two ways of speaking, because they are situated at two distinct levels of comprehension that are not contradictory: on the one hand, we are considering the state of death – the Epicurean proposition – and, on the other hand, the state of being mortal – the proposition of the advocates of death *in* life.

We find a fourth instance of the Epicurean challenge in the goal set for themselves by many thanatologians of the first half of the twentieth century: to denounce the flight from death that takes refuge in the generalization that "people die" and to encourage the human person to lead an authentic life by giving an account of his own death.

The fifth encounter with this challenge in contemporary philosophy is the issue of knowing how – if death as such is hermetically sealed off from all sense experience – one can maintain, as Sartre and Nagel do, that death is an evil. Indeed, do we have the right to claim that death is an evil for someone who is no more and who can no longer experience it? In order to do that it seemed to me necessary, first, to present in minute detail the arguments of the philosopher of the Garden that support his assertion that death is nothing to us. Second, I attempted a critical discussion of the two main presuppositions for that thesis, which are the requirement of experience and the need for a subject; these are some of the underlying presuppositions of the current bioethical debate about the definition of person and about the ethics of interests. In order for it to be possible to characterize a specific event – in this case, death – as an evil, it is necessary, according to Epicurus, that the individual human being have an experience of it and that he himself be present at the moment of its occurrence. And since death does not fulfill these two requirements, one cannot, according to the Greek philosopher, reasonably maintain that human death is perceived as an evil. It is therefore irrational to fear it.

I distanced myself from the Epicurean argument by situating my arguments on the level of the premises presupposed by the "nothingness of death", and by showing that a particular event can be considered an evil independently of the fact that the individual human being experiences it and of the fact that he exists at the moment of the event, as illustrated by posthumous evils. Having set aside experientialism and the need for a subject, I proposed understanding the evil of death from the perspective of privation. This thesis in turn, however, raises several problems when one tries to specify such a privation. Is it a matter of pleasures, desires, interests, projects, the ability to form projects and to project oneself into the future, or, finally, the subject's very existence? A discussion of the contents of the privation inflicted by death necessarily leads to the question that forms the basis of the ethical debate: determining whether death is always an evil or whether that status depends primarily on circumstances (and then one would determine that evil by calculating the subjective value of the subject's life). Another question resulting from this is whether accidental death can be considered as an evil, as opposed to natural death. Starting from an ontology in which the individual is fundamentally capable of projecting himself "indefinitely" into the future and of continually forming new possibilities, one can thus maintain that the human being always dies prematurely, so to speak, that is, before he has exhausted all the possibilities of his being.

This question as to whether death is an evil (for the dead person himself), which I have discussed here on the theoretical level, seems to me to be of paramount importance for the current ethical debate about death, which does not take it sufficiently into account. Indeed, most contemporary moral philosophers accept the opinion that, generally, it is a great misfortune to be killed. If Epicurus was right in asserting that someone's death cannot be considered as an evil for him, how could we maintain that an evil has befallen the person who has been killed? If one wishes to demonstrate satisfactorily that to kill "N." is to do him an injustice, one needs to explain why death is an evil for the person who is dead. In this way the present study leads to new thanatological and ethical speculation.

Bibliography

Adorno, Theodor, *Jargon der Eigentlichkeit. Zur deutschen Ideologie* in *Gesammelte Schriften*, vol. 6, 5th ed. (Frankfurt am Main: Suhrkamp, 1996).

Agazzi, Evandro, *Right, Wrong and Science. The Ethical Dimensions of the Techno-Scientific Enterprise* (Amsterdam, New York: Rodopi, 2004) [*Il bene, il male e la scienza. Le dimensioni etiche dell'impresa scientifico-tecnologica* (Milan: Rusconi, 1992)].

"La mort comme mystère de la vie", in *Idem*, co-ed., *Le sens de la mort. Vom Sinn des Todes* (Fribourg, Switzerland: Editions Universitaires Fribourg Suisse, 1980), pp. 37–52.

"Reductionism as Negation of the Scientific Spirit", in *Idem*, ed., *The Problem of Reductionism in Science* (Dordrecht: Kluwer Academic Publisher, 1991), pp. 1–29.

Agich, George J., "The Concepts of Death and Embodiment", *Ethics in Science and Medicine*, 3 (1976): 2: pp. 95–105.

Agich, George J. and Jones Royce P., "Personal Identity and Brain Death: A Critical Response", *Philosophy and Public Affairs*, 15 (1986): 3: pp. 267–74.

Albert, Karl, *Lebensphilosophie. Von den Anfängen bei Nietzsche bis zur ihrer Kritik bei Lukács* (Freiburg/München: Karl Alber, 1995).

Allen, Colin and Hauser, Marc D., "Concept Attribution in Nonhuman Animals. Theoretical and Methodological Problems in Ascribing Complex Mental Processes", *Philosophy of Science*, 58 (1991): 2: pp. 221–40 [republished in Marc Bekoff and Dale Jamieson, eds., *Readings in Animal Cognition* (Cambridge, Massachusetts: The MIT Press, 1996), pp. 47–62].

Allen, Woody, "Death Knocks", in John Martin Fischer, ed., *The Metaphysics of Death* (Stanford, California: Stanford University Press, 1993), pp. 33–40.

Ambrose of Milan, *Two Orations "On the Death of His Brother Satyrus"*, translated by John J. Sullivan and Martin R. P. McGuire, in *Funeral Orations by St. Gregory Nazianzen and St. Ambrose* (New York: Fathers of the Church, 1953), pp. 161–259.

Apel, Karl-Otto, "Das Problem einer philosophischen Theorie der Rationalitätstypen", in Herbert Schnädelbach, ed., *Rationalität* (Frankfurt am Main: Suhrkamp, 1984), pp. 15–31.

"Ist der Tod eine Bedingung der Möglichkeit von Bedeutung? (Existentialismus, Platonismus oder transzendentale Sprachpragmatik?)", in Jürgen Mittelstrass and Manfred Riedel, eds., *Vernünftiges Denken. Studien zur praktischen Philosophie und Wissenschaftstheorie* (Berlin: Walter de Gruyter, 1978), pp. 407–19.

Arendt, Hannah, *The Human Condition* (Chicago: The University of Chicago Press, 1958).

Ariès, Philippe, *The Hour of Our Death*, translated by Helen Weaver (New York: Knopf, 1981) [*L'homme devant la mort*, 2 vols. (Paris: Seuil, 1977)].

Western Attitudes toward Death: From the Middle Ages to the Present, translated by Patricia Ranum (Baltimore: The John Hopkins University Press, 1974) [*Essais sur l'histoire de la mort en Occident du Moyen Âge à nos jours* (Paris: Seuil, 1975)].

Aristotle, *Nicomachean Ethics*, translated by William D. Ross, in *The Works of Aristotle*, vol. 9 (Oxford: Clarendon Press, 1925).

On Life and Death, translated by William D. Ross, in *The Works of Aristotle*, vol. 3 (Oxford: Clarendon Press, 1931).

Arregui, Jorge V., *El horror de morir. El valor de la muerte en la vida humana* (Barcelona: Tibidabo Ediciones, 1992).

Augustine, *The City of God*, Books VIII–XVI, translated by Gerald G. Walsh and Grace Monahan (New York: Fathers of the Church, 1952). Book XIII is found on pp. 299–346.

Confessions, translated by William Watts (Cambridge, Massachusetts: Harvard University Press, 1968).

Ayer, Alfred Jules, "What I Saw When I Was Dead … ", *Sunday Telegraph*, 28 August 1988, reprinted in Lewis E. Hahn, ed., *The Philosophy of A. J. Ayer* (La Salle, Illinois: Open Court, 1992), pp. 44–53.

Bartlett, Edward T. and Youngner, Stuart J., "Human Death and the Destruction of the Neocortex", in Richard M. Zaner, ed., *Death: Beyond Whole-Brain Criteria* (Dordrecht: Kluwer Academic Publishers, 1988), pp. 199–215.

Bauby, Jean-Dominique, *The Diving Bell and the Butterfly*, translated by Jeremy Leggatt (New York: A. A. Knopf, distributed by Random House, 1997) [*Le scaphandre et le papillon* (Paris: Robert Laffont, 1997)].

Baudrillard, Jean, *L'échange symbolique et la mort* (Paris: Gallimard, 1976).

Baumann, Zygmunt, *Mortality, Immortality and Other Life Strategies* (Cambridge/Oxford: Polity Press/Blackwell Publishers, 1992).

Bayle, Pierre, "Lucrèce", *Dictionnaire historique et critique*, 5th ed. (Amsterdam: La Compagnie des Libraires, 1734), vol. 3, "G–L", pp. 811–30.

Becker, Ernest, *The Denial of Death* (New York: Free Press, 1973).

Belshaw, Christopher, *Annihilation: The Sense and Signification of Death* (Montreal, Kingston, and Ithaca: McGill-Queen's University Press, 2009).

"Asymmetry and Non-Existence", *Philosophical Studies*, 70 (1993): 1: pp. 103–116.

Bergson, Henri, *Creative Evolution*, translated by Arthur Mitchell (New York: The Modern Library, 1944; English edition originally published by Henry

Holt and Co., 1911) [*L'évolution créatrice*, in *Oeuvres*, 5th ed. (Paris: Presses Universitaires de France, 1991), pp. 487–809].

The Two Sources of Morality and Religion, translated by R. Ashley Audra and Cloudesley Brereton (New York: Henry Holt and Company, 1935, 1963) [*Les deux sources de la morale et de la religion*, in *Oeuvres*, 5th ed. (Paris: Presses Universitaires de France, 1991), pp. 979–1247].

Berlinger, Rudolph, *Das Nichts und der Tod* (Frankfurt am Main: Vittorio Klostermann, 1972).

Bernard, Claude, *Leçons sur les phénomènes de la vie communs aux animaux et aux végétaux* (Paris: Baillière, 1878; reprinted Paris: Vrin, 1966).

Bernat, James L., "How Much of the Brain Must Die in Brain Death?", *The Journal of Clinical Ethics*, 3 (1992): 1: pp. 21–6.

Bernat, James L., Culver, Charles M. and Gert, Bernard, "On the Definition and Criterion of Death", *Annals of Internal Medicine*, 94 (1981): 1: pp. 389–94.

Bichat, Xavier, *Recherches physiologiques sur la vie et la mort* (Paris: Flammarion, 1994).

Bigelow John, Campbell, John and Pargetter, Robert, "Death and Well-Being", *Pacific Philosophical Quarterly*, 71 (1990): 1: pp. 119–40.

Birnbacher, Dieter, "Das Dilemma des Personbegriffs", in Peter Strasser and Edgar Starz, eds., *Personsein aus bioethischer Sicht* (Stuttgart: Franz Steiner, 1997), pp. 9–25.

Black, Peter M., "Three Definitions of Death", *The Monist*, 60 (1988): 1: pp. 136–46.

Bloch, Ernst, *Experimentum Mundi. Frage, Kategorien des Herausbringens, Praxis* in *Ernst Bloch Werkausgabe*, 16 vols. (Frankfurt am Main: Suhrkamp, 1969 ff.), vol. 15 (1975).

The Principle of Hope, 3 vols., translated by Neville Plaice, Stephen Plaice and Paul Knight (Cambridge, Massachusetts: The MIT Press, 1986) [*Das Prinzip Hoffnung* in *Ernst Bloch Werkausgabe*, 16 vols. (Frankfurt am Main: Suhrkamp, 1969 ff.), vol. 5 (1985)].

Tübinger Einleitung in die Philosophie in *Ernst Bloch. Werkausgabe*, 16 vols. (Frankfurt am Main: Suhrkamp, 1969 ff.), vol. 13 (1970).

"Der Mensch als Möglichkeit", *Forum. Österreichische Monatsblätter für kulturelle Freiheit*, 12 (1965): 140–1: pp. 357–61.

Bollnow, Otto Friedrich, "Der Tod des andern Menschen", *Universitas*, 19 (1964): 12: pp. 1257–64.

Bouveresse, Renée, *Spinoza et Leibniz. L'idée d'animisme universelle* (Paris: Vrin, 1992).

Bowker, John, *The Meanings of Death* (Cambridge: Cambridge University Press, 1991).

Boyancé, Pierre, *Lucrèce et l'épicurisme* (Paris: Presses Universitaires de France, 1963).

Braddock, Glenn, "Epicureanism, Death, and the Good Life", *Philosophical Inquiry*, 22 (2000), 1–2: pp. 47–66.

Bradley, Ben, *Well Being and Death* (Oxford: Oxford University Press, 2009).

"When Is Death Bad for the One Who Dies?", *Noûs*, 38 (2004): 1: pp. 1–28.

Brock, Dan W., *Life and Death. Philosophical Essays in Biomedical Ethics* (Cambridge: Cambridge University Press, 1993).

Brody, Howard, "Brain Death and Personal Existence: A Reply to Green and Walker", *Journal of Medicine and Philosophy*, 8 (1983): 2: pp. 187–96.

Brueckner, Anthony L. and Fischer, John Martin, "The Asymmetry of Early Death and Late Birth", *Philosophical Studies*, 71 (1993): 3: pp. 327–31.

"Being Born Earlier", *Australasian Journal of Philosophy*, 76 (1988): 1: pp. 110–14.

"Death's Badness", *Pacific Philosophical Quarterly*, 74 (1993): 1: pp. 37–45.

"Why Is Death Bad?", in John Martin Fischer, ed., *The Metaphysics of Death* (Stanford, California: Stanford University Press, 1993), pp. 221–9 [originally published in *Philosophical Studies*, 50 (1986): 2: pp. 213–23].

Bryson, Kenneth A., "Being and Human Death", *The New Scholasticism*, 48 (1974): 3: pp. 343–50.

Buren, John von, *The Young Heidegger: Rumor of the Hidden King* (Bloomington and Indianapolis: Indiana University Press, 1994).

Byrne, Paul A., Nilges, Richard G. and Potts, Michael, "Introduction", in Michael Potts, Paul A. Byrne, and Richard G. Nilges, eds., *Beyond Brain Death: The Case against Brain Based Criteria for Human Death* (Dordrecht: Kluwer Academic Press, 2000), pp. 1–20.

Callahan, Joan C., "On Harming the Dead", *Ethics*, 97 (1987): 2: pp. 341–52.

Campbell, John, Bigelow, John and Pargetter, Robert, "Death and Well-Being", *Pacific Philosophical Quarterly*, 71 (1990): 1: pp. 119–40.

Carey, Susan, *Conceptual Change in Childhood* (Cambridge, Massachusetts: The MIT Press, 1985).

Carruthers, Peter, *Introducing Persons: Theories and Arguments in the Philosophy of Mind* (London: Croom Helm, 1986).

Carse, James P., *Death and Existence: A Conceptual History of Human Mortality* (New York: John Wiley & Sons, 1980).

Caruso, Igor A., *Die Trennung der Liebenden. Eine Phänomenologie des Todes* (Stuttgart: Verlag Hans Huber, 1968).

Cedrins, Janis, *Gedanken über den Tod in der Existenzphilosophie* (Bonn, Ph.D., 1949).

Chauvier, Stéphane, *Qu'est-ce qu'une personne?* (Paris: Vrin, 2003).

Choron, Jacques, *Death and Western Thought* (New York: Collier Books, 1963).

Modern Man and Mortality (New York: The Macmillan Company, 1964).

Cicchese, Gennaro, "L'essere mortale dei mortali. Un'analisi sul problema della morte nel pensiero del secondo Heidegger", *Aquinas*, 34 (1991): 1: pp. 85–102.

Cicero, Marcus Tullius, *De finibus bonorum et malorum*, translated by Harris Rackham (Cambridge, Massachusetts: Harvard University Press, Loeb Library, 1961).

Tusculan Disputations, translated by John E. King (London: William Heinemann, 1966).

Cigman, Ruth, "Death, Misfortune and Species Inequality", *Philosophy and Public Affairs*, 10 (1981): 1: pp. 47–64.

Clay, Diskin, *Lucretius and Epicurus* (Ithaca, New York: Cornell University Press, 1983).

Clements, Colleen, "Death and Philosophical Diversions", *Philosophy and Phenomenological Research*, 39 (1978/79): 4: pp. 524–36.
Clouse, Danner K., Culver, Charles M. and Gert, Bernard, *Bioethics: A Systematic Approach* (Oxford: Oxford University Press, 2006).
Compton, John J., "Death and the Philosophical Tradition", in John Lachs and Charles E. Scott, eds., *The Human Search: An Introduction to Philosophy* (Oxford: Oxford University Press, 1981), pp. 331–51.
Conche, Marcel, *La mort et la pensée* (Villers sur Mer: Éditons de Mégare, 1973).
Condrau, Gion, *Der Mensch und sein Tod. Certa moriendi condicio*, 2nd ed. (Zürich: Kreuz Verlag, 1991).
Cottier, Georges, "Die Todesproblematik bei einigen Existenzialphilosophen", in Norbert A. Luyten, ed., *Tod – Ende oder Vollendung* (Freiburg: Karl Alber, 1980), pp. 111–59.
Courtine, Jean-François, *Heidegger et la phénoménologie* (Paris: Vrin, 1990).
Critchley, Simon, *Very Little ... Almost Nothing: Death, Philosophy, Literature* (London: Routledge, 1997).
Culver, Charles M., Bernat, James L. and Gert, Bernard, "On the Definition and Criterion of Death", *Annals of Internal Medicine*, 94 (1981): 1: pp. 389–94.
Culver, Charles M., Clouse, Danner K. and Gert, Bernard, *Bioethics: A Systematic Approach* (Oxford: Oxford University Press, 2006).
Culver, Charles M. and Gert, Bernard, *Philosophy in Medicine: Conceptual and Ethical Issues in Medicine and Psychiatry* (Oxford: Oxford University Press, 1982).
Dalton, Peter C., "Death and Evil", *The Philosophical Forum*, 11 (1979–80): 2: pp. 193–211.
Dastur, Françoise, *Comment affronter la mort?* (Paris: Fayard, 2005).
La mort. Essai sur la finitude (Paris: Hatier, 1994).
Dauenhauer, Bernard P., "On Death and Birth", *The Personalist*, 57 (1976): 2: pp. 162–70.
Defining Death: A Report on the Medical, Legal and Ethical Issues in the Determination of Death, President's Commission for the Study of Ethical Problems in Medicine and Biomedical and Behavioral Research, 1981 (Washington, D.C.: U.S. Government Printing Office, 1981).
"A Definition of Irreversible Coma. Report of the Ad Hoc Committee of Harvard Medical School to Examine the Definition of Brain Death", *Journal of the American Medical Association*, 205 (1968): 6: pp. 85–8.
DeGrazia, David, *Human Identity and Bioethics* (Cambridge: Cambridge University Press, 2005).
Demske, James M., *Sein, Mensch und Tod. Das Todesproblem bei Martin Heidegger* (Freiburg/München: Karl Alber Verlag, 1963).
Depraz, Natalie, "Naître à soi-même", *Alter. Revue de phénoménologie*, 1 (1993): pp. 81–105.
Deputte, Bertrand L., "Perception de la mort et de la séparation chez les primates", *Nouvelle Revue d'Ethnopsychiatrie*, 10 (1988): pp. 113–50.
Derrida, Jacques, *Aporias*, translated by Thomas Dutoit (Stanford, California: Stanford University Press, 1993) [*Apories. Mourir – s'attendre aux 'limites de la vérité'* (Paris: Galilé, 1996)].

Dickinson, George E., "First Childhood Death Experiences", *Omega: Journal of Death and Dying,* 25 (1992): 3: pp. 169–82.

Donnelly, John, ed., *Language, Metaphysics, and Death,* 2nd ed. (New York: Fordham University Press, 1978, 1994).

Donnelly, John, "The Misfortunate Dead: A Problem for Materialism", in *Idem,* ed., *Language, Metaphysics, and Death,* 2nd ed. (New York: Fordham University Press, 1994), pp. 153–69.

Duchesneau, François, *La physiologie des Lumières: empirisme, modèles et théories* (The Hague: M. Nijhoff, 1982).

Durant, Guy, "Mort, bioéthique de la", *Encyclopédie Philosophique Universelle,* vol. 2: *Les notions philosophiques* (Paris: Presses Universitaires de France, 1990), pp. 1690–1.

Ebeling, Hans, *Rüstung und Selbsterhaltung. Kriegsphilosophie* (Paderborn: Schöningh, 1983).

ed., *Der Tod in der Moderne,* 3rd ed. (Frankfurt am Main: Hain, 1992).

Edwards, Paul, *Heidegger on Death: A Critical Evaluation, in The Monist* (La Salle, Illinois: The Hegeler Institute, 1979).

ed., "Existentialism and Death: A Survey of Some Confusions and Absurdities", in John Donnelly, ed., *Language, Metaphysics, and Death,* 2nd ed. (New York: Fordham University Press, 1978, 1994), pp. 43–79 [originally published in Sidney Morgenbesser, Patrick Suppes, and Morton White, eds., *Philosophy, Science, and Method* (New York: St. Martin's Press, 1969), pp. 473–505].

"Life, Meaning and Value of", in *Idem,* ed., *Encyclopedia of Philosophy* (New York: Macmillan, 1967), vol. 4, pp. 469–70.

"My Death", in *Idem,* ed., *The Encyclopedia of Philosophy* (New York: Macmillan, 1967), vol. 5, pp. 416–19.

Elias, Nobert, *The Loneliness of the Dying,* translated by Edmund Jephcott (New York: Continuum, 2001) [*Über die Einsamkeit der Sterbenden* (Frankfurt am Main: Suhrkamp, 1982)].

Elshtain, Bethke, *Sovereignty: God, State, and the Self,* The Gifford Lectures (New York: Basic Books, 2008).

Emad, Parvis, "Person, Death and World", in Manfred Frings, ed., *Max Scheler (1874–1928). Centennial Essays* (The Hague: Martinus Nijhoff, 1974), pp. 67–77.

Engelhardt, Tristram H., *The Foundations of Bioethics,* 2nd ed. (Oxford: Oxford University Press, 1986, 1996).

"The Counsels of Finitude", in Peter Steinfels and Robert M. Veatch, eds., *Death Inside Out: The Hastings Center Report* (New York: Harper & Row, 1975), pp. 115–25.

"Defining Death: A Philosophical Problem for Medicine and Law", *American Review of Respiratory Disease,* 112 (1975): pp. 587–90.

"Medicine and the Concept of Person", in Michael F. Goodman, ed., *What Is a Person?* (Clifton, New Jersey: Humana Press, 1988), pp. 169–84.

"Redefining Death: The Mirage of Consensus", in Stuart J. Youngner, Robert M. Arnold, and Renie Schapiro, eds., *The Definition of Death: Contemporary Controversies* (Baltimore: The Johns Hopkins University Press, 1999), pp. 319–31.

Epicurus, *La philosophie épicurienne sur pierre. Les fragments de Diogène d'Oenoanda*, translated by Alexandre Etienne and Dominic O'Meara (Paris/Fribourg: Cerf/Editions Universitaires Fribourg Suisse, 1996).

Letter to Menoeceus, translated by Cyril Bailey, in Whitney J. Oates, ed., *The Stoic and Epicurean Philosophers* (New York: Modern Library, 1940), pp. 30–3.

Principal Doctrines, translated by Cyril Bailey, in Whitney J. Oates, ed., *The Stoic and Epicurean Philosophers* (New York: Modern Library, 1940), pp. 35–9.

Fackler, James C. and Truog, Robert D., "Rethinking Brain Death", *Critical Care Medicine*, 20 (1992): 12: pp. 1705–13.

Fagot-Largeault, Anne, "Vie et mort", in Monique Canto-Sperber, ed., *Dictionnaire d'éthique et de philosophie morale* (Paris: Presses Universitaires de France, 1996), pp. 1583–90.

Feifel, Herman, ed., *The Meaning of Death* (New York: McGraw-Hill, 1959).

ed., *New Meanings of Death* (New York: McGraw-Hill, 1977).

"Death", in Norman L. Farberow, ed., *Taboo Topics* (New York: Atherton Press, 1963), pp. 8–21.

Feinberg, Joel, *Harm to Others* (Oxford: Oxford University Press, 1984).

"Harm and Self-Interest", in *Idem, Rights, Justice and the Bounds of Liberty. Essays in Social Philosophy* (Princeton, New Jersey: Princeton University Press, 1980), pp. 45–68.

"Harm to Others", in John Martin Fischer, ed., *The Metaphysics of Death* (Stanford, California: Stanford University Press, 1993), pp. 171–90.

"The Rights of Animals and Unborn Generation(s)", in William Blackstone, ed., *Philosophy and Environmental Crisis* (Athens: University of Georgia Press, 1974), pp. 43–68.

Feit, Neil, "The Time of Death's Misfortune", *Noûs*, 36 (2002): 3: pp. 359–83.

Feldman, Fred, *Confrontations with the Reaper: A Philosophical Study of the Nature and Value of Death* (Oxford: Oxford University Press, 1992).

"Death", in Edward Craig, ed., *Routledge Encyclopedia of Philosophy* (London: Routledge, 1998), pp. 817–23.

"F. M. Kamm and the Mirror of Time", *Pacific Philosophical Quarterly*, 17 (1990): 2: pp. 23–7.

"On Dying as a Process", *Philosophy and Phenomenological Research*, 50 (1989): 2: pp. 375–90.

"Some Puzzles about the Evil of Death", *The Philosophical Review*, 100 (1991): 2: pp. 205–27.

Ferrater Mora, Jose, *El Ser y la muerte. Bosquejo de filosofia integracionista* (Madrid: Allianza, 1988; originally published (Madrid: Aguilar, 1962)).

Fetscher, Iring, "Vom Sinn der Endlichkeit menschlichen Lebens", in Reiner Marx and Gerhard Stebner, eds., *Perspektiven des Todes. Interdisziplinäres Symposium I* (Heidelberg: Carl Winter Universitätsverlag, 1990), pp. 33–52.

Feuerbach, Ludwig, *Die Unsterblichkeitsfrage vom Standpunkt der Anthropologie*, in Wilhelm Bolin and Frierich Jodl, eds., *Sämtliche Werke*, vol. 1: *Gedanken über Tod und Unsterblichkeit* (Stuttgart: Frommanns, 1903).

Todesgedanken, in Wilhelm Bolin and Friedrich Jodl, eds., *Sämtliche Werke*, vol. 1: *Gedanken über Tod und Unsterblichkeit* (Stuttgart: Frommanns, 1903).

Figal, Günther, *Martin Heidegger. Phänomenologie der Freiheit* (Frankfurt am Main: Athenäum, 1988).

Filosofia e religione di fronte alla morte in *Archivio di Filosofia* (Padova: CEDAM, 1981).

Fink, Eugen, *Metaphysik und Tod* (Stuttgart: W. Kohlhammer Verlag, 1969).

"Vergegenwärtigung und Bild. Beiträge zur Phänomenologie der Unwirklichkeit", *Studien zur Phänomenologie 1930–1939* (The Hague: M. Nijhoff, 1966), pp. 1–78.

Finnis, John, "The Fragile Case for Euthanasia: A Reply to John Harris", in John Keown, ed., *Euthanasia Examined: Ethical, Clinical and Legal Perspectives*, 4th ed. (Cambridge: Cambridge University Press, 1995, 1999), pp. 46–55.

"Misunderstanding the Case against Euthanasia", in John Keown, ed., *Euthanasia Examined: Ethical, Clinical and Legal Perspectives*, 4th ed. (Cambridge: Cambridge University Press, 1995, 1999), pp. 62–71.

Fischer, John Martin, ed., *The Metaphysics of Death* (Stanford, California: Stanford University Press, 1993).

"Death, Badness, and the Impossibility of Experience", *The Journal of Ethics*, 1 (1997): 4: pp. 341–53.

"Why Immortality Is Not So Bad", *International Journal of Philosophical Studies*, 2 (1994): 2: pp. 257–70.

Fischer, John Martin and Brueckner, Anthony L., "The Asymmetry of Early Death and Late Birth", *Philosophical Studies*, 71 (1993): 3: pp. 327–31.

"Being Born Earlier", *Australasian Journal of Philosophy*, 76 (1988): 1: pp. 110–14.

"Death's Badness", *Pacific Philosophical Quarterly*, 74 (1993): 1: pp. 37–45.

"Why Is Death Bad?", in John Martin Fischer, ed., *The Metaphysics of Death* (Stanford, California: Stanford University Press, 1993), pp. 221–29 [originally published in *Philosophical Studies*, 50 (1986): 2: pp. 213–23].

Fleischer, Margot, *Die Zeitanalyse in Heideggers Sein und Zeit: Aporien, Probleme und ein Ausblick* (Würzburg: Königshausen and Neumann, 1991).

Flew, Anthony, *The Logic of Mortality* (Oxford: Basil Blackwell, 1987).

"Can a Man Witness His Own Funeral?" *The Hibbert Journal*, 54 (1956): pp. 242–50.

Fortner, B. and Neimeyer, Robert A., "Death Attitudes in Contemporary Perspective", in Stephen Stark, ed., *Death and the Quest for Meaning: Essays in Honor of Herman Feifel* (Northvale, New Jersey: Jason Aronson, 1997), pp. 3–29.

Fossel, Michael, *Reversing Human Aging* (New York: William Morrow and Company, 1996).

Freud, Sigmund, "Thoughts for the Times on War and Death", translated by E. C. Mayne, in James Strachey, ed., vol. 14 of *The Standard Edition of the Complete Psychological Works of Sigmund Freud* (London: The Hogarth Press and the Institute of Psycho-analysis), pp. 273–302 [*Zeitgemässes über Krieg und Tod, Studienausgabe*, vol. 9 (Frankfurt am Main: Fischer Verlag, 1974), pp. 35–60].

Frings, Manfred, *Person und Dasein. Zur Frage der Ontologie des Wertseins* (The Hague: Martinus Nijhoff, 1969).

Frydman, René, *Dieu, la Médecine et l'Embryon* (Paris: Odile Jacob, 1999, 2003).
Fuchs, Werner, *Todesbilder in der modernen Gesellschaft* (Frankfurt: Suhrkamp, 1969).
Furley, David, "Nothing to Us?", in Malcolm Schofield and Gisela Striker, eds., *The Norms of Nature. Studies in Hellenistic Ethics* (Cambridge: Cambridge University Press, 1986), pp. 75–91.
Gadamer, Hans-Georg, "La mort comme question", in Gary B. Madison, ed., *Sens et existence. En hommage à Paul Ricoeur* (Paris: Seuil, 1975), pp. 9–22.
"Schlussbericht", in *Idem* and Paul Vogler, eds., *Neue Anthropologie. Philosophische Anthropologie. Zweiter Teil* (Stuttgart: Georg Thieme Verlag Stuttgart/ Deutscher Taschenbuch Verlag, 1975), vol. 7, pp. 374–92.
Gaulupeau, Serge, "André Malraux et la Mort", *Archives des Lettres Modernes*, 98 (1969): 4: pp. 322–5.
Geach, Peter, *God and the Soul*, 2nd ed. (South Bend, Indiana: St. Augustine's Press, 2001).
Genova, Anthony C., "Death as a Terminus ad Quem", *Philosophy and Phenomenological Research*, 34 (1973/74): 2: pp. 270–7.
Gert, Bernard, Bernat, James L. and Culver, Charles M., "On the Definition and Criterion of Death", *Annals of Internal Medicine*, 94 (1981): 1: pp. 389–94.
Gert, Bernard, Clouse, Danner K. and Culver, Charles M., *Bioethics: A Systematic Approach* (Oxford: Oxford University Press, 2006).
Gert, Bernard and Culver, Charles M., *Philosophy in Medicine: Conceptual and Ethical Issues in Medicine and Psychiatry* (Oxford: Oxford University Press, 1982).
Gervais, Karen Granstrand, *Redefining Death* (New Haven, Connecticut: Yale University Press, 1986).
Glannon, Walter, "Temporal Asymmetry, Life, and Death", *American Philosophical Quarterly*, 31 (1994): 3: pp. 235–44.
Glover, Jonathan, *Causing Death and Saving Lives* (New York: Penguin Books, 1977).
Goldfarb, Alvin I., "Discussion", in *Death and Dying: Attitudes of Patient and Doctor* (New York: Group for the Advancement of Psychiatry, 1965).
Gombay, André, "What You Don't Know Doesn't Hurt You", *Proceedings of the Aristotelian Society*, 79 (1978–79): pp. 239–49.
Gorer, Geoffrey, "The Pornography of Death", *Encounter*, October 1955, reprinted in *Idem, Death, Grief and Mourning* (New York: Anchor Books, Doubleday, 1967), pp. 192–9].
Goulon, Maurice and Mollaret, Pierre, "Le coma dépassé", *Revue neurologique*, 101 (1959): 1: pp. 3–15.
Gray, Glenn J., "The Idea of Death in Existentialism", *The Journal of Philosophy*, 48 (1951): 5: pp. 113–27.
Green, Michael B. and Wikler, Daniel, eds., "Brain Death and Personal Identity", *Philosophy and Public Affairs*, 9 (1980): 2: pp. 105–33.
Green, O. Harvey, "Fear of Death", *Philosophy and Phenomenological Research*, 43 (1982): 1: pp. 99–105.
Greisch, Jean, *Ontologie et temporalité. Esquisse d'une interprétation intégrale de Sein und Zeit* (Paris: Presses Universitaires de France, 1994).

Grey, William, "Epicurus and the Harm of Death", *Australasian Journal of Philosophy*, 77 (1999): 3: pp. 358–64.

Grimaldi, Nicolas, *Le désir et le temps* (Paris: Presses Universitaires de France, 1971).

Grover, Dorothy L., "Death, and Life", *Canadian Journal of Philosophy*, 17 (1987): 4: pp. 711–33.

"Posthumous Harm", *Philosophical Quarterly*, 39 (1989): 156: pp. 334–53.

Habermas, Jürgen, *The Future of the Human Nature*, translated by William Rehg, Max Pensky, and Hella Beister (Cambridge: Polity Press, 2003) [*Die Zukunft der menschlichen Natur: Auf dem Weg zu einer liberalen Eugenik?* (Frankfurt am Main: Suhrkamp, 2005)].

Hahn, Alois, *Einstellung zum Tod und ihre soziale Bedingtheit. Eine soziologische Untersuchung* (Stuttgart: Ferdinand Enke Verlag, 1968).

"L'idée de la mort chez Max Scheler", in Christine Montandon-Binet and Alain Montandon, eds., *Savoir mourir* (Paris: L'Harmattan, 1993), pp. 219–31.

Haji, Ishtiyaque, "Pre-Vital and Post-Vital Times", *Pacific Philosophical Quarterly*, 72 (1991): 3: pp. 171–80.

Hall, Harrison, "Love and Death: Kierkegaard and Heidegger on Authentic and Inauthentic Human Existence", *Inquiry*, 27 (1984): 1: pp. 179–97.

Han, Byung-Chul, *Todesarten. Philosophische Untersuchungen zum Tod* (Munich: Wilhelm Fink Verlag, 1998).

Harris, John, *Clones, Genes and Immortality: Ethics and the Genetic Revolution* (Oxford: Oxford University Press, 1998).

The Value of Life (London: Routledge and Kegan Paul, 1985).

"Euthanasia and the Value of Life", in John Keown, ed., *Euthanasia Examined: Ethical, Clinical and Legal Perspectives*, 4th ed. (Cambridge: Cambridge University Press, 1999), pp. 7–22.

"A Reply to John Finnis", in John Keown, ed., *Euthanasia Examined: Ethical, Clinical and Legal Perspectives*, 4th ed. (Cambridge: Cambridge University Press, 1995, 1999), pp. 36–45.

Hauser, Marc D. and Allen, Colin, "Concept Attribution in Nonhuman Animals: Theoretical and Methodological Problems in Ascribing Complex Mental Processes", *Philosophy of Science*, 58 (1991): 2: pp. 221–40 [reprinted in Marc Bekoff and Dale Jamieson, eds., *Readings in Animal Cognition* (Cambridge, Massachusetts: The MIT Press, 1996), pp. 47–62].

Hayflick, Leonard, *How and Why We Age* (New York: Ballantine Books, 1994, 1996).

"The Cell Biology of Human Aging", *Scientific American*, 242 (1980): 1: pp. 58–65.

Heidegger, Martin, *Being and Time*, translated by John Macquarrie and Edward Robinson (New York: Harper & Row, 1962) [*Sein und Zeit*, 16th ed. (1927) (Tübingen: Max Niemeyer, 1986)].

History of the Concept of Time: Prolegomena, translated by Theodore Kisiel (Bloomington: Indiana University Press, 1985) [*Prolegomena zur Geschichte des Zeitbegriffs* (Frankfurt am Main: Klostermann, 1979)].

On the Way to Language, translated by Peter D. Hertz (New York: Harper & Row Publishers, 1971) [*Unterwegs zur Sprache* (Pfullingen: Neske, 1959)].

Phänomenologische Interpretation von Kants Kritik der reinen Vernunft (Frankfurt am Main: Vittorio Klostermann, 1977).

Über den Humanismus (Frankfurt am Main: Klostermann, 1947).

"Phénoménologie et Théologie / Phänomenologie und Theologie", translated by M. Méry, *Archives de Philosophie*, 32 (1969): 3: pp. 356–95.

Henry, Michel, *The Essence of Manifestation*, translated by Girard Etzkorn (The Hague: Martinus Nijhoff, 1973) [*L'essence de la manifestation*, 2 vols. (Paris: Presses Universitaires de France, 1963)].

"Phénoménologie de la naissance", *Alter. Revue de phénoménologie* 2 (1994): pp. 295–312.

Hershbell, Jackson P., *Pseudo-Plato: Axiochus* (Chico, California: Scholars Press, 1981).

Hinton, John M., *Experiences: An Inquiry into Some Ambiguities* (Oxford: Clarendon Press, 1973).

Hoerster, Norbert, *Abtreibung im säkularen Staat. Argumente gegen den § 218* (Frankfurt am Main: Suhrkamp, 1995).

Hoff, Johannes and Schmitten, Jürgen, eds., *Wann ist der Mensch tot? Organverpflanzung und 'Hirntod'-Kriterium* (Reinbeck bei Hamburg: Rowohlt, 1994).

Hoffman, John C., "Clarifying the Debate on Death", *Soundings*, 62 (1979): 4: pp. 430–47.

Hottois, Gilbert, *Essais de philosophie bioéthique et biopolitique* (Paris: Vrin, 1999).

Hügli, Anton, "Zur Geschichte der Todesdeutung. Versuch einer Typologie", *Studia Philosophica*, 32 (1973): pp. 1–28.

Humphreys, Sarah C. and King, Helen, eds., *Mortality and Immortality: The Anthropology and the Archaeology of Death* (London: Academic Press, 1981).

Huntington, Richard and Metcalf, Peter, eds., *Celebrations of Death: The Anthropology of Mortuary Ritual* (Cambridge: Cambridge University Press, 1979).

Husserl, Edmund, "Die anthropologische Welt" (1936), *Idem, Husserliana*, vol. 29 *[Die Krisis der europäischen Wissenschaften und die transzendentale Phänomenologie. Ergänzungsband. Texte aus dem Nachlass 1934–1937]* (Dordrecht: Kluwer Academic Publishers, 1993), pp. 320–38.

Illich, Ivan, *Medical Nemesis: The Expropriation of Death* (London: Calder and Boyars, 1975) [*Némésis médicale. L'expropriation de la santé* (Paris: Seuil, 1975)].

"The Political Uses of Natural Death", in Peter Steinfels and Robert M. Veatch, eds., *Death Inside Out* (New York: Harper & Row, 1975), pp. 25–42.

Jankélévitch, Vladimir, *La mort* (Paris: Flammarion, 1977).

Penser la mort? (Paris: Liana Lévi, 1994).

Jaspers, Karl, *Philosophie* (Berlin: Springer, 1932).

Psychologie der Weltanschauungen, 5th ed. (Berlin: Springer, 1960).

Johnstone, Henry W., "Discussion: Toward a Phenomenology of Death", *Philosophy and Phenomenological Research*, 35 (1974/75): 3: pp. 396–7.

"Does Death Have a Nature?", *The Journal of Medicine and Philosophy*, 3 (1978): 1: pp. 8–23.

"Sleep and Death", *The Monist*, 59 (1976): 2: pp. 218–33.

"Toward a Philosophy of Sleep", *Philosophy and Phenomenological Research*, 34 (1973/74): 1: pp. 73–81.

Jolivet, Régis, *Le problème de la mort chez M. Heidegger et J.-P. Sartre* (Abbaye Saint Wandrille: Editions de Fontenelle, 1950).
Jonas, Hans, *The Phenomenon of Life: Toward a Philosophical Biology* (Chicago: The University of Chicago Press, 1966, 1982).
"The Burden and Blessing of Mortality" in *Idem, Mortality and Morality: A Search for the Good after Auschwitz*, Lawrence Vogel, ed. (Evanston, Illinois: Northwestern University Press, 1996), pp. 87–98.
"Gehirntod und menschliche Organbank: Zur pragmatischen Umdefinierung des Todes", in *Idem, Technik, Medizin und Ethik. Zur Praxis des Prinzips Verantwortung* (Frankfurt am Main: Suhrkamp, 1987), pp. 219–41.
Jones, Royce P. and Agich, George J., "Personal Identity and Brain Death: A Critical Response", *Philosophy and Public Affairs*, 15 (1986): 3: pp. 267–74.
Jüngel, Eberhardt, *Der Tod* (Stuttgart: Kreuz Verlag, 1971).
Kamlah, Wilhelm, *Meditatio mortis. Kann man den Tod 'verstehen' und gibt es ein 'Recht auf den eigenen Tod'?* (Stuttgart: Ernst Klett Verlag, 1976).
Kamm, Frances M., *Morality, Mortality*, vol. 1: *Death and Whom to Save from It* (Oxford: Oxford University Press, 1993).
"Why Is Death Bad and Worse than Pre-natal Non-existence?", *Pacific Philosophical Quarterly*, 69 (1988): 2: pp. 161–4.
Kant, Immanuel, *Anthropology from a Pragmatic Point of View*, translated by Mary J. Gregor (The Hague: Martinus Nijhoff, 1974) [*Anthropologie in pragmatischer Hinsicht*, in Wilhelm Weischedel, ed., *Werke in zehn Bänden*, vol. 10 (Darmstadt: Wissenschaftliche Buchgesellschaft, 1983)].
Critique of Pure Reason, translated and edited by Paul Guyen and Allen W. Wood (Cambridge: Cambridge University Press, 1997) [*Kritik der reinen Vernunft*, in Wilhelm Weischedel, ed., *Werke in zehn Bänden*, vol. 3 (Darmstadt: Wissenschaftliche Buchgesellschaft, 1983)].
Kass, Leon R., "Death as an Event", in Robert F. Weir, ed., *Ethical Issues in Death and Dying* (New York: Columbia University Press, 1977), pp. 70–81 [originally published in *Science*, 173 (1971): 1: pp. 698–702].
Kaufman, Frederik, "An Answer to Lucretius' Symmetry Argument against the Fear of Death", *The Journal of Value Inquiry*, 29 (1995): 1: pp. 57–64.
"Death and Deprivation; or, Why Lucretius' Symmetry Argument Fails", *Australasian Journal of Philosophy*, 72 (1996): 2: pp. 305–12.
"Pre-Vital and Post-Mortem Non-Existence", *American Philosophical Quarterly*, 36 (1999): 1: pp. 1–19.
Kenney, Edward John, *Lucretius* (Oxford: Clarendon Press, 1977).
Kerr, Fergus, *Theology after Wittgenstein* (Oxford: Blackwell, 1986).
Kierkegaard, Søren, "At a Graveside", in *Three Discourses on Imagined Occasions*, translated and edited by Howard V. Hong and Edna H. Hong (Princeton, New Jersey: Princeton University Press, 1993), pp. 69–102.
King, Helen and Humphreys, Sarah C., eds., *Mortality and Immortality: The Anthropology and the Archaeology of Death* (London: Academic Press, 1981).
Kisiel, Theodore, *The Genesis of Heidegger's Being and Time* (Berkeley, Los Angeles: University of California Press, 1993).
Knörzer, Guido, *Tod ist Sein? Eine Studie zu Genese und Struktur des Begriffs 'Tod' im Frühwerk Martin Heidegger* (Bern: Peter Lang, 1990).

Kojève, Alexandre, *Introduction à la lecture de Hegel. Leçons sur la phénoménologie de l'esprit* (Paris: Gallimard, 1947).
Koninck, Thomas de, *De la dignité humaine* (Paris: Presses Universitaires de France, 2002).
Korein, Julius, "The Problem of Brain Death: Development and History", *Annals of the New York Academy of Sciences*, 315 (1978): 2: pp. 19–38.
Kraus, Michael Rupert, *Das Todesbewusstsein als Dimension des menschlichen Selbstbewusstseins. Eine philosophisch-anthropologiche Bestimmung der Sinnkonstitution* (Würzburg, Ph.D., 1995).
Krell, David Farrell, *Daimon Life: Heidegger and Life-Philosophy* (Bloomington/Indianapolis: Indiana University Press, 1992).
Kripke, Saul A., *Naming and Necessity* (Oxford: Blackwell, 1980).
Kroy, Moshe, "Les paradoxes phénoménologiques de la mort", *Revue de Métaphysique et de Morale*, 97 (1982): 4: pp. 531–50.
Kuhse, Helga and Singer, Peter, "Individuals, Humans, and Persons: The Issue of Moral Status", in Helga Kuhse, ed., *Unsanctifying Human Life: Essays on Ethics: Peter Singer* (Oxford: Blackwell, 2002), pp. 188–98.
"Should All Seriously Disabled Infants Live?", in Helga Kuhse, ed., *Unsanctifying Human Life: Essays on Ethics: Peter Singer* (Oxford: Blackwell, 2002), pp. 233–45.
Lachs, John, "The Element of Choice in Criteria of Death", in Richard M. Zaner, ed., *Death: Beyond Whole-Brain Criteria* (Dordrecht: Kluwer Academic Publishers, 1988), pp. 233–51.
Lafontaine, Céline, *La société postmortelle* (Paris: Seuil, 2008).
Lamb, David, *Death, Brain Death and Ethics* (London: Croom Helm, 1985).
Lamont, Julian, "A Solution to the Puzzle of When Death Harms Its Victims", *Australasian Journal of Philosophy*, 76 (1998): 2: pp. 198–212.
Landsberg, Paul-Louis, *Einführung in die philosophische Anthropologie*, 2nd ed. (Frankfurt am Main: Vittorio Klostermann, 1960).
The Experience of Death; The Moral Problem of Suicide, translated by Cynthia Rowland (New York: Arno Press, 1977) [*Essai sur l'expérience de la mort et Le problème moral du suicide* (Paris: Seuil, 1951, 1993)].
Laudan, Larry, *Science and Values. The Aims of Science and Their Role in Scientific Debate* (Berkeley: University of California Press, 1984).
Lavados, Manuel M. and Serani, Alejandro M., *Etica Clinica. Fundamentos y Aplicaciones* (Santiago: Ediciones Universidad Catolica de Chile, 1993).
Lavin, Michael, "How Not to Define Death: Some Objections to Cognitive Approaches", *The Southern Journal of Philosophy*, 23 (1985): 3: pp. 313–24.
Ledure, Yves, "L'acte philosophique et la pensée de la mort dans la philosophie de Schopenhauer", *Revue des Sciences Philosophiques et Théologiques*, 65 (1981): 3: pp. 373–86.
"La philosophie comme mémoire de la mort", *Nouvelle Revue Théologique*, 108 (1986): 4: pp. 555–70.
Lehmann, Karl, *Der Tod bei Heidegger und Jaspers* (Heidelberg: Jakob Comtesse, 1938).
Leman-Stefanovic, Ingrid, *The Event of Death: A Phenomenological Enquiry* (Dordrecht: Martinus Nijhoff Publishers, 1987).

Levenbook, Barbara Baum, "Harming Someone after His Death", *Ethics*, 94 (1984): 3: pp. 407–19.

"Harming the Dead, Once Again", *Ethics*, 96 (1985): 1: pp. 162–4.

Levinas, Emmanuel, *En découvrant l'existence avec Husserl et Heidegger* (Paris: Vrin, 1982).

God, Death, and Time, translated by Bettina Bergo (Stanford, California: Stanford University Press, 2000) [*La mort et le temps* (Paris: L'Herne, 1991)].

Le Temps et l'Autre (Paris: Presses Universitaires de France, 1991).

Totality and Inifinity: An Essay on Exteriority, translated by Alphonso Lingis (Pittsburgh: Duquesne University Press, 1969) [*Totalité et Infini. Essai sur l'extériorité* (Paris: Librairie Générale Française, 2006; The Hague: Martinus Nijhoff, 1971].

"Le philosophe et la mort", in Christian Chabanis, *La mort, un terme ou un commencement?* (Paris: Fayard, 1982), pp. 341–52.

Lévy, Bernard and Sartre, Jean-Paul, *Hope Now: The 1980 Interviews*, translated by Adrian van den Hoven (Chicago: University of Chicago Press, 1996) [*L'espoir maintenant* (Paris: Verdier, 1991)].

Lewis, Hywel D., *The Self and Immortality* (London: MacMillan, 1985).

Li, Jack, *Can Death Be a Harm to the Person Who Dies?* (Dordrecht/Boston/London: Kluwer Academic Publishers, 2002).

Lingis, Alphonso, *Deathbound Subjectivity* (Bloomington/Indianapolis: Indiana University Press, 1989).

Linschoten, Jan, "On Falling Asleep", in Joseph J. Kockelmans, ed., *Phenomenological Psychology: The Dutch School* (Dordrecht: Martinus Nijhoff Publishers, 1987), pp. 79–117.

Lizza, John P., *Persons, Humanity, and the Definition of Death* (Baltimore: The John Hopkins University Press, 2006).

"Conceptual Basis for Brain Death Revisited", in Calixto Machado and Alan Shewmon, eds., *Brain Death and Disorders of Consciousness* (Dordrecht: Kluwer Academic, 2004), pp. 51–9.

"Persons and Death: What's Metaphysically Wrong with Our Current Statutory Definition of Death?", *The Journal of Medicine and Philosophy*, 18 (1993): 4: pp. 351–74.

Locke, John, "Identity and Diversity", in *Idem, An Essay Concerning Human Understanding*, Book 2, chapter 27 (Oxford: Oxford University Press, 1979), pp. 328–48.

Lohner, Alexander, *Der Tod im Existentialismus. Eine Analyse der fundamentaltheologischen, philosophischen und ethischen Implikationen* (Paderborn: Ferdinand Schöningh, 1997).

Lotz, Johannes B., *Tod als Vollendung. Von der Kunst und Gnade des Sterbens* (Frankfurt am Main: Josef Knecht, 1976).

Löwith, Karl, "Die Freiheit zum Tode", in Klaus Stichweh and Marc Buhot de Launay, eds., *Sämtliche Schriften* (Stuttgart: Metzlersche Verlagsbuchhandlung, 1981), vol. 1, pp. 418–25.

Lucretius, Titus, *De rerum natura*, translated by William H. D. Rouse, 3rd ed. (Cambridge, Massachusetts: Harvard University Press, 1959).

Luper, Steven, *The Philosophy of Death* (Cambridge: Cambridge University Press, 2009).

"Annihilation", in John Martin Fischer, ed., *The Metaphysics of Death* (Stanford, California: Stanford University Press, 1993), pp. 269–90 [originally published in *The Philosophical Quarterly*, 37 (July 1987): 148: pp. 233–52].

Machado, Calixto and Shewmon, Alan, eds., *Brain Death and Disorders of Consciousness* (Dordrecht: Kluwer Academic, 2004).

Macho, Thomas, *Todesmetaphern* (Frankfurt am Main: Suhrkamp, 1987).

MacIntyre, Alasdair, *Dependent Rational Animals: Why Human Beings Need the Virtues* (Chicago and La Salle, Illinois: Open Court, 1999, 2008).

Macklin, Ruth, "Dignity Is a Useless Concept", *British Medical Journal*, 327 (December 20, 2003), pp. 1419–20.

Malpas, Jeff and Solomon, Robert C., eds., *Death and Philosophy* (London: Routledge, 1998).

Manser, Josef, *Der Tod des Menschen. Zur Deutung des Todes in der gegenwärtigen Philosophie und Theologie* (Bern: Peter Lang, 1977).

Mant, Keith A., "The Medical Definition of Death", in Arnold Toynbee, ed., *Man's Concern with Death* (London: Hodder and Stoughton, 1968), pp. 13–24.

Marcel, Gabriel, *Creative Fidelity*, translated by Robert Rosthal (New York: Fordham University Press, 2002) [*Du refus à l'invocation* (Paris: Gallimard, 1940)].

Homo viator: Introduction to a Metaphysic of Hope, translated by Emma Craufurd (Chicago: Regnery, 1951) [*Homo viator. Prolégomènes à une métaphysique de l'espérance* (Paris: Aubier, 1944)].

Mystery of Being, translated by George S. Fraser (vol. 1) and René Hague (vol. 2) (South Bend, Indiana: Regnery/Gateway, 1964) [*Le Mystère de l'être*, 2 vols. (Paris: Aubier, 1951)].

Presence and Immortality, translated by Michael A. Machado (Pittsburgh: Duquesne University Press, 1967) [*Présence et immortalité* (Paris: Flammarion, 1959)].

Marcuse, Herbert, "The Ideology of Death", in Herman Feifel, ed., *The Meaning of Death* (New York: McGraw-Hill, 1959), pp. 64–76.

Marion, Jean-Luc, "L'*ego* et le *Dasein*", in *Idem, Réduction et Donation. Recherches sur Husserl, Heidegger et la phénoménologie* (Paris: Presses Universitaires de France, 1989), pp. 119–61.

Marquis, Don, "Harming the Dead", *Ethics*, 96 (1985): 1: pp. 159–61.

Marten, Rainer, *Der menschliche Tod. Eine philosophische Revision* (Paderborn: Ferdinand Schöningh, 1987).

Marx, Werner, "Die Sterblichen", in Ute Guzzoni, ed., *Nachdenken über Heidegger. Eine Bestandsaufnahme* (Hildesheim: Gerstenberg Verlag, 1980), pp. 160–175.

Matthews, Gareth B., "*De Anima* B2–4 and the Meaning of *Life*", in Martha Nussbaum and Amélie Rorty, eds., *Essays on Aristotle's De Anima* (Oxford: Oxford University Press, 1997), pp. 185–93.

McMahan, Jeff, *The Ethics of Killing: Problems at the Margins of Life* (Oxford: Oxford University Press, 2002).

"An Alternative to Brain Death", *Journal of Law, Medicine and Ethics*, 34 (Spring 2006): 1: pp. 44–8.

"Brain Death, Cortical Death and Persistent Vegetative State", in Helga Kuhse and Peter Singer, eds., *A Companion to Bioethics* (Oxford: Blackwell, 1998), pp. 250–60.

"Death and the Value of Life", in John Martin Fischer, ed., *The Metaphysics of Death* (Stanford, California: Stanford University Press, 1993), pp. 233–66 [originally published in *Ethics*, 99 (October 1988), 1: pp. 32–61].

Mehl, Roger, *Le vieillissement et la mort* (Paris: Presses Universitaires de France, 1956).

Melchiore, Virgilio, *Sul senso della morte* (Milano: Università Cattolica, 1994).

Melhuish, George, *Death and the Double Nature of Nothingness* (London: Duckworth, 1994).

Merleau-Ponty, Maurice, *Phenomenology of Perception*, translated by Colin Smith (London: Routledge, 2002) [*Phénoménologie de la perception* (Paris: Gallimard, 1945)].

Merrill Thomas W., Pellegrino Edmund D. and Schulman Adam, eds., *Human Dignity and Bioethics: Essays Commissioned by the President's Council on Bioethics* (Notre Dame, Indiana: University of Notre Dame Press, 2009).

Metcalf, Peter and Huntington, Richard, eds., *Celebrations of Death: The Anthropology of Mortuary Ritual* (Cambridge: Cambridge University Press, 1979).

Metzger, Arnold, *Freiheit und Tod* (Tübingen: Max Niemeyer Verlag, 1955).

Milanesi, Claudio, *Mort apparente, mort imparfaite. Médecine et mentalités au XVIIIème* (Paris: Payot, 1991).

Mill, John Stuart, *Utilitarianism*, in Mary Warnock, ed., *Utilitarianism, On Liberty, Essay on Bentham* (Cleveland/New York: Meridian Books, 1968), pp. 251–321.

Miller, Fred D., "Epicurus on the Art of Dying", *Southern Journal of Philosophy*, 14 (1976): 2: pp. 169–77.

Mitsis, Phillip, "Epicurus on Death and the Duration of Life", in John J. Cleary and Daniel C. Shartin, eds., *Proceedings of the Boston Area Colloquium in Ancient Philosophy* (New York: University Press of America, 1989), vol. 4, pp. 303–22.

Mollaret, Pierre and Goulon Maurice, "Le coma dépassé", *Revue neurologique*, 101 (1959): 1: pp. 3–15.

Moller, David Wendell, *Confronting Death: Values, Institutions, and Human Mortality* (Oxford: Oxford University Press, 1996).

Life's End: Technocratic Dying in an Age of Spiritual Yearning (Amityville, New York: Baywood Publishing Company, 2000).

Momeyer, Richard W., *Confronting Death* (Bloomington/Indianapolis: Indiana University Press, 1988).

Montaigne, Michel de, *The Complete Essays of Montaigne*, translated by Donald M. Frame (Stanford, California: Stanford University Press, 1948) [*Essais* (Paris: Bibliothèque de la Pléiade, 1940)].

Moreau, Denis, *Les voies du salut* (Paris: Bayard, 2010).

Morin, Edgar, *L'homme et la mort* (Paris: Seuil, 1970, 1976).

Morison, Robert S., "Death: Process or Event", Robert F. Weir, ed., *Ethical Issues in Death and Dying* (New York: Columbia University Press, 1977), pp. 57–69 [originally published *Science*, 173 (August 20, 1971): pp. 694–8].

Mothersill, Mary, "Death", in James Rachels, ed., *Moral Problems* (1971), pp. 83–92 [reprinted in Oswald Hanfling, ed., *Life and Meaning: A Reader* (Oxford: Blackwell, 1989), pp. 83–92].

Müller-Lauter, Wolfgang, *Möglichkeit und Wirklichkeit bei Martin Heidegger* (Berlin: Walter de Gruyter, 1960).

Murphy, Jeffrie, "Rationality and the Fear of Death", *The Monist*, 59 (1976): pp. 187–203 [reprinted in John Martin Fischer, ed., *The Metaphysics of Death* (Stanford, California: Stanford University Press, 1993), pp. 41–58].

Nagel, Thomas, *Mortal Questions* (Cambridge: Cambridge University Press, 1979).

Other Minds: Critical Essays 1969–1994 (Oxford: Oxford University Press, 1995).

The View from Nowhere (Oxford: Oxford University Press, 1986).

What Does It All Mean: A Very Short Introduction to Philosophy (Oxford: Oxford University Press, 1987).

"Death", in *Idem, Mortal Questions* (Cambridge: Cambridge University Press, 1979), pp. 1–10.

"What Is It Like to Be a Bat?", in *Idem, Mortal Questions* (Cambridge: Cambridge University Press, 1979), pp. 165–80.

Nassehi, Armin and Weber, Georg, *Tod, Modernität und Gesellschaft. Entwurf einer Theorie der Todesverdrängung* (Opladen: Westdeutscher Verlag, 1989).

Neimeyer, Robert A. and Fortner, Barry, "Death Attitudes in Contemporary Perspective", in Stephen Stark, ed., *Death and the Quest for Meaning: Essays in Honor of Herman Feifel* (Northvale, New Jersey: Jason Aronson, 1997), pp. 3–29.

Nietzsche, Friedrich, *The Birth of Tragedy*, translated by Walter Kaufmann (New York: Vintage Books, 1967) [*Die Geburt der Tragödie* in *Sämtliche Werke. Kritische Studienausgabe in 15 Bände*, vol. 1 (München/Berlin: Deutscher Taschenbuch Verlag/Walter de Gruyter, 1980)].

Nilges, Richard G., Byrne, Paul A. and Potts, Michael, "Introduction", in Michael Potts, Paul A. Byrne, and Richard G. Nilges, eds., *Beyond Brain Death: The Case against Brain Based Criteria for Human Death* (Dordrecht: Kluwer Academic Press, 2000), pp. 1–20.

Nozick, Robert, *The Examined Life: Philosophical Meditations* (New York: Touchstone/Simon & Schuster, 1989).

Philosophical Explanations (Cambridge, Massachusetts: The Belknap Press of Havard University Press, 1981).

"Dying", in *Idem, The Examined Life: Philosophical Meditations* (New York: Touchstone/Simon & Schuster, 1989), pp. 20–33.

"On the Randian Argument", in Paul Jeffrey, ed., *Reading Nozick: Essays on Anarchy, State, and Utopia* (Oxford: Basil Blackwell, 1981), pp. 206–31.

Nuland, Sherwin B., *How We Die: Reflections on Life's Final Chapter* (New York: Vintage Books, 1993).

Nussbaum, Martha C., "Mortal Immortals: Lucretius on Death and the Voices of Nature", *Philosophy and Phenomenological Research*, 50 (1989): 2: pp. 303–51.

Olson, Eric T., *The Human Animal: Personal Identity without Psychology* (Oxford: Oxford University Press, 1997).

What Are We? A Study in Personal Ontology (Oxford: Oxford University Press, 2007).

Onfray, Michel, *Féeries anatomique: Généalogie du corps faustien* (Paris: Grasset, 2003).

Pallis, Chris, *The ABC of Brain Death* (London: British Medical Journal Publishers, 1996).

Parfit, Derek, *Reasons and Persons* (Oxford: Clarendon Press, 1984).

Pargetter, Robert, Bigelow, John and Campbell, John, "Death and Well-Being", *Pacific Philosophical Quarterly*, 71 (1990): 1: pp. 119–40.

Partridge, Ernest, "Posthumous Interests and Posthumous Respect", *Ethics*, 91 (1981): 2: pp. 243–64.

Pascal, Blaise, *Pensées*, translated by W. F. Trotter (New York: Modern Library, 1941) [*Pensées*, Edition Brunschvicg (Paris: Garnier, 1961)].

Paskow, Alan, "The Meaning of My Own Death", *International Philosophical Quarterly*, 14 (1974): 2: pp. 51–69.

"What Do I Fear in Facing My Death?", *Man and World: An International Philosophical Review*, 8 (1975): 2: pp. 146–56.

Paterson, Ronald W. K., *Philosophy and the Belief in a Life after Death* (London: MacMillan Press LTD, 1995).

Paus, Ansgarm, ed., *Grenz-Erfahrung Tod* (Graz: Styria, 1976).

Pelikan, Jaroslav Jan, *The Shape of Death* (Westport, Connecticut: Greenwood Press, 1971, 1978).

Pellegrino Edmund D., Merrill Thomas W. and Schulman, Adam, eds., *Human Dignity and Bioethics: Essays Commissioned by the President's Council on Bioethics* (Notre Dame, Indiana: University of Notre Dame Press, 2009).

Penelhum, Terence, *Survival and Disembodied Existence* (London: Routledge and Kegan Paul, 1970).

Perrett, Roy W., *Death and Immortality* (Dordrecht: Martinus Nijhoff Publishers, 1987).

Peters Ted, Russell John and Welker, Michael, eds., *Resurrection: Theological and Scientific Assessments* (Grand Rapids, Michigan: W. B. Eerdmans, 2002).

Pfeiffer, Helmut, "Die Wirklichkeit des Todes in der Philosophie", *Stimmen der Zeit*, 196 (1978): 11: pp. 772–84.

Pieper, Josef, *Death and Immortality*, translated by Richard and Clara Winston (South Bend, Indiana: St. Augustine's Press, 2000) [*Tod und Unsterblichkeit* in *Werke in acht Bänden*, edited by Berthold Wald (Hamburg: Felix Meiner Verlag, 1997), vol. 5, pp. 280–397].

Pinker, Steven, "The Stupidity of Dignity", *The New Republic*, May 28, 2008.

Pitcher, George, "The Misfortunes of the Dead", in John Martin Fischer, ed., *The Metaphysics of Death* (Stanford, California: Stanford University Press, 1993), pp. 159–68 [originally published *American Philosophical Quarterly*, 21 (April 1984): 2: pp. 183–8].

Plato, *The Collected Dialogues*, edited by Edith Hamilton and Huntington Cairns, Bollingen Series LXXI (Princeton, New Jersey: Princeton University Press, 1961).
Gorgias, pp. 229–307.
Philebus, pp. 1086–1150.
Republic, pp. 575–844.
Socrates' Defense (Apology), pp. 3–26.
Plato-pseudo, *Axiochus*, translated by Jackson P. Hershbell (Chico, California: Scholars Press, 1981).
Plessner, Helmuth, "Über die Beziehung der Zeit zum Tode", in *Eranos-Jahrbuch*, 20 (1951): pp. 349–86.
Plutarch, Lucius Mestrius, *A Letter of Condolence to Apollonius*, in *Moralia*, vol. 2, translated by Frank Cole Babbitt (Cambridge, Massachusetts: Harvard University Press, 1928), pp. 109–211.
Plutarch's Morals, translation revised by William W. Goodwin (Boston: Little Brown and Co., 1871).
That Epicurus Actually Makes a Pleasant Life Impossible, in *Moralia*, vol. 14, translated by Benedict Einarson and Phillip H. DeLacy (Cambridge, Massachusetts: Harvard University Press, 1967), pp. 15–149.
Portmore, Douglas, "Desire Fulfillment and Posthumous Harm", *American Philosophical Quarterly*, 44 (2007): 1: pp. 27–38.
Poteat, William H., "'I Will Die': An Analysis", *The Philosophical Quarterly*, 9 (1959): 34: pp. 46–58.
Potts, Michael, Byrne, Paul A. and Nilges, Richard G., "Introduction", in Michael Potts, Paul A. Byrne, and Richard G. Nilges, eds., *Beyond Brain Death: The Case against Brain Based Criteria for Human Death* (Dordrecht: Kluwer Academic Press, 2000), pp. 1–20.
Pritzl, Kurt, "Aristotle and Happiness after Death: *Nicomachean Ethics* 1, 10–11, *Classical Philology*, 78 (1983): 2: pp. 101–11.
Puccetti, Roland, "Does Anyone Survive Neocortical Death?", in Richard M. Zaner, ed., *Death: Beyond Whole-Brain Criteria* (Dordrecht: Kluwer Academic Publishers, 1988), pp. 75–90.
"The Conquest of Death", *The Monist*, 59 (1976): 2: pp. 249–63.
"The Life of a Person", in William B. Bondeson, Tristram H. Engelhardt, Stuart F. Spicker, and Daniel H. Winship, eds., *Abortion and the Status of the Fetus* (Dordrecht: Reidel, 1983), pp. 169–82.
Quante, Michael, *Personales Leben und menschlicher Tod. Personale Identität als Prinzip der biomedizinischen Ethik* (Frankfurt am Main: Suhrkamp, 2002).
Rachels, James, *The End of Life: Euthanasia and Morality* (Oxford: Oxford University Press, 1986).
Rager, Günter, "Données biologiques et réflexions sur la personne", in François-Xavier Putallaz and Bernard N. Schumacher, eds., *L'humain et la personne* (Paris: Cerf, 2008), pp. 97–114 [also in German: "Biologische Fakten und personales Denken", François-Xavier Putallaz and Bernard N. Schumacher, eds., *Der Mensch und die Person* (Darmstadt: Wissenschaftliche Buchgesellschaft, 2008), pp. 63–72].

Ramsey, Ian T., "Persons and Funerals: What Do Person Words Mean?", *The Hibbert Journal*, 54 (1956): pp. 330–8.

Ricoeur, Paul, *Living Up to Death*, translated by David Pellauer (Chicago: University of Chicago Press, 2009) [*Vivant jusqu'à la mort. Suivi de Fragments* (Paris: Seuil, 2007)].

Time and Narrative, translated by Kathleen McLaughlin and David Pellauer, vols. 1 and 3 (Chicago: University of Chicago Press, 1984) [*Temps et récit* (Paris: Seuil, vol. 1, 1983 and vol. 3, 1985)].

"Vraie et fausse angoisse", in *Idem, L'angoisse du temps présent et les devoirs de l'esprit* (Neuchâtel: Editions de la Baconnière, 1953), pp. 33–53.

Rilke, Rainer Maria, *Von der Armut und von dem Tod*, from *Das Stunden-Buch* in *Sämtliche Werke in 6 Bänden* (Frankfurt am Main: Rilke Archiv, 1955–66; reprinted Insel Taschenbuch, 1986).

Rist, John M., *Stoic Philosophy* (Cambridge: Cambridge University Press, 1969).

Roger, Jacques, *Les sciences de la vie dans la pensée française du XVIIIème siècle. La génération des animaux de Descartes à l'Encyclopédie* (Paris: Albin Michel, 1993).

Rorty, Amélie Oksenberg, "Fearing Death", *Philosophy*, 58 (1983): 2: pp. 175–88 [reprinted in John Donnelly, ed., *Language, Metaphysics and Death* (New York: Fordham University Press, 1994), pp. 102–16].

Rorty, Richard, "The Contingency of Selfhood", *London Review of Books*, 8 May 1986, pp. 11–15.

Rosenbaum, Stephen E., "Epicurus and Annihilation", in John Martin Fischer, ed., *The Metaphysics of Death* (Stanford, California: Stanford University Press, 1993), pp. 293–304 [originally published *The Philosophical Quarterly*, 39 (1989): 154: pp. 81–90].

"The Harm of Killing: An Epicurian Perspective", in Robert M. Baird, William F. Cooper, Elmer Duncan, and Stuart Rosenbaum, eds., *Contemporary Essays on Greek Ideas: The Kilgore Festschrift* (Waco, Texas: Baylor University Press, 1987), pp. 207–26.

"How to Be Dead and Not Care: A Defense of Epicurus", in John Martin Fischer, ed., *The Metaphysics of Death* (Stanford, California: Stanford University Press, 1993), pp. 119–34 [originally published *American Philosophical Quarterly*, 23 (1986): 2: pp. 217–25].

"The Symmetry Argument: Lucretius against the Fear of Death", *Philosophy and Phenomenological Research*, 1 (1989): 2: pp. 353–73.

Rosenberg, Jay F., *Thinking Clearly about Death* (Englewood Cliffs, New Jersey: Prentice-Hall, 1983).

Ross, William D., *Foundations of Ethics* (Oxford: Clarendon Press, 1939).

Royce, Jones P. and Agich, George J., "Personal Identity and Brain Death: A Critical Response", *Philosophy and Public Affairs*, 15 (1986): 3: pp. 267–74.

Russell, Bertrand, *Portraits from Memory and Other Essays* (London: George Allen and Unwin LTD, 1956).

Russell John, Peters Ted and Welker, Michael, eds., *Ressurection: Theological and Scientific Assessments* (Grand Rapids, Michigan: W. B. Eerdmans, 2002).

Russell, Tom, *Brain Death: Philosophical Concepts and Problems* (Aldershot, England: Ashgate, 2000).

Salem, Jean, *La mort n'est rien pour nous. Lucrèce et l'éthique* (Paris: Vrin, 1990).

Tel un Dieu parmi les hommes. L'éthique d'Epicure (Paris: Vrin, 1989).

Sartre, Jean-Paul, *Being and Nothingness: A Phenomenological Essay on Ontology*, translated by Hazel E. Barnes 1956 (New York: Washington Square Press, 1992) [*L'Être et le Néant: Essai d'ontologie phénoménologique* (Paris: Gallimard, 1943)].

Critique of Dialectical Reason I, translated by Alan Sheridan-Smith (London/ Atlantic Highlands, New Jersey: NLB/Humanities Press, 1976) [*Critique de la raison dialectique* (Paris: Gallimard, 1985)].

No Exit, translated by Stuart Gilbert, in *No Exit and Three Other Plays* (New York: Vintage International, 1989), pp. 1–46 [*Huis clos* (Paris: Gallimard, Folio, 1994)].

Notebooks for an Ethics, translated by David Pellauer (Chicago: University of Chicago Press, 1992) [*Cahiers pour une morale* (Paris: Gallimard, 1983)].

The Words, translated by Bernard Fretchman (New York: Vintage Books, 1964, 1981) [*Les mots* (Paris: Gallimard, 1994)].

"Interview with Jean-Paul Sartre", in Paul A. Schilpp, ed., *The Philosophy of Jean-Paul Sartre* (La Salle: Open Court, 1981), pp. 3–51.

Sartre, Jean-Paul and Lévy, Bernard, *Hope Now: The 1980 Interviews*, translated by Adrian van den Hoven (Chicago: University of Chicago Press, 1996) [*L'espoir maintenant* (Paris: Verdier, 1991)].

Scare, Geoffrey, *Death* (Montreal, Kingston, and Ithaca: McGill-Queen's University Press, 2007).

Schaerer, René, "Le philosophe moderne en face de la mort", in *L'homme face à la mort* (Paris/Neuchâtel: Niestlé/Delechaux, 1952), pp. 125–54.

Scheler, Max, *Tod und Fortleben* (1911–4) in *Gesammelte Werke*, vol. 10: *Schriften aus dem Nachlass*, vol. 1 (Bern: Francke, 1957), pp. 9–64.

Das Wesen des Todes (1923–4) in *Gesammelte Werke*, vol. 3: *Schriften aus dem Nachlass, Philosophische Anthropologie* (Bern: Francke, 1987), pp. 253–327.

"Idealism and Realism", David R. Lachterman, ed., *Max Scheler: Selected Philosophical Essays*, translated by David R. Lachterman (Evanston, Illinois: Northwestern University Press, 1973), pp. 288–356 ["Idealismus-Realismus", *Philosophischer Anzeiger*, 2 (1927–8): 3: pp. 255–324].

"Zur Unsterblichkeit" (1925–6) in *Gesammelte Werke*, vol. 3: *Schriften aus dem Nachlass, Philosophische Anthropologie* (Bern: Francke, 1987), pp. 333–41.

Scherer, Georg, *Das Problem des Todes in der Philosophie*, 2nd ed. (Darmstadt: Wissenschaftliche Buchgesellschaft, 1988).

Der Tod als Frage an die Freiheit (Essen: Fredebeul/Koenen, 1971).

Sinnerfahrung und Unsterblichkeit (Darmstadt: Wissenschaftliche Buchgesellschaft, 1985).

"Philosophie des Todes und moderne Rationalität", in Hans H. Jansen, ed., *Der Tod in Dichtung, Philosophie und Kunst*, 2nd ed. (Darmstadt: Steinkopff Verlag, 1989), pp. 505–21.

Schmitten, Jürgen and Hoff, Johannes, eds., *Wann ist der Mensch tot? Organverpflanzung und 'Hirntod'-Kriterium* (Reinbeck bei Hamburg: Rowohlt, 1994).

Schopenhauer, Arthur, "On Death", in *The World as Will and Idea*, vol. 3, translated by Richard B. Haldane and John Kemp (London: Kegan, Paul, Trench,

Trübner and Co., 1906), pp. 249–308 [*Die Welt aus Wille und Vorstellung* in *Arthur Schopenhauer. Sämtliche Werke,* edited by Wolfgang Frhr. Von Löhneysen (Frankfurt am Main: Suhrkamp, 1986), vol. 2, pp. 590–651].

Schulman Adam, Merrill Thomas W. and Pellegrino, Edmund D., eds., *Human Dignity and Bioethics: Essays Commissioned by the President's Council on Bioethics* (Notre Dame, Indiana: University of Notre Dame Press, 2009).

Schulz, Walter, *Subjektivität im nachmetaphysischen Zeitalter. Aufsätze* (Pfullingen: Neske, 1992).

"Wandlungen der Einstellung zum Tode", in Johannes Schwartländer, ed., *Der Mensch und sein Tod* (Göttingen: Vandenhoeck and Ruprecht, 1976), pp. 94–107.

"Zum Problem des Todes", in Alexander Schwan, ed., *Denken im Schatten des Nihilismus. Festschrift für Wilhelm Weischedel zum 70. Geburtstag* (Darmstadt: Wissenschaftliche Buchgesellschaft, 1975), pp. 313–33.

Schumacher Bernard N., *Confrontations avec la mort. La philosophie contemporaine et la question de la mort* (Paris: Cerf, 2005).

A Philosophy of Hope (New York: Fordham University Press, 2003).

ed., *Jean-Paul Sartre. Das Sein und das Nichts* (Berlin: Akademie Verlag, 2002).

"Deux ennemies irréductibles: la philosophie et la théologie selon Heidegger", *Freiburger Zeitschrift für Philosophie und Theologie,* 44 (1997): 3: pp. 279–96.

"L'aporie de la mort. Derrida interprète de l'être-vers-la-mort heideggérien", *Freiburger Zeitschrift für Philosophie und Theologie,* 45 (1998): 3: pp. 568–75.

"La dictature de la conscience", *Nova et Vetera,* 85 (2010): 2: pp. 153–82.

"La mort: événement naturel ou accidentel?", *Laval Théologique et Philosophique,* 54 (1998): 1: pp. 5–22.

"La mort comme la possibilité de l'impossibilité d'être. Une analyse critique de Heidegger", *Archives de Philosophie,* 62 (1999): 1: pp. 71–94.

"La mort comme un mal. Défi épicurien à la lumière de la philosophie analytique contemporaine", in Jean-Gabriel Rueg, ed., *Le mystère du mal* (Toulouse: Editions du Carmel, 2001), pp. 177–216.

"La mort dans la vie. La thanatologie de Max Scheler", *Phänomenologischen Forschungen – Phenomenological Studies – Recherches phénoménologiques,* Neue Folge 4 (1999): 2: pp. 238–55.

"La mort sous l'angle de la structure de l'être-pour-autrui", *Etudes phénoménologiques,* 17 (2001): 33–4: pp. 163–95.

"La personne comme conscience de soi performante au cœur du débat bioéthique: Analyse critique de la position de John Locke", *Laval Théologique et Philosophique,* 64 (2008), 3: pp. 709–43.

"Le défi d'une définition séculière de la personne pour l'éthique", *Nova et Vetera,* 59 (2004): 4: pp. 49–64.

"Philosophische Interpretationen der Endlichkeit des Menschen", in Hans Kessler, ed., *Auferstehung der Toten* (Darmstadt: Wissenschaftliche Buchgesellschaft, 2004), pp. 113–36.

"Tout être humain est-il une personne? Controverse autour de la définition de la personne dans la discussion éthique médicale contemporaine", *Laval Théologique et Philosophique,* 61 (2005): 1: pp. 107–34.

Schwartländer, Johannes, ed., *Der Mensch und sein Tod* (Göttingen: Vandenhoeck and Ruprecht, 1976).

"Der Tod und die Würde des Menschen", in *Idem*, ed., *Der Mensch und sein Tod* (Göttingen: Vandenhoeck and Ruprecht, 1976), pp. 14–33.
Segal, Charles, *Lucretius on Death and Anxiety: Poetry and Philosophy in De Rerum Natura* (Princeton, New Jersey: Princeton University Press, 1990).
Seifert, Josef, *What Is Life? The Originality, Irreducibility and Value of Life* (Amsterdam: Rodopi, 1997).
"Is 'Brain Death' Actually Death?", *The Monist*, 76 (1993): 2: pp. 175–202 [reprinted in Robert J. White, Heinz Angstwurm, and Ignacio Carrasco de Paula, eds., *Working Group on the Determination of Brain Death and Its Relationship to Human Death* (Rome: Pontificia Academia Scientiarum, 1992), pp. 95–143].
Seneca, *Letters to Lucilius (Ad Lucilium Epistulae Morales)*, translated by Richard M. Gummere, 3 vols. (Cambridge, Massachusetts: Harvard University Press, 1917–25, reprinted 1961–3), vol. 1 of 3.
To Marcia on Consolation, in Moral Essays, translated by John W. Basore (Cambridge, Massachusetts: Harvard University Press, 1958), vol. 2, pp. 3–97.
To Polybius on Consolation, in Moral Essays, translated by John W. Basore (Cambridge, Massachusetts: Harvard University Press, 1958), vol. 2, pp. 357–415.
Serani, Alejandro M. and Lavados, Manuel M., *Etica Clinica. Fundamentos y Aplicaciones* (Santiago: Ediciones Universidad Catolica de Chile, 1993).
Shann, Frank, "The Cortically Dead Infant Who Breathes", in K. Sanders and B. Moore, eds., *Anencephalics, Infants and Brain Death: Treatment Options and the Issue of Organ Donation*, Proceedings of Consensus Development Conference, February 28–March 1, 1991 (Melbourne: The Law Reform Commission of Victoria Australian Association of Paediatric Teaching Centres Royal Children's Hospital, Melbourne, 1991), pp. 28–30.
Sheets-Johnstone, Maxine, "On the Conceptual Origin of Death", *Philosophy and Phenomenological Research*, 47 (1986): 1: pp. 31–58.
Shewmon, Alan, "The Brain and Somatic Integration: Insights into the Standard Biological Rationale for Equating 'Brain Death' with Death", *Journal of Medicine and Philosophy*, 26 (2001): 5: pp. 457–78.
"'Brainstem Death', 'Brain Death' and Death: A Critical Re-Evaluation of the Purported Equivalence", *Issues in Law and Medicine*, 14 (1998): 2: pp. 125–45.
Shewmon, Alan and Machado, Calixto, eds., *Brain Death and Disorders of Consciousness* (Dordrecht: Kluwer Academic, 2004).
Shneidman, Edwin S., *Deaths of Man* (New York: Jason Aronson, 1983).
Silverstein, Harry S., "The Evil of Death", in John Martin Fischer, ed., *The Metaphysics of Death* (Stanford, California: Stanford University Press, 1993), pp. 95–116 [originally published *Journal of Philosophy*, 77 (1980): 7: pp. 401–24].
"The Evil of Death Revisited", *Midwest Studies in Philosophy*, 24 (2000): 1: pp. 116–34.
Siméon, Georges, "La naissance et la mort", *Revue de Métaphysique et de Morale*, 27 (1920): pp. 495–515.
Simmel, Georg, *Lebensanschauung. Vier metaphysische Kapitel* (München/Leipzig: Duncker and Humblot, 1918).

"Zur Metaphysik des Todes", in *Idem, Das Individuum und die Freiheit. Essais* (Berlin: Verlag Klaus Wagenbach, 1957, 1984), pp. 28–35.

Singer, Peter, *Applied Ethics* (Oxford: Oxford University Press, 1986).

Practical Ethics, 2nd ed. (Cambridge: Cambridge University Press, 1993).

Rethinking Life and Death: The Collapse of Our Traditional Ethics (New York: St. Martin's Press, 1994).

Singer, Peter and Helga Kuhse, "Individuals, Humans, and Persons: The Issue of Moral Status", in Helga Kuhse, ed., *Unsanctifying Human Life: Essays on Ethics: Peter Singer* (Oxford: Blackwell, 2002), pp. 188–98.

"Should All Seriously Disabled Infants Live?", in Helga Kuhse, ed., *Unsanctifying Human Life: Essays on Ethics: Peter Singer* (Oxford: Blackwell, 2002), pp. 233–45.

Skegg, Peter D. G., *Law, Ethics and Medicine* (Oxford: Clarendon Press, 1984).

Slote, Michael, "Existentialism and the Fear of Dying", *American Philosophical Quarterly*, 12 (1975): 1: pp. 17–28.

Smart, Ninian, "Philosophical Concepts of Death", in Arnold Toynbee, ed., *Man's Concern with Death* (London: Hodder and Stoughton, 1968), pp. 25–35.

Soll, Ivan, "On the Purported Insignificance of Death: Whistling before the Dark?", in Jeff Malpas and Robert C. Solomon, eds., *Death and Philosophy* (London: Routledge, 1998), pp. 22–38.

Solomon, Robert C., "Is There Happinness after Death?", *Philosophy*, 51 (1976): 196: pp. 189–93.

Solomon, Robert C. and Malpas, Jeff, eds., *Death and Philosophy* (London: Routledge, 1998).

Sorabji, Richard, *Time, Creation and the Continuum: Theories in Antiquity and the Early Middle Ages* (Ithaca, New York: Cornell University Press, 1983).

Spaemann, Robert, *Persons: The Difference between 'Someone' and 'Something'*, translated by Oliver O'Donovan (Oxford: Oxford University Press, 2007) [*Personen. Versuche über den Unterschied zwischen 'etwas' und 'jemand'* (Stuttgart: Klett-Cotta, 1996)].

Spinoza, *Ethics*, translated by Andrew Boyle (London: Everyman's Library, revised ed. 1959).

Sprumont, Pierre, "La mort comme condition de la vie" in *Idem*, co-ed., *Le sens de la mort. Vom Sinn des Todes* (Fribourg: Editions Universitaires Fribourg Suisse, 1980), pp. 8–21.

Steiner, M., "Der Tod as biologisches Problem", in Norbert A. Luyten, ed., *Tod-Preis des Lebens* (Freiburg/München: Karl Alber, 1980), pp. 11–50.

Steinfeld, Peter and Veatch, Robert M., eds., *Death Inside Out*, The Hastings Center Report (New York: Harper & Row, 1974–5).

Sternberger, Dolf, *Der verstandene Tod. Eine Untersuchung zu Martin Heideggers Existenzial-Ontologie in Über den Tod, Schriften I* (Frankfurt am Main: Insel, 1977), pp. 69–264.

Stoecker, Ralf, *Der Hirntod. Ein medizinethisches Problem und seine moralphilosophische Transformation* (Freiburg/München: Karl Alber, 1999).

Stork, Traudel, *Nil igitur mors est ad nos. Der Schlussteil des dritten Lukrezbuches und sein Verhältnis zur Konsolationsliteratur* (Bonn: Rudolf Habelt Verlag, 1970).

Ströker, Elisabeth, "Der Tod im Denken Schelers", in Paul Good, ed., *Max Scheler im Gegenwartsgeschehen der Philosophie* (Bern/München: Francke, 1975), pp. 199–213.

Suits, David B., "Why Death Is Not Bad for the One Who Died", *American Philosophical Quarterly*, 38 (2001): 1: pp. 69–84.

Sumner, Leonard W., *Abortion and Moral Theory* (Princeton, New Jersey: Princeton University Press, 1981).

"A Matter of Life and Death", *Noûs*, 10 (1976): 2: pp. 145–71.

Taylor, Charles, *Sources of the Self: The Making of the Modern Identity* (Cambridge, Massachusetts: Harvard University Press, 1989).

Theognis, *Elegies*, in Hesiod, *Theogony – Works and Days and Theognis, Elegies*, translated by Dorothea Wender (Harmondsworth, England: Penguin Books, 1973).

Theunissen, Michael, "Die Gegenwart des Todes im Leben", in *Idem, Negative Theologie der Zeit*, 2nd ed. (Frankfurt am Main: Suhrkamp, 1992), pp. 197–217.

Thomas, Louis-Vincent, *Anthropologie de la mort* (Paris: Payot, 1975, 1994).

Tilliette, Xavier, "Le moi et la mort", in *Qu'est-ce que l'homme? Hommage à Alphonse De Waelhens* (Bruxelles: Facultés universitaires Saint-Louis, 1982), pp. 185–204.

Tooley, Michael, *Abortion and Infanticide* (Oxford: Clarendon Press, 1983).

"Abortion and Infanticide", *Philosophy and Public Affairs*, 2 (1972), 1: pp. 37–65.

"Decisions to Terminate Life and the Concept of Person", in John Ladd, ed., *Ethical Issues Relating to Life and Death* (Oxford: Oxford University Press, 1979), pp. 62–93.

"Personhood", in Helga Kuhse and Peter Singer, eds., *A Companion to Bioethics* (Blackwell: Oxford, 1988), pp. 117–26.

"Why a Liberal View Is Correct", in Michael Tooley, Celia Wolf-Devine, Philip E. Devine, and Alison M. Jaggar, eds., *Abortion: Three Perspectives* (Oxford: Oxford University Press, 2009), pp. 3–64.

Toynbee, Arnold, ed., *Man's Concern with Death* (London: Hodder and Stoughton, 1968).

Troisfontaines, Claude, "Y a-t-il une expérience de la mort?", *La foi et le temps*, 6 (nouvelle série, november–december 1979): 9 : pp. 504–14.

Truog, Robert D., "Is It Time to Abandon Brain Death?", *Hastings Center Report*, 27 (1997): 1: pp. 29–37.

Truog, Robert D. and Fackler, James C., "Rethinking Brain Death", *Critical Care Medicine*, 20 (1992): 12: pp. 1705–13.

Tugendhat, Ernst, *Über den Tod* (Frankfurt am Main: Suhrkamp, 2006).

Türk, Hans Joachim, "Der Hirntod in philosophischer Sicht", *Zeitschrift für medizinische Ethik*, 43 (1997): 1: pp. 17–29.

Ugazio, Ugo Maria, *Il problema della morte nella filosofia di Heidegger* (Milano: Mursia, 1976).

Uhlig, Ludwig, *Der Todesgenius in der deutschen Literatur von Winckelmann bis Thomas Mann* (Tübingen: Max Niemeyer Verlag, 1975).

Unamuno, Miguel de, *Del sentimiento trágico de la vida* (Buenos Aires: Orbis, 1984).

Diario intimo (Madrid: Alianza, 1986).
Van Evra, James W., "On Death as a Limit", *Analysis*, 31 (1971): 5: pp. 170–6.
Veatch, Robert M., *Death, Dying and the Biological Revolution: Our Last Quest for Responsibility* (New Haven, Connecticut: Yale University Press, 1976, 1977; also revised 3rd ed. 1989).
"The Impending Collapse of the Whole Brain Definition of Death", *Hasting Center Report*, 23 (1993): 4: pp. 18–24.
"Whole-Brain, Neocortical, and Higher Brain Related Concepts", in Richard M. Zaner, ed., *Death: Beyond Whole-Brain Criteria* (Dordrecht: Kluwer Academic Publishers, 1988), pp. 171–86.
Veatch, Robert M. and Steinfeld, Peter, eds., *Death Inside Out*, The Hastings Center Report (New York: Harper & Row, 1974–5).
Velleman, David J., "Well-Being and Time", in John Martin Fischer, ed., *The Metaphysics of Death* (Stanford, California: Stanford University Press, 1993) pp. 329–57 [originally published *Pacific Philosophical Quarterly*, 72 (1991): 1: pp. 48–77].
Vernant, Jean-Pierre, *L'individu, la mort, l'amour. Soi-même et l'autre en Grèce ancienne* (Paris: Gallimard, 1989).
Vogl, Gabriele, *Das Problem des Todes bei Heidegger ("Sein und Zeit") und Augustinus* (Vienna, Ph.D., 1966).
Voltaire, *Dictionnaire philosophique*, in *Oeuvres complètes*, XVII–XX (Paris: Reprint Nendeln/Liechtenstein, 1967).
Vuillemin, Jules, *Essai sur la signification de la mort* (Paris: Presses Universitaires de France, 1948).
Wach, Joachim, *Das Problem des Todes in der Philosophie unserer Zeit* (Tübingen: Mohr, 1934).
Wallach, Barbara Price, *Lucretius and the Diatribe against the Fear of Death. De Rerum Natura III, 830–1094* (Leiden: Brill, 1976).
Walter, Tony, *The Revival of Death* (London: Routledge, 1994).
Walton, Douglas N., *Brain Death: Ethical Considerations* (West Lafayette, Indiana: Purdue University Press, 1980).
On Defining Death: An Analytic Study of the Concept of Death in Philosophy and Medical Ethics (Montreal: McGill-Queen's University Press, 1979).
Warren, James, *Facing Death: Epicurus and His Critics* (Oxford: Oxford University Press, 2004, 2008).
Warren, Mary Anne, *Moral Status: Obligations to Persons and Other Living Things* (Oxford: Oxford University Press, 2005).
"On the Moral and Legal Status of Abortion", *The Monist*, 57 (1973): 1: pp. 43–61.
Weber, Georg and Nassehi, Armin, *Tod, Modernität und Gesellschaft. Entwurf einer Theorie der Todesverdrängung* (Opladen: Westdeutscher Verlag, 1989).
Weir, Robert F., ed., *Ethical Issues in Death and Dying* (New York: Columbia University Press, 1977).
Weismann, August, *Über Leben und Tod. Eine biologische Untersuchung* (Jena: Gustav Fischer, 1884).
Welker Michael, Peters Ted and Russell, John, eds., *Resurrection: Theological and Scientific Assessments* (Grand Rapids, Michigan: W. B. Eerdmans, 2002).

Wennberg, Robert, *Life in the Balance: Exploring the Abortion Controversy* (Grand Rapids, Michigan: W. B. Eerdmans, 1985).
Wikler, Daniel and Green, Michael B., eds., "Brain Death and Personal Identity", *Philosophy and Public Affairs*, 9 (1980): 2: pp. 105–33.
Williams, Bernard, "The Makropulos Case", in *Idem, Problems of the Self: Philosophical Papers 1956–1972* (Cambridge: Cambridge University Press, 1973, 1995), pp. 82–100.
Wiplinger, Fridolin, *Der personal verstandene Tod. Todeserfahrung als Selbsterfahrung* (Freiburg/München: Karl Alber, 1970).
Wittgenstein, Ludwig, *Tractatus Logico-Philosophicus*, German text with a new translation by David F. Pears and Brian F. McGuinness, 2nd ed. (London: Routledge and Kegan Paul, 1963) [*Schriften 1* (Frankfurt am Main: Suhrkamp, 1969)].
Wollheim, Richard, *The Thread of Life* (Cambridge: Cambridge University Press, 1984).
Wreen, Michael J., "The Definition of Death", *Public Affairs Quarterly*, 1 (1987): 4: pp. 87–99.
Wulf, Christoph, "Körper und Tod", in Dietmar Kamper and *Idem*, eds., *Die Wiederkehr des Körpers* (Frankfurt am Main: Suhrkamp, 1982), pp. 259–73.
Wyschogrod, Edith, "Death and Some Philosophies of Language", *Philosophy Today*, 22 (1978): pp. 255–65.
Youngner, Stuart J. and Bartlett, Edward T., "Human Death and the Destruction of the Neocortex", in Richard M. Zaner, ed., *Death: Beyond Whole-Brain Criteria* (Dordrecht: Kluwer Academic Publishers, 1988), pp. 199–215.
Yourgrau, Palle, "The Dead", in John Martin Fischer, ed., *The Metaphysics of Death* (Stanford, California: Stanford University Press, 1993), pp. 137–56 [originally published *Journal of Philosophy*, 84, (1987): 2: pp. 84–101].
Zacher, Klaus-Dieter, *Plutarchs Kritik an der Lustlehre Epikurs. Ein Kommentar zu 'Non posse suaviter vivi secundum Epicurum: Kap. 1–8* (Königstein/Ts.: Anton Hain, 1982).
Zaner, Richard M., ed., *Death: Beyond Whole-Brain Criteria* (Dordrecht: Kluwer Academic Publishers, 1988).
"Introduction", in *Idem*, ed., *Death: Beyond Whole-Brain Criteria* (Dordrecht: Kluwer Academic Publishers, 1988), pp. 1–14.
Ziegler, Jean, *Les vivants et les morts* (Paris: Seuil, 1975).

Index of Names

Index of Concepts